GLOBAL MONITORING REPORT 2009

GLOBAL MONITORING REPORT 2009

A Development Emergency

ISBN: 978-0-8213-7859-5
eISBN: 978-0-8213-7860-1
DOI: 10.1596/978-0-8213-7859-5

Cover photo: © Jason Hosking/Zefa/Corbis.

Cover design by Critical Stages.

The annex to this book contains **DataLinks**, a feature that provides access to the Excel files corresponding to each figure. To make use of this feature, simply locate the link below each figure (beginning with http://dx.doi.org), and type it into your Internet browser.

Contents

Boxes

Figures

Tables

Foreword

The title of this year's *Global Monitoring Report* is "A Development Emergency." Appropriately so. We are in the midst of a global financial crisis for which there has been no equal in over 70 years. It is a dangerous time. The financial crisis that grew into an economic crisis is now becoming an unemployment crisis. It risks becoming a human and social crisis—with political implications. No region is immune. The poor countries are especially vulnerable, as they have much less cushion to withstand events. This poses serious threats to the hard-won gains in boosting the economic growth of many developing countries, especially in Africa, as well as achieving progress toward the Millennium Development Goals (MDGs). It also poses a threat to global recovery, because developing countries can provide a growth platform to help the global economy pull out of the crisis.

Middle-income countries were the first among developing countries to feel the impact of the financial crisis, given their heavier reliance on private capital flows. Private capital flows to the developing world are seeing their sharpest decline in many decades. Both middle- and low-income countries will be hit hard in 2009 by a second wave of effects reflecting the global recession and declining world trade. Poor countries will be affected through reductions in export volumes, commodity prices, remittances, tourism, foreign direct investment, and possibly even foreign aid. These shocks will hurt public revenues, constricting fiscal space for public programs.

Economic growth in developing countries has declined sharply to the lowest rates for some decades; per capita incomes will fall in many countries. Sub-Saharan Africa will see a rise in the poverty count in 2009, with the more fragile and low-growth economies especially at risk. Globally, we estimate that because of the crisis there will be more than 50 million additional people living in extreme poverty in 2009 than expected before the crisis, compounding the impact from soaring food and fuel prices of recent years.

These numbers have a human face. We estimate that as a result of sharply lower economic growth rates, about 200,000 to 400,000 more babies may die each year. School enrollments will suffer—especially for girls. The prospect of reaching the MDGs by 2015, already a cause for serious concern, now looks even more distant.

A global crisis requires a global solution. The crisis began in the financial markets of developed countries, so the first order of business must be to stabilize these markets and counter the recession that the financial turmoil has triggered. This calls for timely, adequate, and coordinated actions by developed countries to restore confidence in the financial system and counter falling demand. At the same time, we need strong and urgent actions to counter the impact of the crisis on developing countries by helping them to boost growth while protecting the poor. The report sets out six priority areas for action to confront the development emergency that now faces many of these countries.

First, we must ensure an adequate fiscal response in developing countries to protect the poor and vulnerable groups and to support economic growth. Priority areas must be strengthening social safety nets and protecting infrastructure programs that can create jobs while building a foundation for future productivity and growth. The precise fiscal response needs to be tailored to individual country circumstances, consistent with maintenance of macroeconomic stability. Second, we must provide support for the private sector and improve the climate for recovery and growth in private investment, including paying special attention to strengthening financial systems. Helping small and medium enterprises get access to finance for trade and investment is vital for job creation. But the crisis has also underscored the importance of broader reforms to improve the stability and soundness of the financial system. Third, we must redouble efforts in human development and recover lost ground in progress toward the MDGs.

We can do this not only by strengthening key public programs for health and education, but also by better leveraging the private sector's role in the financing and delivery of services.

In support of these efforts to help developing countries, the report emphasizes three key global priorities. Donors must deliver on their commitments to increase aid. Indeed, the increased needs of poor countries hit hard by the crisis call for going beyond existing commitments. National governments must hold firm against rising protectionist pressures and maintain an open international trade and finance system. Completing the Doha negotiations expeditiously would provide a much-needed boost in confidence to the global economy at a time of high stress and uncertainty. Finally, multilateral institutions must have the mandate, resources, and instruments to support an effective global response to the global crisis. The international financial institutions will need to play a key role in bridging the large financing gap for developing countries resulting from the slump in private capital flows, including using their leverage ability to help revive private flows.

World leaders made important progress in coordinating a global response to the crisis at the recently held summit of the Group of Twenty countries. This must be followed by strong, concerted actions. The need for international cooperation has never been greater.

Robert B. Zoellick
President
The World Bank Group

Dominique Strauss-Kahn
Managing Director
International Monetary Fund

Acknowledgments

This report has been prepared jointly by the staff of the World Bank and the International Monetary Fund. In preparing the report, staff have collaborated closely with partner institutions—the African Development Bank, the Asian Development Bank, the European Bank for Reconstruction and Development, the Inter-American Development Bank, the Organisation for Economic Co-operation and Development, the World Trade Organization, the United Nations Conference on Trade and Development, and other UN agencies. The cooperation and support of staff of these institutions are gratefully acknowledged.

Zia Qureshi was the lead author and manager of the report. The core team for the report included Felipe Barrera, Peter Berman, Jean-Pierre Chauffour, Punam Chuhan-Pole, Stefano Curto, Mary Hallward-Driemeier, and Homi Kharas (World Bank) and Stijn Claessens, Richard Harmsen, Laura Kodres, Andrea Maechler, and Axel Palmason (IMF). Other significant contributions were made by Katharina Gassner, Arthur Karlin, and Linda Lee (World Bank) and Alberto Espejo, Emmanuel Hife, and Ioana Niculcea (IMF). Sachin Shahria assisted with the overall preparation and coordination of the report. The work was carried out under the general guidance of Justin Yifu Lin, Senior Vice President and Chief Economist, World Bank.

A number of other staff and consultants made valuable contributions, including the following from the World Bank: Philippe Ambrosi, Uranbileg Batjargal, Amie Batson, Iwona Borowik, Penelope Brooks, Andrew Burns, Shaohua Chen, Robert Cull, Susan Davis, Asli Demirgüç-Kunt, Shanthi Divakaran, Simeon Djankov, Sharon Felzer, Ariel Fiszbein, Vivien Foster, Caroline Freund, Boris Gamarra, Alan Gelb, Navin Girishankar, Neil Gregory, Juliana Guaqueta, April Harding, Masako Hiraga, Bernard Hoekman, Ludwina Joseph, Johannes Sebastian Kiess, Stephen Knack, Gerard Martin La Forgia, Gina Lagomarsino, Benjamin Loevinsohn, Knut Lonnroth, Mattias Lundberg, Frank Lysy, Mariem Malouche, Aaditya Mattoo, Dominique van der Mensbrugghe, Inez Mikkelsen-Lopez, Dominic Montague, Marisela Montoliu-Munoz, Joyce Msuya, Richard Newfarmer, Israel Osorio-Rodarte, Harry Patrinos, Emilio Porta, Abha Prasad, Alexander Preker, Martin Ravallion, Lulu Shui, Eric Swanson, Nigel Twose, Marilou Uy, Daniel Villar, Dileep Wagle, and Elizabeth White.

Other contributors from the IMF included Elif Aksoy, Alexandre Chailloux, Peter Dattels, and Deniz Igan.

Contributors from other institutions included: Gaston Gohou, Ellen Goldstein, Josephine Kiyenje, and Timothy Turner (AfDB); Indu Bhushan, Christopher Maccormac, Manju Senapaty, and Gina Marie Umali (ADB); Yannis Arvanitis, Gary Bond, and James Earwicker (EBRD); Nathaniel Jackson and Max Pulgar-Vidal (IDB); Yasmin Ahmad, Simon Scott, and Suzanne Steensen (OECD); and Alessandro Nicita (UNCTAD).

Guidance received from the Executive Directors of the World Bank and the IMF and their staff during discussions of the draft report is gratefully acknowledged. The report also benefited from many useful comments and suggestions received from the Bank and Fund management and staff in the course of its preparation and review.

The World Bank's Office of the Publisher managed the editorial services, design, production, and printing of the report, with Susan Graham anchoring the process. Others assisting with the report's publication included Denise Bergeron, Martha Gottron, Nancy Lammers, Stephen McGroarty, Santiago Pombo-Bejarano, Kirsten Dennison and associates of Precision Graphics, and Bill Pragluski of Critical Stages.

The report's dissemination and outreach was coordinated by Merrell Tuck-Primdahl, working with Prianka Nandy, Kavita Watsa, and Roula Yazigi.

Abbreviations

ACP	African, Caribbean, and Pacific countries	FDI	Foreign direct investment
ADB	Asian Development Bank	FSAP	Financial Sector Assessment Program
AfDB	African Development Bank	G-8	Group of Eight
AIDS	Acquired immune deficiency syndrome	G-20	Group of Twenty
AMC	Advanced Market Commitment	GAVI	Global Alliance for Vaccines and Immunizations
CCT	Conditional cash transfer	GDP	Gross domestic product
CDM	Clean Development Mechanism	GEF	Global Environmental Facility
CERs	Certified emissions reductions	GFATM	Global Fund to Fight AIDS, Tuberculosis, and Malaria
COMPAS	Common preference assessment system	GHG	Greenhouse gases
CPA	Country programmable aid	GNI	Gross national income
CPIA	Country Policy and Institutional Assessment	HIPC	Heavily indebted poor country/countries
CRS	Creditor Reporting System (of the OECD DAC)	HIV	Human immunodeficiency virus
CSR	Corporate social responsibility	IBRD	International Bank for Reconstruction and Development
DAC	Development Assistance Committee	ICP	International Comparison Program
DRF	Debt Reduction Facility (of the World Bank)	IDA	International Development Association (of the World Bank)
EBRD	European Bank for Reconstruction and Development	IDB	Inter-American Development Bank
EC	European Commission	IEA	International Energy Agency
EITI	Extractive Industries Transparency Initiative	IFC	International Finance Corporation
FAO	Food and Agriculture Organization (of the UN)	IFI	International financial institutions

IFFIm	International Finance Facility for Immunizations	OECD	Organisation for Economic Co-operation and Development
IHP	International Health Partnership	OTRI	Overall Trade Restrictiveness Index
ILO	International Labour Organization	PFM	Public financial management
IMF	International Monetary Fund	PPIAF	Public-Private Infrastructure Advisory Facility
ITC	International Trade Centre	PPP	Purchasing power parity
LDCs	Least-developed countries	PTA	Preferential trade agreement
MDBs	Multilateral development banks	SIAP	Sustainable Infrastructure Action Plan
MDG	Millennium Development Goal	SME	Small and medium enterprises
MDRI	Multilateral Debt Relief Initiative	SWF	Sovereign wealth fund
MFIs	Microfinance institutions	TTRI	Tariff Trade Restrictiveness Index
MSE	Micro- and small enterprise	UN	United Nations
NAMA	Nonagricultural market access	UNDP	UN Development Programme
NEPAD	New Partnership or African Development	UNFCCC	UN Framework Convention on Climate Change
NGOs	Nongovernmental organizations	WFP	World Food Programme
NTM	Nontariff measure	WHO	World Health Organization
ODA	Official development assistance	WTO	World Trade Organization

Overview

The global financial crisis, the most severe since the Great Depression, is rapidly turning into a human and development crisis. The financial crisis originated in the developed world, but it has spread quickly and inexorably to the developing world, sparing no country. Increasingly it appears that this will not be a short-lived crisis. The poor countries are especially vulnerable, as they lack the resources to respond with ameliorative actions. The crisis poses serious threats to their hard-won gains in boosting economic growth and achieving progress toward the Millennium Development Goals (MDGs). Poor people typically are the hardest hit, and have the least cushion. For millions of them, the crisis puts at risk their very survival.

At high-level meetings held in 2008 to mark the MDG halfway point, world leaders expressed grave concern that the world was falling behind most of the MDGs, with the shortfalls especially serious in human development, and issued an MDG Call to Action to step up development efforts. The UN secretary general noted that "we face nothing less than a development emergency." The U.K. prime minister spoke of a "global poverty emergency." These concerns were expressed before the onset of the full-blown global financial crisis. If there was a development emergency then, there surely is one now. The financial crisis threatens serious further setbacks and greatly increases the urgency for action.

A Crisis upon Crisis

For poor countries, this is a crisis upon crisis. It comes on the heels of the food and fuel crises. The triple jeopardy of the food, fuel, and financial crises is pushing many poor countries into a danger zone, imposing rising human costs and imperiling development prospects.

With the seizing-up of the international financial markets in 2008, emerging market countries were the first among developing countries to feel the impact of the financial crisis, given their heavier reliance on private capital flows. Private capital flows to the developing world are seeing their sharpest slump ever, with net flows likely turning negative in 2009—a more than $700 billion drop from the peak in 2007. Many low-income countries are also affected by the private credit crunch; private flows to these countries, including several in Africa, that had increased in recent years are now falling. But these countries are expected to be hit particularly hard in 2009 by a second round of impacts reflecting the global recession and declining world trade: world gross domestic product (GDP) is projected to decline in 2009 for the first time since World War II and world trade is projected to register its largest decline in the post-war period.

Low-income countries will be affected through reductions in export volumes, commodity prices, remittances, tourism, foreign direct investment, and possibly even foreign aid. These shocks in turn will hurt public revenues, adding to the sizable negative fiscal impact of the food and fuel crises on many countries and putting further pressure on public expenditure programs. In addition, financial systems in low-income countries, even when relatively shielded from the international financial contagion because of less exposure to international financial markets, may be hit by second-round effects as the economic downturn increases problem loans, limiting the availability of domestic financing to businesses.

The impact of the global financial crisis on developing countries is reflected in sharp reductions in their projected GDP growth to rates that are the lowest since the 1990s. Average projected GDP growth in developing countries in 2009 is now only about a quarter of what was expected before the financial turmoil intensified into a full-blown crisis in the latter half of 2008 and a fifth of that achieved in the period of strong growth up to 2007. For developing countries as a whole, growth is now projected to fall to 1.6 percent in 2009, from an average of 8.1 percent in 2006–07. Growth in Sub-Saharan Africa is projected to slow to 1.7 percent in 2009, from 6.7 percent in 2006–07, breaking the momentum of the region's very promising growth revival of recent years. Even these low projections are subject to further downside risks. Countries in Eastern Europe and Central Asia that entered the global crisis with weaker macroeconomic fundamentals are most severely hit, with average growth in the region in 2009 now projected to be negative. Average growth in Latin America and the Caribbean

also is projected to be negative in 2009. The current growth projections, adjusted for terms-of-trade changes, imply declining real per capita incomes for more than 50 developing countries in 2009.

Impact on Poverty Reduction and Other MDGs

The sharp slowdown in growth can seriously set back progress on poverty reduction and other MDGs. Food price increases between 2005 and 2008 pushed around 200 million more people into extreme poverty, and about half of them will remain trapped in poverty in 2009 even as food prices recede from their peaks. While food prices have fallen since mid-2008, they remain high by historical standards, and the food crisis is by no means over. The slowdown in growth resulting from the financial crisis will add to the poverty impact of high food prices. The International Labour Organization projects that some 30 million more people around the world may be unemployed in 2009, of whom 23 million could be in developing countries. A worse-case scenario envisages as many as 50 million more people becoming unemployed in 2009. Estimates of the poverty impact of the growth slowdown range from 55 million to 90 million more extreme poor in 2009 than expected before the crisis. These numbers will rise if the crisis deepens and growth in developing countries falters further.

In Sub-Saharan Africa and South Asia, which have high poverty rates, the growth slowdown essentially eliminates the pre-crisis prospect of continued reductions in the poverty count in 2009. Indeed, the poverty count is likely to rise in Sub-Saharan Africa in 2009, with the more fragile and low-growth economies especially at risk. While poverty rates on average are much lower in Europe and Central Asia and in Latin America and the Caribbean, these regions could also see an increase in the number of the poor in 2009. Overall, on current growth projections, more than one-half of all developing countries could experience a rise in the number of extreme poor in 2009; this proportion is likely to be still higher among low-income countries and countries in Sub-Saharan Africa—two-thirds and three-quarters, respectively.

Experience suggests that growth collapses are costly for human development outcomes, which tend to deteriorate more quickly during growth decelerations than they improve during growth accelerations. Countries that suffered economic contractions of 10 percent or more between 1980 and 2004 experienced more than 1 million additional infant deaths. It is estimated that the sharply slower economic growth resulting from the current financial crisis may cause as many as 200,000 to 400,000 more infant deaths per year on average between 2009 and the MDG target year of 2015, which translates into 1.4 million to 2.8 million additional infant deaths during the period. In poor countries, education outcomes, such as school enrollment, also tend to deteriorate during economic crises—especially for girls.[1]

The long-run consequences of the crisis for human development outcomes may be more severe than those observed in the short run. For example, the decline in health status among children who suffer from reduced (or inferior) food consumption can be irreversible, retarding growth as well as cognitive and learning abilities. Estimates suggest that the food crisis has already caused the number of people suffering permanent damage from malnutrition to rise by 44 million. The financial crisis will exacerbate this impact as poor households respond to decreases in income by further cutting the quantity and quality of food consumption.

The overall outlook for the MDGs, already a cause for serious concern, has become still more worrisome. Strong economic growth in developing countries in the past decade had put the MDG for poverty reduction within reach at the global level, but the triple punch of the food, fuel, and financial crises creates new risks. In the medium term, the proportion of people in extreme poverty in the developing world is still expected to decline, but at a slower pace than envisaged before the crisis because of the slowdown in economic growth.

The food crisis, and now the global financial crisis, are reversing past gains in fighting hunger and malnutrition. Before the onset of the food crisis in 2007, there were about 850 million chronically hungry people in the developing world. This number rose to 960 million people in 2008 and is expected to climb past 1 billion in 2009, breaking the declining trend in the proportion of hungry people in the developing world and seriously jeopardizing the goal of halving this proportion by 2015. These trends call for maintaining the momentum of recent efforts to boost agricultural investment and productivity.

The goal of gender parity in primary and secondary education has seen relatively good progress and is expected to be achieved at the global level. However, prospects for gender parity in tertiary education and other targets that empower women—such as increased participation of women in wage employment in the non-agricultural sector—are less promising. The gender goals face added risks as evidence from past crises shows that women are in general more vulnerable to impact—heightening the need for attention to the gender aspects in policy responses.

Of greatest concern are the human development goals. Based on current trends, most human development goals are unlikely to be met at the global level. Despite substantial improvements in primary school enrollment and completion rates, the world is likely to miss the goal of universal primary school completion, although it could come close. Prospects are gravest in health. Large shortfalls are likely in reducing child and maternal mortality. There have been some encouraging gains in halting and beginning to reverse the spread of major communicable diseases, such as HIV/AIDS and malaria, but progress must be accelerated if the MDG targets are to be met. Large shortfalls are also likely in improving access to basic sanitation, although there is greater progress on the related goal of improving access to safe drinking water.

At the regional level, Sub-Saharan Africa lags on all MDGs, including the goal for poverty reduction. South Asia lags on most human development MDGs; it will likely meet the poverty reduction goal, although barely. At the country level, a majority of countries will fall short of most MDGs. Middle-income countries have made the most progress toward the MDGs. Many of these countries, however, continue to have large concentrations of poverty and face major challenges in achieving the non-income human development goals. Overall progress toward the MDGs has been weaker in low-income countries, although performance varies considerably across countries within this group. Progress has been slowest in countries in fragile situations. Wracked by conflict and hampered by weak governance and capacities, fragile states present difficult political and governance contexts for effective delivery of development finance and services.

Even at the MDG halfway point, around 75 million children of primary school age were not in school; 190,000 children under five died every week from preventable disease; 10,000 women died every week from treatable complications of pregnancy; more than 2 million people died from AIDS annually, close to 2 million from tuberculosis, and about 1 million from malaria; around 1 billion people suffered from hunger and twice as many were undernourished; and about half of the developing world lacked access to basic sanitation—grim numbers that would be far lower if the world were on track on the MDGs. The world can, and should, do better. Acceleration of progress requires a shared commitment to pursue this development agenda with greater vigor and urgency.

A Development Emergency

A global crisis must be met with a global response. Much of the attention initially was understandably focused on the impact of the crisis and the policy response in developed countries and in major emerging market countries that are closely integrated with international financial markets. But as the crisis has engulfed other, lower-income countries, it has become truly global. It has become clear that the impact on these countries, and the resulting grave risks to development prospects, must be addressed as part of a global response to the crisis. The challenge for the international community is to overcome the global financial crisis and respond to the deepening human and development crisis in poor countries.

The development emergency that now confronts many poor countries calls for commitment to a set of actions that signal a clear resolve to avert the potentially large human costs of the crisis and assist these countries to lay the ground for a recovery of strong growth and accelerated progress toward the MDGs. The stakes are high, and the need for action urgent.

Leaders of the Group of Twenty (G-20), at their summit held in London on April 2, 2009, made important progress in coordinating a global response to the crisis. The summit's outcome showed a clear concern with the serious development dimension of the crisis. Agreements reached at the summit have laid a good foundation for follow-up. Other major meetings in the period ahead—the Spring Meetings of the World Bank and the International Monetary Fund (IMF), the UN International Conference on the Global Financial Crisis and its Impact on Development, and the G-8 summit—can build on the progress made at the G-20 summit by elaborating a fuller agenda and developing momentum in implementation.

The crisis calls for a reaffirmation of the world's commitment to the promise of the MDGs, in the spirit of the international cooperation that gave birth to the MDGs at the turn of the century and to the Monterrey framework for the mutual accountability of both developing and developed countries for the achievement of these goals. It is fitting, therefore, that the G-20 leaders stated in their London summit communiqué that "we reaffirm our historic commitment to meeting the Millennium Development Goals." In the current context, international cooperation for development is needed more than ever.

Priorities for Action

Because the global crisis originated in the financial markets of developed countries, the first order of business is to stabilize these markets and counter the recession that the financial turmoil has triggered. This calls for timely, adequate, and coordinated actions by developed countries to restore confidence in the financial system and unfreeze the flow of credit and to counter falling demand. Major actions have been taken by these countries on both counts as they have responded with financial sector rehabilitation measures and fiscal stimulus packages. The challenge ahead is to ensure that the actions are commensurate with the scale and depth of the crisis and are appropriately coordinated internationally. Action is also needed to deal with the flaws in financial sector regulation and supervision revealed by the crisis and to establish a more solid foundation for stability in a world of globalized financial markets.

At the same time, strong and urgent actions are needed to counter the impact of the global crisis on poor countries and help them restore strong growth and recover lost ground in their progress toward the MDGs. The report sets out six priorities for action (box 1).

Ensuring an Adequate Fiscal Response

A global slowdown in growth calls for a global fiscal stimulus. Those developing countries with strong fiscal and external positions should make use of the room for fiscal stimulus that they possess. However, most developing countries faced with sharply declining growth and consequent major social disruptions lack the resources to mount any fiscal response, and will in fact experience a further erosion of their fiscal space as public revenues fall and external financing dries up. Let alone implement a fiscal stimulus, many may be forced to cut valuable infrastructure spending and social programs. Additional financing, on appropriate terms, would help them support growth and protect the poor and vulnerable from the impact of the crisis. Enabling an adequate fiscal response in developing countries would be a win-win for all. If financing were available, many of these countries have the opportunities for high-return investments that break bottlenecks to growth, quality of economic management, and institutional capacity to increase spending that would both benefit their future growth and contribute to global demand and hence

---

BOX 1   Responding to a development emergency: priorities for action

- Ensure an adequate fiscal response to support economic growth and protect poor and vulnerable groups from the impact of the crisis—consistent with maintenance of macroeconomic stability
- Shore up the private sector and improve the climate for recovery and growth in private investment, including paying special attention to strengthening financial systems
- Redouble efforts toward the human development goals, including leveraging the private sector role
- Scale up aid to poor and vulnerable countries hit hard by the crisis
- Maintain an open trade and finance system—including quick action on the Doha Round
- Ensure that the multilateral system has the mandate, resources, and instruments to support an effective global response to the global crisis

recovery in developed countries. Easing the fiscal constraint on developing countries should thus be part of the equation as the world fashions a coordinated fiscal response to the global crisis.

As many as 90 percent of developing countries are assessed to be highly or moderately exposed to the impact of the crisis, as they face slowing growth, high levels of poverty, or both. Three-quarters of the exposed countries lack the fiscal capacity to finance programs to curb the effects of the downturn. Those among them with good macroeconomic management and institutional capacities should be assisted with financing to enhance their fiscal space to respond to the crisis. Thanks to their efforts over the past decade to improve macroeconomic policies and governance, at least one-half of developing countries today have the macroeconomic conditions (taking into account fiscal and external sustainability considerations) and institutional capacities to underpin some fiscal expansion were financing on appropriate terms available. At the individual country level, fiscal response will of course need to be tailored to specific country circumstances.

Countries must also use available scope for domestic resource mobilization. The crisis calls for an even sharper focusing of expenditures on core priorities—infrastructure for growth, key investments in human capital, and social safety nets. Investment projects for new spending must be carefully chosen to address key bottlenecks to growth and maximize development impact. Spending on social safety nets must be targeted to reach the intended beneficiaries—through programs such as conditional cash transfers to poor households, workfare schemes, and maternal-child or school feeding programs.

Supporting the Private Sector

Economic growth is central to poverty reduction and to the achievement of the MDGs more broadly. A vibrant private sector is key to economic growth and job creation. Fiscal stimulus will catalyze sustainable economic growth only if there is a vigorous private sector response. The private sector, in turn, will rebound only if supported by an appropriate enabling environment. Access to finance and infrastructure and the quality of business regulation are three key determinants of the private sector enabling environment.

In the current credit crunch, particular urgency attaches to shoring up the private sector's access to finance for investment and trade, both of which have contracted sharply. Governments, working with development partners, need to move quickly on this front, with a special focus on access to finance for small and medium enterprises that are critical for job creation and that are finding themselves particularly squeezed by the credit contraction. At the same time, the crisis has underscored the importance of broader reforms to improve financial system stability and soundness, including strengthening financial regulation and supervision. Some countries will likely face the need to recapitalize distressed financial institutions and must prepare for that in advance.

The most urgent issues with respect to infrastructure development in the current context also pertain to financing, as both governments and private investors face increased financial constraints. Multilateral financial institutions will need to play a stronger supporting role, including most immediately in shoring up viable ongoing public-private partnership projects facing financial distress. However, more financing is only part of what is needed to meet the longer-term infrastructure challenge in developing countries. For example, it is estimated that Sub-Saharan Africa could reduce its infrastructure financing gap of about $40 billion annually by as much as 45 percent through improved management of investments, reduction of operating inefficiencies, and better cost recovery. Also, even with the tighter financing conditions, countries implementing reforms of the regulatory and institutional framework for public-private partnerships in infrastructure can expect to attract more private investment—and enhance its development effectiveness. Investments in energy-efficient infrastructure offer the dual benefits of contributing to economic recovery and growth and mitigating climate change. Going forward, carbon markets can play an increasingly important role in mobilizing private financing in support of investments that promote environmental sustainability.

Measured by the World Bank Group's Doing Business and Enterprise Surveys, developing countries have implemented significant reforms to improve their regulatory environments for private sector activity. However, progress has been uneven, and much scope for regulatory improvements remains. The crisis has reinforced findings from research that the aim should be better, not necessarily fewer, regulations. Simplification of regulations—to make them more efficient and streamlined—must ensure adequate protection of public interests. The crisis has underscored the role of appropriate regulatory oversight.

Research also finds complementarity between regulatory reforms and broader improvements in governance. Regulatory reforms have greater impact in better institutional environments. Weak institutional capacities for enforcement undermine the effectiveness and credibility of the regulatory framework. In many countries, firms report corruption as a major constraint to business. Strong institutions and good governance, therefore, are an important underpinning of a conducive environment for private activity—and of development effectiveness more broadly.

Redoubling Efforts toward Human Development Goals

Progress toward the human development goals must be accelerated. The crisis gives added urgency to reinforcing key programs in health and education, such as control of major diseases including HIV/AIDS and malaria, health systems strengthening, and the Fast Track Initiative in education. It also creates pressing short-term challenges, as it calls for a special focus on social protection programs and services that shield poor and vulnerable households from the likely severe human impacts, such as a rise in child mortality. This implies a high priority for primary health care and nutrition programs in rural areas and in poor urban neighborhoods, including paying special attention to gender needs. A strengthening of the social safety nets will bring immediate relief but, in concert with improvement of key services in health and education, it will also help safeguard health and education outcomes in the medium term. Financing these needs will require increased donor support, but countries will also need to create fiscal space by pruning lower-priority spending and seeking efficiency gains in existing programs.

The crisis also calls for better leveraging the role of the private sector in human development. Governments are key actors in the financing and delivery of human development services, but the private sector (for-profit and non-profit) is playing an increasingly significant role. For example, one-half of health spending in many developing countries comes from private sources. Recent surveys in Sub-Saharan Africa and South Asia find that more than half of the MDG-related maternal, reproductive, and child health services used are privately provided. In South Asia, the share of private enrollment in primary and secondary education averages about 30 percent. The scale of the MDG challenge calls for mobilization of resources from all sources, and there is significant potential for greater private sector contributions—not only of more resources but also innovation, flexibility, and improvements in quality that private participation can bring. There are successful examples of different combinations of government and private partnerships in service delivery and financing, and countries can consider options that best suit their circumstances. To work effectively with the private sector, governments need to develop requisite capacities for regulation and oversight, use incentives judiciously, and improve governance and accountability arrangements.

The expanded potential of private international financing (from non-governmental organizations, foundations, and business corporations) for human development in poor countries and related innovations in financing modalities and delivery vehicles also needs to be effectively tapped. Important examples of private giving include sizable contributions, from the Bill and Melinda Gates Foundation, for example, into the Global Alliance for Vaccines and Immunization and the Global Fund to Fight AIDS, Tuberculosis, and Malaria. The Advanced Market Commitment mechanism represents an innovative way to leverage corporate finance in development of treatments for diseases in poor countries.

Scaling Up Aid to Poor Countries

The urgency for donors to deliver on their aid commitments cannot be overemphasized in the current context. Official development assistance (ODA) from members of the Development Assistance Committee (DAC) of the Organisation for Economic Co-operation and Development (OECD) rose by about 10 percent in real terms in 2008. This is a welcome development, following declines in ODA in both 2006 and 2007. In real terms, ODA from DAC donors in 2008 was about $29 billion short of the Gleneagles target of $130 billion per annum by 2010. ODA to Sub-Saharan Africa was about $20 billion short of the 2010 target of $50 billion per annum. Donors should scale up rapidly to deliver on these commitments. Although the crisis has put donors' fiscal positions under increased pressure, the additional sums needed to meet the Gleneagles commitments amount to a fraction of the support they have provided to rescue individual financial institutions in their countries and a miniscule proportion of the fiscal stimulus packages they have announced.

Indeed, the crisis calls for going beyond the commitments made at Gleneagles as

the needs of poor countries have increased sharply. One option for additional support is the proposal by President Zoellick of the World Bank that developed countries invest 0.7 percent of their stimulus packages, or about $15 billion based on the packages announced to date, in a Vulnerability Fund to help developing countries. The fund would support three crisis-response priorities in developing countries that lack the resources to act on their own—strengthening social safety nets, funding investments in essential infrastructure, and supporting financing for small and medium enterprises and microfinance institutions. The resources would be channeled through multilateral and bilateral agencies, in programs backed by safeguards to ensure that they are well spent.

As donors pick up the pace in delivering aid, progress on the Accra Agenda for Action to improve aid effectiveness—better aid alignment and harmonization, improved aid predictability and timeliness, and a stronger focus on results—should also be expedited. Improving the effectiveness of the use of resources is even more important in times of crisis and related budget constraints. Moreover, as the aid landscape changes with a growing role of non-DAC official donors and private sources of aid and an increasing array of aid modalities, aid coordination frameworks will need to encompass a broader range of development partners.

Private aid has emerged as an increasingly important player in development finance. The OECD estimated private international giving at $18.6 billion in 2007, but this is widely considered to be an underestimate. Alternative estimates place private international giving from the United States alone at $34.8 billion in 2006. The sources of private giving are various—foundations, corporations, and civil society organizations of different types. The rising role of private assistance has spawned innovative public-private partnerships in development activities, especially in health, education, and climate change. There is some concern that the financial crisis may interrupt the rising trend in private aid. Nonetheless, private aid today represents a source that, if effectively deployed, can be an important complement to public aid and a partner in development.

Maintaining an Open Trade and Finance System

It is vitally important to maintain trade openness and resist the recent rise in protectionist pressures. The food, fuel, and financial crises have put great strain on the world trading system. In early 2008, sharp increases in food prices triggered some harmful trade policy responses, including the imposition of trade taxes, quotas, and even outright export bans.[2] Protectionism risks have intensified with the financial crisis as economic activity collapses and unemployment rises. A number of countries have raised border barriers or subsidized export or import-competing industries such as automotive and steel, and there has been a rise in inward-looking "buy national" policies. Such responses retard needed market corrections, distort trade, and risk retaliation. The world can ill-afford competitive beggar-thy-neighbor policies that would only deepen the slump in global trade and undercut prospects for economic recovery for all.

At the London summit, G-20 leaders reaffirmed their commitment to refrain from raising new barriers to investment or trade in goods and services, imposing new export restrictions, or implementing World Trade Organization (WTO)-inconsistent measures to stimulate exports, and agreed to rectify promptly any such measures. This commitment must be followed through with firm resolve—in contrast to a similar commitment made by the G-20 leaders at their summit in Washington, DC, in November 2008 that was not adhered to by a majority of G-20 members.

The crisis increases the urgency of bolstering multilateral cooperation in trade. A quick and successful conclusion to the Doha Round of trade negotiations would help to ease protectionist pressures, keep markets

open, and strengthen the rules-based multilateral trading system. It would also provide a much-needed boost in confidence to the global economy at a time of high stress and uncertainty.

Trade has been a powerful force for growth and poverty reduction, and in turn for progress toward the MDGs, in developing countries. Maintaining and improving developing countries' access to international markets is therefore a key element of the development agenda. A complementary priority is the strengthening of support for trade facilitation to address behind-the-border constraints to trade—improvement of trade-related infrastructure, finance, regulations, and logistics such as customs services and standards compliance. To take advantage of trade opportunities, developing countries need to enhance their competitiveness by reducing the high trade costs associated with the behind-the-border barriers. The ease of moving goods internationally has become an increasingly important determinant of competitiveness in the globalized marketplace. Research shows that in many low-income countries trade facilitation can be at least as important as further reduction in trade tariffs in boosting trade.

In support of trade facilitation, aid for trade should be scaled up substantially. While rising overall, aid for trade from bilateral sources declined in 2007. More of such aid needs to be directed to low-income and the least developed countries, which currently receive only about one-half and one-quarter of the total, respectively.

It is also important to preserve the openness of the international financial system. There are widespread concerns that government interventions in financial systems in advanced countries may be accompanied by pressures on financial institutions to curtail cross-border lending. A shift toward such financial mercantilism must be resisted. It would particularly hurt financial flows to developing countries, which are already under increasing stress as a result of the financial contagion and the potential crowding-out implications of the sharply increased borrowing requirements of advanced country governments.

The international community has recognized the importance of addressing the crunch in trade finance in a coordinated fashion. The G-20 leaders agreed at their London summit to ensure the availability of at least $250 billion of trade finance over the next two years through their export credit and investment agencies and through the multilateral development banks (MDBs)—including up to $50 billion of trade liquidity support over the next three years through the new Global Trade Liquidity Pool introduced by the International Finance Corporation (IFC).

Empowering Multilateral Institutions

The international financial institutions (IFIs) have a crucial role to play in supporting an effective response to the global crisis and the development emergency that now confronts many poor countries. They are essential to forging a coordinated global response to a global crisis. Two key priorities are meeting the sharply increased needs of developing countries for balance of payments financing and budget support for critical public spending such as social safety net programs and key infrastructure investments, and shoring up the private sector in these countries through support for trade financing, recapitalization of banks, and financing for small and medium enterprises. The IFIs are responding with increased financing and facilities and processes designed to accelerate the speed of response, including facilities with a special focus on support to the poor and vulnerable, such as the World Bank's Vulnerability Financing Facility. But they will need more resources to meet the needs.

The IFIs are facing an unprecedented rise in demand for financing. With the slump in private capital flows, estimates of developing countries' financing gap in 2009 reach as high as $1 trillion. The IFIs will need to play a role in filling some of this gap,

including using their leverage ability to help revive private capital flows. In this context, the G-20 leaders at their London summit took timely action in agreeing to support a sizable increase in resources available to the IMF and the MDBs.

The G-20 leaders agreed to support a tripling of resources available to the IMF to $750 billion. They also supported a general allocation of the Special Drawing Rights (SDRs) equivalent to $250 billion to increase global liquidity, $100 billion of which will go directly to emerging market and developing countries ($19 billion to low-income countries). The IMF has moved quickly to strengthen its lending framework, including establishing a new Flexible Credit Line to provide large and upfront financing to emerging market economies with strong fundamentals and policies, enhancing the flexibility of the regular stand-by arrangements, doubling access limits for emerging markets and low-income countries, and reforming conditionality to make it more focused and tailored to country circumstances. The IMF plans to step up its lending to low-income countries to around $3 billion a year over the next two years—triple last year's level.

The G-20 leaders also supported an increase in MDB lending of $100 billion to a total of around $300 billion over the next three years and agreed to ensure that all MDBs have the appropriate capital. They supported a 200 percent general capital increase at the Asian Development Bank (ADB) and reviews of the need for capital increases at several other MDBs. They also agreed to support, through voluntary bilateral contributions, the World Bank's Vulnerability Framework, including the Infrastructure Crisis Facility and the Rapid Social Response Fund. The concessional windows of the African Development Bank, the ADB, and the World Bank have received significant increases in resources through recent replenishments. Also, debt relief provided through the Heavily Indebted Poor Countries (HIPC) Initiative and the Multilateral Debt Relief Initiative (MDRI) has increased fiscal space in many poor countries. Nonetheless, the rise in the financing needs of low-income countries hit hard by the crisis will test the adequacy of available resources. An immediate need is for donors to honor existing pledges to the MDB concessional windows and to the MDRI.

The MDBs will also need to review existing financing instruments and constraints on capital utilization to increase the flexibility of response and make the capital go further. Areas that may be considered include increasing individual country limits on lending; raising limits on the proportion of quick-disbursing financing; front-loading commitments; accelerating disbursements on existing projects; and allowing low-income countries access to non-concessional windows while ensuring debt sustainability. Increased demand for risk mitigation and public-private partnerships will call for more fully exploiting the leverage of the MDBs' private sector arms, such as the IFC, and guarantee instruments.

The role of the IFIs, of course, extends beyond financing. Knowledge is a core IFI comparative advantage. A crucial role for IFIs in the context of the current global crisis is to inform policy making by analyzing the international spillovers of national policy actions and showing the interconnected nature of the challenges, and to highlight the need to ensure that national responses are consistent with the global good. Amid rising pressures for policies to turn inward, the IFIs' role in warning against the risks of trade protectionism and financial mercantilism is indispensable. Drawing policy lessons from the current crisis, especially but not only in financial regulation, will be another key area. The IMF will have a particularly important role in enhanced surveillance of risk in the globalized financial markets, in collaboration with a new Financial Stability Board.

The crisis has highlighted the need to reform the IFIs—to align their governance with today's economic realities—and more broadly to reconfigure 20th-century global institutions to match 21st-century global challenges. As an old Chinese proverb says, a crisis is an opportunity riding the dangerous wind. The present crisis can set the stage for a new multilateralism that supports sustainable and inclusive globalization.

Notes

1. Currently available information provides only a partial picture of the impact of the crisis on poverty and human development outcomes. A recent proposal by the United Kingdom seeks to establish a Global Poverty Alert to capture fuller, real-time information to underpin the design of policy responses. The communiqué of the recent G-20 summit in London called on the UN, working with other global institutions, to establish an effective mechanism to monitor the impact of the crisis on the poorest and most vulnerable.

2. Distorted trade policies are part of the reason for the emergence of the food crisis in the first place.

Goals and Targets from the Millennium Declaration

GOAL 1	ERADICATE EXTREME POVERTY AND HUNGER
TARGET 1.A	Halve, between 1990 and 2015, the proportion of people whose income is less than $1.25 a day
TARGET 1.B	Achieve full and productive employment and decent work for all, including women and young people
TARGET 1.C	Halve, between 1990 and 2015, the proportion of people who suffer from hunger

GOAL 2	ACHIEVE UNIVERSAL PRIMARY EDUCATION
TARGET 2.A	Ensure that by 2015, children everywhere, boys and girls alike, will be able to complete a full course of primary schooling

GOAL 3	PROMOTE GENDER EQUALITY AND EMPOWER WOMEN
TARGET 3.A	Eliminate gender disparity in primary and secondary education, preferably by 2005, and at all levels of education no later than 2015

GOAL 4	REDUCE CHILD MORTALITY
TARGET 4.A	Reduce by two-thirds, between 1990 and 2015, the under-five mortality rate

GOAL 5	IMPROVE MATERNAL HEALTH
TARGET 5.A	Reduce by three-quarters, between 1990 and 2015, the maternal mortality ratio
TARGET 5.B	Achieve by 2015 universal access to reproductive health

GOAL 6	COMBAT HIV/AIDS, MALARIA, AND OTHER DISEASES
TARGET 6.A	Have halted by 2015 and begun to reverse the spread of HIV/AIDS
TARGET 6.B	Achieve by 2010 universal access to treatment for HIV/AIDS for all those who need it
TARGET 6.C	Have halted by 2015 and begun to reverse the incidence of malaria and other major diseases

GOAL 7	ENSURE ENVIRONMENTAL SUSTAINABILITY
TARGET 7.A	Integrate the principles of sustainable development into country policies and programs and reverse the loss of environmental resources
TARGET 7.B	Reduce biodiversity loss, achieving by 2010 a significant reduction in the rate of loss
TARGET 7.C	Halve by 2015 the proportion of people without sustainable access to safe drinking water and basic sanitation
TARGET 7.D	Have achieved a significant improvement by 2020 in the lives of at least 100 million slum dwellers

GOAL 8	DEVELOP A GLOBAL PARTNERSHIP FOR DEVELOPMENT
TARGET 8.A	Develop further an open, rule-based, predictable, nondiscriminatory trading and financial system (including a commitment to good governance, development, and poverty reduction, nationally and internationally)
TARGET 8.B	Address the special needs of the least-developed countries (including tariff- and quota-free access for exports of the least-developed countries; enhanced debt relief for heavily indebted poor countries and cancellation of official bilateral debt; and more generous official development assistance for countries committed to reducing poverty)
TARGET 8.C	Address the special needs of landlocked countries and small island developing states (through the Programme of Action for the Sustainable Development of Small Island Developing States and the outcome of the 22nd special session of the General Assembly)
TARGET 8.D	Deal comprehensively with the debt problems of developing countries through national and international measures to make debt sustainable in the long term
TARGET 8.E	In cooperation with pharmaceutical companies, provide access to affordable, essential drugs in developing countries
TARGET 8.F	In cooperation with the private sector, make available the benefits of new technologies, especially information and communications

Source: United Nations. 2008. *Report of the Secretary-General on the Indicators for Monitoring the Millennium Development Goals.* E/CN.3/2008/29. New York.

Note: The Millennium Development Goals and targets come from the Millennium Declaration, signed by 189 countries, including 147 heads of state and government, in September 2000 (http://www.un.org/millennium/declaration/ares552e.htm) and from further agreement by member states at the 2005 World Summit (Resolution adopted by the General Assembly–A/RES/60/1). The goals and targets are interrelated and should be seen as a whole. They represent a partnership between the developed countries and the developing countries "to create an environment—at the national and global levels alike—which is conducive to development and the elimination of poverty."

MDGs: Crisis Impact and Outlook

Assessment of the progress toward the Millennium Development Goals (MDGs) at the halfway point in 2008 showed major shortfalls in several of them. At high-level meetings held during the year, world leaders noted the substantial progress that had been made toward some of the goals, especially poverty reduction, but expressed grave concern at the prospect that most of the other goals, in particular the human development goals, would not be achieved if past trends continued. At the UN General Assembly's High-Level Event on the MDGs held in September 2008, Secretary General Ban Ki-moon noted that "we face nothing less than a development emergency," and the meeting resulted in a call to action to scale up development efforts and put the world back on track to achieve the MDGs.[1] A similar assessment was echoed in the report of the MDG Africa Steering Group comprising all major multilateral development organizations that focus on the region facing the most serious shortfalls.[2] Since then, the global financial crisis, coming on the heels of the food and fuel crises, threatens further setbacks, making the achievement of the goals still more challenging and the need for stronger action still more urgent.[3]

Crisis Impact on MDGs

The global financial crisis can seriously retard progress toward the MDGs. The impact will be felt on all MDGs, including the goals for poverty reduction and human development. Poor countries that are vulnerable to shocks and have the least capacity to respond with ameliorative actions are at particular risk of falling further behind. A recent assessment by the World Bank found that almost 40 percent of developing countries were highly exposed to the poverty effects of the crisis (with both declining growth rates and high levels of poverty); most of the others were moderately exposed, with fewer than 10 percent facing little risk. Three-quarters of the exposed countries had limited fiscal capacity to expand programs to curb the effects of the economic downturn. Within countries, the poor typically are more vulnerable and have the least cushion.[4]

Strong economic growth in developing countries in the past decade had put the MDG for poverty reduction (halving the proportion of extreme poor in the population between 1990 and 2015) within reach at the global level. But the triple jeopardy of the food, fuel, and financial crises adds new challenges. The rise in food prices between 2005 and 2008 pushed an estimated 160 million to 200 million more people into extreme poverty. Falling food prices since mid-2008 are helping to reduce this number. However, because changes in local prices lag behind changes in international prices, not all of the benefits of lower international prices have been felt yet. Preliminary projections suggest that as local prices come into line with international prices, between 90 million and 120 million people who were pushed into poverty by high food prices by 2008 may emerge from poverty in 2009. Still, up to 100 million people pushed into poverty by the high food prices would remain poor in 2009.

The growth slowdown resulting from the financial crisis will add to the poverty impact of high food prices. Projected economic growth in developing countries in 2009 on average is now only about a quarter of that forecast before the onset of the financial crisis. Past trends show that a decline in the average GDP growth rate in developing countries by one percentage point can trap as many as 20 million more people in poverty. Estimates of the poverty impact of the growth slowdown in developing countries as a result of the financial crisis range from 55 million to 90 million more poor people in 2009 than anticipated before the crisis.[5] At current growth projections, overall poverty rates in the developing world are still expected to fall in 2009 but at a much slower pace than before the crisis. The poverty impact of the crisis will vary across regions and countries. In Sub-Saharan Africa and South Asia (except India), the growth slowdown essentially eliminates the prospect of continued reductions in the poverty count in 2009. Within these regions, which already have high poverty rates, rising poverty can be expected in some of the more fragile and low-growth economies, which may experience declines in per capita incomes as a result of the growth slowdown.

The poverty impact of the crisis would be even greater if the crisis deepens and growth in developing countries falters further than currently anticipated. Severe financial crises in the past that caused growth to turn negative produced sharp increases in poverty rates in the affected countries. During the East Asian crisis of the late 1990s, for example, the sharp reversal in growth and the associated rise in unemployment and decline in wages caused the poverty headcount index in Indonesia to rise by 11 percent in 1997 and a further 19.9 percent in 1998. In Thailand, the increases in the same crisis years were 9.8 percent and 12.9 percent, respectively.[6]

Progress in reducing hunger and malnutrition, which along with poverty reduction is part of MDG 1, has also been affected. Although the proportion of people who suffer from hunger has fallen since 1990, there are serious shortfalls in achieving the goal of halving the incidence of hunger and malnutrition. The recent food crisis is eroding some of the hard-won past gains. High prices have increased the number of people without sufficient access to food because the majority of the world's poor, particularly those who live in urban areas, are net food buyers and spend over half of their income on food. About 1 billion people now suffer from hunger, and about 2 billion are undernourished. The food crisis is estimated to have caused the number of people suffering permanent damage resulting from early childhood malnutrition to rise by 44 million in 2008. The financial crisis and the resulting fall in economic growth are likely to exacerbate this impact. Decreases in household incomes can reduce both the quantity and quality of food consumption. Children and women are particularly vulnerable to such impacts.

With the world already off track on most of the MDGs in human development, the financial crisis threatens to further set back progress. In the face of economic crises, both household and public investments in human capital tend to suffer. With falling employment, wages, and asset values, and with weak social insurance systems, poor households in developing countries may not be able to cope with the economic shocks without cutting investments in human capital. Faced with declining revenues and limited financing options, government social sector spending is also likely to come under pressure. For example, Argentina and Indonesia cut public health expenditures by two-thirds during the crises of the 1990s. Experience suggests that growth collapses from financial crises are costly for human development outcomes. Countries that suffered economic contractions of 10 percent or more between 1980 and 2004 experienced more than 1 million additional infant deaths. During the crisis of the late 1990s, infant mortality in Indonesia increased 1.8 percentage points. In Peru, during the economic crisis of the late 1980s, the infant mortality rate rose by 2.5 percentage points for children born during the crisis, implying about 18,000 more infant deaths.[7]

Human development outcomes tend to deteriorate more quickly during growth decelerations than they improve during growth accelerations.[8] The projected slowdown in growth in developing countries is likely to sharply slow progress in reducing infant mortality. Based on current projections of lower growth, preliminary analysis shows that infant deaths in developing countries may be 200,000 to 400,000 per year higher on average between 2009 and the MDG target year of 2015 than they would have been in the absence of the crisis; that translates into an additional 1.4 million to 2.8 million infant deaths during the period.[9] In poor developing countries, education outcomes such as school enrollment also tend to deteriorate during economic crises. Evidence indicates that fluctuations in income have a larger impact on survival and school enrollment among girls than among boys. The intensity of the impacts of the financial crisis on health and education outcomes will vary across countries, depending on their initial conditions, exposure to crisis impact, and policy response.

The long-run implications of the crisis for human development outcomes may be more severe than those observed in the short run. When poor households withdraw their children from school, there is a significant risk that they will not return once the crisis is over or that they will be unable to fill the learning gaps resulting from lack of attendance. And the decline in nutritional and health status among children who suffer from reduced (or lower-quality) food consumption can be irreversible, retarding their growth and cognitive and learning abilities.

Overall MDG Progress and Outlook

Even though the global economic crisis will slow progress, the target for reducing income poverty remains within reach at the global level based on current growth projections, which envisage a recovery in growth starting in 2010. The goals for gender parity in primary and secondary education and for access to safe water have also seen relatively good progress and are expected to be met at the global level by 2015, although prospects for gender parity in tertiary education and other targets about empowerment of women are less promising. Of greatest concern are the nonincome human development goals. Based on current trends, most human development MDGs—especially for child and maternal mortality, but also for primary school completion, nutrition, and sanitation—are unlikely to be met at the global level (figure 1).

Within this global picture, considerable variation occurs across regions and countries. At the regional level, Sub-Saharan Africa lags on all MDGs, including the goal for poverty reduction, which on current trends will be achieved or nearly achieved in all other regions. Thanks to rapid growth,

FIGURE 1   MDGs at the global level: serious shortfalls loom on human development goals

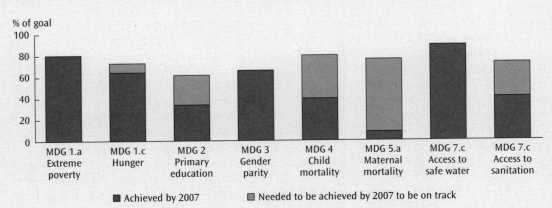

% of goal

Legend: ■ Achieved by 2007   ■ Needed to be achieved by 2007 to be on track

Source: Staff calculations based on World Development Indicators database.
Note: Calculations are based on the most recent year for which data are available. MDG 1.a: Poverty headcount ratio (PPP2005 US$1.25 a day); MDG 1.c: Underweight under-five children (U.S. child growth standards); MDG 2: Primary education completion rate; MDG 3: Gender parity in primary and secondary education; MDG 4: Under-five mortality rate; MDG 5.a: Maternal mortality ratio (modeled estimates); MDG 7.c: Access to improved water source; MDG 7.c: Access to improved sanitation facilities.

especially in China, the East Asia region has already succeeded in halving extreme poverty. South Asia is on track to achieve the poverty reduction goal, but it is seriously off track on most human development goals. On the goals relating to health, most regions are off track, though the rate of progress varies substantially across regions, with East Asia, Europe and Central Asia, and Latin America in general doing better than the other regions.

Middle-income countries have made the most rapid progress toward the MDGs. These countries as a group are on track to achieve the target for poverty reduction. Many of these countries, however, continue to have large concentrations of poverty, in part reflecting high levels of income inequality. This factor, together with the large population size of some middle-income countries, means that these countries remain home to a majority of the world's poor in absolute numbers. Many of these countries also continue to face major challenges in achieving the nonincome human development goals. Overall progress toward the MDGs has been weaker in low-income countries, although

here too performance varies considerably across countries within the group. Progress toward the MDGs has been slowest in fragile and conflict-affected states (figure 2). Wracked by conflict and hampered by weak capacities, these states—more than half of which are in Sub-Saharan Africa—present difficult political and governance contexts for effective delivery of development finance and services. Fragile states account for close to one-fifth of the population of low-income countries but more than one-third of their poor people. Looking ahead, the challenge to achieve the MDGs will increasingly be concentrated in low-income countries, especially fragile states.

Review of data for individual countries reveals that many countries will achieve a few of the MDGs, but that on current trends a majority are likely to fall short of most of the goals. Among countries for which data are available, the proportion of off-track countries exceeds that of on-track countries for all MDGs except those for poverty reduction and gender parity at school (figure 3). In many countries MDG data continue to suffer from large gaps.

FIGURE 2 Fragile states have made the least progress toward the MDGs

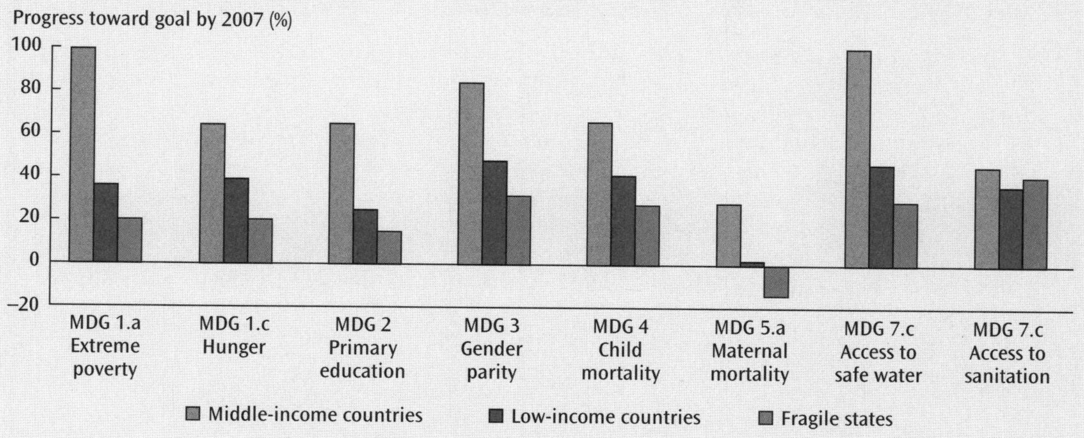

Progress toward goal by 2007 (%)
100
80
60
40
20
0
–20
MDG 1.a Extreme poverty
MDG 1.c Hunger
MDG 2 Primary education
MDG 3 Gender parity
MDG 4 Child mortality
MDG 5.a Maternal mortality
MDG 7.c Access to safe water
MDG 7.c Access to sanitation
Middle-income countries
Low-income countries
Fragile states

Source: Staff calculations based on World Development Indicators database.

Closer Look at Progress by Goal

New data on poverty show that the number of people living in extreme poverty in developing countries fell from about 1.8 billion in 1990 to 1.4 billion in 2005, decreasing from 42 percent to 25 percent of the population (box 1). Much of this progress is attributable to East Asia, which reduced the incidence of poverty from 55 percent in 1990 to 17 percent in 2005. In China, the proportion declined from 60 percent to 16 percent, and the absolute number of extreme poor fell from 683 million to 208 million (figure 4). The number of people living in extreme poverty in India rose between 1990 and 2005, from 436 million to 456 million, but their share in total population declined from 51 to 42 percent. Thanks to a resurgence of growth in this decade, Sub-Saharan Africa also was able to reduce the proportion of poor people, from 58 percent in 1990 to 51 percent in 2005, but the absolute number of poor people rose from 296 million to 388 million. Of all developing regions, Sub-Saharan Africa alone remains seriously off track to achieve the poverty reduction MDG, and the global economic crisis threatens to interrupt the region's recent progress in picking up the pace on economic growth and poverty reduction. For developing countries as a whole, the proportion of extreme poor is projected to fall to 15 percent by 2015, below the MDG target of 21 percent,

FIGURE 3 Most countries are falling short of most MDGs

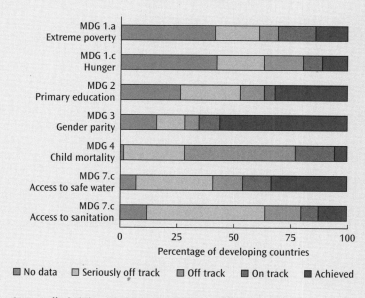

MDG 1.a Extreme poverty
MDG 1.c Hunger
MDG 2 Primary education
MDG 3 Gender parity
MDG 4 Child mortality
MDG 7.c Access to safe water
MDG 7.c Access to sanitation
0
25
50
75
100
Percentage of developing countries
No data
Seriously off track
Off track
On track
Achieved

Source: Staff calculations based on World Development Indicators database.
Note: The graph covers 144 developing countries.

BOX 1   New estimates of global poverty

The *Global Monitoring Report 2009* uses new estimates of global poverty based on recently released data on purchasing power parities (PPPs) compiled by the International Comparison Program (ICP) and on an expanded set of household income and expenditure surveys covering 115 developing countries. As part of this revision, the international poverty line has been recalibrated to $1.25 a day. This new poverty line, measured in 2005 prices, replaces the $1.08 a day poverty line, measured in 1993 prices, often described as "a dollar a day," which has been widely accepted as the international standard for extreme poverty. The new poverty line maintains the same standard for extreme poverty—the poverty line typical of the poorest countries in the world—but updates it using the latest information on the cost of living in developing countries.

2005 ICP benchmark

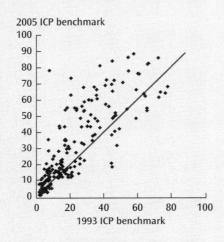

1993 ICP benchmark

Note: The diamonds represent old and new poverty rates for individual countries.

Proportion of people below old and new poverty lines (%)

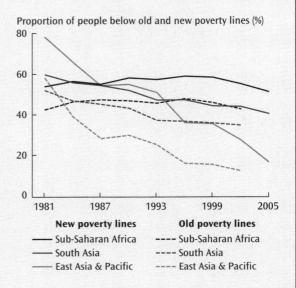

The new estimates change our view of poverty in the world (see the two figures above). There are more poor people than previously estimated, and the incidence of poverty reaches further into middle-income countries. Previous rounds of the ICP underestimated average price levels in developing countries (perhaps because they did not fully adjust for quality differences) and thus overestimated their standards of living. By the new measurements, about 1,375 million people in developing countries (25 percent of the population) were living in extreme poverty in 2005, compared with the previous estimate of 935 million (17 percent) using the old measurements. The new, higher estimates for poverty imply that the target poverty rate to achieve the poverty MDG is 20.9 percent (half of the now higher estimate of 41.7 percent in 1990), rather than the previous 14.4 percent (half of the previous estimate of 28.7 percent in 1990). The upward revision of the poverty level does not imply that the rate of poverty reduction since 1990 has been less rapid that estimated previously.[a]

a. Chen and Ravallion 2008.

but the economic crisis adds serious new risks to the prospects for achieving the poverty goal in many countries.

The developing world is not on track to achieve the target of halving the proportion of people who suffer from hunger, and the food crisis can slow progress further. Reducing malnutrition has a multiplier effect, because it is essential to success on several other MDGs, including those relating to infant mortality, maternal mortality, and education. Child malnutrition accounts for 35 percent of the disease burden of children under age five. More than 20 percent of maternal mortality is attributable to malnutrition during pregnancy. The proportion of under-five children in developing countries who are underweight declined from 33 percent in 1990 to 26 percent in 2006, a much slower pace than needed to halve this proportion by 2015. While some regions have achieved stronger gains, progress has been slowest in Sub-Saharan Africa and South Asia. These regions have the highest incidence of child malnutrition, with severe to moderate stunting affecting as many as 35 percent of children under five. Currently, more than 140 million children under five in developing countries suffer from malnutrition.

Despite substantial improvements in primary school net enrollment and completion rates, the world is likely to miss the goal of universal primary school completion (MDG 2), though it will come close. In 2006 the primary school completion rate reached 85 percent for all developing countries and 93 percent in middle-income countries but was just 65 percent in low-income countries. Even with rising enrollments, as many as 75 million children of primary school age were not in school in 2007. Whereas other regions have shown good progress toward MDG 2, sizable shortfalls are likely in Sub-Saharan Africa and South Asia.

Gender equality and female empowerment are not only important in themselves as the third MDG, they are also effective ways

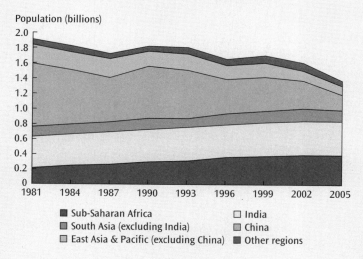

FIGURE 4 The decline in the number of people living in extreme poverty is largely attributable to East Asia, China in particular

Source: World Development Indicators, Poverty Data 2008.

to improve progress on the other MDG targets related to poverty, hunger, disease, and education. Considerable progress has been made in reducing gender disparity in education. Almost two-thirds of developing countries reached gender parity at the primary school level by 2005, and the MDG 3 target of achieving gender parity in primary and secondary education can be met by 2015. However, Sub-Saharan Africa is likely to fall short, even though it is making notable progress. MDG 3 also calls for gender parity in tertiary education, gender equality in employment, and increased political representation of women. Progress toward these goals has been slower and more uneven. The gender goals face added risks from the current crisis because evidence from past crises suggests that women in general are more vulnerable to impact.

Prospects are gravest for the MDGs relating to health. The under-five mortality rate in developing countries declined from 93 to 72 deaths per 1,000 live births between 1990 and 2006, showing notable but insufficient progress to meet the MDG 4 of reducing under-five mortality by two-thirds. In 2006, 10 million children died before age five from preventable diseases, compared with 13 million in 1990. The HIV/AIDS epidemic and civil conflicts have hampered Sub-Saharan Africa's progress in reducing child mortality, adding to other contributory factors such as malnutrition, lack of access to water and sanitation, and lack of mothers' education. The under-five mortality rate in the region in 2007 was still as high as 146 deaths per 1,000 live births, though down from the 1990 level of 183. Sub-Saharan Africa accounts for 20 percent of the world's children under age five but 50 percent of all child deaths. Progress in reducing infant mortality is also well short of the target in South Asia.

Relatively little progress has been made in reducing maternal mortality. The maternal mortality ratio declined by less than 1 percent per year between 1990 and 2005, much slower than the 5.5 percent annual decline needed to achieve the MDG 5 of reducing maternal mortality by three-quarters between 1990 and 2015. Most regions are off track on this goal, Sub-Saharan Africa and South Asia most seriously. Sub-Saharan Africa has the highest maternal mortality ratio at 900 deaths per 100,000 births, which is twenty times greater than the maternal mortality ratio in Europe and Central Asia. Progress in reducing the region's high maternal mortality rate has been negligible. Globally, the maternal health improvement goal has seen the least progress among all the MDGs. As many as 10,000 women die every week in developing countries from treatable complications of pregnancy and childbirth.

Progress toward MDG 6 targets for halting and beginning to reverse the spread of major communicable diseases has been mixed. An estimated 33 million individuals were living with HIV/AIDS at the global level in 2007, about two-thirds of them in Sub-Saharan Africa. Annual deaths from AIDS are estimated at more than 2 million

a year. The HIV prevalence rate has shown some decline in Sub-Saharan Africa, but it has risen in other regions, albeit from much lower levels than in Africa. The coverage of antiretroviral treatment for HIV-infected individuals has improved significantly, and now almost one-third of people living with HIV in developing countries receive the treatment. However, most countries are struggling to meet the target of achieving by 2010 universal access to HIV treatment for those who need it. The prevalence of tuberculosis, a disease that killed 1.8 million people in 2006, has been declining in all regions except Sub-Saharan Africa. Mortality from malaria remains high—at about 1 million annually, 80 percent of whom are children under five in Sub-Saharan Africa—but lack of data makes it difficult to monitor the incidence over time.

Substantial progress has been made toward the targets of halving the proportion of people without access to clean water and basic sanitation, part of MDG 7 on environmental sustainability. On current trends, the water access target is likely to be achieved at the global level and in most regions. However, the target for improving access to sanitation, where progress has been much slower, will be missed. Almost half of the developing world's population lacks sanitation. In Sub-Saharan Africa, the proportion of population with access to sanitation rose from 26 percent in 1990 to only 31 percent in 2006. South Asia also lags far behind. MDG 7 also calls for integration of sustainable development principles into country policies and programs and reversal of the loss of environmental resources. Progress on this broader environmental agenda has been relatively slow but is picking up as the world focuses increased attention on environmental sustainability and climate change.[10]

Progress has been made toward the MDG 8 goal of developing a global partnership for development but is falling short of targets in several areas. The goal covers cooperation in the areas of aid, trade, debt relief, and access to technology and essential drugs. Net ODA (official development assistance) disbursements from the Development Assistance Committee of the Organisation for Economic Co-operation and Development rose during 2003–05 but fell in both 2006 and 2007, dropping from 0.33 percent of donors' gross national income (GNI) in 2005 to 0.28 percent in 2007. The ODA-to-GNI ratio increased to 0.30 percent in 2008, but to meet donors' aid commitments, larger and sustained increases in ODA will be needed than seen so far. Donors will need to demonstrate resolve in shielding aid budgets from the fiscal impact of the financial crisis. The largest implementation gap in the trade area is the failure to date to conclude the Doha Round of trade negotiations. Greater progress has been achieved in the provision of debt relief to poor countries, thanks to the Heavily Indebted Poor Countries Initiative and the Multilateral Debt Relief Initiative.[11] A challenge in monitoring progress in improving the transfer of technology to developing countries and their access to essential drugs is the lack of specific targets for commitments in these areas.[12]

the poor and vulnerable. At the same time, countries and their development partners

need to recommit to the longer-term development objectives and redouble efforts to generate stronger and broader momentum toward the MDGs and related development outcomes. This report addresses key elements of that agenda.

Notes

1. United Nations. 2008. "Committing to Action: Achieving the Millennium Development Goals." Background note by the Secretary-General for the High-Level Event on the Millennium Development Goals. New York.

2. United Nations. 2008. "Achieving the Millennium Development Goals in Africa: Recommendations of the MDG Africa Steering Group." MDG Africa Steering Group. New York.

3. What follows provides a summary assessment of the outlook for the MDGs. More details on trends in progress toward the MDGs, including a listing of the goals, are provided in the annex to this report.

4. High exposure denotes that countries are experiencing the combined effects from both declining growth rates and high initial poverty levels, whereas moderate exposure denotes that they are affected by either decelerating growth or high poverty levels. Low exposure to the financial crisis is defined as having economic growth at rates similar to precrisis conditions and low initial poverty levels. See "The Global Economic Crisis: Assessing Vulnerability with a Poverty Lens." A note prepared by the World Bank's Poverty Reduction and Economic Management Network in February 2009.

5. See "The Expected Impact of the Global Financial Crisis on the World's Poorest." A note prepared by the World Bank's Development Economics Vice Presidency in February 2009; and International Labour Organization, *Global Employment Trends: January 2009*, Geneva.

6. Fallon, Peter, and Robert Lucas. 2002. "The Impact of Financial Crises on Labor Markets, Household Incomes, and Poverty: A Review of Evidence," *World Bank Research Observer* 17 (1): 21–45.

7. Baird, Sarah, Jed Friedman, and Norbert Schady 2007. "Infant Mortality over the Business Cycle in the Developing World," Policy Research Working Paper 4346, World Bank, Washington, DC.

8. Arbache, Jorge, and John Page. 2007. "More Growth or Fewer Collapses? An Investigation of the Growth Challenges of Sub-Saharan African Countries." Policy Research Working Paper 4384, World Bank, Washington, DC.

9. See "The Impact of the Financial Crisis on Progress towards the Millennium Development Goals in Human Development." A note prepared by the World Bank's Development Economics and Human Development vice presidencies in February 2009.

10. Environmental sustainability and its links to the MDGs were a major focus of *Global Monitoring Report 2008*.

11. Developments in aid, debt relief, and trade are discussed in more detail in chapters 4 and 5.

12. United Nations. 2008. "Delivering on the Global Partnership for Achieving the Millennium Development Goals." *MDG Gap Task Force Report*. New York: United Nations.

The Global Financial Crisis and Its Impact on Developing Countries

The deepening global recession, rising unemployment, and high volatility of commodity prices in 2008 and 2009 have severely affected progress toward poverty reduction (Millennium Development Goal [MDG] 1). The steady increases in food prices in recent years, culminating in exceptional price shocks around mid-2008, have thrown millions into extreme poverty, and the deteriorating growth prospects in developing countries will further slow progress in poverty reduction. The prospects for an economic recovery, essential for alleviating poverty, are highly dependent on effective policy actions to restore confidence in the financial system and to counter falling international demand. While much of the responsibility for restoring global growth lies with policy makers in advanced economies, emerging and developing countries have a key role to play in improving the growth outlook, maintaining macroeconomic stability, and strengthening the international financial system.

The main messages in this chapter can be summarized as follows:

- The world faces the severest credit crunch and recession since the Great Depression. Developing countries' growth prospects and access to external financing are subject to unusually large downside risks.

- Though originating in advanced countries, the crisis is hitting developing countries hard.
- While transmission channels may differ, both emerging market and low-income countries will be severely impacted.
- Economic policy responses should be adapted to country circumstances: countries with strong fundamentals may have room for monetary and fiscal stimulus, while those in weaker macroeconomic positions and with limited access to external financing will have less room for policy maneuver; some may need to undertake fiscal consolidation.
- Advanced, emerging, and developing countries should take comprehensive action to resolve liquidity and solvency problems in the banking system and strengthen prudential supervision.
- Development aid must be increased to help countries cope with the crisis.
- It is crucial to maintain an open trade and exchange system.

Emerging and Developing Countries and the Weakening Global Economic Environment

The global economic downturn is much deeper than expected, and the recovery will be gradual and uncertain. During the second half of 2008, the global economy came to a halt: on an annualized basis, global GDP growth slowed to 2 percent after an average growth rate of 5 percent over 2003–07. International trade flows collapsed in the last quarter of 2008, with world exports projected to decline in 2009 for the first time since 1982

FIGURE 1.1 World trade in goods and services

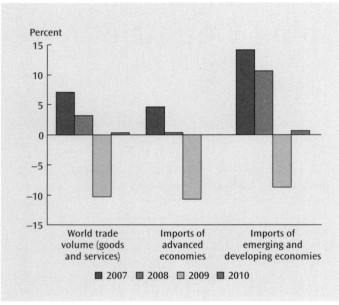

Source: IMF.

(figure 1.1). The contraction in economic activity is most sharply felt in advanced economies, which have decidedly entered the severest recession since the Great Depression, with consumer and investor confidence indicators at historic lows following the dramatic broadening of the confidence crisis in financial markets in October 2008. While bold actions by governments and central banks in advanced economies have helped to mitigate strains in the interbank money markets (box 1.1), they have been insufficient to address reduced access to private sector credit and wide interest spreads in advanced economies. While relatively strong balance sheets in the U.S. corporate sector and the western European household sector initially eased the drag from liquidity and credit strains in financial markets, advanced economies are now experiencing rapidly rising default rates, with a damaging feedback loop further undermining the solvency of the banking sector. As a result, advanced economies are expected to contract in 2009 by 3.8 percent, compared with 0.9 percent growth in 2008.

Emerging and developing countries are increasingly affected by the recession in advanced economies through trade and financial market channels; earlier expectations that these countries would be able to

---

BOX 1.1 The financial crisis

Financial conditions will remain difficult in 2009 and could deteriorate further if the adverse feedback loop between the slowdown in the real economy and financial markets intensifies.

- Systemic financial risks again appear elevated and policy measures, although aggressive and unprecedented, have failed to restore confidence in banks. Bank equity prices and credit premiums reflect serious solvency concerns, and in the absence of private sector willingness to provide bank capital, the policy debate has shifted toward the form and degree of public intervention. Recent borrowings have been confined to those that bear government guarantees.
- Even with significant public capital injections, the pressure for banks in advanced economies to delever will remain high as loan losses continue to accumulate, limiting the supply of credit into 2010. Other sources of financing also appear limited in the short term, apart from those supported by government programs.
- Firms will be under increasing stress in 2009, as earnings deteriorate. Conditions will be especially difficult for firms with lower credit ratings, which will face significantly higher financing costs, if they can borrow at all.
- One risk is that an increase in the supply of government debt will lead to a rise in long-term rates, choking off demand for financing by creditworthy borrowers.

- There has been a structural reassessment of credit risk as a result of the crisis. The amount of financial leverage that markets are allowing will be reduced for a sustained period. In addition, counterparty risks that were once deemed trivial are now foremost in traders' minds, and this will be one factor contributing to keeping risk premiums elevated.

The widespread process of deleveraging and risk retrenchment is continuing to weaken a broad range of financial markets and institutions.

- Funding markets continue to be dominated by central bank operations and, despite measures to alleviate credit risk, residual counterparty concerns are limiting interbank activity.
- Cross-border bank financing has contracted sharply. This has placed significant pressure on some European banking systems reliant on cross-border flows to meet dollar refinancing needs, especially in emerging Europe.
- Securitization markets remain severely hampered but are being supported by government guarantees or asset purchases that are being extended to a widening range of securities.
- Institutional investors have faced significant redemptions from retail clients while hedge funds' assets under management have fallen substantially due to losses and redemptions, and their access to financing has declined markedly. These have led to a sharp unwinding of risk positions and falls in asset prices in both advanced and emerging economies.
- Declining asset prices are spreading strains to other nonbank financial institutions such as insurance companies and pension funds. Although liquidity pressures on such institutions are less than on banks and hedge funds, they may face solvency risks that force them into asset sales that further add to adverse feedback loops.

Market volatility has dropped from the levels of late 2008, but equity markets remain near multiyear lows and credit spreads near multiyear highs. In fact, corporate credit spreads have started to widen further, reflecting severe credit deterioration stemming from the global economic downturn.

- Coordinated interventions and swap arrangements by global central banks have eased short-term liquidity conditions and offshore dollar shortages, but conditions have not normalized and liquidity remains very limited at longer maturities.
- Asset purchase programs have led to some tightening of spreads in several markets (for instance, U.S. agency securities, commercial paper, and consumer asset-backed securities), but spreads are rising further for corporate debt and commercial mortgages for which no government support is in place, and reflect a serious decline in credit quality and a rise in defaults stemming from the global economic downturn.

Emerging markets are coming under serious pressure from the global credit and economic crisis, particularly in emerging Europe.

- Emerging market financing costs remain significantly higher than precrisis levels, and bond issuance, which was extremely low in the fourth quarter of 2008, has recovered only marginally, largely confined to higher-quality borrowers. Emerging market corporates are facing extremely serious financing constraints, and some will almost certainly be unable to meet rollover needs.

Advanced economy banks undergoing severe pressures to shrink balance sheets are likely to scale back lending to emerging markets, particularly in Europe. Local banks, facing their own pressures to deleverage, will be hard-pressed to substitute for the drop in financing of corporate clients from international banks and credit markets.

"decouple" and weather the storm through rising domestic demand have turned out to be overly optimistic. With contracting world trade, slowing domestic demand, and sharply reduced access to external financing, emerging market growth is expected to decline sharply to 1.5 percent in 2009, from 6.1 percent in 2008, which would be the weakest growth rate since the 1990s. In general, low-income countries have been less affected by the financial contagion, but slowing exports and deteriorating terms of trade for commodity exporters will increasingly hit growth prospects in 2009: growth in Sub-Saharan Africa, for instance, will drop to 1.7 percent, from 5.5 percent in 2008.

Commodity and food prices have come down considerably from their peaks in mid-2008 (figure 1.2), reflecting the sharp downturn in global demand for nonfood commodities,[1] the resolution of weather-related supply disruptions in agriculture, and the removal of export restrictions on food products. Overall, however, commodity and food prices are projected to rise again once global growth picks up, because demand pressures from rapidly industrializing emerging economies will continue to have their effects on world markets.

Headline inflation rates have come down from their peaks in mid-2008 as the sharp drop in economic activity and the declines in commodity prices affect consumer prices. In the advanced economies, headline inflation receded to around 3.5 percent in December 2008 (12-month rate), down from 4.5 percent in mid-2008. With rapidly rising unemployment and output gaps, risks of deflation have become a concern in some countries. Developments in emerging and developing countries show a mixed picture. While inflation has declined in most countries, price pressures in some countries remain strong, reflecting price stickiness in markets for food products and the lagged effects of rising wages and input cost.

A gradual recovery will not become visible before the end of 2009: with advanced economies in recession and growth in emerging and developing economies rapidly declining, the April 2009 World Economic Outlook (WEO) projects a contraction of global output by 1.3 percent in 2009, compared with 3.2 percent growth in 2008 (table 1.1). This baseline scenario, however, is subject to unusually large downward risks, because weakening confidence and continuing solvency problems in the financial sector may cause a longer and deeper contraction of global economic activity than currently projected.

Financial Turmoil Spreading to Emerging Markets

The financial market turmoil is spreading to emerging markets, but thus far low-income countries have been less affected by the financial contagion. Weakening global

FIGURE 1.2   Commodity price indexes

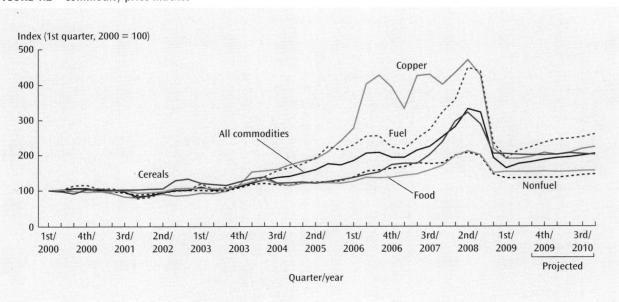

Source: IMF.
Note: Indexes are in U.S. dollars.

TABLE 1.1 Summary of world output
annual percent change

| | 2002 | 2003 | 2004 | 2005 | 2006 | 2007 | 2008 | Projections | |
								2009	2010
World Output	**2.8**	**3.6**	**4.9**	**4.5**	**5.1**	**5.2**	**3.2**	**−1.3**	**1.9**
Advanced Economies	**1.6**	**1.9**	**3.2**	**2.6**	**3.0**	**2.7**	**0.9**	**−3.8**	**0.0**
of which									
United States	1.6	2.5	3.6	2.9	2.8	2.0	1.1	−2.8	0.0
Euro Area	0.9	0.8	2.2	1.7	2.9	2.7	0.9	−4.2	−0.4
Japan	0.3	1.4	2.7	1.9	2.0	2.4	−0.6	−6.2	0.5
Canada	2.9	1.9	3.1	2.9	3.1	2.7	0.5	−2.5	1.2
United Kingdom	2.1	2.8	2.8	2.1	2.8	3.0	0.7	−4.1	−0.4
Other advanced countries	3.9	2.5	4.8	4.0	4.6	4.7	1.6	−4.1	0.6
Emerging markets and developing countries	**4.8**	**6.3**	**7.5**	**7.1**	**8.0**	**8.3**	**6.1**	**1.6**	**4.0**
Emerging markets	4.6	6.3	7.5	7.1	8.0	8.3	6.1	1.5	3.9
Other developing countries	7.5	6.2	7.4	7.6	8.2	8.3	6.5	3.2	4.7
Africa	6.5	5.7	6.7	5.8	6.1	6.2	5.2	2.0	3.9
of which									
Sub-Saharan Africa	7.3	5.4	7.1	6.2	6.6	6.9	5.5	1.7	3.8
Central and Eastern Europe	4.4	4.9	7.3	6.0	6.6	5.4	2.9	−3.7	0.8
Commonwealth of Independent States	5.2	7.8	8.2	6.7	8.4	8.6	5.5	−5.1	1.2
Developing Asia	6.9	8.2	8.6	9.0	9.8	10.6	7.7	4.8	6.1
South Asia	4.4	6.5	7.6	8.7	9.1	8.7	7.0	4.3	5.3
East Asia	7.9	8.8	9.0	9.2	10.1	11.4	8.0	5.1	6.4
Middle East	3.8	7.0	6.0	5.8	5.7	6.3	5.9	2.5	3.5
Western Hemisphere	0.6	2.2	6.0	4.7	5.7	5.7	4.2	−1.5	1.6
Memorandum items:									
China	*9.1*	*10.0*	*10.1*	*10.4*	*11.6*	*13.0*	*9.0*	*6.5*	*7.5*
India	*4.6*	*6.9*	*7.9*	*9.2*	*9.8*	*9.3*	*7.3*	*4.5*	*5.6*

Source: IMF.

growth prospects, the financial deleveraging process in advanced economies, and the unintended effects of some of the recent policy measures taken by advanced economy governments have severely affected emerging economies in recent months.

Banks and investors in advanced economies have sharply reduced their exposure to emerging markets and developing countries. The global repricing of risk and the deleveraging process in advanced economies have led to sharp drops in the availability of funding for sovereigns and corporations and steep increases in interest margins. While external financing conditions remained relatively stable through most of 2008, especially in comparison with previous crises, market access for emerging and developing countries virtually collapsed in October 2008 with the intensification of the turmoil in advanced economies: the Emerging Markets Bond Index Global (EMBIG) sovereign spread jumped by around 200 basis points in October 2008 and remains well above the levels seen in 2007 (figure 1.3). Most affected are countries with large current account deficits and countries in which the banking sector relies heavily on foreign funding, such as emerging Europe. Countries with solid external and fiscal positions, such as Brazil, have seen increases in spreads as well but by much less than in the more vulnerable countries.

Corporate sectors in emerging and developing countries are particularly hard hit by increasing funding problems and, in some cases, foreign exchange losses. While some recovery of access for sovereign borrowers has become visible since early 2009, funding conditions for the corporate sector remain extremely difficult, especially in light of high refinancing needs this year. In addition, exporters and other firms in several countries have taken substantial open currency positions against the U.S. dollar. Many of these positions have given rise to liquidity

and solvency problems in the nonfinancial sector following the appreciation of the U.S. dollar in the second half of 2008. Many companies have high refinancing needs in 2009 that may be hard to meet in the current environment.

The pernicious effects of reduced access to external financing are exacerbated by the sharp tightening in domestic credit conditions; banks are hoarding cash because of increasing concerns about counterparty risks. Overall, banking systems in emerging and developing countries are not facing the solvency problems affecting banks in advanced economies, but vulnerabilities are rising, especially for those banks dependent on foreign funding in the wholesale markets.

Policy measures in advanced economies aimed at stabilizing the financial sector may have had the unintended effect of contributing to the weakness in emerging markets. There are indications that the enhancement of deposit insurance schemes and government actions to strengthen financial institutions' capital, aimed at restoring confidence in advanced economies, have had the side

FIGURE 1.3 Bond spreads and issues of international bonds in emerging markets and developing countries

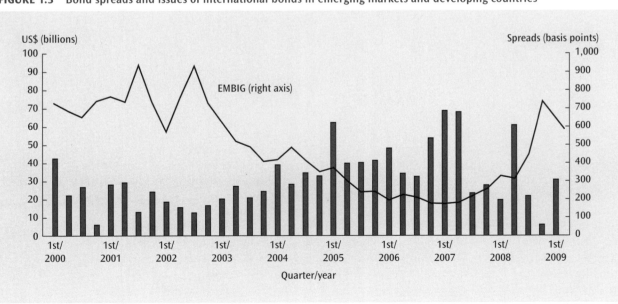

Source: Dealogic; Bloomberg.

effect of generating a flight to banks benefiting from state guarantees.

It is expected that the full effect of reduced market access will become visible in deteriorating capital account balances in 2009, and the risks are firmly on the downside. For the year 2008 as a whole, private financial flows to emerging markets declined by about 2 percentage points of GDP in comparison with 2007, while flows to other developing countries continued to rise (table 1.2). As the deleveraging process in advanced economies

TABLE 1.2 Net capital flows
% of GDP

	Average 1991–2001	2002	2003	2004	2005	2006	2007	2008	2009
Emerging market economies	**7.1**	**6.4**	**7.9**	**7.5**	**8.6**	**9.0**	**10.8**	**8.4**	**3.8**
Private capital flows, net	3.5	2.4	4.1	4.0	5.5	5.7	7.3	4.9	−0.6
of which									
private direct investment	2.6	3.0	2.6	3.3	3.5	4.5	4.3	3.8	2.4
private portfolio flows	0.5	−0.1	0.1	0.7	0.7	0.7	0.8	−0.8	−0.6
Private current transfers	2.2	3.1	3.4	3.5	3.5	3.5	3.4	3.2	2.9
Official capital flows and transfers (net)	1.3	1.0	0.3	0.0	−0.4	−0.3	0.1	0.3	1.4
Memorandum item:									
Reserve assets	*−1.4*	*−1.1*	*−3.3*	*−2.5*	*−3.0*	*−4.1*	*−4.3*	*−1.8*	*1.3*
Other developing countries[a]	**13.7**	**14.4**	**14.9**	**14.2**	**17.0**	**15.6**	**16.8**	**18.3**	**16.2**
Private capital flows, net	2.6	2.7	3.0	2.2	3.6	3.5	5.1	6.8	4.9
of which									
private direct investment	3.0	4.0	4.6	4.4	4.5	5.6	6.0	5.7	5.2
private portfolio flows	0.1	0.1	−0.2	−0.2	−0.1	0.0	−0.1	−0.1	−0.2
Private current transfers	3.3	4.3	4.9	5.7	6.2	6.0	5.9	5.8	5.3
Official capital flows and transfers (net)	7.8	7.4	6.9	6.3	7.2	6.2	5.9	5.7	6.0
Memorandum item:									
Reserve assets	*−1.1*	*−1.6*	*−1.4*	*−1.8*	*−2.5*	*−4.1*	*−3.9*	*−2.3*	*0.4*
Memorandum items (US$ billions):									
Private capital flows, net	*112*	*94*	*171*	*257*	*312*	*280*	*647*	*307*	*−82*
of which									
private direct investment:	*106*	*152*	*142*	*186*	*231*	*238*	*392*	*467*	*311*
private portfolio flows	*33*	*−22*	*27*	*63*	*60*	*−7*	*136*	*−55*	*−136*
liabilities to foreign banks	*5*	*−16*	*23*	*32*	*25*	*73*	*190*	*177*	*142*
Private current transfers	*60*	*106*	*135*	*156*	*187*	*217*	*250*	*279*	*262*
Total net private financial flows including current transfers	*172*	*200*	*306*	*413*	*499*	*497*	*898*	*586*	*180*

Source: IMF.
Note: Percentage numbers represent unweighted averages.
a. Includes fragile states, but excludes Timor-Leste, Zimbabwe, Sierra Leone, Liberia, and the Solomon Islands.

is continuing and as private investment plans are being scaled back, all groups of countries will be faced with sharply reduced syndicated bank lending, portfolio flows, and foreign direct investment this year.

Emerging market currencies have seen sharp declines in recent months (figure 1.4), while some other countries have lost large amounts of reserves in attempts to stabilize exchange rates. Countries with highly liquid markets that in the past experienced short-term capital inflows from carry trades, such as Brazil and South Africa, and countries with external vulnerabilities have been hit hardest (most recently in eastern Europe). Market volatilities have risen to levels not seen after the Asian crisis of the 1990s, a reflection in some cases of extremely illiquid and dysfunctional market conditions (box 1.2).

Financial systems in low-income countries are less affected by the turmoil in advanced economies, although financial sector vulnerabilities are rising as a result of weakening domestic economic activity. Domestic banks in low-income countries usually fund their lending activities in relatively stable domestic savings markets and often have ample liquidity reserves parked at the central bank. Domestic interbank money markets and derivatives markets are in general small or nonexistent, while capital controls and the limited size of other financial markets (such as treasury bill markets) have often limited participation by foreign market operators. Credit markets have therefore not witnessed the instabilities seen in some advanced economies, although foreign parent banks have withdrawn capital from subsidiaries in some countries, stock markets have dropped sharply, and nonperforming loan portfolios may rise if economic activity weakens further. Some low-income countries have shown signals of sagging confidence in the banking system, but this appears to be

FIGURE 1.4 Daily spot exchange rates, national currency per U.S. dollar

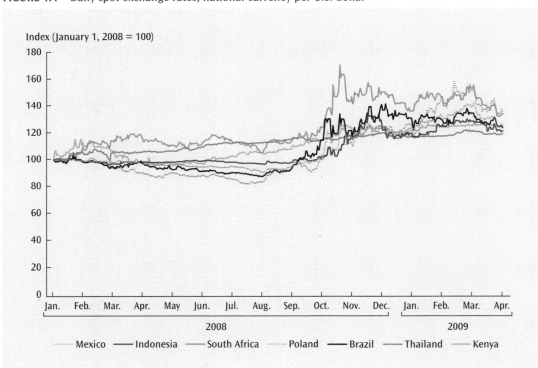

Source: Bloomberg.

BOX 1.2 Increasing exchange rate volatility and the financial market crisis

Following several years of relatively stable currency market developments, exchange rate volatility in some emerging and developing countries has increased recently, approaching levels not seen since the Asian crisis of the 1990s. As measured by the normalized standard deviation of daily exchange rates, volatility of the Indonesian rupee, for instance, increased almost fivefold in 2008 in comparison with 2007.

Several factors may explain this phenomenon. Perceptions of increased external vulnerabilities in an environment of slowing global growth and weakening commodity prices certainly play a role. Technical market factors related to the financial crisis in advanced economies may have an impact as well.

First, the overall risk budget of international banks acting as market makers on emerging market currencies has been shrunk, because banks have generally scaled down their risk appetite and lowered their stop-loss thresholds across trading books. Some large market makers, including Lehman Brothers and Bear Stearns, have also withdrawn from the market. The recent bank mergers have also in general resulted in lower aggregated risk budgets, because banks taking over usually slim down the risk budget of the entity taken over.

Another factor that might have depressed market makers' trading turnover, and therefore their cushioning impact on daily volatility, is the U.S. dollar liquidity squeeze on offshore markets. Although a large part of the turnover does not result in overnight exposure, all positions taken beyond the horizon of a trading session involve the need to access some overnight (or longer-term) funding. In principle higher funding costs should simply affect forward rates. But this assumes that funding is available without restriction. In the current circumstances, however, some individual banks have been deprived of any access to U.S. dollar lending from their correspondent banks. This disruption has been mitigated by the recent swap arrangements between the Federal Reserve and Brazil, the Republic of Korea, Mexico, and Singapore. In the context of a dollar funding squeeze, most emerging market currency trading is affected, because most emerging market currencies are traded against the U.S. dollar. It is also likely that foreign exchange activities on emerging market currencies involving some U.S. dollar funding needs have been curtailed to lower the overall funding needs of market makers. Investment banks, which were among the main liquidity providers on the foreign exchange market, have been hit very hard because of their lack of a deposit base and reliance on the interbank market. In this context, the higher volatility could be the consequence of the withdrawal of key market makers, resulting in a smaller cushion of risk capital available in the market to absorb the price impact of the normal commercial order book.

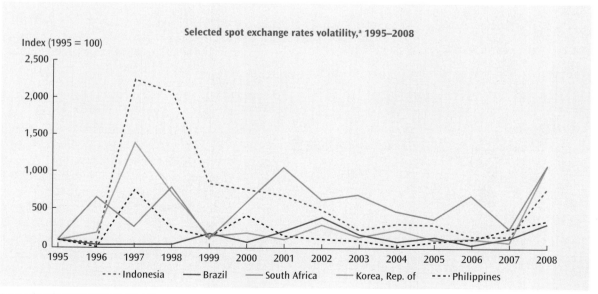

Selected spot exchange rates volatility,[a] 1995–2008

Index (1995 = 100)

Source: Bloomberg and IMF staff calculations.
a. Volatility is calculated as the index of the annual coefficients of variation (standard deviation/mean) of daily spot exchange rates.

FIGURE 1.5 Vulnerabilities in emerging and developing countries

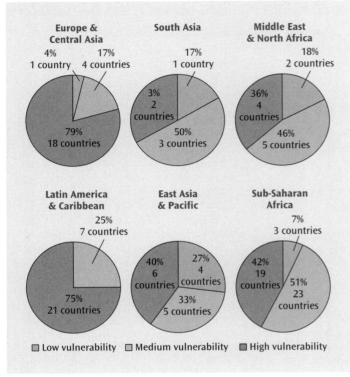

Source: IMF.
Note: Vulnerabilities are measured on the basis of developments in exports, foreign direct investment, remittances flows, external debt ratios (emerging markets), and aid flows (low-income countries). For a detailed explanation of the methodology, see IMF 2009.

FIGURE 1.6 Terms-of-trade changes per quintile group

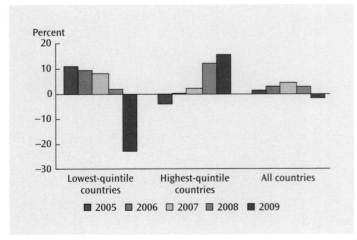

Source: IMF.
Note: Quintile groups are based on the average of terms-of-trade changes in 2007–08 and 2008–09.

related to domestic factors rather than the international crisis.

Increasing Vulnerabilities in Emerging and Developing Countries

The confluence of weak economic activity, sharp swings in commodity prices, and financial market instability is causing increasing vulnerabilities in emerging and developing countries. The sharp downturn in advanced economies and the fluctuations in commodity prices are affecting current account and fiscal balances in emerging and developing economies. Countries that entered the global crisis with weak macroeconomic fundamentals are most severely hit, but other countries are affected as well (figure 1.5). Several factors are contributing to increased vulnerabilities.

Recent movements in commodity prices are having strong—and often divergent—effects on emerging and developing countries' terms of trade. Notwithstanding the sharp movements in commodity prices, the terms of trade for emerging and developing countries as a group have not changed much in recent years, but these averages conceal sharp contrasts dependent on countries' composition of imports and exports (figure 1.6). While commodity-importing emerging markets with large manufacturing industries and net fuel importers are benefiting from lower commodity input prices, countries highly dependent on exports of fuels, metals, and some other commodities are experiencing a weakening of their terms of trade.

Reflecting rising unemployment and weak earnings growth among migrant workers in advanced economies, remittance flows to developing countries began to slow down in the third quarter of 2008. Although in U.S. dollar terms they are still up for 2008 as a whole, overall flows are projected to fall by 5 percent to 8 percent in 2009 (table 1.3). Migration from developing countries may slow as a result of the global growth downturn, but the number of foreign workers living in destination countries is unlikely to

TABLE 1.3 Inflows of international remittances[a]
US$ (billions)

	Annual average 1992–2002	2003	2004	2005	2006	2007	2008[b]	2009[c]	2010[c]
Emerging market economies	56.8	114.4	128.0	153.5	179.1	218.9	240.5	229.1	227.5
Other developing countries	16.8	27.5	33.8	39.2	47.3	59.2	62.0	58.1	66.0
Fragile states	1.2	2.7	3.1	2.7	3.1	4.1	4.3	4.2	5.2

Source: World Bank remittances data.
a. Remittances include workers' remittances, compensation of employees, and migrant transfers.
b. Estimate.
c. Base case scenario forecast,

decrease. Countries in Latin America, the Middle East and North Africa, and South Asia that rely on remttance flows are most affected.[2]

Per capita income adjusted for terms of trade will decline in 2009 in a number of countries (figure 1.7). As a group, Sub-Saharan African countries are particularly affected: 13 countries will experience decline in per capita income in 2009 on the order of 11 percent on average. The situation is comparable in North Africa and the Middle East, but other regions are less affected.

Official transfers are expected to either remain broadly unchanged or decline in 2009, at a time when the flow of private capital is slowing rapidly (figure 1.8). On current trends, official aid will not play a countercyclical role in developing countries as it should. To prevent a reversal of years of development progress, official aid should be increased substantially in 2009 and later years.

As a result of these factors, weak export markets, and the divergent terms-of-trade effects of recent commodity price declines,

FIGURE 1.7 Real 2009 per capita growth rate adjusted for terms-of-trade changes

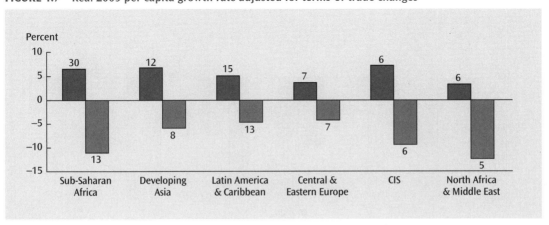

Source: IMF.
Note: Simple average percentage change for developing country regional groups.

FIGURE 1.8 Official current transfers, 2008–09

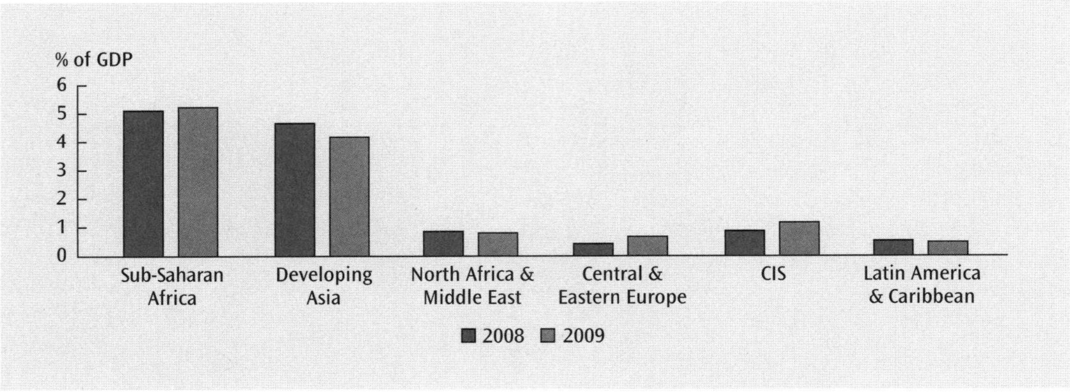

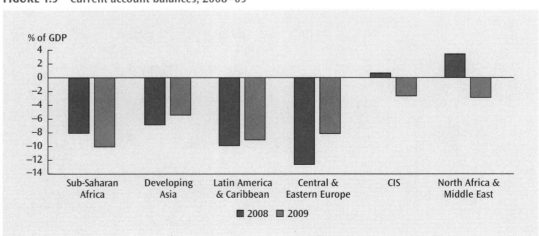

Source: IMF.

the current accounts of many emerging and developing countries are deteriorating. Oil exporters in the Middle East and North Africa are hardest hit, with a weakening in current account balances by 6 percentage points of GDP in 2009, followed by Europe and the Commonwealth of Independent States (CIS) of about 3.5 percentage points (figure 1.9). In other regions, the net balance-of-payments effects are projected to remain limited, although some countries are strongly affected: 14 countries are projected to see a deterioration in the current balance

of more than 10 percent of GDP. Overall, more than half of the emerging and developing countries can expect a weakening of current account balances in 2009.

The sharp declines in capital flows to emerging and developing countries will exarcerbate the strains and vulnerabilities caused by deteriorating current accounts. Many countries will find themselves in situations where it will be impossible to square the circle of deteriorating current account balances, reversing capital flows, and declining aid. As a result, following years of steady

FIGURE 1.9 Current account balances, 2008–09

Source: IMF.

reserve accumulation, many countries will experience steep declines in foreign exchange reserves in 2009, especially in Europe and Sub-Saharan Africa, and the risks of debt defaults are rising.

Overall, fiscal positions in emerging and developing countries are weakening in 2009. Several factors are contributing to this outcome, including slowing domestic revenue growth, increased spending on social programs in response to the crisis, and deteriorating terms of trade in commodity exporters (figure 1.10). Fuel-exporting economies are hardest hit, with an average deterioration in the overall government balance of just over 10 percentage points in 2009, but they are often well positioned to mitigate the domestic effects. Overall, fiscal balances in nonfuel commodity exporters will deteriorate as well, but less than in fuel exporters, because sources of government revenue in nonfuel commodity producers are often more diversified.

The rise in demand for raw materials from emerging markets in recent years and supply bottlenecks have led to marked increases in price volatility for a number of commodities, complicating macroeconomic and fiscal management in countries highly dependent on commodity exports (box 1.3).

Macroeconomic and Social Policy Choices in Emerging and Developing Countries

Emerging and developing countries are facing difficult macroeconomic policy choices in the current environment. Because economic circumstances and developments differ from country to country, the optimal policy responses are not uniform across emerging and developing countries. The World Bank and the International Monetary Fund (IMF) stand ready to assist countries in addressing these policy challenges.[3]

Macroeconomic Policies

Macroeconomic policies should be adapted to the specific circumstances of countries. The most pressing need is to address in a comprehensive way the continuing confidence crisis in financial markets and stop its fallout in the real economy. Although this is primarily a responsibility of policy makers in advanced economies, the authorities in emerging and developing countries have a key role to play in restoring confidence and preventing a more serious downturn in global economic activity. In particular, they should adapt economic policies to support economic growth while keeping inflation under control; strengthen the liquidity of the banking system; ensure that an efficient framework is in place allowing the prompt resolution of liquidity and solvency problems, especially for systemically important financial institutions; clarify to what extent further strengthening of domestic prudential supervision and market regulation is needed to set their domestic financial systems on a firm footing; and dress up contingency plans to deal with sudden stops in capital flows and shocks in the domestic banking system. These issues are discussed in more detail in the next section.

In most emerging and developing countries, the balance of risks has firmly shifted from inflation to financial instability and deteriorating growth prospects. In light of this, several countries, especially emerging markets, have taken steps to stimulate economic

FIGURE 1.10   Government balances, 2008–09

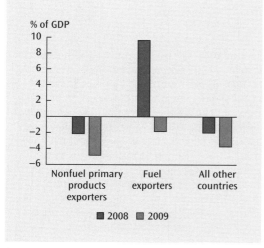

Source: IMF.

BOX 1.3 Commodity exporters: how to deal with increased price volatility?

The past year has witnessed significant increases in market volatility in emerging and developing countries. As a result of the deleveraging process in advanced economies and concerns about growth prospects and vulnerabilities, emerging market currencies have shown wide swings since October 2008. In many commodity-exporting countries, the macroeconomic policy challenges posed by currency instability are compounded by increased volatility in U.S. dollar prices for commodities. The chart below shows that price volatility (as measured by the normalized standard deviation of daily prices) jumped in 2008 for several key commodities. For example, the standard deviation of rice prices in 2008 more than tripled in comparison with 2007, and medium-term price projections are more uncertain than usual.

Because many of the underlying causes of higher volatility are still at work, volatility could remain elevated in the coming years. In the commodity markets, supply constraints and short-term demand inelasticities may cause new price fluctuations once global demand picks up.

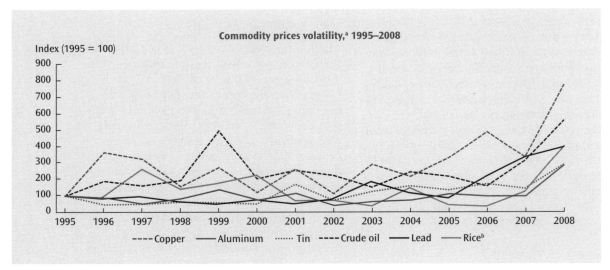

Commodity prices volatility,[a] 1995–2008

Index (1995 = 100)

- - - - Copper   —— Aluminum   ········ Tin   - - - - Crude oil   —— Lead   —— Rice[b]

Source: Bloomberg and IMF staff calculations.
a. Volatility is calculated as the index of the annual coefficients of variation (standard deviation/mean) of daily commodity prices.
b. Due to the lack of data for rice, calculations use monthly commodity prices (for rice, the index is 1996 = 100).

The increased uncertainties surrounding commodity prices have implications for fiscal policy formulation and the size of foreign exchange reserves in countries highly dependent on revenue from commodity exports. In principle, a commodity exporter will maximize its social welfare if primary government spending is based on an estimate of "permanent income" derived from the exploitation of commodity wealth.[a] The practical implementation of this principle, however, is not straightforward because of the many uncertainties related to, among other things, long-term price projections, extraction costs, and estimates of the volume of exploitable commodity reserves. In many commodity-exporting countries, therefore, governments have based their fiscal policies on price projections linked to actual spot prices, or to a combination of spot and forward market prices, which may lead to sizable over- or underspending in relation to permanent income. In addition, intra-annual price fluctuations may lead to the need for sizable unexpected adjustments in government spending and borrowing, with negative effects on macroeconomic stability and the poverty reduction effort. To avoid this type of stop-and-go policy, relatively simple rules of thumb have been proposed to smooth primary government spending over time based on conservative price projections.[b] In a recent IMF working paper on Nigeria, Bartsch (2006) proposes to base annual government spending on moving averages of past oil prices in combination with a stabilization fund that is fed in good times and used as a source of financing for government spending in times of low prices. Building on this approach, the following conclusions can be drawn:

■ The recent increase in price volatility strengthens the case for establishing stabilization funds in countries highly dependent on commodity exports. To accumulate assets in such a fund, governments would initially need to base fiscal policy on a prudent, relatively low projection of export prices. As assets grow to the targeted level, the export price projection could move closer to a path linked to a moving average. Simulation results for Nigeria show that with a three-year moving average price, a stabilization fund asset level of about 75 percent of 2004 government revenue from oil production would reduce the probability of a forced adjustment of government spending to below 20 percent.

■ The optimal size of a stabilization fund is sensitive to export price variability. In light of the higher volatility seen in recent years, countries with a stabilization fund should consider an increase in its average size to deal with potentially larger revenue shortfalls in the future.

■ The timing of the buildup or increase of the stabilization fund should be consistent with macroeconomic policies: to avoid procyclical polices, the shift to larger buffers should take place during periods of rising commodity prices and economic growth and not during periods of distress.

■ Commodity exporters should consider a more extensive use of the forward markets and long-term contracts to reduce short-term price risks. The liquidity of forward markets for major fuel and nonfuel commodities has grown considerably over the past decade, especially for crude oil (with hedging possible for periods up to seven years) and precious metals, but also for some base metals and agricultural commodities.[c]

Higher price volatility also has implications for the optimal size of foreign exchange reserves.[d] Sharp fluctuations in export prices will affect not only the central government but also the broader economy, with potentially large effects in terms of lost output. Foreign exchange reserves allow the monetary authorities to smooth the effects of export price fluctuations on the economy similar to the role of stabilization funds in smoothing government spending; optimal reserves levels will be higher if export prices fluctuate more sharply. On the basis of a two-good model, Drummond and Dhasmana (2008) concluded that foreign exchange reserves in almost one-half of 44 commodity-exporting countries in Sub-Saharan Africa faced with large terms-of-trade shocks were, on average, roughly one-third below optimal levels at the end of 2007. The recent increases in commodity price fluctuations, therefore, have underlined the need to strengthen foreign exchange reserves in many countries.

a. The optimal noncommodity primary budget deficit is equivalent to the sum of the projected permanent income stream from extraction and the income from foreign assets acquired from the receipts of commodity exports. For a discussion of the permanent income approach, see Davis, Ossowsky and Fedelino (2003).
b. See, for instance, box 1.4 in the *Global Monitoring Report 2008*.
c. See also The World Bank 2008, chapter 3.
d. As foreign exchange reserves constitute self insurance against various external shocks to the economy, their optimal size is determined by factors such as terms-of-trade fluctuations; unexpected changes in the volumes of exports and imports; sudden reversals in capital flows and official aid; and developments in remittances, etc.

activity through expansionary monetary and fiscal policies this year, and further stimulus may be needed in 2010. Notwithstanding the deterioration in financial market conditions since October 2008, a number of economies with rapidly declining inflation, sustainable fiscal balances, strong international reserve positions, and limited external vulnerabilities have scope for monetary easing and discretionary fiscal policies to support domestic demand. Fiscal measures should be selected in a way that allows a gradual withdrawal of stimulus once domestic activity picks up. Temporary tax measures or quick-disbursing public expenditure of a nonrecurrent nature that can be relatively quickly reversed (such as increased spending on infrastructure maintenance) would therefore be preferable to measures leading to sizable future liabilities that may eventually undermine fiscal sustainability (such as large increases in the public wage bill through new hires or pay awards).

Countries facing unsustainable fiscal and current account deficits, reduced access to international financing, and vulnerable external debt positions have no choice but to give priority to improving the fiscal and external accounts, while seeking to mitigate negative effects on domestic growth prospects. The optimal policy mix in these cases will depend on the circumstances but could include tighter monetary policy and fiscal deficit reduction, accompanied by a depreciation of the exchange rate to support economic growth and external viability. Increasing fiscal constraints heighten the need for improved expenditure management to protect core spending, including infrastructure spending for growth and better social safety nets.

Many countries with sound macroeconomic fundamentals may also be better off continuing a medium-term policy aimed at maintaining stable economic conditions, even if they are facing slowing domestic and external demand. Notwithstanding good policies, many governments, especially in low-income countries, face external financing constraints limiting the scope for using monetary and fiscal instruments to stimulate domestic demand. While the quality of fiscal policies in most low-income countries has improved somewhat in recent years (box 1.4), many lack the administrative capacity to implement a successful domestic demand management policy, because economic data are insufficiently comprehensive and up-to-date to assess accurately the most recent developments in economic activity. Governments in these countries often do not have the capacity or sufficient policy credibility to implement effective short-term stimulus measures that can be easily reversed. In these circumstances, policies that give priority to maintaining fiscal and debt sustainability while allowing automatic stabilizers to work are likely to have more positive growth effects than short-term stimulus measures.

Support from the International Community

The international community must act decisively to support low-income countries. Most low-income countries, will not be able to address the effects of the international crisis through adjustment alone without laying unacceptable burdens on the poorest in society. While adjustment to the realities of contracting world trade and the sharp declines in financial flows may be unavoidable, donor countries must step up their efforts to help developing countries mitigate the effects on the poor and protect spending critical for future growth, such as on essential infrastructure. On current indications, total foreign exchange receipts by low-income countries will drop sharply in 2009 (box 1.5), causing an additional financing need of at least $25 billion,[4] which may increase significantly if the downside risks to the growth projections materialize. This underscores the urgency of increasing official development aid.

The Importance of an Open International Trade and Exchange System

Maintaining an open international trade and exchange system remains crucial. In 2008 many countries responded to the food crisis by imposing export restrictions.[5] These restrictions aggravated the sharp increases in world market food prices in 2008 and undermined confidence in the international trade system. More recently, some countries have introduced, or are considering, trade and exchange measures in an attempt to raise tax revenue or protect domestic industries from the effects of the global downturn. Also, there are widespread concerns that government intervention in advanced country financial systems is associated with pressures to curtail cross-border bank lending. If followed on a larger scale, these restrictions could deepen the current global recession and undermine the prospects for a global recovery—reminiscent of the vicious cycle of trade protection and production declines during the Great Depression. Rapid and substantial progress in opening markets at the multilateral level remains a priority. All parties involved should therefore make strong efforts to reinvigorate the Doha Round (see chapter 5).

BOX 1.4   The quality of macroeconomic policies in low-income countries

Since 2003 IMF staff have conducted surveys among mission chiefs to gauge their assessments of the quality of macroeconomic policies in low-income countries. While substantial progress has been made in many areas of economic policy since 2003, the quality of policies in two areas (monetary policy and governance in monetary and financial institution) declined in 2008. At the same time, progress was made in the areas of fiscal policy and fiscal transparency.

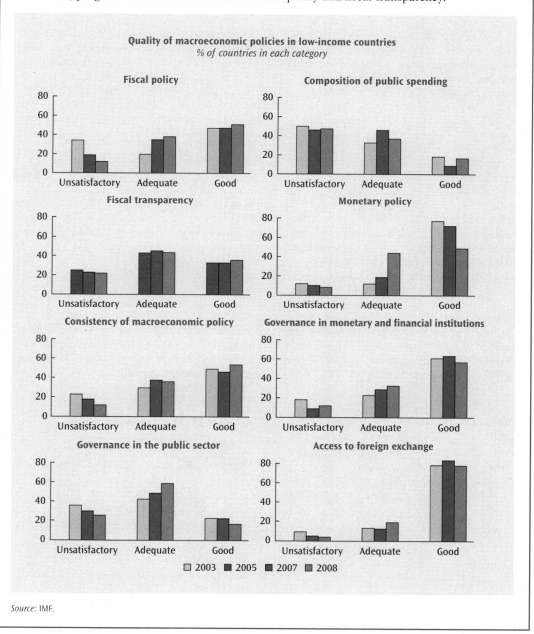

Quality of macroeconomic policies in low-income countries
% of countries in each category

Source: IMF.

Maintaining Longer-Term Priorities

The financial crisis should not distract policy makers from longer-term priorities. The food crisis is not over. Even though commodity prices may weaken further in 2009, food prices remain relatively high in comparison to levels seen in the first half of the decade, and upward price pressures may reappear once the global economy picks

---

BOX 1.5   The impact of the crisis on selected countries

The economic downturn in advanced economies has decidely spread to emerging markets and other developing countries. The collapse of world trade and declining net capital flows have led to sharp declines in the availability of foreign exchange resources in emerging and developing countries, causing dismal growth, deteriorating fiscal balances, and sharp declines in private demand (see the left figure).

To combat the downturn, many governments have announced fiscal packages to boost their economies. But only countries that have created fiscal space in recent years through debt reduction and strong policies have scope for fiscal stimulus. In others, this scope is limited by debt sustainability or financing constraints. Hence, many emerging and developing countries are facing the need to adjust. While the impact of the crisis is felt around the globe, some economies are especially hard hit.

Examples of negatively impacted countries grappling with seemingly unrelated challenges in the context of the crisis, include Tanzania, Kazakhstan, Chile, and Latvia (see the figure to the right). A worldwide recession impacts negatively on Tanzania's fast-growing tourism and export sectors, while cutbacks in foreign financing pose a threat to business investment. Lower growth dampens government revenues, suggesting that the current path of spending may lead to widening fiscal deficits and financing gaps. The year 2009 will likely be very difficult for Kazakhstan's economy. Lower oil and commodity prices, adverse conditions in international financial markets, and developments in neighboring countries are negatively affecting confidence, credit availability, and foreign exchange inflows. In response, substantial fiscal easing has provided important support to growth over the past year. However, with the outlook for oil prices uncertain, some scaling-back of nonessential expenditures may be called for, notwithstanding the need to protect social safety net spending. While the Chilean economy enters the crisis from a position of fiscal and external stability, and its GDP growth has become increasingly resilient to copper price booms and busts, its fiscal and current account balances are nonetheless expected to deteriorate significantly in 2009 as a result of the crisis. In Latvia, years of unsustainably high growth and large current account deficits have coalesced into a financial and balance-of-payments crisis, brought to a head by the current international financial turmoil. Declines in private sector deposits have sparked severe liquidity problems. The Latvian authorities have launched a decisive economic reform program and sought substantial international financial assistance to quell this crisis.

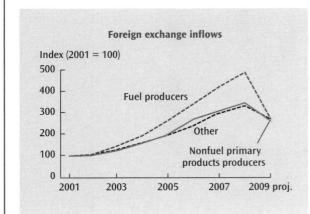

Source: IMF.

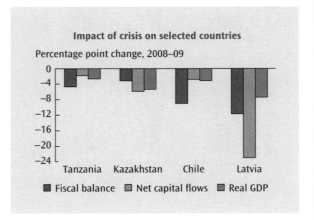

Source: IMF.
Note: For Latvia, the fiscal balance includes estimated bank restructuring costs, 12.4 percent of GDP in 2009.

up pace. Food demand, particularly from emerging and developing economies, is likely to remain robust over the medium term, while continued strong demand for corn for ethanol use will also bolster price pressures. In light of these factors, policy makers in emerging and developing countries should continue to plan for enhancing food security through increased investment in the agricultural sector and domestic reforms aimed at developing commercial farming and increasing small holder productivity.

Governments in emerging and developing economies are also faced with difficult choices when addressing the social effects of high food prices. Countries have responded in different ways, including reductions in fuel and food taxes and tariffs, increases in universal subsidies, expansions in transfer programs, and public sector wage increases.

Some of these measures, however, are often cost ineffective and may even be counterproductive over the medium term. About one-third of developing countries have increased fuel price subsidies in 2008. These subsidies may create unsustainable fiscal positions, even at current lower oil prices, and are inconsistent with longer-term objectives to mitigate climate change. Governments should therefore give high priority to phasing out these subsidies and replacing them with more finely tuned social protection schemes to protect the poor. Well-targeted and flexible measures, such as direct income support, workfare, and food-for-work programs, that help the poorest while keeping a cap on government spending are highly preferable to measures that also benefit those who do not need government support (box 1.6).

Prudential Supervision and Market Regulation in Emerging and Developing Countries

The financial crisis has exposed a number of shortcomings in countries' supervisory frameworks that need to be addressed to restore confidence in the financial system and reduce the likelihood of financial instability in the future. While many of the lessons of the crisis focus on the more mature financial markets, where the problems began, most of them are also relevant for emerging and developing countries.

The globalization of financial institutions has complex implications for financial stability.[6] From the perspective of individual institutions, globalization helps diversify risks and may well have improved financial stability, particularly in the face of relatively small shocks. As recent events have shown, however, severe crises can be more easily transmitted across borders and therefore more difficult to deal with. To address wider systemic risk, a comprehensive approach to prudential supervision and market regulation is needed. Emerging and developing countries are thus presented with new challenges to strengthen institutions and improve coordination.

Drawing from recent reports under the Financial Sector Assessment Program (box 1.7) and the new lessons emerging from the current global financial turmoil, it appears that policies aimed at strengthening the robustness of financial systems should be tailored along four dimensions: policies that seek to strengthen the soundness of individual institutions; policies that solidify the contingency planning and crisis management framework; policies that mitigate the risks from cross-border exposures and spillover effects; and policies that adopt a broader macroeconomic orientation for financial surveillance.

Further Strengthening Prudential Frameworks

Supervisors must have adequate expertise and resources to monitor banks' risk management models and develop their own assessment tools. This recommendation applies to all supervisory regimes, from the emerging countries with the more developed banking systems that use the internal risk-based approach under the Basel II framework, to the developing countries where banks continue to work under the more traditional Basel I regime. The financial crisis has highlighted the need for financial institutions and supervisors to contemplate low-probability risks in their stress test assumptions. Supervisors must have at their disposal the discretion to use a range of tools to reduce financial risks, including a gradual increase in overall capital requirements.

Supervisors must give equivalent weight to the supervision of liquidity risk and solvency risk. The current crisis has demonstrated that during times of extreme stress, there is little distinction between illiquidity and insolvency. While emerging countries that already have a sound systemic liquidity framework may focus more on monitoring banks' internal liquidity risks management processes (as Kazakhstan and Sri Lanka have done), low-income countries may need to focus their efforts on strengthening their broader systemic liquidity framework, including the role of the central bank as a lender of last resort and the degree of cooperation between the fiscal and monetary authorities to ensure a coherent debt management policy.

In countries where nonbank financial institutions (such as pension funds and insurance companies) pose systemic risks, nonbank regulatory regimes should be strengthened. For example, risks can build up and go unrecognized where there is insufficient information on exposures through nonbank subsidiaries, such as leasing companies, and opaque ownership linkages (such as Botswana and Haiti).

National authorities must actively encourage improvements in the resilience of financial infrastructure. Strengthening the resilience and efficiency of domestic clearing and settlement systems, including those for retail electronic payments and foreign exchange

---

BOX 1.6   Bailing out the world's poorest

As the financial crisis spills over to the developing world in 2008–09, many governments and citizens are asking what can be done to help protect the poorest.

The starting point for many developing countries will be a weak safety net, with limited potential for protecting the poor from an economywide crisis. There will also be limited information concerning the likely profile of welfare impacts, although an effort should still be made to anticipate the types of households and places that will be most vulnerable, using the best available data and analytic tools. Crises have often presented opportunities for setting up better information systems for monitoring progress and for future preparedness.

Expanding the coverage and increasing the benefit levels on conditional cash transfer programs (CCTs) has been one response to crises, particularly in Latin America. There are several examples of effective CCTs in developing countries. The Food-for-Education Program in Bangladesh, Mexico's PROGRESA program (now called Oportunidades) and Bolsa Escola in Brazil require the children of the recipient family to demonstrate adequate school attendance (and health care in some cases). Impact evaluations show evidence that such programs bring non-negligible benefits to poor households in terms of both current and future incomes, through higher investments in child schooling and health care. Mexico was able to help redress the adverse welfare impacts of the recent rise in food prices by implementing a one-time top-up payment to Oportunidades participants.

There has been some evaluative research on specific programs introduced during past crises. One example studied a CCT program in Indonesia, the Jaring Pengamanan Sosial, and found that it appreciably reduced school dropout rates among beneficiaries during the 1998 financial crisis; the program had the greatest impact at the lower secondary school level where children are most susceptible to dropping out.

A common drawback of targeted cash transfer schemes in practice is that they tend to be relatively unresponsive to changes in the need for assistance. A previously ineligible household that is hit by, say, unemployment of the main breadwinner may not find it easy to get help from such schemes. Temporary expansion in the transfer payments to existing beneficiaries can help in a crisis, though a temporary expansion in coverage will probably also be needed and this can be harder to achieve.

markets, should become a key priority for countries with less developed financial systems (such as Haiti and Moldova).

Governments must be fully cognizant of the risks inherent in direct intervention. The breadth of public responses to address troubled institutions witnessed during the current crisis has no historic parallel (table 1.4). Policy makers must ensure that these interventions are credible, both in terms of their funding and implementation, and that they do not aggravate market distortions. For example, encouraging banks to lend in the face of a credit crunch could weaken the prospects of a return to normalcy when the financial turmoil recedes. Similarly, the use of government guarantees and expenditures on

fiscal deficits and public debt markets need to be carefully monitored.

Off-balance-sheet items and derivatives should also be monitored. Even though the originate-to-distribute model had flaws that led to overexpansion in credit in mature markets, emerging markets have used some forms of securitization to expand credit. Emerging market securitization should also incorporate appropriate safety nets to avoid problems similar to those in mature markets.

Strengthening Contingency Planning

The current crisis has demonstrated that existing contingency planning and crisis preparedness arrangements have been

One way to ensure that the safety net provides effective insurance—a genuine safety net—is to build in design features that only encourage those in need of help to seek out the program and encourage them to drop out of it when help is no longer needed given better options in the rest of the economy.

The classic example of such self-targeting is a workfare program (variously called relief work or public works programs; food-for-work programs also fall under this heading). Workfare has been widely used in crises and by countries at all stages of development. Famously, workfare programs were a key element of the New Deal introduced in the United States in 1933 in response to the Great Depression. They were also a key element of the Famine Codes introduced in India around 1880 and have continued to play an important role to this day in the subcontinent. Relief work programs have helped in responding to, and preventing, famines in Sub-Saharan Africa. During the East Asian financial crisis of the late 1990s, both Indonesia and the Republic of Korea introduced large workfare programs, as did Mexico in the 1995 "Peso crisis," Peru during its recession of 1998–2001, and Argentina in the 2002 financial crisis. These programs can be responsive to differences in need—both between people at one date and over time for a given person—provided the program is designed and implemented well.

The Employment Guarantee Scheme in Maharashtra, India, which started in the early 1970s, aims to ensure income support in rural areas by providing unskilled manual labor at low wages to anyone who wants it. The scheme is financed domestically, largely from taxes on the relatively well-off segments of Maharashtra's urban population. In 2004 India introduced an ambitious national version of this scheme under the National Rural Employment Guarantee Act. This program promises to provide up to 100 days of unskilled manual labor per family per year, at the statutory minimum wage rate for agricultural labor, to anyone who wants it in rural India.

An ideal workfare scheme guarantees low-wage work on community-initiated projects. The low-wage rate ensures that the scheme is self-targeted in that the nonpoor will rarely want to participate. The federal or state government announces that it is willing to finance up to, say, 15 days a month of work on community projects for any adult at a wage rate no higher than the market wage rate for unskilled manual labor in a normal year. The work is available to any adult at any time, crisis or not. This would extend the coverage of the public works schemes often found in current relief efforts to include normal times at which demand would be much lower, but almost certainly not zero. It would also relax the eligibility restrictions often found on relief work. Access to the program would rely very little on administrative discretion (either in turning it on and off, or determining who gets help.) As long as the guarantee is credible, it will also help reduce the longer-term costs of risks facing the poor. Thus it can help in fighting chronic poverty as well as transient poverty in a crisis.

Source: Ravallion 2008.

BOX 1.7   The Financial Sector Assessment Program

The FSAP is a joint IMF–World Bank program that aims at synthesizing a relatively comprehensive and detailed view of a country's financial sector risks, vulnerabilities, and development needs in an overall report. With over two-thirds of the countries having been covered by a first-round FSAP or FSAP update, the FSAP is now recognized as an essential cornerstone of the World Bank and the IMF's financial sector surveillance work, and demand for this voluntary program by member countries remains strong. The FSAP coverage remains uneven across regions and levels of development, with mainly developing countries covered by an FSAP. Nonetheless, the coverage of developing countries is rising, reflecting the initial emphasis on systemically important countries and the greater capacity of high-income countries to undertake the exercise.

A sound and well-functioning financial system rests on three pillars, which constitute the basis of the assessment framework:

■ Macroprudential surveillance and financial stability analysis by the authorities to monitor the impact of potential macroeconomic and institutional factors (both domestic and external) on the risks, vulnerabilities, and stability of financial systems.
■ Financial system supervision and regulation to help manage the risks and vulnerabilities, protect market integrity, and provide incentives for strong risk management and good governance for financial institutions.
■ Financial system infrastructure, including the legal infrastructure for finance; the systemic liquidity infrastructure (monetary and exchange operations; payments and securities settlement systems; and the structure of money, exchange, and securities markets); and issues related to governance and transparency (such as the accounting and auditing framework, market monitoring arrangements, and credit reporting systems).

The FSAP assessments carefully consider the complementarities and trade-offs between financial stability and development. Policies to foster financial stability also support orderly financial development. Nevertheless, in specific contexts, the benefits of stability policies in terms of increased soundness and containment of risks have to be weighed against the costs of regulatory compliance and the possible side effects of prudential regulations on market functioning and access. Similarly, policies to foster financial development necessarily involve some increase in both macroeconomic and financial risks, which need to be managed. Thus, promoting an orderly process of financial development alongside stability necessarily involves a proper sequencing and coordination of a range of financial policies.

The FSAP assessments have also proven to be a powerful tool in helping shape policy advice on prudential supervision and market regulation during the financial market crisis. Since August 2007, 21 FSAPs (mostly updates) have taken place, including in advanced and emerging market countries that could be expected to be susceptible to the turmoil. In these assessments, particular attention was paid to crisis management frameworks and cross-border supervisory cooperation, as well as to exposures to subprime-related financial instruments and tighter funding conditions.

---

inadequate in responding to systemic risk and has underscored the need to strengthen these arrangements.

The roles and responsibilities between relevant authorities must be clear. Certain conditions are of critical importance during a financial crisis: a clear hierarchy in the decision-making structure, up-to-date supervisory information, and a true ability to act swiftly. As events have demonstrated, these conditions are not in place in many countries. Greater coordination among central banks, financial regulators, and their respective

governments, both domestically and on a cross-border basis, would contribute to better monitoring of liquidity and solvency risks.

National authorities must ensure that a robust legal process exists for early intervention in, and resolution of, failing financial institutions. Recent FSAP reports found prompt corrective action and bank resolution systems to be weak in a broad range of countries (box 1.8). Regulatory authorities need to have the power to close or restructure a troubled financial institution. For this, the authorities must be clear about the main

TABLE 1.4 Measures implemented during financial turmoil, by country

Country	Higher deposit insurance coverage	Other debt guarantee provision	Bank recapitalization	Foreign exchange liquidity support	Domestic liquidity support	Capital controls
Argentina	...	...	...	✔	✔	...
Brazil	...	...	...	✔	✔	...
Bulgaria	✔	...	...	...	✔	...
China	...	...	...	✔	✔	✔
Colombia	...	...	...	...	✔	✔
Croatia	✔	...	...	...	...	...
Czech Republic	✔	...	...	...	✔	...
Ecuador	...	...	...	...	...	✔
Estonia	✔	...	...	...	...	...
Hong Kong, China[a]	✔	...	✔	...	...	...
Hungary	...	✔	...	✔	✔	...
India[a]	...	...	✔	✔	✔	...
Indonesia	✔	✔	✔	✔	...	✔
Kazakhstan	✔	✔	✔	...	✔	...
Korea, Rep. of	✔	✔	...	✔	✔	...
Latvia	✔	...	...	...	...	...
Lithuania	✔	...	...	...	...	...
Malaysia[a]	✔	✔	✔	...	✔	...
Mexico	...	...	...	✔	✔	...
Mongolia	✔	...	...	...	...	...
Nigeria	...	...	...	...	✔	...
Peru	...	...	...	✔	✔	...
Poland	✔	...	...	✔	✔	...
Philippines	✔	...	...	✔	✔	...
Romania	✔	...	...	...	✔	...
Russian Federation	✔	✔	✔	✔	✔	✔
Singapore	✔	...	...	✔	...	...
Slovakia	✔	...	...	...	...	...
Slovenia	✔	...	...	...	...	...
Turkey	✔	...	...	✔	...	...
Ukraine	✔	...	...	✔	✔	✔
Total	**21**	**6**	**6**	**15**	**19**	**6**

Source: IMF.
Note: This is a summary of key measures taken by authorities.
a. Bank recapitalization not yet implemented, possibly only as contingency.

BOX 1.8 Common regulatory and supervisory shortcomings identified in recent FSAP reports

Publicly available information drawn from a sample of 16 FSAPs and FSAP updates conducted in emerging and developing countries in 2007–08, shows common shortcomings emerging across different levels of development and/or geographical regions. For illustration purposes, in what follows, each of the common shortcomings identified during an FSAP is associated with some of the sample countries. This does not suggest, however, that these shortcomings were particularly severe in the cited country, but only that they were discussed in the FSAP. The economies included are Algeria, Botswana, Costa Rica, Croatia, Arab Republic of Egypt, Haiti, Kazakhstan, Lithuania, Moldova, Mongolia, Morocco, Namibia, Sri Lanka, Thailand, Ukraine, and the Western African Economic Monetary Union (WAEMU).

- *Insufficient independence and enforcement powers of supervisory agencies.* Many FSAP reports highlighted the need to strengthen supervisors' powers to enforce prudential requirements, including through stronger bank licensing frameworks and "fit and proper" rules (Haiti, Mongolia, WAEMU) and through more resources to attract and retain high-skilled staff (Lithuania, Namibia) and achieve operational independence (Costa Rica, Kazakhstan).
- *Insufficient tools to assess borrower's creditworthiness and quality of collateral.* Weak auditing, reporting, and accounting standards (WAEMU), lack or incomplete credit registries (Egypt, Haiti), and limited judicial capacity to enforce foreclosure rules (Haiti, Thailand) were found to substantially hamper banks' ability to assess borrowers' creditworthiness.
- *Weak risk management.* Key recommendations in this area focused on strengthening supervisors' ability to ensure the quality of banks' assets, including through adequate provisioning rules and capital risk weights (Kazakhstan, Morocco, Ukraine), a proper connected-lending and concentration risk regulation (Haiti, Mongolia, WAEMU), and effective consolidated supervision for groups and their offshore subsidiaries (Botswana, Costa Rica, Kazakhstan, Namibia, Sri Lanka, Ukraine). Other shortcomings included weak internal controls (Haiti, Morocco) and limited liquidity risk management (Algeria, Kazakhstan, Mongolia).
- *Limited coordination between bank and nonbank supervisory authorities.* Key issues related to weak information exchange on risk exposures and ownership linkages (Croatia, Ukraine) and unequal level-playing field (Botswana, Egypt, Haiti, Namibia, Sri Lanka).
- *Distortionary role of the state in the financial system.* Some FSAP reports highlighted weak supervision of state-owned banks, including capital deficiencies and unresolved problem loans (Algeria, Sri Lanka, Thailand). Many reports pressed for scaling back government ownership and interference (Botswana, Egypt, Mongolia).
- *Weak payment infrastructure.* Many countries were found to have weak payment and settlements systems.
- *Insufficient contingency planning.* The FSAP recommended revamping early remedial actions and bank resolution systems (Costa Rica, Haiti, Kazakhstan, Sri Lanka, Ukraine); initiating formal cross-border crisis management arrangements with foreign supervisors (Lithuania); and clarifying the role of different agencies in contingency planning (Croatia).
- *Underdeveloped infrastructure in capital markets.* FSAP reports recommended increasing disclosure standards and transparency practices of nonfinancial and financial institutions (Algeria, Ukraine); simplifying legal procedures for equity share listings and bond issuances (Egypt, Namibia); and establishing a benchmark yield curve (Algeria, Botswana, Ukraine).
- *Limited capacity to assess financial stability.* Key recommendations focused on the need to improve financial sector data and analytical capacity to monitor systemwide risks and vulnerabilities, including through stress testing (Egypt, Namibia, Ukraine).

objectives to achieve (maintaining public confidence in the banking system, for example), the methods of bankruptcy prevention, and the crisis resolution tools (such as liquidation or merger).[7]

National authorities must ensure clarity over deposit insurance responsibility and coverage, including for cross-border institutions. In all countries, depositors must receive clear information on who is responsible for safeguarding their claims and the coverage of their deposit insurance. The coverage must be credible, and the payouts in the event of a failure must be provided promptly to minimize disruptions in the payments system.

The Need for Greater International Cooperation

Reflecting the links between financial markets and institutions, the current crisis is calling for greater international policy cooperation among countries with international banks.

National authorities need to cultivate closer cooperation between home and host supervisors. A number of countries, particularly in Eastern and Central Europe and Sub-Saharan Africa, have banking systems dominated by foreign-owned banks. The behavior of foreign subsidiaries could depend largely on their parent groups, whose management and supervisory authorities are located abroad. This calls for coordinated inspections of international banks, joint risk assessments, and the preparation of plans to deal with a major bank failure. Going forward, the role of international supervisory colleges for cross-border financial institutions needs to be augmented to achieve a more effective information exchange.

Close cross-border coordination in crisis management is necessary to forestall beggar-thy-neighbor policies with damaging cross-border spillover effects and market distortions. This is particularly important in countries where large international banks are established. Recent unilateral increases in deposit insurance coverage are examples of how a lack of policy coordination can cause serious spillover effects.

Emphasis on Systemic Risks

Financial surveillance should have a greater emphasis on systemic risks and their wider implications for economic stability. Financial surveillance needs to pay closer attention to the sources of financing of domestic credit and their macroeconomic implications.

Specifically, surveillance should consider the composition of private sector credit, its impact on a country's external position, and the ability of its banking system to absorb shocks from a sharp unwinding of external funding. This is particularly true for countries (such as the Baltics, Hungary, and some Sub-Saharan African countries) with a large foreign ownership component, because they could face the effects of a credit crunch in the event of a sharp capital flow reversal.

Central banks must have access to adequate institution-specific information to assess financial stability risks. Central banks should have access to all necessary supervisory information to assess systemic risks to their economy, including to the payments system and emergency liquidity operations.

Regulators must ensure that market participants are fully informed of the risks inherent in financial products, and financial supervisors must ensure that capital buffers are commensurate with the risks.[8]

Prudential regulations should explicitly counter cyclical tendencies, including through larger liquidity and capital buffer requirements and dynamic loan loss provisioning to account for the inherent underpricing of risk in upturns.

National authorities must counteract institutions' tendency to become "too big to fail" or "too connected to fail" to better internalize the economic costs of financial instability. Authorities need to protect taxpayers' interests by seeking to reduce risks posed by large and complex institutions. This can be promoted through competition policy, restrictions on activities, or prudential measures (such as capital requirement or deposit insurance premiums).

Capital Restrictions as a Last Resort

Capital restrictions might be unavoidable as a last resort to prevent or mitigate the crisis effects. A few emerging countries have introduced capital controls and other measures to better monitor and, in some cases, limit the conversion of domestic currency into foreign exchange (see table 1.4). Capital controls, however, typically result in economic distortions that are harmful for longer-term growth and lose their effectiveness quickly, as market participants find ways to circumvent them and undermine investors' confidence. Nonetheless, capital controls might need to be imposed as a last resort to help mitigate a financial crisis and stabilize macroeconomic developments

The Poverty Effects of the Crisis

As a result of the food and financial crises, the pace of poverty reduction has slowed. The positive effects on poverty of the high global growth in recent years have been partly offset by the rise in food prices, which pushed an estimated 160 million to 200 million people into extreme poverty between 2005 and 2008. Although international food prices have declined since the middle of 2008, all of the benefits of the lower prices will not be felt immediately because local prices lag behind changes in international prices. As a result, no more than 90 million to 120 million people who had been pushed

into poverty by the high food prices may emerge from poverty in 2009.

The slowdown in economic growth resulting from the global financial crisis will add to the poverty impact of high food prices. On current growth projections, there will be about 55 million more extreme poor (those living below the international poverty line of $1.25 a day in 2005 purchasing power parity terms) in developing countries in 2009 than expected before the financial crisis.[9] The poverty rate is still expected to decline in 2009, but at a much slower pace because of the sharply lower growth. Table 1.5 presents poverty projections for 2009 based on current growth projections.[10] The proportion of people living in extreme poverty is projected to decline in 2009 by 0.6 percentage point. This compares with an average annual decline of 1.3 percentage points in the three-year period preceding 2009. All regions of the developing world are affected, although to a varying degree. Sub-Saharan Africa will see a rise in the poverty count. Rising poverty is likely especially in the more fragile and low-growth economies. While poverty rates on average are much lower in Europe

TABLE 1.5 Short-term poverty outlook
people living below the international poverty line of $1.25/day (2005 PPP)

	Number of people (millions)		Change in number of people (millions)		% of population		Change (percentage points)	
	2008	2009	2005–08[a]	2009	2008	2009	2005–08[a]	2009
East Asia and the Pacific	222.5	203.0	−31.2	−19.5	11.5	10.4	−1.8	−1.1
Europe and Central Asia	15.1	15.5	−0.7	0.4	3.2	3.3	−0.2	0.1
Latin America and the Caribbean	37.6	40.3	−2.5	2.7	6.6	7.0	−0.5	0.4
Middle East and North Africa	8.6	8.3	−0.8	−0.3	2.7	2.5	−0.3	−0.2
South Asia	536.3	530.6	−19.8	−5.7	34.8	33.9	−1.8	−0.9
Sub-Saharan Africa	382.7	385.9	−1.9	3.2	46.7	46.0	−1.4	−0.7
Total	1,202.8	1,183.6	−56.9	−19.2	21.3	20.7	−1.3	−0.6
Low-income countries	952.3	947.8	−26.9	−4.5	38.0	37.2	−1.8	−0.8
Middle-income countries	262.1	247.2	−33.1	−14.9	8.3	7.8	−1.2	−0.5

Source: World Bank (model-based projections).
Note: PPP = purchasing power parity.
a. Simple annual average change for the three-year period 2005–08.

and Central Asia and in Latin America and the Caribbean, these regions could also see an increase in the number of poor in 2009. If the crisis deepens and growth in developing countries falters further, the impact on poverty would be still stronger. Overall, on current growth projections, more than half of all developing countries could experience a rise in the number of extreme poor in 2009; this proportion could be still higher among low-income countries and countries in Sub-Saharan Africa—two-thirds and three-fourths, respectively.

Estimates by the International Labour Organization (ILO), which focus on the impact of the growth slowdown on employment and wages, indicate a still stronger impact on poverty. The ILO estimates that some 30 million more people around the world may be unemployed in 2009, compared with 2007, of which 23 million could be in developing countries. The labor market

impact is estimated to be associated with 93 million additional people classified as extreme poor.[11]

The MDG 1 for poverty reduction remains achievable at the global level, but the crisis adds new risks. Current growth projections envisage a gradual recovery of growth in developing countries starting in 2010. Per capita GDP growth in developing countries is expected to rebound to an average of about 4.5 percent per year during 2011–15. On the basis of these projections, the proportion of people living below $1.25 per day is expected to reach 15.1 percent by 2015, surpassing the MDG target of 20.8 percent (half of the 1990 level) for developing countries as a whole (table 1.6). These projections, however, are subject to considerable uncertainty and downside risks stemming from the crisis. Within this overall picture, there are major differences in performance among regions and countries. In Sub-Saharan Africa, the

TABLE 1.6 Longer-term poverty outlook
people living below the international poverty line of $1.25 (2005 PPP)

	Number of people (millions)			% of population			Over/under[a]
	1990	2005	2015	1990	2005	2015	MDG[b]
East Asia & Pacific	873.3	316.2	103.6	54.7	16.8	5.1	22.3
East Asia & Pacific, excluding China	190.1	108.5	43.5	41.3	18.7	6.7	14.0
Europe & Central Asia	9.1	17.3	12.8	2.0	3.7	2.7	−1.7
Latin America & the Caribbean	49.6	45.1	33.4	11.3	8.2	5.4	0.3
Middle East & North Africa	9.7	11.0	6.7	4.3	3.6	1.8	0.4
South Asia	579.2	595.6	416.1	51.7	40.3	24.5	1.4
South Asia, excluding India	143.7	139.8	97.7	53.1	36.6	21.2	5.4
Sub-Saharan Africa	295.7	388.4	352.6	57.6	50.9	36.6	−7.8
Total	1,816.6	1,373.5	925.2	41.7	25.2	15.1	5.7
Total, excluding China	1,133.5	1,165.8	865.1	35.2	28.1	18.2	−0.6
Low-income countries	920.4	1,032.9	789.3	52.8	43.5	28.0	−1.6
Middle-income countries	914.2	361.5	143.5	35.0	11.8	4.3	13.2

Source: World Bank (model-based projections).
Note: PPP = purchasing power parity.
a. The difference in percentage points between the MDG target and the projected poverty rate in 2015. Negative numbers indicate underperformance.
b. Relates to MDG 1, target 1.A, which calls for halving, between 1990 and 2015, the proportion of people living below the poverty line.

share of people living in extreme poverty will remain well above the MDG target of 28.8 percent in 2015. South Asia will barely meet the MDG target. In contrast, the East Asia and Pacific region has already surpassed the target. The Latin America and the Caribbean region is on track. The Middle East and North Africa and Europe and Central Asia regions are likely to miss the MDG target, but they started from much lower poverty levels.

Low-income countries as a group are likely to fall short of the MDG target. The poverty rate in these countries is projected to fall from 52.8 percent to 28.0 percent between 1990 and 2015. The middle-income countries do much better, with the poverty rate declining from 35 percent to 4.3 percent. Within these groupings, however, there is considerable variation in performance among individual countries.

The effects of growth volatility are not symmetric. Research shows that growth accelerations and decelerations have an asymmetric impact on poverty and human development outcomes. These outcomes tend to deteriorate more quickly during growth decelerations than they improve during growth accelerations. This finding suggests that preventing growth collapses is essential for a region such as Sub-Saharan Africa to attain the MDGs. Sub-Saharan Africa has had a number of growth acceleration episodes in the past 30 years, but also nearly a comparable number of growth collapses, offsetting much of the benefit of the bursts in growth. Had Africa avoided its growth collapses, its GDP per capita would have grown at 1.7 percent a year instead of 0.7 percent between 1975 and 2005, and it would have been more than 30 percent higher by the end of the period.[12]

Notes

1. Commodity prices are sensitive to growth prospects, because output in commodity-intensive sectors (manufacturing and construction) tends to contract more in recessions than output in other sectors.

2. World Bank 2008b.

3. Details of World Bank and IMF response to the crisis are discussed in chapter 6.

4. IMF 2009.

5. By August 2008, 35 countries had some form of export restriction on food items in place. The most distortionary measures have been removed since then.

6. For a detailed discussion on financial stability implications of globalization of financial institutions, see Chapter 3 of the 2007 Global Financial Stability Report (Washington, International Monetary Fund).

7. A good review of banking crises resolution can be found in Hoggarth and Reidhill (2003).

8. These issues are the focus of a Financial Stability Forum Working Group on enhancing market and institutional resilience, and of discussions within the Basel Committee.

9. World Bank 2009.

10. These poverty projections are based on projections of economic growth; they do not include the effects of food price changes.

11. ILO 2009. Geneva. The report also presents a worse-case scenario that projects an increase in the number of unemployed at 51 million globally and at 40 million in developing countries.

12. Arbache and Page 2007.

2

Improving the Private Investment Climate for Recovery and Growth

Economic growth is central to achieving the Millennium Development Goals (MDGs) and related development outcomes, and a vigorous private sector is vital for strong and sustainable growth. The private sector drives job creation, increases in productivity, and economic growth.[1] Private sector jobs provide most of the income in developing as well as developed countries. Revenues from private sector transactions and incomes pay for many of the public goods provided by governments. Competition can help spur technological advancements and productivity gains that are the key to sustained long-term growth.

Private-sector-led growth also benefits the poor. The expansion of job opportunities is identified as the single most important pathway out of poverty.[2] When average household incomes rise by 2 percent, poverty rates fall by about twice as much on average.[3] The poverty effects of income growth are often associated with a shift in employment from traditional sectors with low productivity to those with higher productivity growth, such as manufacturing, mining, and utilities. The poor also benefit from expanding public goods provision associated with higher revenue collection.

The current international financial crisis has sharpened the focus on the private sector. With credit hard to come by almost

everywhere in the world, private firms are having to downsize, lay off workers, and delay if not cancel investment plans. Fear that economic hardships in the private sector could widen and lead to deeper recession globally has heightened the need to ensure that the private sector has the tools it needs and the fiscal and monetary policies that will make it grow. Addressing key constraints in the private sector is necessary to ensure that firms can respond and expand once the recovery is under way.

The agenda involves improving the enabling environment facing businesses of all types and sizes, from small farmers to sophisticated technology firms, and increasing the attractiveness of economies to investors, both foreign and domestic. This chapter assesses progress and the policy agenda regarding three key elements of the private investment climate: the regulatory and institutional environment; access to financial services; and access to infrastructure. The latter two elements are both important inputs to private sector development, and the private sector itself can play an important role in their provision.

The current crisis reinforces lessons from research on regulatory reform: the aim should be better, not necessarily fewer, regulations; and the quality of enforcement and broader governance matter greatly for the effectiveness of regulations. The crisis underscores the need to pay special attention to the financial sector. It is also vitally important to protect infrastructure investment from the impact of the crisis as much as possible. Infrastructure investment can both help with economic recovery in the short term and strengthen foundations for future growth.

Quality of Investment Climate Key to Private Sector Contributions

The investment climate, or broader business environment, in which firms operate can be critical in shaping the incentives and opportunities for, and rewards from, investment and productive efforts. Taxation directly affects the return on investment, while regulations influence the types of activities one

can or cannot engage in and who can engage in them. A firm's access to finance can determine the opportunities it can pursue. And the availability of infrastructure services can affect the costs of production and delivery of goods and services to consumers. Indeed, by influencing the barriers to entry, the risks, and the costs facing firms, the investment climate affects the scope for private sector growth and productivity.

The World Bank's Enterprise Surveys, now completed in over 100 countries, provide insights into the current investment climate. The information includes subjective rankings of constraints, which can be corroborated with more objective, quantitative measures. Thus, if firms report electricity to be a problem, information is also available on the frequency of outages, the costs of running a generator, and the production lost as a result of interruptions in the public grid.

Firm responses show that the regulatory environment, access to finance, and infrastructure are three key constraints affecting private business around the world.[4] Figure 2.1 illustrates a number of patterns shown in these surveys.

Firms in high-income countries report facing fewer constraints. The share of firms that see the various potential issues as a major or severe constraint to the growth of their business is much lower in high-income countries than it is in developing countries. The share is often half that of lower-income countries, with the exception of licenses and permits and labor regulations, where the share is only marginally lower than for middle-income countries. Because the objective conditions in higher-income countries are generally better—that is, electrical outages are less common, the financial system is more developed, and procedures to comply with regulations are often more streamlined—this finding is not too surprising.

Access to electricity and finance are the top two issues in low-income countries. The importance of these constraints decreases

FIGURE 2.1 Key constraints on firms vary by country income level

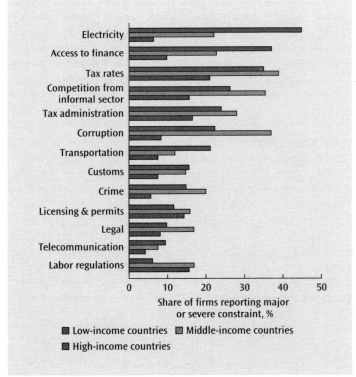

Source: Enterprise Surveys database.

dramatically as a country's income rises. This is true for the other infrastructure variables too—although telecommunications is not reported as a major constraint in any income category, thanks to rapid progress in this area in recent years.

Several areas related to regulations and governance are reported as most significant in middle-income countries. These are tax rates, tax administration, competition from the informal sector, and corruption. As discussed below, it is often the low-income countries that have the most regulatory procedures and time delays associated with compliance. As income rises, these tend to fall. However, enforcement of these regulations often strengthens as income rises. So, while the formal requirements may be decreasing, the greater enforcement could well explain why entrepreneurs in middle-income countries report being more constrained by regulation. The results also suggest that corruption and regulatory constraints may go together.

Many studies show that these areas of the investment climate—regulatory and institutional environment, finance, and infrastructure services—are closely associated with firm performance.[5] Weaknesses in the business environment have been shown to shift the size distribution of firms downward.[6] Interruptions in access to power are particularly significant in reducing the growth of large firms while encouraging the spread of small, more labor-intensive firms. A lack of access to finance lowers growth across the size distribution. Because the benefits of finance are particularly strong for small firms, a lack of access hurts them disproportionately.[7]

Regulatory and Institutional Environment for Private Sector Development

Regulations are generally justified as addressing market failures. A common one involves externalities, cases where activities

have spillover effects on others that are not taken into account by the original actor. A second market failure is information asymmetry, where the producer, for example, may have more information about the safety or reliability of its products than the consumer. A third is monopoly power, market power that can be used to raise prices and lower output to maximize a firm's rents at the expense of the consumer.

These market failures drive a wedge between the private interests of firms and those of broader society. They can also inhibit productive investments and growth. Thus regulations can play a critical role in protecting society and consumers and in promoting greater equity and access to a level playing field for private sector development.

The challenge to governments, however, is that they not overreach in correcting these failures. While underregulation may fail to address social interests or externalities, overregulation can stifle the ability to pursue opportunities, curtailing growth. Government failures, from limited capacity or its own rent-seeking incentives, can also be harmful. Such risks reinforce the case for keeping regulations simple, transparent, and enforceable.

The goal is not simply to have fewer regulations. Rather it is to have better regulations. And one of the lessons of experience is that enforcement matters in assessing the quality of regulations. The effectiveness of regulations can depend on the capacity of local officials as well as on budget constraints. The broader quality of governance plays a role as well.

Substantial Scope Exists for Regulatory Improvements

Looking at what is known about regulations in practice, there appears to be substantial room for improvements without compromising broader public interests. Too often governments pursue regulations that fail to meet intended social interests or impose unnecessary costs, risks, or barriers to entry and competition. Demonstrating a commitment to improve the regulatory environment can lead to substantial results—without requiring a perfect business environment. Examples from China to India to Uganda show how tackling regulatory costs and strengthening property rights can generate significant increases in investment and productivity.[8]

One source of data on regulations is the World Bank's Doing Business project, benchmarking specifically defined areas of business regulations in most countries of the world. The ability to compare formal requirements of regulatory compliance across countries can be useful in encouraging officials to undertake reforms. And the data can be used to analyze their associations with outcomes of interest, such as

investment, job creation, and growth (see box 2.1 for a recent evaluation of the Doing Business project and follow-up actions).

The Doing Business measure of the ease of doing business covering 10 regulatory areas shows that the ease of doing bussiness varies widely across countries (figure 2.2).[9] Richer countries tend to have more efficient and streamlined regulations. But there is considerable variation in this relationship. What matters for the quality of the business environment is the quality of the regulations, including their enforceability, not just the number of regulating procedures. Enforceability is a particularly important consideration in poorer countries, which tend to have less control of corruption and more limited administrative capacities. A heavy

BOX 2.1 Independent Evaluation Group reviews Doing Business

In 2008 the World Bank's Independent Evaluation Group (IEG) released its report on the Doing Business project. The evaluation recognized that the project has been effective in spurring dialogue on reforms and motivating interest and action. "For country authorities, it sheds a bright, sometimes unflattering, light on regulatory aspects of their business climate. For business interests, it has helped to catalyze debates and dialogue about reform." However, the evaluation also found that business is affected not only by laws and regulations, but also by a host of other variables outside the scope of the Doing Business indicators. In response, the 2009 report on Doing Business is careful to strengthen the caveats about what the indicators do and do not capture.

The IEG evaluation found little evidence that the Doing Business indicators distorted policy priorities or encouraged policy makers to make superficial changes solely to improve rankings. It also concluded that a country's legal origin, whether civil or common law, does not determine its score in the Doing Business indicators. The evaluation's recommendations to further develop the transparency of the data collection, data revisions, and the respondent selection process have been accepted and are being implemented by the Doing Business team.

Within indicator areas, the IEG evaluation addressed concerns that the rankings may appear to reward less regulation without necessarily capturing the quality of the regulations or the social values they might reflect. The 2009 report clarifies Doing Business's focus on efficient, streamlined, and accessible regulation. In the case of labor regulation, Doing Business specifically endorses the International Labour Organization's (ILO) core labor standards, and the Employing Workers indicator is designed to be consistent with all relevant ILO conventions. No economy can achieve a better score by failing to comply with these conventions. The Paying Tax indicator generated more debate about whether to include the tax rates in addition to the administrative time and costs of paying taxes. The tax rates remain as an indicator, but it is noted that they reflect in part the social and political preferences of a country.

The IEG cautioned that the Bank Group, by so prominently recognizing highly ranked countries in the Doing Business index, may be inadvertently signaling that it values reduced regulatory burdens more than other development goals. The Bank Group's approach entails helping countries achieve a wide range of objectives, yet it has no comparable way of celebrating improvements in other important development outcomes. One response could be to apply cross-country rankings to spur dialogue and motivate interest in and action on other development issues—those for which actionable indicators can serve as proxies for the target outcomes and for which there is a clear consensus on what constitutes an improvement.

regulatory burden in situations of poor enforcement capacities can produce perverse outcomes, including undermining the credibility and effectiveness of the government.

Improvements in Doing Business Indicators Are Common across Countries

A great many countries have seen improvements in their Doing Business indicators over time. Across all indicators and over the six years of data now available, 126 of the 178 economies for which there is at least two years of data register an improvement of 10 percent or more in at least one indicator. Fifty-two countries report such an improvement in more than three indicators. Only 18 countries report an overall reversal in an indicator.

Figure 2.3 shows the share of countries by region that report an improvement of 10 percent or more in an indicator. The Europe and Central Asia region has had a higher share of countries with improving indicators.[10] Sub-Saharan Africa has had a somewhat smaller improvement over time. However, the majority of countries there saw their indicators improve in 2007–08, and three of the world's top ten economies that reformed their business regulations were from the region: Botswana, Burkina Faso, and Senegal. Mauritius moved up to 24 in the global rankings on the regulatory ease of doing business. The runner-up in these overall rankings was South Africa at 32, followed by Botswana at 38. Other economies in Africa making the most reforms of business regulations include some postconflict countries, such as Liberia, Rwanda, and Sierra Leone.

More specialized analysis of Arab countries illustrates that reforms can have an impact. Six months after the Arab Republic of Egypt reformed its property registry, title registrations increased and related revenue rose by 39 percent. Commercial registrations in Oman increased by 93 percent during the year after Oman implemented a one-stop shop for business start-ups. In Saudi Arabia, reducing minimum capital requirements led

FIGURE 2.2   The ease of doing business varies widely

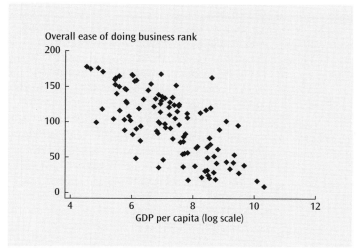

Source: World Bank Doing Business database and World Development Indicators.

FIGURE 2.3   Most regions are improving their regulatory indicators over time

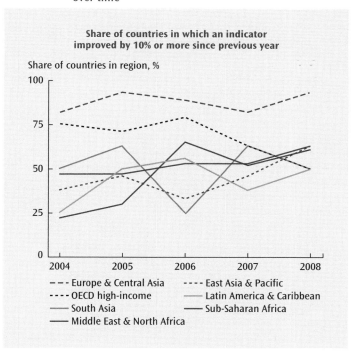

Source: World Bank, Doing Business database.
Note: Additional indicators were added in later years, contributing to the probability that an indicator would improve. The figure excludes coverage of credit registries that could be expanding without any reforms having been initiated. Cost variables are normalized as a share of GNI per capita. As countries grow, the same fixed cost will decline as a share. However, looking at annual changes (rather than the whole period), few countries would register an improvement based solely on growth.

to an 81 percent increase in new company registrations.[11]

The analysis also shows that geographical challenges in many landlocked and small island economies are compounded by a bureaucratic regulatory environment that hinders business. More isolated, such countries need to make their business environments all the more attractive if they are to be successful in encouraging new investments. However, this is not always the approach taken in many such economies. Compared with coastal economies, landlocked countries tend to rank lower in starting a business, dealing with construction permits, getting credit, protecting investors, paying taxes, trading across borders, and closing a business. Overall, landlocked economies have an average ranking of 107 out of 181 economies covered by the global *Doing Business 2009* report. But again, improvements are possible. The Dominican Republic was the top small-island reformer in 2008, as well as a top-10 reformer globally.

An expanded number of countries, including China, Mexico, Nigeria, and the Philippines, have developed subnational indicators of regulations. This has allowed for more tailored messages, improved the ability to benchmark, and made it easier to demonstrate what is actually feasible within the country. In Mexico these subnational indicators have revealed wide differences from city to city and state to state. For example, the time to enforce a contract varies significantly from 248 days in Zacatecas to 560 days in Quintana Roo. Zacatecas and other states are reducing the backlog by creating specialized commercial courts. Other states are increasingly using electronic platforms to share information and manage cases.

But Reforms Are Not Equally Common across Regulatory Areas

In which areas of business regulation are reforms most common? With six years of data now available, it is possible to look in

FIGURE 2.4 Regulatory reform is more common in some areas than in others

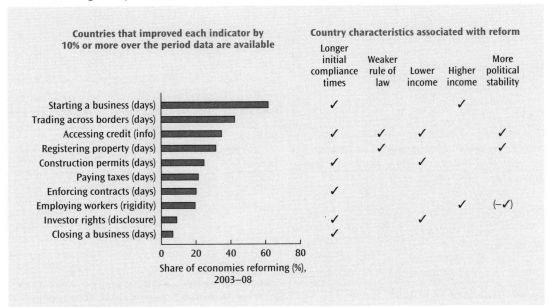

Source: World Bank, Doing Business database.
Note: Not all indicators are covered for the full period of 2003–08. Property was introduced in 2004; construction permits, tax, investor rights, and trade indicators were introduced in 2005.

more detail at the trends. Figure 2.4 illustrates the share of countries that have posted an improvement of at least 10 percent in each indicator. The most common area is starting a business, followed by improving trading across borders and expanding access to credit.[12] In contrast, labor regulations, closing a business, and investor rights are areas experiencing more limited reform, in large part because political economy considerations are particularly challenging.

Figure 2.4 also shows those country characteristics that are associated with particular regulatory areas being reformed. Of particular interest is knowing whether countries that started out with weaker Doing Business indicators were more or less likely to reform in the subsequent years. For six of the areas, countries with longer initial times to complete the regulatory processes have been more likely to make subsequent reforms. This is encouraging; much of the motivation for providing the benchmarks is to encourage those with higher burdens to tackle them. Low-income countries have been more likely to reform access to credit, construction permits, and disclosure rules, while high-income countries have been relatively more focused on reforms regarding starting a business and employing workers. Other country characteristics do not show much pattern. The data on reform patterns over time show that countries that reform are more likely to have subsequent improvements too.[13] Less encouraging, there is no significant evidence that reformers are concentrated in countries that are improving their broader policy or political environments.[14]

The impact of these regulations and their reform has been a growing area of research—aided in part by the expanded coverage of the Doing Business indicators and Enterprise Surveys. The findings of this research underscore the importance of improving regulations and strengthening enforcement (box 2.2).

BOX 2.2 Business environment reforms matter

Numerous studies have found examples of regulations that hamper business and of reforms that have improved the business climate. Barseghyan (2008) looks at output per worker in 157 countries and total factor productivity in 97 countries. He finds that an increase in entry costs by 80 percent of income per capita, which is one half of their standard deviation in the sample, decreases total factor productivity and output per worker by 22 percent and 29 percent, respectively. The magnitudes are large: one reason may be that an increase in entry costs decreases entry pressure, allowing existing firms with lower productivity to survive.

Klapper, Laeven, and Rajan (2006) find that the difference in real growth rates of value added per worker between the retail and pulp wood industries in the Czech Republic (whose entry costs put it at the 25th percentile in the sample of 40 countries) is 0.7 percentage points higher than the difference in real growth rates between the same industries in Italy (which is at the 75th percentile in entry costs). In other words, moving from Italy to the Czech Republic benefits the growth rate of the high-entry retail sector relatively more. With the average real growth rate in value added per worker at 1 percent, this is a sizable magnitude.

Similar measures have been constructed and used to look at reforms within specific countries. Chari (2008) looks at the simplification of entry regulation in India in 1984–90 and finds that when entry costs were cut by approximately 65 percent, the resulting productivity increase was as much as 28 percent over the six years covered by the data, of which 16 percent was directly contributed by the entry reforms (the remainder results from reforms in licensing of already-established businesses).

Bruhn (2008) uses information on the simplification of entry regulations initiated in Mexico in 2002 to look at the effects of entry. She finds a 5 percent increase in entry in eligible industries. However, little of this effect was attributable to already-established informal firms registering for the first time. Rather, former wage earners opened new businesses. Moreover, employment in eligible industries went up by 2.8 percent, and the results imply that competition from new entrants lowered prices by 0.6 percent and decreased the income of incumbent businesses by 3.2 percent.

The Effects of Regulations Can Vary within a Country

Another strand of research analyzing the impact of regulations has focused on how effects can vary across firms, particularly by the size of the firm, whether the firm is formal or informal, and the gender of the entrepreneur. Lifting the burden from small firms, encouraging informal firms to become formal, and drawing more women into the marketplace can strengthen the private sector and promote growth and progress toward the MDGs.

Effects on firm size. Regulatory reform can make small businesses more effective participants in the economy. In many areas, small and medium (10 to 50 employees) enterprises, which typically are the main motor of job creation in an economy, are the most affected by weaknesses in the investment climate.[15] In contrast, microfirms—those with 10 or fewer employees—are often able to stay below the bureaucratic radar screen and avoid the costs of taxation and regulatory compliance. Larger firms, while hampered by weak property rights, often can provide their own solutions to problems such as weak infrastructure (by purchasing their own generator, for example) or limited local finance (by attracting a foreign partner or drawing on their larger volume of retained earnings). They are also often best positioned to negotiate favorable tax treatments.

Smaller firms face many fixed costs that are proportionally higher for them, resulting in greater constraints on their being able to do business. Smaller firms are also more likely to face difficulties accessing finance, because of the higher relative transaction costs and greater information uncertainty involved, although the evidence shows that small firms that do get access to finance benefit the most from it.[16]

Effects on formality. The regulatory burden faced by small firms has particular influence on a second dimension of differences across firms, namely, whether they operate in the formal or informal sectors. Cross-country correlations show that countries with more regulatory burdens often have large informal sectors. Onerous regulations can reinforce the incentives informal firms have to remain small and informal and thus prevent them from realizing their full potential. To encourage small firms to grow and to participate in the formal sector, it is important to strengthen those areas that will benefit formal firms. Improving property rights is one such benefit. This can reduce uncertainty, encourage transactions with a wider set of suppliers and customers, and, by strengthening control of collateral, expand access to credit.

Burdensome regulations can affect informality on another dimension—compliance. Noncompliance is higher where regulations are more stringent and also where enforcement is more lax. Reducing the time requirements and the costs of regulations is only part of the solution. Improving transparency about what is required and making sure the information is readily available are important steps. It is important too to overcome the "culture of informality."[17] Widespread noncompliance can undermine the legitimacy of the state and reduce the likelihood that reforms will be effective at changing behaviors of firms. A broader goal of improving the quality and fairness of state institutions and policies can help ensure specific reforms will be effective.

Effects on women's participation. One of the MDGs is women's economic empowerment, and greater participation of women in business is one indicator of that goal. Data from the Enterprise Surveys confirm that participation rates are lower for women than men. Women's participation as owners in formal firms varies across countries but generally ranges between 20 and 30 percent of firms. Participation rates, both as owners and as workers, are generally highest among the smallest firms and in the informal sector. These gaps signal an important untapped resource for economic growth.

Evidence suggests that as regulatory burdens fall, women's participation as entrepreneurs tends to rise.[18] Some of this may stem from decreases in practices that explicitly restrict women's economic rights. A new Gender Law Library documents where gender-differentiation exists in formal regulations around the world (box 2.3). More generally though, lower regulatory burdens make entry easier and can encourage more part-time businesses where women's participation is higher.

Effects of Broader Institutional Environment Can Undermine Regulatory Reforms

Regulatory reforms will have little impact on the economic outcomes of interest if the surrounding institutional and governance environment is weak, inefficient, and corrupt. The six years of available data indicate that associations between *changes* in individual Doing Business indicators and the economic outcomes of interest are stronger for countries that are well-governed (controlling for income).[19] That the governance of a country affects the impact of business reforms should not be surprising. Changing what is on the books is not likely to have much impact if there is a large gap between de jure and de facto regulations. With better governance,

the changes are likely to be seen as credible and thus more likely to generate a response.

Data from the World Bank's Enterprise Surveys reinforce the importance of governance in implementing and enforcing regulations. These surveys are based on information firms themselves report and show the gaps that can exist between a regulation as it is meant to work and the actual experience on the ground.

Weak and ineffective regulatory implementation and enforcement create incentives for firms to circumvent the regulations, by failing to report all their revenues to the tax authorities, for example, or by not registering all their employees with the social security office. As table 2.1 shows, there is indeed a range of responses to regulations across regions. One measure is the time managers have to spend with government officials dealing with regulatory requirements. The time varies across countries, but patterns also emerge across regions and income groups. These indicators corroborate the earlier findings from the subjective rankings that some of the regulatory burdens are felt most strongly in middle-income countries. Management time is highest in middle-income countries, particularly in Latin America and to a lesser extent in the Middle East and North Africa. Respondents in middle-income countries were also

---

BOX 2.3   Adding a gender dimension to the measures of regulation

Given the MDG on women's economic empowerment, and the recognition that some regulations are not neutral in their impact on men and women, the Gender Law Library was launched in October 2008 (http://www.doingbusiness.org/elibrarydata/elibrary.aspx?libID=1). Topics covered in the library include national legal statutes on property and inheritance rights, business registration, and employment. The library also identifies countries that are signatories of gender-related international conventions. This new resource is a starting point for governments, civil society, and researchers to gain a better picture of the legal framework shaping a woman's ability to do business.

According to World Bank studies, better economic opportunities for women are associated with higher incomes, higher literacy, better health, and faster economic growth.[a] While the empowerment of women is the subject of MDG 3, progress on this goal contributes to the achievement of all of the other MDGs.

a. Mason and King 2001; Buvinic and King 2007.

TABLE 2.1 Weak implementation and enforcement can increase the regulatory burden
percent

Income group or region	Management time with officials	Firms that report regulations are interpreted consistently	Firms that believe courts will uphold property rights	Firms that make payments to "get things done"
Low income	9.0	47.5	52.2	57.5
Middle income	10.6	40.5	55.2	30.4
High income	4.7	53.3	70.9	23.0
East Asia and Pacific	9.8	56.1	69.4	49.6
Europe and Central Asia	7.1	40.8	50.3	38.3
Europe high-income	3.4	56.6	75.0	20.7
Latin America and Caribbean	13.9	34.0	49.2	20.2
Middle East and North Africa	11.3	47.4	60.7	26.0
South Asia	10.8	57.5	52.3	72.7
Sub-Saharan Africa	7.9	42.0	56.5	44.6

Source: Enterprise Surveys database.

least likely to report that regulations were enforced consistently.

The importance of the quality of implementation in determining the impact of regulations and regulatory reforms raises questions about what optimal regulations would look like. Regulations that are simple rather than complex and that reduce the discretion of officials are likely to be more desirable in countries with lower enforcement capacity.

Improvements in the Broader Institutional Environment Are Possible

Better governance not only improves the climate for investment, but it also helps in the fight against poverty and the achievement of the MDGs more broadly. The World Bank's World Governance Indicators comprise indicators in six areas (voice, political stability, rule of law, government effectiveness, regulatory quality, and control of corruption) for 212 countries, beginning in 1996.[20] Research over the past decade shows that improved governance helps raise incomes.

When governance is improved by one standard deviation, infant mortality declines by two-thirds and incomes rise about threefold in the long run. Such an improvement in governance is within reach.[21]

Good governance can be found at all income levels. Some emerging economies are even matching the performance of rich countries. More than a dozen emerging countries, including Botswana, Chile, Costa Rica, the Czech Republic, Estonia, Hungary, Latvia, Lithuania, Mauritius, Slovenia, and Uruguay score higher on key dimensions of governance than some industrial countries. And in many cases these differences are statistically significant.[22]

Improvements in governance can and do occur. From 1998 to 2007 countries in all regions have shown substantial improvements in governance, even if at times starting from a very low level. Examples include Ghana, Indonesia, Liberia, and Peru in voice and accountability; Algeria, Angola, and Rwanda in political stability and restoration of peace; Afghanistan, Ethiopia, and Serbia in government effectiveness; the Democratic Republic of Congo and Georgia in regulatory quality; Tajikistan in rule of law; and Liberia and Serbia in control of corruption. Supporting and encouraging improved governance has broad benefits. As the research shows, it is an essential foundation for an investment climate conducive to private sector development and economic growth.

Moving Regulatory Reform Forward

The current financial crisis is rightly putting attention on appropriate regulatory oversight. While the case is particularly compelling in the financial sector, it would be a mistake to assume the lessons should be limited to the regulation of financial institutions. One broad lesson is that regulations need to be effective and that enforcement matters. While many countries are focusing their efforts on the immediate challenge of restoring financial stability, conditions that shape the growth of private sector activities will be important in affecting how well the private sector can cope with the downturn and take advantage of new opportunities as recovery begins.

The foregoing review of progress on the private sector regulatory and institutional environment suggests three areas of emphasis for future efforts:

- *Simplifying regulations while ensuring adequate protection of public interests.* Regulations are governments' way of protecting legitimate social interests. The objective of reform is not to remove regulations. Rather the goal is to ensure that regulations are indeed addressing the underlying public interests they are meant to safeguard. In many cases, streamlining requirements can actually help ensure greater compliance. Setting standards too high can mean not only that few firms meet them but that many are discouraged from even trying to comply. Simplification can also help close loopholes or exceptions that benefit only a few, more connected, firms, thus helping to level the playing field for all firms.

- *Strengthening broader governance environment and building capacity for enforcement.* The evidence on the impact of regulations stresses the importance of the broader governance environment for reform effectiveness. Changing formal regulations can have little impact in the face of weak governance and enforcement capacity. Building capacity by hiring and training officials can improve enforcement, an effort in which external assistance can help. But part of the solution can also be to reform implementation. In particular, reducing discretion in how regulations are implemented can lower uncertainty and address a significant concern reported by firms.

- *Expanding inclusive public-private dialogue in shaping reform priorities.* Members of the private sector can identify issues that they experience as most constraining. Clearly, all of their preferences cannot be automatically followed; they need to be weighed against public interests that may not align with their private ones. But tools like the Enterprise Surveys can highlight the extent of various constraints—and how they can vary across different actors (by size, location, and gender). The variation in impact within a country across different types of firms underscores the importance of making public-private dialogue inclusive. This approach can help target priorities for reform and better ensure results.

Financial Sector Development

Finance is an essential part of the development process. When financial markets work well, they provide opportunities for a wider set of market participants to take advantage of the best investments by channeling funds to their most productive uses, hence boosting growth, improving income distribution, and reducing poverty. When they do not work well, growth opportunities are missed, inequalities persist, risks and volatility rise, and in the extreme case crises follow with high fiscal and real costs.[23]

Improved Access to Finance Contributes to Reaching the MDGs

A growing body of evidence—country and cross-country studies and, more recently, experimental analyses—shows that access to financial services can contribute significantly to reaching the MDGs. Financial development and greater access to financial services lead not only to income growth but also to reductions in poverty and undernourishment; they are also associated with better health, education, and gender equality outcomes.

The most researched and arguably the most important direct effect of financial sector development is its impact on economic growth and poverty. Research implies that if India, for example, had increased its average ratio of private credit to gross domestic product (GDP)—a commonly used metric of financial sector development—from 19.5 percent to 25 percent (the mean value for developing countries), its average real annual GDP per capita growth would have accelerated by an additional 0.6 percentage point per year over the period 1960–95.[24] Another, more recent study finds that a 10 percentage point increase in the private-credit-to-GDP ratio reduces poverty ratios by 2.5 to 3 percentage points.[25] Similar effects have been found for the development of capital markets and other forms of nonbank financing as important drivers of economic growth.[26]

Financial development also affects the nonpoverty MDGs, both indirectly, through the income channel, and directly. For instance, a 1 percentage point increase in the private-credit-to-GDP ratio has been shown to reduce the prevalence of undernourishment by 0.22–2.45 percentage points.[27] These findings imply that much can be gained from financial sector development: the ratio of private credit to GDP is around 16 percent in low-income countries compared with 88 percent in high-income countries.

The relationships between financial development and health, education, and gender equality have not been researched much to date, but cross-country regression analyses show positive relationships, with some evidence of causal relationships, although the quality of data does not allow for strong tests. Supporting case-study evidence, using household and firm surveys and specific interventions, suggests, however, that financial development does have beneficial causal impacts on these MDGs.[28] The contribution of finance to MDGs relative to other policies is large: the evidence suggests that financial development accounts for one-quarter to one-half of the impact of GDP per capita on several of the MDG indicators (box 2.4).

Financial sector development is not without risks, however. The recent financial crisis underscores the need for appropriate regulation and supervision to ensure financial system soundness and stability.

Financial Sector Development Is Key for Private Sector Development

Finance is important for many key private sector activities. Investment, domestic and international trade, and other private sector activities all require financial services. Recent research using detailed firm-level data and survey information provides direct evidence on the role of access to finance in affecting firm growth. The Enterprise Surveys show that small and medium enterprises (SMEs) in low-income countries rank finance as an especially high barrier for growth (figure 2.5).

Corroborative evidence for this comes from the responses of some 10,000 firms in 80 countries to the World Business Environment Survey. Respondents who identified finance as a constraint are more likely to experience slow output growth.[29] Finance is a general obstacle to firm growth, but that growth is also significantly constrained by barriers that capture more specific aspects of financing, such as high interest payments, collateral requirements, bank paperwork and bureaucracy, as well as bank corruption. Other important business environment obstacles are often interrelated with finance. Even when controlling for these interactions,

BOX 2.4   Relative impact of economic and financial development on MDGs

To illustrate the significant impact of financial development on the MDGs, the chart below compares the impact of financial development, as measured by private credit as a percentage of GDP, and the impact of GDP per capita on several MDG indicators in 2015, the target date for the MDGs. In this analysis, both private credit and GDP per capita are assumed to follow their past growth trends of 1.6 and 1.1 percentage points per year, respectively.

Impact of financial development and GDP per capita on selected MDGs in 2015 when they follow their past growth trends[a]

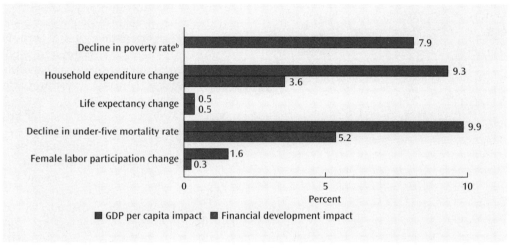

Source: Claessens and Feijen 2006.
a. All analyses are based on elasticities calculated by using time series fixed-effects regressions. Elasticity of poverty and GDP per capita is taken from Besley and Burgess (2003). Educational variables are not shown for lack of sufficient time-series data.
b. There is insufficient data to calculate the impact of financial development on the poverty rate.

access to finance seems to emerge consistently as one of the most important and robust underlying factors constraining firm growth.[30] And some evidence also suggests that lack of finance makes other barriers more binding for firms.

Research shows that small firms benefit the most from financial development—both in terms of entry and in seeing their growth constraints relaxed. At any given level of financial development, smaller firms have more difficulty accessing external finance than larger ones. But with financial development and greater availability of external finance, those that were formerly excluded are given new opportunities.

Cross-country data also show innovation to be an important channel through which finance affects firm performance. A survey of some 17,000 firms in 47 countries found that firms' use of external finance was significantly associated with more innovation.[31] This finding was even more strongly evident when access to finance came from foreign banks.[32]

Where Are Countries Today in Their Financial Sector Development?

A country's financial sector development should be assessed on four dimensions—size, access, efficiency, and stability. Analysis

FIGURE 2.5   Access to finance varies by country income and size of firm

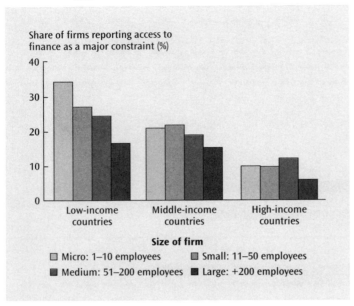

Source: Enterprise Surveys database.

of the effects of different aspects of financial sector development makes clear that all dimensions of financial sector development matter, but in different ways, for growth and development. This recognition is important because countries can vary in each of these dimensions. Although data are limited, the main finding is that while the size of the financial sector has grown in many countries, access generally remains weak.

In most of Sub-Saharan Africa, fewer than 20 percent of households have an account in a financial institution, and this figure is less than 50 percent in many other developing countries. While business access to financial services is less of a constraint in some regions, in almost all developing countries in Sub-Saharan Africa, more than 50 percent of firms complain about lack of finance (figure 2.6).

All forms of finance matter for firms' access. Bank finance is typically the major source of external finance for firms of all sizes, no matter how small. Nonbank finance remains much less important in most developing countries, but it can play an important role in improving the price and availability of longer-term credit to smaller borrowers. Leasing and other forms of collateral-based lending can be of particular importance for getting small firms going. And nonbank financing can be a source of competition for banking systems that often favor lending to large, connected enterprises. Bond finance can provide a useful alternative to bank finance. Supply of external equity (including portfolio equity investments, foreign direct investment, and private equity) requires strong investor rights; where these are present, a country that opens itself to capital inflows can improve access and lower the cost for large firms, with spillover effects for smaller firms.

While the depth and efficiency of financial systems are good indicators of overall development, they do not necessarily capture access. Comparing the use of financial services (by households) with financial depth indicators shows a positive but imperfect correlation (figure 2.7a). Economic development does not guarantee access to finance for households (figure 2.7b). Similar patterns exist for comparisons of access to financial services for small firms with financial depth. For instance, low-income countries in South Asia typically have a higher proportion of use of financial services than low-income countries in Sub-Saharan Africa.

There is some evidence that access to finance in developing countries is increasing. On the household side, data on the use of microfinance suggest an expansion of the use of financial services (box 2.5). Some evidence also suggests increasing financial service provision by commercial banks, as competitive forces and technology lead them to reach the lower-income segments of the population. Examples in developing countries include the ICICI Bank and the SHG Bank Linkage program in India and commercial banks in Brazil and South Africa. On the firm side, the evidence on increased access to credit and other financial services is more mixed. It appears to

FIGURE 2.6 Many firms say lack of access to financing hampers their growth
percentage of firms

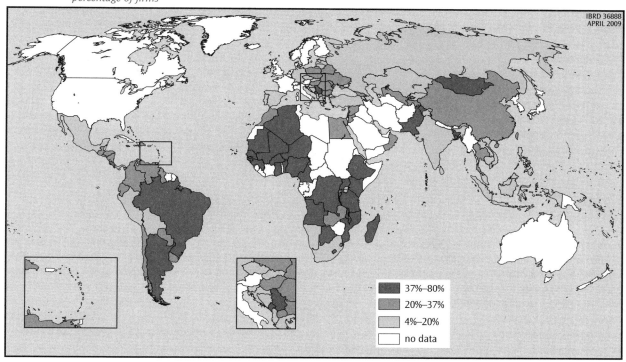

Source: Enterprise Surveys database.

FIGURE 2.7 Financial and economic development does not guarantee access to finance

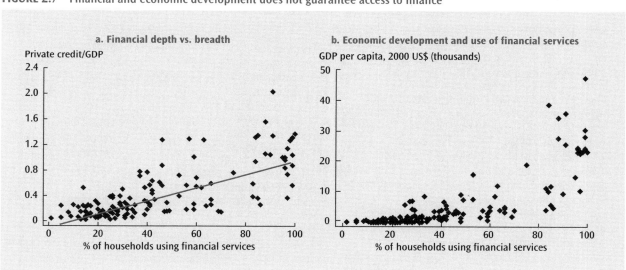

Source: World Bank 2008a.

BOX 2.5   Microfinance: reaching out to the poor but with limits

Thirty years after the establishment of Grameen Bank, the microfinance movement has attained a certain maturity. Yet there remains a lack of scale in microfinance; only in eight countries do microfinance borrowers account for more than 2 percent of the population. One reason is that these programs can be very costly to operate, making many of them dependent on subsidies and not sustainable on their own. Indeed, in a sample of 124 microfinance institutions (MFIs) in 49 countries representing around half of all microfinance clients around the globe, only half were profitable and self-sustainable.

The lack of self-sustainability might result from scale. Many MFIs have found that the poorest of the poor are difficult to reach even with a subsidy. Also, focusing on finance for the very poor shifts the attention to subsidies and charity, which hurts the quality of services. As a result many MFIs remain small. At the same time, those MFIs that grow and mature seem to focus less on the poor, which could be interpreted either as a success story for their borrowers or as mission drift. In any case, broadening access to the middle class makes it more likely that promotion of access will receive higher political priority.

More generally, shifting the focus to building inclusive financial systems and improving access for all underserved groups is likely to have a greater impact on development outcomes. Indeed, the attention of the development community has shifted to focus not only on microcredit institutions but on an array of other financial institutions, such as postal savings banks, consumer credit institutions, and most importantly the banking system. Here a broader approach is taken, focusing on overall financial system efficiency and outreach to the whole population. In this process, it will remain important, however, to apply the valuable lessons of the microcredit movement on technologies and methodologies.

The characteristics of microcredit lending most cited for their contributions to success include dynamic incentives, repayment in public, forced savings, notional collateral, and targeting of women (85 percent of the poorest 93 million MFI clients are women). Dynamic incentives, such as the promise of repeat lending, has been a mechanism to overcome moral hazard in lender relationships with risky and high-transaction-cost borrowers. Repayment in public is said to increase social pressure and the threat of stigma while at the same time reducing transaction costs for lenders. The requirement to keep a certain fraction of the credit as savings with the microfinance institution, and the use of assets with "notional" rather than resale or salvage value, such as refrigerators and televisions, have often been cited as success factors but have not yet been evaluated properly. Targeting women has not only contributed to women's greater economic empowerment, but studies have shown wider contributions to expanding health and educational outcomes.

Source: Honohan 2004; Cull, Demirgüç-Kunt, and Morduch 2007; Armendariz de Aghion and Morduch 2005; World Bank 2007a.

Microfinance penetration across countries

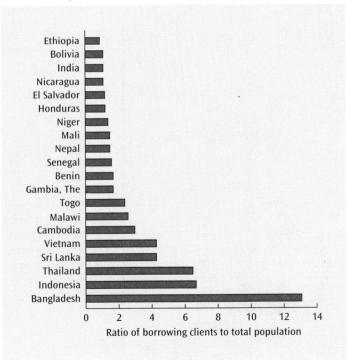

Ratio of borrowing clients to total population

Source: Honohan 2004.
Note: This figure shows the ratio of borrowing clients to total population for the 20 countries with the highest microfinance penetration.

be increasing in some countries, but mostly in consumer finance forms and less so in credit to SMEs.[33]

Increasing access to financial services to low-income groups is not easy and can involve risks. Increased competition can, for example, lead to more access but also to weaker lending standards. Furthermore, when amplified through opaque financial engineering, problems with even a small segment of the financial system can have devastating effects on confidence in the overall financial system. Recent experiences with the subprime lending market in the United States underline the importance of designing regulation and supervision in developing countries in such a way as to allow for increased access in a sustainable manner (box 2.6).

Why Is Access to Finance Still Limited in Developing Countries?

What are the most important barriers to access, and how can they be reduced? The barriers derive from the size and reach of the financial system, institutional constraints, ownership structures, technology hurdles, and political economy constraints.

BOX 2.6 Access to financial services: evidence from the subprime mortgage market

The recent global financial crisis has placed the U.S. subprime mortgage industry in the spotlight. Over the last decade, this market expanded rapidly and witnessed the entry of major players, evolving from a small niche segment to a major portion of the U.S. mortgage market. Evidence suggests that this growth was accompanied by a decline in credit standards and excessive risk taking by lenders. Indeed, major mortgage lenders are experiencing increased delinquency rates of subprime mortgages and insolvency problems.

Analysis using data from over 50 million individual mortgage applications in the United States combined with information on local and national economic variables shows that the credit expansion in the subprime mortgage market led to a decrease in lending standards, as measured by a decline in application denial rates and an increase in loan-to-income ratios not explained by an improvement in the underlying economic fundamentals. Specifically, denial rates declined more and loan-to-income ratios rose more in areas where the number of loan applications rose faster. These areas subsequently experienced a sharper increase in delinquency rates. Also, changes in market structure affected lending standards, with denial rates declining more in areas with a larger number of competitors, evidence that local lenders cut lending standards when facing competition from new entrants. But evidence also shows that lax regulation and supervision, in part attributable to the lobbying efforts of firms involved in subprime lending, led to poor lending, with the effectiveness of laws in place suffering as a result of such industry actions.

Obviously, more households were able to get financing for their homes but in many cases on unaffordable terms. And when the bubble burst, mortgage defaults fed a vicious cycle that led to a downward spiral in housing prices. What does this mean for overall welfare? Analysis of the impact of mortgage market transformation on the well-being of households is difficult. Before the crisis, the perception was that the developments were welfare-enhancing because they increased households' access to housing finance. A widely cited statistic was the home ownership ratio that hit an all-time high in 2006. Many viewed the fact that home ownership rose faster among households that historically had difficulty gaining access to credit as a sign of benefits associated with financial innovation and fast growth in mortgage credit. However, many also warned that these mortgages were going to be problematic.

Following the increase in delinquency rates and a wave of foreclosures, however, more questions on the optimality of the mortgage credit boom, the opaqueness and risks associated with the increasingly complex financial instruments, and the very existence of public institutions supporting mortgage credit have been raised. A better assessment of lending quality and overall exposures and risks of the financial system is needed, and these will be important areas of focus for future financial sector regulations.

Source: Dell'Ariccia and others 2008; Igan and Okada 2009.

Many financial systems are too small—in absolute and relative terms—and lack outreach to poorer households and smaller firms. Indeed, many systems are smaller than a small bank in most advanced economies—thus lacking the scale to operate more efficiently (figure 2.8). In financially less-developed countries with limited outreach, poorer households and smaller firms use fewer financial services than richer households and larger firms do. As a consequence, smaller firms experience higher obstacles to growth than larger firms do.

Policy and institutional environment barriers also play important roles. Macro-economic instability, a weak institutional environment, extensive government intervention, and a lack of competition can act as barriers to accessing financial services or make financial services more expensive or incapable of being provided in a viable way. Analysis of the wide variation across countries shows that barriers are lower for both households and firms in countries with more open and competitive banking systems characterized by private ownership of banks and foreign entry; stronger legal, information, and physical infrastructures; regulatory and supervisory approaches that reinforce

market discipline; and greater transparency and freedom for the media.[34]

The ownership structures of the banking system can matter as well. Evidence shows that state-owned banks can reduce overall financial sector development, leading to lower efficiency and reduced access to financial services. The performance of state-owned banks in subsidized lending aimed at enhancing access has tended to be poor as well.[35] Governments with greater checks and balances and better institutional development might be expected to have more positive results from state ownership.

The balance of a large body of evidence suggests that opening to foreign banks improves access for SMEs. Even if foreign banks often confine their lending to large firms and governments, they can enhance access to SMEs through competitive pressures. Indeed, firms in countries with more foreign banks are less likely to rate high interest rates and access to long-term loans as major obstacles. An analysis of borrowers' perceptions across 36 countries finds that financing obstacles are lower in countries with higher levels of foreign bank penetration.[36] While at times the internationalization of financial services can

FIGURE 2.8 Most financial systems are small

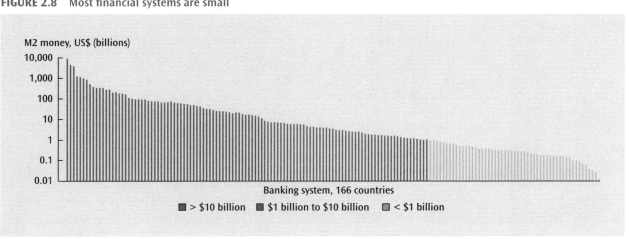

Source: World Bank 2007a.
Note: M2 money is a measure of the money supply. It includes currency in circulation plus demand deposits or checking accounts and net time deposits.

introduce more volatility, in the long run, the gains in access are significant.

Supply and demand mismatches can also hinder access. From the supply side, financial services providers often do not target the poor and small firms because of problems of information, high transaction costs, and poor enforcement of contracts. From the demand side, poor households and smaller firms often lack financial sophistication and literacy, do not trust financial institutions, simply do not realize their need for financial services, or think that products offered can be ill suited to their needs. But technological improvements and competition are broadening the access frontier, as evidenced by the rapid expansion of specialized microfinance firms.[37]

The largest barriers to broadening access may be the influence of special interests. Powerful insiders may oppose financial development because it creates a level playing field and enables newcomers to finance and implement their ideas and defy the economic status quo.[38]

Improving Access to Finance

The recent financial crisis has reconfirmed some old lessons in how to develop sound financial systems that expand access to finance in a sustainable manner. But it has also provided some new lessons, particularly in how to manage risks.[39] In many developing countries, achieving broad-based access requires deep institutional reforms. Because expanding access remains an important challenge even in some developed economies, it is likely that governments everywhere have an important role to play in building inclusive financial systems.

Reforms should foremost ensure security of property rights against expropriation by the state. This will typically be a longer-term challenge. Prioritizing institutional reforms, however, would help focus reform efforts and could produce impact in the short to medium term. Recent evidence suggests that, in low-income countries, it is the information infrastructures that generally matter most, while enforcement of creditor rights is more important in high-income countries.[40]

Another finding is that in relatively underdeveloped institutional environments, procedures that enable the individual lenders to recover on debt contracts (for example, those related to collateral) are much more important in boosting bank lending than procedures such as bankruptcy codes that are mainly concerned with resolving conflicts between multiple claimants. These are important findings because building credit registries and reforming procedures related to collateral are potentially easier to achieve than making lasting improvements in the enforcement of creditor rights and bankruptcy codes.

Consequently, encouraging specific infrastructures, particularly in information and debt recovery, can be particularly important, given the large deficiencies today in many countries (figure 2.9). Institutional reforms that can lower transaction costs include establishing credit registries or issuing individual identification numbers to establish credit histories, reducing costs of registering or repossessing collateral, and introducing specific legislation to underpin modern financial technology—from leasing and factoring to electronic finance and mobile finance.

Encouraging openness and competition, including by internationalization of financial services, is an essential part of broadening access because it encourages incumbent institutions to seek out profitable ways of providing services to previously excluded segments of the population and increases the speed with which access-improving new technologies are adopted. Achieving the full gains from increased competition and internationalization of financial services does, however, often require some convergence of regulations and legal and other institutional infrastructure.

In this process, providing the private sector with the right incentives is key; hence the

FIGURE 2.9 Availability of credit information varies greatly

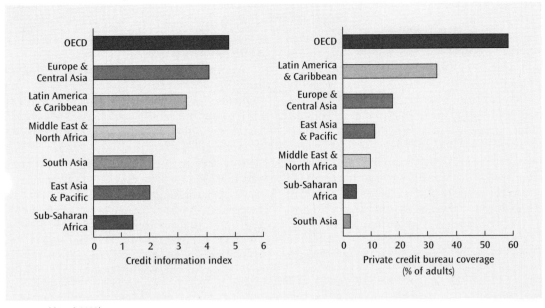

Source: World Bank 2008b.
Note: The number of individuals or firms listed by the private credit bureau with current information on repayment history, unpaid debts, or credit outstanding.

importance of good prudential regulations. Competition that helps foster access can also result in reckless or improper expansion if not accompanied by proper regulatory and supervisory framework (see box 2.6). At the same time, the increasingly complex international regulations imposed on banks to help minimize the risk of costly bank failures should not inadvertently penalize small borrowers.

The scope for beneficial direct government interventions in improving access must be carefully assessed. A large body of evidence suggests that interventions to provide credit through government-owned subsidiaries have generally not been successful.[41] In nonlending services, the experience has been more mixed. A handful of government financial institutions have moved away from credit and evolved into providers of more complex financial services, entering into public-private partnerships to help overcome coordination failures, first-mover disincentives, and obstacles to risk sharing and distribution. Ultimately private capital can take over the successful initiatives, but the state

can have a useful role in jump-starting these services.[42]

Direct intervention through taxes and subsidies can be effective in certain circumstances. If poorly designed and implemented, however, it can have large unintended consequences. The government-underwritten credit guarantees for SME lending are a good example. Experience shows that these are often poorly structured, embody hidden subsidies, and benefit mainly those who do not need the subsidy. With direct and directed lending programs having generally performed less well, partial credit guarantees have been the direct intervention mechanism of choice for SME credit in recent years.[43] In the absence of thorough economic evaluations, however, the net effects of many such schemes in cost-benefit terms remain unclear.

Finally, as noted, political economy concerns are key in implementing policies to expand access. If the interest of powerful incumbents is threatened by the emergence of new entrants financed by a system that has improved access and outreach, lobbying by those incumbents can block the needed reforms. A comprehensive approach to financial sector reform aiming at better access must take these political realities into account. Given that challenges of financial inclusion and benefits from broader access go well beyond ensuring financial services for the poor, defining the access agenda more broadly to include the middle class will help mobilize greater political support.

Infrastructure

Cost-effective, reliable, and affordable infrastructure services are critical for private sector development and economic growth. The role electricity and transport play in economic activity is well understood, yet infrastructure services in many developing countries remain woefully inadequate. Progress in closing the infrastructure gap has been made in the past decade, but many challenges remain. A lack of financial resources is only part of the story. Equally important is the need to address below-cost price structures that make revenue streams insufficient to support even the operation and maintenance of existing assets, weak governance and regulatory frameworks that lead to misuse of resources, and inadequate sector policies and planning and implementation capacities that slow investment programs. Both financial and nonfinancial factors must be part of an integrated strategy for infrastructure development.

Infrastructure Is Important for Growth and the MDGs

Infrastructure directly affects progress in achieving MDG 7, part of which is to "halve, by 2015, the proportion of the population without sustainable access to safe drinking water and basic sanitation." Indirectly, infrastructure influences the achievement of most MDGs, be they health, education, gender equality, or income poverty, through its effect on household opportunities. Each year 529,000 women die from childbirth complications. Most of these deaths could

be prevented through timely access to essential childbirth-related care, but to physically reach that care, an adequate road network is crucial.[44] The construction of an all-weather road in Morocco increased school attendance by girls from 28 percent to 68 percent; in parallel, the quality of education improved, because it became possible to recruit teachers to staff the schools, and absenteeism of both teachers and students dropped.[45] Every year 1.8 million people die from diarrheal diseases, including cholera. Improved water supply reduces diarrheal morbidity by 21 percent, improved sanitation by 37.5 percent.[46]

An adequate supply of infrastructure has long been viewed as a key ingredient for economic development.[47] By one estimate, raising infrastructure services of all Sub-Saharan countries to the level of the regional leader Mauritius could add 2.2 percentage points to per capita growth. Catching up to the level in the Republic of Korea would raise economic growth per capita by up to 2.6 percent percentage points per year.[48] Infrastructure has also received much attention in the context of reducing poverty and inequality.[49] In rural Ethiopia, improvements in access to quality roads increased consumption growth by an estimated 16 percent and reduced poverty by 7 percent.[50]

Infrastructure is an important part of the investment climate enabling the emergence and success of private entrepreneurs. Many case studies provide evidence of the beneficial impact of infrastructure on business performance. After an upgrade of the highway system connecting the four largest cities in India, firms in the beneficiary cities reported that they encountered fewer transportation obstacles to production, that they were able to reduce their average stock of input inventories by about a week's worth of production, and that they had greater flexibility in choosing their primary input suppliers.[51]

Yet Infrastructure Needs Remain Large

Since the start of this decade, there has been a renewed focus on infrastructure. For example, World Bank financing for the infrastructure sectors totaled $33 billion for the 2004–07 period, compared with $22 billion over the preceding four-year period.[52] Nonetheless, large infrastructure gaps remain in areas crucial for the MDGs: 1.1 billion people are without safe access to water, 1.6 billion without electricity, 2.4 billion without sanitation, and more than 1 billion without access to telephones (table 2.2). South Asia and Sub-Saharan Africa confront the largest gaps in essential infrastructure for households and businesses.

Competition and technology developments have reduced the costs associated with some infrastructure development. Gas-fired combined-cycle gas turbines and the emergence of smaller, more modular technologies have decreased the capital cost of power plants and the time needed to plan and build them. The generation sector has seen growth and private entry by independent power producers in many developing countries.[53] But it is in the information and communications technology sector that the role of technological progress has had the largest impact. In the mid-1990s, installing a satellite telephone cost $60,000, whereas in 2002 it cost between $2,000 and $4,000.[54] As a consequence, mobile usage and associated information services, such as Internet access, have increased exponentially in all developing regions (figure 2.10). In Africa infrastructure improvements added nearly one percentage point to per capita economic growth between 1990 and 2005, almost entirely attributable to advances in the penetration of telecommunication services.[55]

Despite progress in recent years, the region with the greatest infrastructure challenge remains Sub-Saharan Africa (table 2.3). It lags behind other low- and middle-income countries in infrastructure coverage for paved roads, telephone mainlines,

TABLE 2.2 Access to infrastructure is improving but still lags seriously in some regions
percent of population unless otherwise indicated

Type of infrastructure	East Asia & Pacific		Europe & Central Asia		Latin America & Caribbean		Middle East & North Africa		South Asia		Sub-Saharan Africa	
	2000	2006	2000	2006	2000	2006	2000	2006	2000	2006	2000	2006
Access to electricity	87	89	—	99	87	90	—	78	41	52	23	26
Access to improved water supply	80	87	93	95	89	91	89	89	81	87	55	58
Urban	95	96	98	99	96	97	96	95	93	94	81	81
Rural	72	81	85	88	69	73	80	81	77	84	42	46
Access to improved sanitation	60	66	89	89	75	78	74	75	27	33	29	31
Urban	71	75	94	94	85	86	86	89	54	57	41	42
Rural	52	59	79	79	47	51	58	59	17	23	22	24
Access to rural transport	—	90	—	82	—	59	—	59	—	57	—	34
Mainline telephone density (per 100 people)	0.0	3.0	—	3.0	0.0	2.6	—	—	0.0	0.2	—	—

Source: For water and sanitation, World Energy Outlook 2002 for 2000 figures; International Energy Agency for 2006. China is included in data for East Asia and Pacific; North African countries are excluded from data for the Middle East and North Africa. For access to rural transport, see Joint Monitoring Program database (wssinfo.org), 2004 data.
Note: — = Not available.

FIGURE 2.10   Exponential growth of telecommunications services in all regions

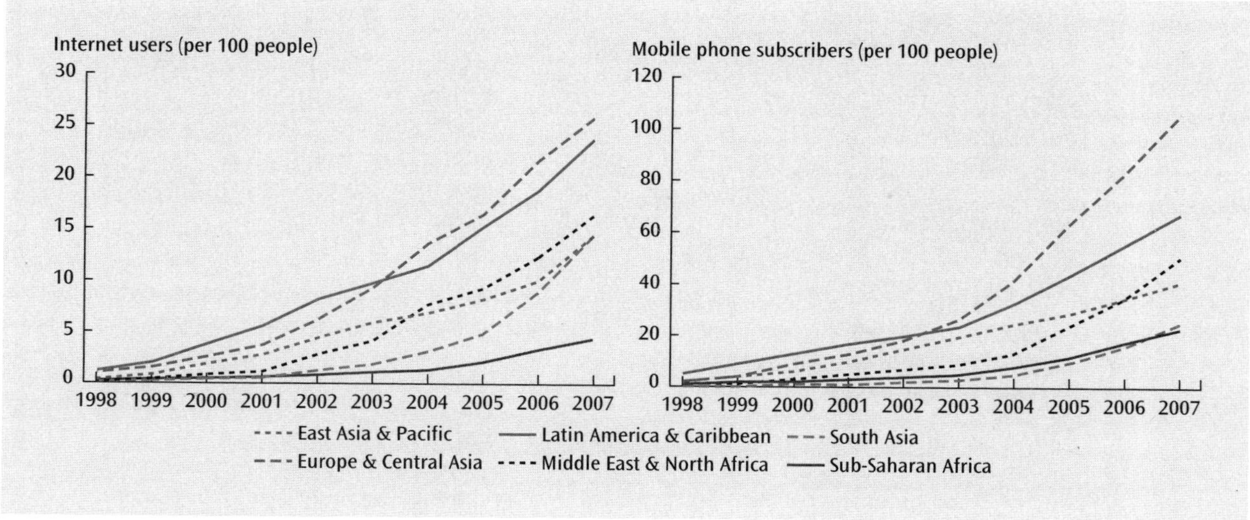

Internet users (per 100 people)

Mobile phone subscribers (per 100 people)

- - - - East Asia & Pacific   —— Latin America & Caribbean   - - - South Asia
- - - Europe & Central Asia   - - - - Middle East & North Africa   —— Sub-Saharan Africa

Source: World Development Indicators.

and power generation capacity. The Africa Infrastructure Country Diagnostic reports that for these three key infrastructures, Africa has been expanding stocks much more slowly than other developing regions, implying a widening gap over time.[56] In 1970 Sub-Saharan Africa had almost three times as much generating capacity per million people as South Asia, a region with similar per capita income. Three decades later, in 2000, South Asia had left Sub-Saharan Africa far behind: it now has almost twice the generation capacity per million people. Similarly, in 1970 Sub-Saharan Africa had twice the mainline telephone density of South Asia, but by 2000 the two regions had drawn even.

Geography and population patterns play a role in the particularly challenging situation of infrastructure in Africa. The low economic density of the continent makes transport networks and power grids, which exhibit economies of scale and density, more expensive to build and maintain.[57] According to one report, the national power systems in 21 of 48 Sub-Saharan countries fall below the minimum efficient scale of 200 megawatts for electricity generation.[58] As a result, their operating costs are nearly double those

found in the continent's larger power systems. Geography also matters in the transport area: Africa has a large number of landlocked countries, which are home to about 40 percent of the region's population. Poor infrastructure compounds the growth challenge

TABLE 2.3   Africa's infrastructure deficit is widening compared with other regions

Normalized units	Low-income countries	
	Sub-Saharan Africa	Other
Paved road density	31	134
Total road density	137	211
Mainline telephone density	10	78
Mobile telephone density	55	76
Internet density	2	3
Generation capacity	37	326
Electricity coverage	16	41
Improved water	60	72
Improved sanitation	34	51

Source: AICD 2009.
Note: Road density is in kilometers of road per thousand square kilometers; telephone density is in lines per thousand population; generation capacity is in megawatts per million population; electricity, water and sanitation coverages are in percentage of population.

for these countries, because it results in high transport costs that hamper trade both within and outside the region. One recent estimate suggests that a feasible upgrading of the transnational road network in Sub-Saharan Africa would increase overland trade from $10 billion annually to $30 billion.[59] Over a 15-year period, this research suggests the region would gain $250 billion in additional intra-African trade at a cost of $32 billion (upgrade and annual maintenance).

Infrastructure Gaps Hinder Private Sector Growth

Enterprise Surveys show that firms in developing countries often rate infrastructure as one of their biggest problems (figure 2.11). In African countries the infrastructure constraint on doing business is found to be associated with 40 percent lower firm productivity.[60] For most countries the negative impact of deficient infrastructure is at least as large as that associated with crime, red tape, corruption, and financial market constraints.

Enterprise Surveys underscore the importance of unreliable power as a major obstacle to growth and business development. Businesses in East Asia, South Asia, and Sub-Saharan Africa report numerous power outages per month. The unreliability of service leads a majority of firms in low-income countries to generate their own power, thus

missing out on the efficiencies, cost savings, and environmental benefits that a well-designed and centrally operated power network brings (figure 2.12). On average, African firms report losing more than 5 percent of their sales as a result of frequent power outages; this rises to 20 percent for informal sector firms unable to afford backup generation facilities.[61]

The Lack of Financial Resources Is a Major Constraint

The gaps in infrastructure coverage reflect a large unmet need for infrastructure investment in developing countries. This in turn is often attributed to a lack of financial resources to fund these investments.

Estimates of "required" future spending on infrastructure are very large. Each year developing countries require around $900 billion (7–9 percent of their GDP) both to maintain existing infrastructure and to undertake new projects, yet only half of the required amount is actually spent.[62] By one estimate, the investment effort implicit in catching up would require as much as 15 percent of GDP in the low-income countries of East and Central Africa.[63] Trade-offs are inescapable in countries with limited resources: more money spent on infrastructure means less money spent on health, education, and other valuable services.

Inadequate Investment Is Not the Only Challenge

Financial constraints are a part of the story, but they are far from the whole story. Several factors other than investment have emerged as important in designing a strategy for sustainable infrastructure provision in developing countries. Addressing them would lower the unit costs of supply, free resources for increasing capacity, and improve the business environment. Among the most important issues to be tackled are below-cost tariffs, ill-targeted subsidies, weak governance and regulatory frameworks, systematic

FIGURE 2.11   Inadequate infrastructure constrains business

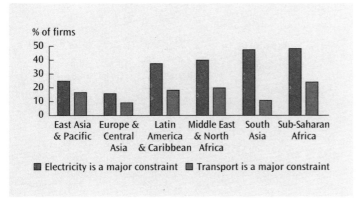

Source: Enterprise Surveys database.

FIGURE 2.12   The business cost of inadequate infrastructure can be high

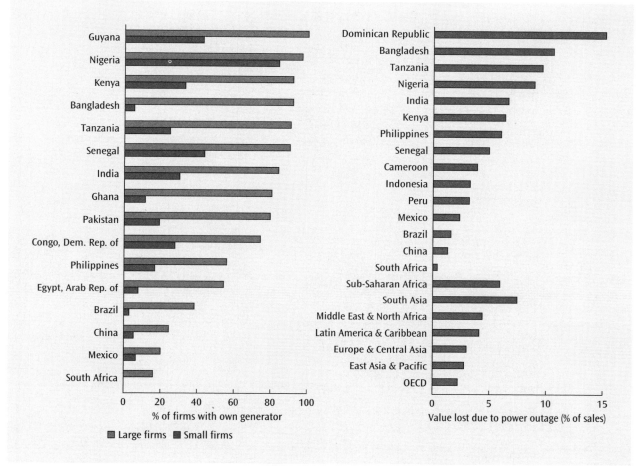

Source: Enterprise Surveys database.

inefficiencies, and inadequate sector policies and planning capacities.

The tariff challenge: getting prices right. The essential nature of infrastructure services and their monopoly provision make tariff setting political, and politics as well as affordability concerns often keep tariffs below costs. Tariff revenues that do not cover costs result in a vicious cycle of underperformance, low-quality services, and ensuing lack of goodwill among the population for tariff increases. Because their fundamentals are unsound, infrastructure service providers often lack the cash flow and creditworthiness needed to secure investment commitments.

The underpricing of utility services is not a phenomenon of low-income countries alone. Even in upper-middle-income countries, a significant portion of water services are priced too low to cover basic operations and maintenance (O&M) costs (table 2.4).[64]

Subsidies to service providers, in particular to state-owned enterprises, can fill the revenue gap left by low tariffs (and are particularly important when the infrastructure creates positive externalities, as in the case of sanitation), but their costs often compromise the fiscal position of low-income countries. Evidence from Europe and Central Asia shows that the hidden costs of electricity tariffs set below cost recovery totaled

TABLE 2.4 Water and electricity services are often underpriced
percent

Country income level	Water tariffs		Electricity tariffs	
	Too low to cover basic O&M	Covers O&M and partial capital	Too low to cover basic O&M	Covers O&M and partial capital
High	8	50	0	83
Upper-middle	39	39	0	29
Lower-middle	37	22	27	23
Low	89	3	31	25

Source: Foster and Yepes 2006.
Note: Figures are the percent of countries at an income level that fall in each category.

$10.6 billion in 2003, or 2.6 percent of GDP; the figure for the gas sector was 0.6 percent of GDP, and for water 0.4–0.5 percent of GDP.[65] In Indonesia, the government's explicit subsidy to PLN, the state-owned power company, to cover the gap between electricity tariffs and actual costs reached 1.4 percent of GDP in 2005 (not including the additional subsidy received in the form of below-cost fuel for generation).[66]

On the demand side, price subsidies are often poorly targeted and regressive. Although tariffs are lowest for the low-voltage connections typically used by the poorest consumers, the poorest consumers also purchase only small quantities of electricity. The subsidy design thus gives the poorest consumers relatively less of the total subsidy than the richest consumers, whose consumption is greater.[67] An in-depth study of 22 cases of quantity-based subsidies in water and electricity across developing regions concluded that not a single case achieved a progressive, or even neutral, subsidy distribution.[68]

The high cost of corruption, red tape, and operational inefficiency. Corruption in infrastructure reduces the funds available for essential services as well as the returns from investments. The characteristics of infrastructure sectors such as transport, which relies heavily on construction services, and utility sectors, which are regulated natural monopolies with significant fixed costs and which award complex contracts through nonstandard procedures, suggest that there are many opportunities for corruption and that it is relatively easy to hide the crime.[69] For example, the Business Environment and Enterprise Performance Survey (BEEPS), which covers 4,000 firms in 22 transition countries, provides evidence that construction firms pay considerably more than the average firm in bribes, with a focus on bypassing regulation and obtaining government contracts.[70] One study finds corruption to be the most important explanatory factor behind variation in efficiency among 80 electricity distribution companies in Latin America.[71]

The three key components of hidden costs affecting infrastructure—poor bill collection rates, excessive losses resulting from inefficient operations or theft from networks, and tariffs set below cost-recovery rates—averaged 4.4 percent of GDP in 2003 in the power sector in Europe and Central Asia, down from double that figure in 2000. Hidden costs in the gas and water sectors were 1 percent and 1.2 percent of GDP respectively in 2003, with little change since 2000.[72] In Bangladesh and the Indian state of Orissa, an estimated 45 percent of generated power is lost to technical and commercial inefficiencies.[73] The Africa Infrastructure Country Diagnostic finds that addressing existing system inefficiencies would almost halve the amount of funding required for Sub-Saharan Africa to close its infrastructure gap (table 2.5).[74]

Recent research into landlocked countries in Africa shows that physical constraints are not the only source of high transportation costs: widespread rent-seeking activities and flaws in the implementation of the transit systems also prevent the emergence of reliable logistics services.[75] One report on transport services in West Africa reveals that trucking wares from Bamako, the capital of Mali, to a port in Ghana over 2,000 kilometers away costs about $200 in bribes to various groups of officials, including police, customs, and gendarmerie.[76] The nearly 50 stops along the way delay the journey by almost four hours (figure 2.13). The situation is not unique to Africa; during the 637 kilometer trip from Medan to Meulaboh in Aceh province, Indonesia, one study found that drivers typically passed through

TABLE 2.5 Closing the infrastructure financing gap in Sub-Saharan Africa

	US$ (billions) annually
Financing gap	+40
Reallocate spending across categories	−8
Raise capital budget execution	−3
Reduce operating inefficiencies	−3
Improve cost recovery	−4
Remaining gap	+22

Source: AICD 2009.

27 checkpoints and paid a total of $23 in bribes, representing roughly 13 percent of the cost of the trip and more than the wages of those driving the truck.[77]

Such findings have helped to focus attention on the governance agenda in improving

FIGURE 2.13 First priority corridors in West Africa: Checkpoints, bribes, and delays

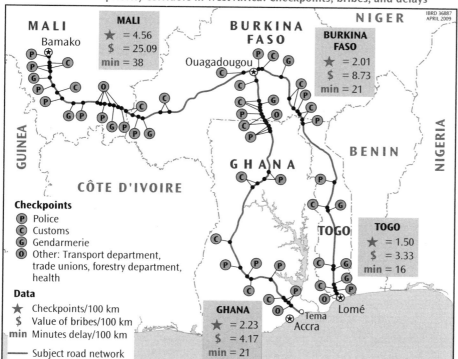

Source: West Africa Trade Hub 2007.

the quality of public spending on infrastructure. Strategic medium- and long-term planning and transparent procedures for the identification and implementation of projects have emerged as critical in improving the performance of public investment. Public expenditure reviews and budget tracking procedures improve the monitoring of spending against identified needs. The performance of state-owner enterprises (SOEs) plays a key role in improving infrastructure service delivery. SOE governance and financial management are receiving increasing attention, including appropriate incentive and control mechanisms to strengthen performance and reduce the risk of misallocation of funds. Reforms span benchmarking approaches, corporatization, and improvements in internal governance.[78]

Private Participation in Infrastructure

Considering the persistent investment gap, many governments see the private sector as a solution. However, private financing, while offering additional resources, does not change the fundamentals of infrastructure provision: customers or taxpayers (domestic or foreign) must ultimately pay for the investments; and cost-covering tariffs (and well-targeted subsidies) remain the centerpiece of all sustainable infrastructure provision, public or private. Indeed, private provision reinforces the need to address governance issues around contracting and concession decisions.

In addition to financing, mitigating the efficiency gap observed in service delivery is another benefit offered by the private sector. A recent global study comparing public and private operators in water and electricity distribution found that private operators provided significant efficiency gains over comparable public enterprises, including a 12 percent increase in residential connections for water utilities, a 19 percent increase in residential coverage for sanitation services, a 45 percent increase in electricity bill collection rates, an 11 percent reduction in distribution losses, as well as significant improvements in labor productivity.[79] Table 2.6 summarizes experience with private sector participation in different infrastructure sectors in Africa.

During the 1990s, there were widespread expectations that the private sector would play a much larger role in financing infrastructure in the developing world. While private investment in infrastructure has risen, it has fallen short of these expectations. The volume of investments with private sector involvement in developing countries expanded in the 1990s, reaching a peak of about $140 billion in 1997 (figure 2.14). However, private financing flows were concentrated in relatively few countries and sectors, with telecommunications absorbing 46 percent of investment and energy 33 percent.[80] During the period of optimism in the 1990s, bilateral official development assistance (ODA) for infrastructure declined and, in parallel, World Bank lending dropped from $10.6 billion in 1993 to $5.4 billion in 2003.[81] Following the Latin American financial crisis and then the Asian crisis, as well as the Enron and other corporate scandals, private investment in infrastructure declined sharply, even in developing countries previously successful in attracting capital.

In recent years, however, a resurgence of private participation in infrastructure has been observed.[82] Investment commitments in developing countries grew in real terms over several years, reaching a level in 2007 that was 10 percent higher than the previous peak 10 years earlier. Still, private funding of infrastructure remains limited: 70 percent of infrastructure investment in the 2000–05 period originated from governments and state-owned enterprises, 22 percent from the private sector, and 8 percent from ODA. In International Development Association (IDA)-eligible countries, only 10 percent of infrastructure was funded from the private sector in 2007, and the number is likely to fall in the immediate future in light of the current financial crisis.

TABLE 2.6 Overview of experience with private participation in infrastructure in Sub-Saharan Africa

	Extent of PPI	Nature of experience	Prospects
ICT			
Mobile telephony	Over 90 percent of countries have licensed multiple mobile operators	Extremely beneficial with exponential increase in coverage and penetration	A number of countries still have potential to grant additional licenses
Fixed telephony	60 percent of countries have undergone divestiture of SOE telecom incumbent	Controversial in some cases, but has helped to improve overall sector efficiency	A number of countries still have potential to undertake divestitures
Power			
Power generation	34 IPPs provide 3,000 MW of new capacity investing US$2.5 billion	Few cancellations but frequent renegotiations, PPA have proved costly for utilities	Likely to continue given huge unsatisfied demands and limited public sector capacity
Power distribution	16 concessions and distribution; 17 management or lease contracts in 24 countries	Problematic and controversial with one quarter of contracts cancelled before completion	Movement toward hybrid models involving local private sector in similar frameworks
Transport			
Airports	4 airport concessions, investing <US$0.1 billion, plus some divestitures	No cancellations but some lessons learned	Limited number of additional airports viable for concessions
Ports	26 container terminal concessions, investing US$1.3 billion	Processes can be controversial but cancellations have been few and results positive	Good potential to continue
Railroads	14 railroad concessions, investing US$0.4 billion	Frequent renegotiations, low traffic and costly PSOs keep investment below expectations	Likely to continue but model needs to be adapted
Roads	10 toll road projects almost all in RSA, investing US$1.6 billion	No cancellations reported	Limited as only 8 percent of road network meets minimum traffic threshold, almost all in RSA
Water			
Water	26 transactions, mainly management or lease contracts	Problematic and controversial with 40 percent of contracts cancelled before completion	Movement toward hybrid models involving local private sector in similar frameworks

Source: AICD 2009.

An interesting feature of recent private investment in infrastructure is that many more of the transactions are "South-South," with private investors coming from Brazil, China, India, the Philippines, and the Russian Federation. A recent survey of emerging market investors and operators, defined as companies domiciled or incorporated in low- and middle-income countries, found that their role has been steadily increasing.

For infrastructure projects reaching financial closure in 1998–2006, these investors mobilized about 44 percent of private funds.[83]

Research confirms that institutional factors matter greatly in the success of the private sector in infrastructure. Studies suggest that market reform, governance, and regulatory framework play an important part in attracting private investment and ensuring its effectiveness. Straub documents that ex

FIGURE 2.14 The rise and fall of private investment in infrastructure
investment commitments in infrastructure projects with private participation in developing countries

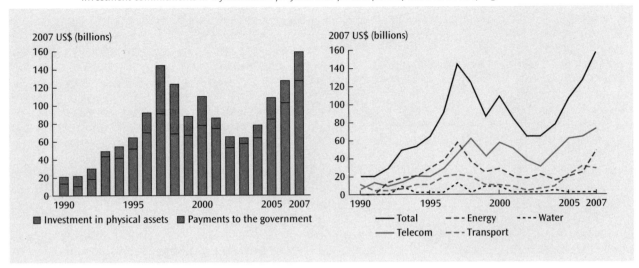

Source: World Bank and PPIAF, PPI Project database.

ante market restructuring makes privatization more successful.[84] In the case of the telecommunications sector, for example, regulatory and institutional arrangements such as transparency and autonomy increase the efficiency gains brought by the private sector.[85] The introduction of competition where feasible is one of the key means for governments to leverage the benefits of private investment in infrastructure.

Crisis Increases Challenge of Meeting Infrastructure Needs

Addressing the infrastructure challenge is made more difficult by the current financial crisis. Previous crises have shown that infrastructure is among the expenditure categories cut most severely by governments under financial stress. In Latin America, some 50 percent of the fiscal adjustment in the 1990s was borne by cuts in public infrastructure spending. According to one study, lack of infrastructure investment in the 1990s in Latin America reduced long-term growth by an estimated 1–3 percent.[86] The Asian crisis also resulted in precipitous declines in

infrastructure spending in many countries, forced the postponement of long-gestation infrastructure projects, and significantly retarded economic growth—leading to what is often referred to as the "lost decade" for many Asian countries. Indonesia's total public investment in infrastructure dropped from about 7 percent of GDP in 1995–97 to 2 percent in 2000; private investment fell from 2.5 percent of GDP to 0.09 percent during the same period.

Such responses come at great developmental cost as subsequent rehabilitation of facilities is exponentially more costly than regular maintenance. In the medium and long term, inadequate infrastructure slows economic development and hinders poverty reduction. In its response to the current crisis, the World Bank is strengthening its existing instruments to help maintain spending in the infrastructure sectors and is establishing new facilities to assist governments and private investors to refinance infrastructure projects. At the same time, safety nets to help the poorest absorb the current shocks are being developed and existing subsidy schemes scaled up.

In the current crisis situation, governments and international financial institutions are facing exponentially increasing requests for public assistance. While a few countries with deep financial markets are turning to domestic debt, most private infrastructure projects in developing countries are facing financing constraints in reaching closure and rolling over debt. The rate of closure on such projects was already 15 percent lower in the latter half of 2008 than in the same period in 2007. The crisis is likely to reinforce the importance of institutional quality in determining which developing countries will receive rarified private capital. Because around 80 percent of infrastructure spending in the developing world is done by the public sector, much of the attention, certainly in the short run, is on how to support the sector's ability to maintain needed infrastructure spending.

Yet a number of countries are interested in going further and increasing spending on infrastructure. Indeed, infrastructure spending has been identified as an important means of addressing the crisis itself. Expanding infrastructure spending can provide an important countercyclical stimulus by boosting demand and employment while also supporting longer-term growth. China's $586 billion spending package announced at the end of 2008, the largest stimulus plan in China's history, specifically targets infrastructure investment. India's infrastructure sector is recognized as a major employment generator in the country, accounting for 12 percent of total jobs created during the first three months of fiscal 2008–09.[87]

Through its recent Infrastructure Recovery and Assets (INFRA) Platform initiative, the World Bank response aims at both addressing immediate needs and strengthening an asset base for the future. It includes the protection of existing infrastructure assets and the preservation of the project pipeline and priority projects. Jointly with the International Finance Corporation's Infrastructure Crisis Facility, resources are being made available to support and refinance public-private partnerships at risk.

The concern with crisis response, however, should not distract attention from the broader goals of addressing the institutional and regulatory framework governing infrastructure. Indeed, extraordinary circumstances, such as an emergency situation triggered by the financial crisis, often increase the risk of misallocation of resources and corruption. To avoid inefficient spending, the challenge of combining quick decisions with sound policy solutions needs to be faced. Indeed, the crisis can even be used as an opportunity to strengthen the legal, regulatory, and contracting frameworks.

Looking Forward

Addressing the infrastructure challenge in the developing world means mobilizing additional funds for capital and maintenance spending. However, it also requires tackling inefficiencies in current spending. The revenue gap in infrastructure delivery needs to be made transparent and tariff policy reviewed to address the often regressive nature of tariffs. Explicit performance or output-based subsidies can be used to provide essential services to the poor in situations where cost-covering tariffs are economically undesirable or politically difficult. Better-targeted subsidies mean either lower subsidy budgets or larger discounts or transfers for the poorest people. Efforts to strengthen the regulatory and institutional framework for public-private partnerships, including attention to fiscal issues related to such partnerships, need to continue.

Sustainable development and long-term environmental objectives must continue to play an important role. Going forward, climate change will be increasingly important in driving the infrastructure agenda, with the private sector playing a key role in innovation and financing. Beyond concerns generated by the current crisis, the recent momentum on the promotion of sustainable development solutions and the integration of long-term environmental concerns in policies and programs must be sustained. Indeed, globally, the crisis offers a win-win opportunity—investment in green technology and energy-efficient infrastructure would not only provide a short-run stimulus but also help with longer-term environmental goals (a "green recovery").[88]

The World Bank is actively engaged with countries in climate change mitigation and plans to expand its instruments aimed at fostering clean technology, renewable energy, and energy efficiency. The newly established Climate Investment Funds aim to support innovative solutions in mitigation and adaptation to a changing world climate.

Regional collaboration is an attractive answer to lowering unit costs and pooling scarce resources in some of the poorest developing regions. Regional projects have emerged in a wide variety of infrastructure sectors, spanning regional power markets (such as in Central America or the West African Power Pool), regional gas trading (such as in Central and Eastern Europe or the Middle East), regional transport corridors (in Sub-Saharan Africa), and regional telecom agreements (mobile phone systems in Africa and the Caribbean). Regional infrastructure initiatives allow countries to pool their limited resources and achieve economies of scale in markets. However, the political dimension of regional projects and the challenge posed by aligning national objectives and policies and harmonizing regulations is not to be underestimated.

Notes

1. World Bank 2004.
2. Narayan 2000.
3. Ravallion 2001.
4. Firm responses need to be interpreted with caution—they are subjective measures and do not necessarily reflect social interests. They can also be affected by differences in reference points used and by the firm's own characteristics. But they do provide insights into what private sector actors are thinking. The relative ranking of issues can be particularly informative in this regard. They certainly corroborate the importance of the three areas highlighted here.

5. World Bank 2004; Dollar, Hallward-Driemeier, and Mengistae 2005, and numerous Investment Climate Assessments.

6. Aterido, Hallward-Driemeier, and Pages 2008.

7. Beck, Demirgüç-Kunt, and Maksimovic 2004.

8. World Bank 2004.

9. Two new measures are under development. An infrastructure measure contains two sets of indicators, one on potential consumers (namely, the time and procedures necessary to access the public grid), and one for potential distributors of electricity. A transparency measure captures the disclosure rules for elected officials.

10. The stronger performance of the Europe and Central Asia region on the regulatory indicators in part reflects the concentration of transition economies in the region that faced an especially challenging agenda of regulatory reform at the start of the transition process.

11. World Bank 2008c.

12. The bankruptcy recovery rate is also high but reflects in part some fixed costs that will decline as incomes rise.

13. Hallward-Driemeier and Li 2009.

14. Eifert 2009. The ICRG and Freedom House ratings were used as indicators.

15. Aterido, Hallward-Driemeier, and Pages 2008.

16. Beck and others 2006; World Bank 2008a.

17. Perry and others 2007.

18. World Bank 2008b.

19. Eifert 2009.

20. www.govindicators.org.

21. Kaufmann, Kraay, and Mastruzzi 2008.

22. Ibid.

23. This section draws heavily on World Bank (2007a) and Claessens and Feijen (2006).

24. This is a big effect because per capita growth in India only averaged about 1.6 percentage points per year over this period. See Levine, Loayza, and Beck 2000.

25. Beck, Demirgüç-Kunt, and Levine 2007. See also Honohan 2004.

26. Levine and Zervos 2004. Simultaneity bias is already addressed in these estimates.

27. Claessens and Feijen 2007.

28. Claessens and Feijen 2006.

29. Beck, Demirgüç-Kunt, and Maksimovic 2005. Surveyed businesses were asked (among other things) to rate financing in general as well as some specific financing issues on a scale from 1 (no obstacle) to 4 (major obstacle). The median response was 3 for financing in general, as well as for collateral requirements and lack of availability of long-term loans, and the median response for "high interest rates" was 4. Most of the other specific financing issues—paperwork, the need for special connections, banks' lack of money to lend, credit information, access to foreign banks, to equity, to export finance and to leasing—yielded a median response of "2". For a subset of 56 countries, additional data, including the growth rate of firms' sales, was available, Beck, Demirgüç-Kunt, and Maksimovic show that a firm's response on 7 of 13 perceived financial barriers is negatively and significantly correlated with that firm's growth rate.

30. Ayyagari, Demirgüç-Kunt, and Maksimovic 2006.

31. Ayyagari, Demirgüç-Kunt, and Maksimovic (2007). Specifically, respondents were asked whether they had developed a major new product line; upgraded an existing product line; introduced new technology that has substantially changed the way that the main product is produced; discontinued at least one product (not production) line; opened a new plant; closed at least one existing plant or outlet; agreed to a new joint venture with a foreign partner; obtained a new licensing agreement; outsourced a major production activity that was previously conducted in-house; or brought in-house a major production activity that was previously outsourced.

32. Giannetti and Ongena 2005.

33. de la Torre, Martinez Peria, and Schmukler 2007.

34. Beck, Demirgüç-Kunt, and Martinez Peria 2007.

35. La Porta and others 2003; Caprio and others 2004; Barth, Caprio, and Levine 2006.

36. Cull, Clarke, and Martinez Peria 2001.

37. de la Torre, Gozzi, and Schmukler 2007; de la Torre, Martinez Peria, and Schmukler 2007.

38. Claessens and Perotti 2007.

39. See World Bank (2001) for an overview of the determinants of financial sector development. See IMF (2009) for a discussion of lessons for financial sector policy from the recent crisis. The focus in this section is on improving access to finance; regulatory issues relating to financial sector stability are discussed in more detail in chapter 1.

40. Djankov, McLiesh, and Shleifer 2008.

41. For early evidence, see Caprio and Demirgüç-Kunt 1997.

42. de la Torre, Gozzi, and Schmukler (2007) provide some examples.

43. See further Conference on Partial Credit Guarantee Schemes: Experiences and Lessons, The World Bank, Washington DC, March 13–14, 2008.

44. Wagstaff and Cleason 2004.

45. IEG 1996.

46. WHO 2004.

47. A recent survey of 64 empirical papers on the link between infrastructure and growth in developing countries finds that in two thirds of the specifications used a positive and significant link between infrastructure and growth is supported by the data; see Straub 2008.

48. Calderón and Servén 2008.

49. See for example, Estache Foster, and Wodon 2002.

50. Dercon and others 2007.

51. Datta 2008.

52. World Bank Group 2008.

53. Eberhard and Gratwick (2006) count about 40 IPP independent power provider projects in 15 African countries alone.

54. Galdo and Torero 2006.

55. Calderón and Servén 2008.

56. AICD 2009.

57. Ramachandran, Gelb, and Shah 2009.

58. Eberhard and others 2008.

59. Buys, Deichman, and Wheeler 2006.

60. Escribano, Guasch, and Pena 2008.

61. Eberhard and others 2008.

62. World Bank Group 2008.

63. Calderón and Servén 2008.

64. Foster and Yepes 2006.

65. Ebinger 2006.

66. World Bank 2007b.

67. See World Bank 2007b for a detailed discussion in the case of Indonesia.

68. Komives and others 2005.

69. Kenny 2006; Kenny and Soreide 2008.

70. Kenny 2007.

71. Dal Bo and Rossi 2007.

72. Ebinger 2006.

73. Gulati and Rao 2006.

74. AICD 2009.

75. Arvis, Raballand, and Marteau 2007.

76. West Africa Trade Hub 2007.

77. Olken and Barron 2007.
78. See, for example, Vagliasindi 2008.
79. Gassner, Popov, and Pushak 2008.
80. The top five recipients of private infrastructure investment—Argentina, Brazil, China, Malaysia, and Mexico—received 49 percent of all private investment in 1984–2004. Less than 10 percent of private investment has been made in low-income countries.

81. World Bank Group 2008.
82. PPIAF 2008.
83. Von Klaudy Sanghi, and Dellacha 2008.
84. Straub 2008.
85. Andres and others 2008.
86. Calderón and Servén 2003.
87. *Business Standard*, New Delhi, December 3, 2008.
88. Stiglitz and Stern 2009.

3

Leveraging the Private Sector Role in Human Development

The Millennium Development Goals (MDGs) strongly emphasize human development–related outcomes, with five of the eight MDGs having health, nutrition, and education results as key indicators for monitoring progress. Governments have a special responsibility to their citizens, especially their poorest citizens, to ensure attainment of primary education, basic maternal and child health and nutrition, and control of communicable diseases. Previous *Global Monitoring Reports* have largely focused on strengthening this government role. Yet experience in many countries, including some of the poorest, shows that the private sector is also extensively involved in the delivery of services that address these MDGs.

Governments can act to enhance the contribution of the nongovernment sector to the human development MDGs as an integral part of efforts to accelerate national progress. Recognition of this potential is growing. Important new roles are emerging for private actors in human development, in financing government and nongovernment actions, in new service delivery organizations and strategies, and in innovative partnerships. These opportunities for new approaches to the MDGs require governments to develop new capacities to design, manage, and regulate mixed strategies to achieve better outcomes.

The current global economic crisis makes this discussion about leveraging private sector contributions to human development especially timely. Human development needs have become more acute, both in terms of safeguarding past gains and achieving further progress. At the same time, financial constraints on all sectors have increased, and global interdependence has become more visible. Development partners and national and local actors may want to be more open to thinking about new strategies, including engaging the nongovernment sector in maintaining or increasing the momentum for achieving the MDGs.

Leveraging the private sector to accelerate human development outcomes has potential rewards and risks. Nongovernment partners can be a source of innovation and can help to rapidly expand access to services, which supplement government efforts. But working with the private sector poses new challenges to ensure quality in providers that are not directly under government control and to introduce new mechanisms of incentives and accountability. To maximize the rewards and minimize the risks, governments must choose the most appropriate modalities for partnership, given local needs and conditions, and must devote resources and efforts to acquire new skills and capacities in contracting, monitoring and evaluation, and regulation. Governance and accountability arrangements are critical. They affect what is feasible and what skills and capacities governments need to develop.

Several premises guide this chapter's investigation of the potential for leveraging the private sector's role in health and education. First, one should start with a focus on outcomes. The MDGs themselves provide a list of monitorable outcome indicators against which to assess progress. Second, it is important to be pragmatic rather than normative or ideological. Strategies that improve or increase outcomes sustainably over the long term are desirable, regardless of which sector is carrying them out. Government's role is central, but there are also potentially valuable contributions from the nongovernment sector. Engaging the private sector more in human development will also require government to develop better regulation and learn to manage relationships with new partners. Third, one should draw on the available evidence to support analysis and recommendations wherever possible and to recognize that more evidence is needed.

To explore how to leverage the private sector's role in human development, this chapter examines four topics. It first provides a brief review of concepts needed for clear thinking and discussion about the private sector's role. This is followed by an examination of current patterns of government and private sector roles related to the delivery of services that increase MDG-related outcomes in health and education. Private sector roles in health and education are expanding rapidly, beyond just service delivery, into areas such as insurance, production and distribution of essential inputs, and charitable financing from both for-profit and not-for-profit sources and from both international and domestic agencies. These "new vehicles" are reviewed before the chapter concludes with a discussion of opportunities and challenges for the future in further leveraging private sector roles in health and education.

In working with the private sector, governments have many options to consider and

examples worldwide from which to learn. Considering the large gaps in MDG achievement that need to be spanned, these opportunities should not be ignored.

Framework for Thinking about the Private Sector's Role in Health and Education

What is "the private sector"? It is typically defined in terms of what it is not—that is, the "nongovernment" or "nonstate" sector. A key concept used for these distinctions is ownership.[1] Organizations that belong to (are owned by) government can be distinguished from those that are not government-owned. The people employed directly by those government organizations, the work they do, and the services they provide are those of the government. Everything else is the domain of the nongovernment, nonstate, or private sector.

The private sector includes both for-profit (where for-profit includes proprietary enterprises, recognized or not, and publicly listed companies) and not-for-profit organizations, as well as individuals and community groups operating outside the government's ownership, such as traditional practitioners.

Normative Views of the Private Sector's Role

There is ample evidence to confirm the significant role played by the private sector in health and education. Such observable facts, however, are not always accepted as justifying such arrangements or further efforts to engage with, support, or even enhance them. Discussions about the private sector in human development are often driven by value-based positions about whether this role is a good or bad one. Such normative views influence debates about government action. Understanding the basis for these views is important.

It is helpful to consider at least three different value-based positions that often underpin views about the private sector's role in health and education. The first perspective draws on economic theory centered on the role of markets. According to this view, reasonably well-functioning markets exist for goods and services, and better outcomes for human welfare (which economists define as "efficiency") are obtained when government roles are kept limited and mainly focus on improving the functioning of these markets.[2] This view suggests that the private sector should be encouraged to deliver those goods and services for which there is private demand and little market failure and that the government role should emphasize public goods for which markets may not exist or significantly fail to provide optimal outcomes.

Debate then focuses on whether significant market failures exist for specific health- and education-related goods and services, and, if they do, what are the best strategies for government action? A straightforward example of market failure relates to environmental control of disease-transmitting vectors. The market is unlikely to deliver adequate control services because individuals who do not pay for them cannot be excluded from enjoying the benefits they generate. Government action is needed to ensure the appropriate level of disease control investment. Immunization and primary education provide more complex examples. These services have important externalities—meaning their consumption by some individuals affects the well-being of others; the result is that markets may not produce the optimal level of services for overall social welfare. This market failure provides the justification for dominant government financing and provision, especially in poor countries. Despite the market failure, however, there is some private demand for immunization, and as national incomes rise, private capacity to deliver immunization increases. Government strategies often change as markets develop. In the case of immunization, nongovernment provision may increase, and then governments can shift their efforts to financing and regulation. Similar arguments are given for primary education. Schools require some collective investment. Social benefits exceed private benefits. Yet there is private demand for schooling, and government provision of schooling may not be the only way to ensure education.

A different perspective is propounded by those who argue that all citizens have a right to health and health care as well as education. Rights are typically the responsibility of the state to define and to ensure. Calls for comprehensive and universal health and education services with government financing and delivery are often justified as the appropriate way to fulfill these rights, with the corollary that the private sector's role should be limited. Rights-based arguments need not always promote a central role for government in service provision. Many advanced countries have universal systems with mixed provision.

A third perspective, a pragmatic or results-oriented approach, argues that strong normative positions about government and private sector roles should be avoided. The focus should be on what works to improve outcomes in health, learning, and equity. This approach fosters acceptance of more pluralistic strategies for financing and delivery of health and education services, and this is the position taken in this chapter. This view does not preclude strong conclusions about preferred government and private sector roles in health and education, based on theory and evidence about how markets relevant to human development succeed or fail to produce optimal outcomes, as well as the strengths and weaknesses of government.

Understanding How the Government and Private Sector Roles Relate to Each Other

This debate about government and private sector roles in health and education has been going on for many years. The published literature is extensive.[3] One basic framework of proven utility and wide use emphasizes the different roles government and private sector actors play in the financing and delivery of goods and services. Each actor can act alone—examples are publicly owned and operated facilities such as government hospitals or schools, where the government funds service delivery directly; and private health insurance or out-of-pocket payments, where private financing pays for services delivered by nongovernment providers such as private clinics or private schools.

There are also the widespread examples where government and private roles combine in different ways to produce services. Governments may purchase services from private providers; for example, paying private clinics to provide birthing services to poor mothers, or funding tuition in private schools that offer services unavailable in government schools. Private payers may also fund services delivered in government facilities; examples include user charges in public hospitals or schools or private donations to government facilities.

A display of real-world examples of these cases might look like table 3.1.

Of course, the real world can be much more complex than the one represented in the table 3.1 matrix. Several stages in the delivery of services may be financed in different ways, such as the education of medical personnel, the development of new pharmaceuticals and vaccines, teacher training, and school construction. Government and private organizations themselves display a variety of different ownership arrangements.

The next section explores in more detail what the current global evidence says about the relative importance of these four cells in the delivery of services for the health- and education-related MDGs. The picture is highly variable across countries, and even within countries, where evidence is available for different regions or socioeconomic groups.

It is clear, however, that privately financed and delivered services make up a significant part of all services that address the different MDGs in many low- and middle-income countries, and that is also often true for services being used by the poor. The picture is somewhat different for health and education, with government-financed and -provided education being more prevalent than government-financed and -provided health care. There are also many examples of innovations located in the "mixed" cells of the matrix.

Policy makers and planners want to know which type of arrangements for financing

TABLE 3.1 Matrix of financing and delivery arrangements in health and education

		DELIVERY	
		Government	Private
FINANCING	Government	■ Publicly owned health facilities and schools financed from public budgets	■ Contracting out with nongovernment providers ■ Vouchers and cash subsidies given to poor clients for service use
	Private	■ Out-of-pocket payments for patients and students ■ Private health insurance payments to government providers ■ Community contributions of land, buildings ■ Student loans	■ Privately owned health facilities and schools financed from private sources

and delivery are best. Unfortunately, the available global evidence on this question is limited and often lacking in sound evaluation and valid comparisons. The answer, which is not fully satisfying, is that the performance of the different arrangements depends much more on organizational capacities, incentives, and governance and accountability arrangements than on the simpler variables of structure and ownership. The extreme cases—all unitary financing and provision by either government or private sector—are almost unknown. Rarely is it a choice between exclusively government and exclusively private roles; rather, the question is how to develop and regulate mixed strategies for better outcomes.

Following the pragmatic, results-focused approach described above presents questions on whether and how government should engage with the private sector. This engagement should be based on evidence and sound expectations about whether unitary government, unitary private, or mixed models are most likely to produce better outcomes, given the existing incentive, governance, and accountability arrangements in different countries or even parts of countries. Leveraging the private sector's role can contribute to improving health and education outcomes when certain conditions exist. For example, government contracts or purchasing arrangements with private service providers could enhance MDG achievement and be an efficient alternative strategy to simply expanding government delivery. To succeed, these arrangements must have the right incentives and sufficient monitoring and accountability measures to increase service coverage and ensure adequate quality at a cost equal to or lower than the comparable cost to the government. Even at a higher cost, this approach might be desirable if comparable improvement in government service delivery were not feasible.

Engaging with the private sector could have other advantages as well. Private funds can complement limited public financing, which would increase the overall funding available for health or education. Competition in service delivery markets could increase incentives for the public sector to perform better. Government may be able to share some risks with private partners. Flexibility and innovation could be enhanced through engaging the private sector. Private organizations may be more willing to finance new approaches as well as test new service delivery strategies than governmental systems where innovation is more constrained. In all of these examples, the advantage of leveraging the private sector is conditional on whether government-financed and -delivered services can be made to fulfill the desired objectives at an acceptable cost. If the private sector role is already large, the relative costs and benefits of improving it, compared with efforts to substitute new public capacity for it, may make leveraging the private sector a more attractive strategy.

Implications of the Framework for Government Action to Improve Outcomes

For government to support more pluralistic approaches to financing and provision of MDG-related services it must enhance its capacities to design, regulate, and manage finance and delivery arrangements that differ substantially from government "business as usual." Indeed, one argument against more government engagement with the private sector is that these capacities may not exist in government and may be quite difficult to create. Although government might be able to contract out some of these functions, some base of government capacity to "buy" rather than "make" will be needed.[4] In the absence of such capacities, governments may risk worse outcomes with the private sector than with current government-focused arrangements.

Thus the decision of whether government should try to leverage the private sector role also depends in part on government's current and potential ability to manage new

TABLE 3.2   Matrix of government capacities needed to manage various finance and delivery models

		DELIVERY	
		Government	*Private*
FINANCING	*Government*	▪ Improve financial and operational management and accountability mechanisms for better performance	▪ Ability to design, bid, award, monitor, and evaluate contracts, voucher schemes, and similar arrangements
	Private	▪ Ability to collect, manage, and account for fees and donations without corruption ▪ Ability to use funds effectively including at the local level	▪ Ability to monitor and regulate nongovernmental providers for quality and law-abiding behavior

arrangements. Some of the requirements are illustrated in table 3.2.

Policy makers wanting to follow a more pragmatic approach should consider a number of key questions. Is there in place a large private sector presence that could contribute to access and quality? Can the private operators be effective partners? Should the government focus more on policy, finance, and regulation than on service delivery? Can government service delivery be made to work well at an acceptable cost? Can government carry out new tasks by partnering with the private sector? For many of these questions, ex ante answers may be hard to come by. Trying innovative approaches and evaluating results should contribute to the answers.

The Private Sector's Role in Health and Education Services

Private sector actors are already playing a significant and increasingly diverse role in both the financing and delivery of health and education services. This section looks first at that role in health and then in education.

Private Financing of Health Care

A widely used summary measure for the extent of private health care at the country level is the share of total health expenditure coming from private sources, and more specifically, from out-of-pocket payments. Government services are often delivered free of charge or with low fees, so most out-of-pocket spending usually goes to private providers, including clinical providers of care, pharmacies and drug sellers, and providers of other ancillary health services such as diagnostic tests.

Figure 3.1 presents recent estimates of the share of total health expenditure at the national level that comes from private sources. Across the range of country income levels, private spending accounts for more than half of all health expenditures in about 47 percent of low-income countries and about 51 percent of lower-middle-income countries (figure 3.1 upper). For the low-income countries, private health spending is almost entirely out-of-pocket spending, because private insurance and formal employer-provided benefits are limited. Figure 3.1 (lower) shows that in 80 percent of low-income countries and 93 percent of middle-income countries, out-of-pocket spending makes up over 50 percent of private spending.

Private Delivery of Services Related to the Health MDGs

Despite the widely held view that services supporting the health- and education-related

MDGs should be supplied mainly by government, ample evidence shows that when measured on a population basis, many of these services are being delivered by nongovernment providers. For MDGs 4 and 5—the maternal, reproductive, and child health goals—an excellent source of data on private provider roles is the Demographic and Health Surveys (DHS) supported by the U.S. Agency for International Development (USAID) that have been carried out in 80 countries over the last 23 years, with many countries having multiple surveys.[5] A recent review of these surveys shows the share of services provided by formal and informal private health care givers for four key indicators related to MDGs 4 and 5 for those countries in Sub-Saharan Africa and South Asia where DHS surveys have been done (figure 3.2).[6]

The shares of private formal and informal health care provision vary widely from country to country. Many surveys report private provision at more than 50 percent of MDG-related maternal, reproductive, and child health services in recent years. The levels are high across all the indicators: sources of contraception, most recent delivery, and treatment of childhood infections. The informal sector is supplying a very significant share of privately provided services.

Private providers also play a significant role in the treatment of communicable diseases such as tuberculosis (TB), malaria, and HIV/AIDS. Figure 3.3 summarizes results from a recent survey of 22 countries with a high TB burden regarding the participation of a wide range of government and private providers in TB referral and treatment. Authorities in 22 high TB burden countries were surveyed as to their perceptions about whether "all," "some," or "none" of the government and nongovernment providers are involved in TB case-finding and referral as well as treatment with approved TB drug regimens. The responses indicate that private providers participate in TB-related activities at about the same rate as public providers and that they are involved in both case-finding and referral

FIGURE 3.1 Private and out-of-pocket shares of health expenditure

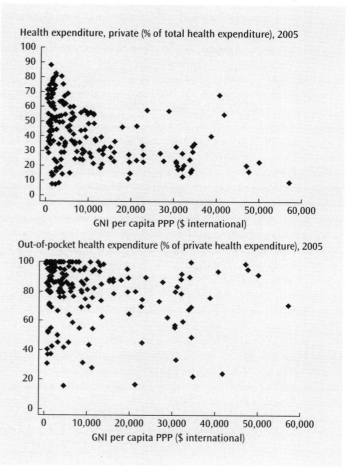

Source: World Bank 2008.

as well as treatment with approved drug regimens. Lonnroth, Uplekar, and Blanc (2006) report positively on experiences in 15 different initiatives to involve private for-profit providers in government-initiated and -supported TB control programs.

Because the DHS surveys have often been done several times in an individual country, it is possible to examine trends in the use of private providers of maternal, reproductive, and child health services. Figure 3.4 summarizes the data for those countries with multiple observations and shows whether the share of private use has increased, decreased, or remained unchanged.

FIGURE 3.2   Use of private maternal and child health care services, Sub-Saharan Africa and South Asia

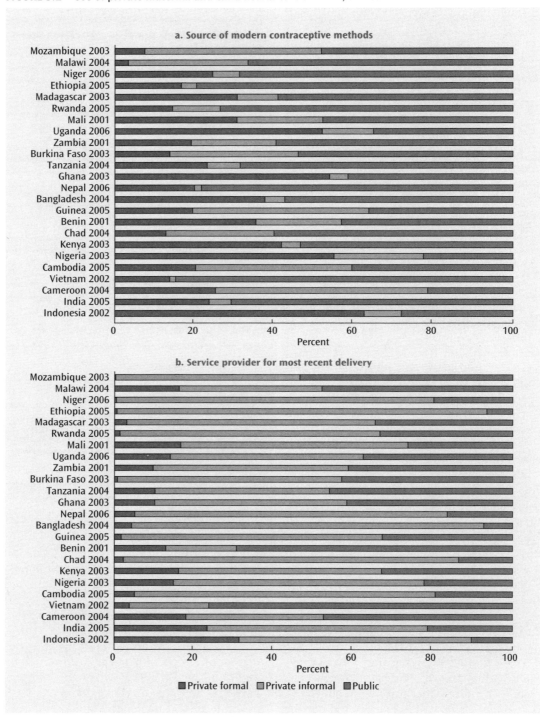

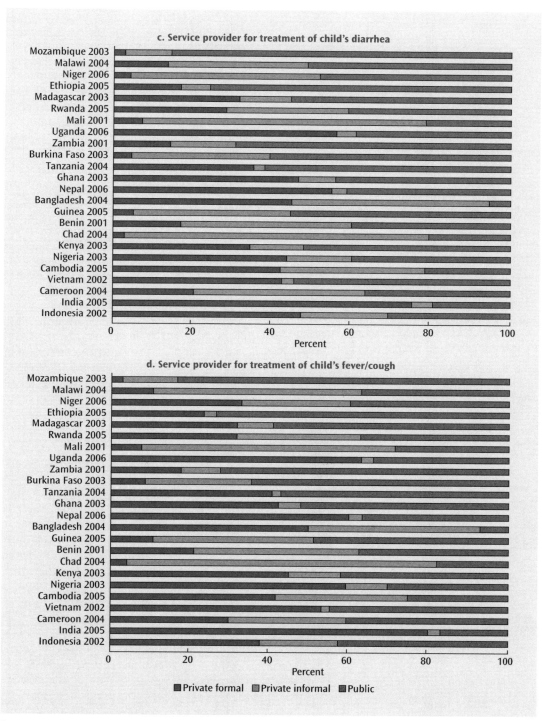

Source: Supon 2008, using most recent DHS data for Sub-Saharan African and South Asian countries. Countries arrayed by purchasing power parity GDP level. Year of survey shown next to name of country.

FIGURE 3.3 Public and private providers of TB services in 22 high-burden countries

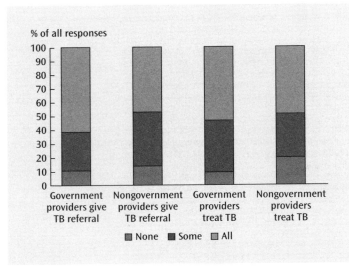

Source: WHO 2009.

FIGURE 3.4 Trends in the use of private providers in Sub-Saharan Africa and South Asia

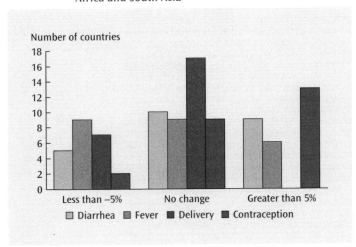

Source: DHS survey data used by Supon (2008).
Notes: The chart shows change in the share of private providers between two recent DHS surveys. Negative change indicates reduction in private sector shares. Changes less than 5 percentage points positive or negative are shown as "no change."

Overall, the chart presents a picture of little significant change in the shares of private providers delivering services related to maternal, reproductive, and child health in low-income countries. The only clear reduction in the private shares has been for delivery, reflecting a shift from traditional birth attendants and home delivery (private informal) to qualified institutional deliveries in government facilities. The absence of widespread reduction in the use of private providers in these surveys is interesting, because most of these surveys were conducted after the mid-1990s during a period of significantly increased effort to expand government roles in service delivery.

Figures 3.2, 3.3, and 3.4 show the highly significant role played by nongovernment providers in delivering services related to the health MDGs. These data indicate the important role of private providers in offering *access* to health care. However, concerns are often raised about whether private providers reach the poor (equity) as well as about the quality of the service they provide.

The data available from the DHS surveys can be used to examine where low-income households (proxied by a ranking based on household assets) obtain MDG-related health services. Figure 3.5 shows results for the four measured services—diarrhea, fever/cough treatment, source of delivery, and source of contraception—comparing the two lowest asset quintiles (or bottom 40 percent of the asset index distribution) with the average for the whole population. Points above the 45 percent line indicate higher use of private providers by the lower quintiles than by the general population. Overall, there is no clear indication that private sector use is mainly among the better-off while the poor largely use government services. In fact, the results point slightly in the other direction with government providers favored by the poor mainly as a source of contraception.

Informal private providers play a large role. When these results are separated for formal and informal private providers, it is clear that the poor rely significantly on the informal sector. In a relatively unregulated market, formal private providers will gravitate to those more able to pay, and informal providers will be more accessible to the poor.

Private providers, formal and informal, account for a large share of service use related to the MDGs, even for the poor. But usage data say little about the *quality* of the services people are receiving from private providers or about how this quality compares with that of government providers. Unfortunately, the evidence on quality is fairly weak.

Anecdotal evidence and casual observation suggest that a lot of the health care available in low-income countries with widespread private provision—including widespread self-treatment and treatment by untrained or unlicensed providers—is of poor quality. But there are few systematic and representative studies of quality of care in low-income countries and even fewer comparing government and nongovernment providers. In general, nongovernment providers are less likely to follow standard diagnostic and treatment protocols for communicable diseases and much more likely to use a wider range of less-preferred and more costly diagnostic and treatment actions.

Researchers distinguish between *technical quality* (the degree to which services adhere to best-practice processes likely to ensure health impact) and *patient-perceived quality* (which relates to the nontechnical characteristics of care that lead to patient satisfaction). Studies of private provider quality often raise concerns about the low quality of treatment practices.[7] Some disease-specific assessments have reported low quality of health care in the private sector, such as in the treatment of TB in India,[8] treatment of sexually transmitted diseases in South Africa,[9] and distribution of antimalarial drugs in Kenya.[10] In many low-income countries where regulation is weak, private providers often do not follow guidelines, may be poorly trained, and may have inadequate drug stocks and low quality drugs. Unsound prescribing, for example, leading to antimicrobial resistance, is one quality problem that is often cited.

Patients themselves often give private providers good marks on characteristics such as flexible working hours, convenient location, better equipment, more confidential care and

FIGURE 3.5 Probability of using private health care providers by whole population and the lowest two asset quintiles in Sub-Saharan Africa and South Asia

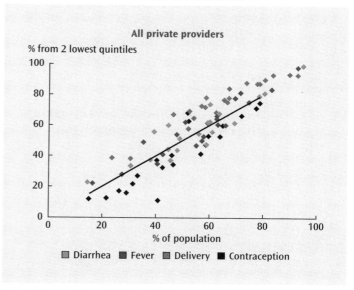

Source: DHS survey data used by Supon (2008).
Note: The diamonds in this chart show the percentages of reported service utilization of private formal and informal health care providers by the whole population (x axis) and the lowest two quintiles in the asset index distribution (y axis) for four MDG-related health care services measured by the DHS surveys.

attentiveness to patients, and greater availability of physicians and pharmaceuticals.

Very few studies compare government and nongovernment providers systematically. A recent study in New Delhi found poor technical quality in both sectors.[11] Some studies have also found the quality of private sector providers to be superior to that of public sector providers. Examples include antenatal care in Tanzania[12] and the quality of care for sexually transmitted diseases in Uganda.[13]

Overall, the limited available evidence suggests that governments and donors should be much more concerned about the quality of health care. There are great risks of poor quality with informal private providers. Recognition of the quality problems in the private sector often leads to simplistic calls for government regulation—but experience suggests that regulation is difficult to implement, especially in weaker states and in less accessible locations. Quality improvement may require more inputs. Increased costs will need to be financed somehow, such as through new purchasing mechanisms, higher volume, or subsidies. More evidence is needed to assess alternative approaches to expanding access and ensuring quality with both government and private providers.[14]

Examples of Innovation in Leveraging the Private Sector's Role in Health

Given the large presence of private providers in many developing countries, there are many examples of private providers engaged in delivering services to enhance

achievement of the health MDGs. The following cases (box 3.1) illustrate some of the innovative ways that have been used to leverage existing private capacity. They also reinforce the messages introduced in table 3.2 that such innovative arrangements require new actions and capacities on the part of governments to design, implement, regulate, and evaluate.

In the first example, the Chiranjeevi scheme in Gujarat, India, the state government has developed an innovative contracting mechanism to pay private obstetricians to provide institutional deliveries to poor women. This example shows how a government committed to ensuring access to

---

BOX 3.1   Examples of innovative approaches to expand access to health services via the nongovernment sector

1. Chiranjeevi Yojana "Long Life of Mothers and Babies": Engaging Private Obstetricians in Improving Access and Quality of Institutional Deliveries in Gujarat, India

To meet the MDG targets for maternal and child health in the state of Gujarat, the state government set up a public-private partnership in 2005 that contracted with private obstetricians already practicing in rural areas to provide pregnancy and birthing care to poor women who otherwise likely would have had their babies at home. The program was initially implemented in five pilot districts within the state. Based on its initial success in raising the share of babies delivered in institutions from 38 percent to 59 percent, this program was expanded to cover the whole state with a total population of 55 million (see source below).

One key to the program's success was an innovative funding mechanism developed by the state government to improve the incentives for private practitioners to participate. Providers were given a contract for assisting with a given quantity of births for Chiranjeevi beneficiaries; a significant advance payment helped to overcome concerns about delays in payment. Payments were also replenished on a regular basis to assure participating doctors that they would be compensated for their work. A small sum from the payments was given to the women to cover their transportation costs. The total value of the contract included an agreed-upon estimate for a share of more complex deliveries, including caesarian sections.

The results of this partnership have been impressive. In less than two years, the number of obstetricians providing delivery care through the government program increased from the original 7 in the public sector to more than 800 in the private sector. Overall, the additional cost of the program for the whole state was estimated to be around 3.5 percent of the total health budget. Funding was provided by both the state and the central governments.

Sources: http://gujhealth.gov.in/Chiranjeevi%20Yojana/M_index.htm; Bhat and others 2006.

2. Child and Family Welfare Stores: Social Franchising of Low-Cost Pharmaceuticals in Kenya

The HealthStore Foundation's Child and Family Welfare (CFW) model is a private network of micro pharmacies and clinics whose mission is to provide access to essential medicines for marginalized populations. The CFW outlets target the most common killer diseases including malaria, respiratory infections, and dysentery, among others. CFW was launched as a nonprofit organization but today is planning to convert to for-profit status.

The CFW model incorporates all the key elements of successful franchising: uniform systems and training; careful selection of locations; and, most importantly, strict controls on quality, backed up by regular monitoring and inspections. Using a centralized procurement operation that works through the Mission for Essential Drugs and Supplies (MEDS) and other suppliers, HealthStore is able to obtain quality medicines at the lowest possible cost.

The network operates two types of outlets: basic drug stores owned and operated by community health workers, and clinics owned and operated by nurses who provide a deeper list of essential medicines as well as basic primary care. As the franchisor, HealthStore can revoke a franchisee's right to operate an outlet if the franchisee fails to comply with the franchise rules and standards.

HealthStore's customers are primarily low- or middle-income women and children subsisting on agriculture, although people of all ages and incomes are treated. CFW outlets are located at market centers in agricultural areas of approximately 5,000 people. The CFW network has 17 drug outlets and 48 basic medical clinics in operation. Central subsidies allow CFW outlets to offer lower prices and more predictable quality than competing private shops. Recently, CFW clinics have supported pilots for the introduction of artemisinin-combination therapy (ACT) for malaria, and the network has been included in the National Malaria Strategy.

Source: www.cfwshops.org.

3. Contracting out with Nongovernmental Organizations (NGOs) in Post-Conflict States

To address the inadequacies in its health care system, the Cambodian government decided to contract out the delivery of primary health care services to NGOs. A randomized trial was carried out starting in 1999 to compare the outcomes in the contracted districts with government provision of health services. Districts were randomly assigned to one of three health care delivery models: (1) contracting out, where the contractors were given full line responsibility for service delivery, including organizing health facilities; hiring, firing, and setting wages; and procuring and distributing essential drugs and supplies; (2) contracting in, where the contractors worked within the Ministry of Health (MOH) system to strengthen the existing administrative structure; they could not hire or fire health workers, although they could request that they be transferred. Drugs and supplies came through normal MOH channels. The contractors also received a nominal budget supplement for staff incentives and operating expenses; and (3) government provision, where the government district health management team (DHMT) continued to manage the services; drugs and supplies came through normal MOH channels, and the DHMT also received a budget supplement for staff incentives and operating expenses. The results showed that by 2003 contracted districts outperformed the government districts in terms of the coverage of services, quality of care, utilization by the poor, and out-of-pocket expenditures on health by the community, especially the poor.

Source: Schwartz and Bhushan 2004.

In Guatemala, a similar effort was launched in 1997 with the goal of extending a basic health care package to 3 million people living in rural, impoverished, and indigenous communities that had previously been involved in conflict. Three different delivery methods were chosen: (1) direct contracting out, where NGOs were contracted to directly provide services; they received payments and were responsible for the purchase of all inputs (apart from vaccines); (2) a "mixed method," where the government contracted with NGOs to act as financial and administrative managers for services delivered by government service providers; these NGOs also received a set payment and were able to hire additional staff and purchase supplies, allowing them to bypass the notoriously slow hiring and procurement process; and (3) the traditional method, where current health posts operated by the government were strengthened. The results showed that women and children serviced by the mixed model had significantly better results for many key health indicators, compared with the other two models. The results also showed that the direct contracting out had higher productivity than either of the other two methods but was more costly, in part because the directly contracted NGOs were assigned to more distant and difficult-to-access areas than those contracted under the mixed model.

Source: Danel and La Forgia 2005.

certain services can creatively combine existing government and private provision capacity. With this scheme, the number of women who use qualified private providers to assist them at birth in public clinics has rapidly expanded. This innovative program also addresses a staffing issue, because public clinics typically encounter difficulties in recruiting and retaining qualified medical staff. The payment arrangement also gives some incentive to providers to avoid unnecessary services. The financial burden on the state government appears to be manageable, and it substitutes for government spending on expanding its own service delivery.

The second example, the Child and Family Welfare (CFW) stores in Kenya, illustrates the strategy of "social franchising," which uses techniques developed in commercial franchising to engage private providers in offering quality-assured, standardized, and branded services under agreed price and service conditions. This is a purely

private initiative, where local entrepreneurs have sought to meet an evident need with a viable but low-cost business model. The HealthStore Foundation's CFW program has expanded access to essential pharmaceuticals to low-income consumers.

The third set of examples, contracting out of primary health care services in post-conflict settings in rural Cambodia and Guatemala, shows government engaging the capacities of the nonprofit sector to expand access to basic health services in rural areas where the government's own capacity to deliver services was very limited. Both programs tested several alternative contracting-out strategies and carried out substantial impact evaluations. The evaluations indicate that the programs performed well in several respects (increasing coverage and achieving a more pro-poor distribution); however, the evidence also suggests that these successes may not necessarily be reproduced in another country setting.

Private Sector in Education

The private sector is also an important provider of education. Over the past two decades, private participation in education has increased dramatically throughout the world, serving all types of communities—from high-income to low-income families.[15]

Unlike for health, information for education is available only for a relatively small set of countries and indicators. Figure 3.6 shows recent data on the share of education expenditure from private sources for countries with available information. In some countries, such as Jamaica, Peru, and Zambia, the private sector contributes more than 40 percent of the total expenditures in education. In several others—such as Chile, Haiti, Kenya, Paraguay, and the Philippines—the percentage fluctuates between 30 and 40 percent.

Although governments remain the main financiers of primary and secondary education, in many countries private agents deliver a sizable share. Table 3.3 shows the

FIGURE 3.6 Private spending on education

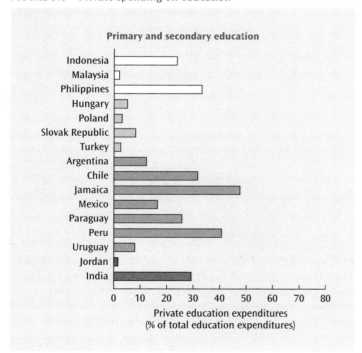

Source: UNESCO, EdStats (www.worldbank.org/education/edstats).

participation of the private sector in primary and secondary education for 1990 and 2006 for those countries with available information. Private enrollment shares at the primary level increased by a large magnitude in countries in most regions, particularly in Sub-Saharan Africa, the Middle East, and Southeast Asia. At the secondary level, private enrollment has also increased, although less uniformly across countries. However, private enrollment shares typically remain higher in secondary education than in primary education.

Figure 3.7 presents data for private enrollment shares by region in 2006, based on the countries with available information, while

TABLE 3.3 Private enrollment shares in education, selected countries, 1990 and 2006
percent

Country	Region	Primary		Secondary	
		1990	2006	1990	2006
Burkina Faso	Sub-Saharan Africa	8.6	13.7	41.1	38.8
Cameroon	Sub-Saharan Africa	25.2	22.5	42.8	28.2
Guinea	Sub-Saharan Africa	2.4	22.0	4.1	15.9
Mauritania	Sub-Saharan Africa	0.7	7.4	2.5	16.8
Indonesia	East Asia & Pacific	17.6	15.9	49.2	43.5
Philippines	East Asia & Pacific	6.7	7.8	36.4	20.4
Thailand	East Asia & Pacific	9.6	16.7	16.2	15.0
Poland	Europe & Central Asia	0.1	1.9	0.4	2.8
Turkey	Europe & Central Asia	0.6	1.8	2.8	2.3
Chile	Latin America & Caribbean	38.8	52.9	49.0	53.7
Costa Rica	Latin America & Caribbean	4.7	7.0	7.9	9.8
Mexico	Latin America & Caribbean	6.2	8.1	16.6	15.0
Peru	Latin America & Caribbean	12.6	17.6	14.6	24.3
Jordan	Middle East & North Africa	22.9	31.2	6.1	17.0
Morocco	Middle East & North Africa	3.6	7.3	2.7	5.2
Syria	Middle East & North Africa	3.5	4.3	5.6	4.0
Tunisia	Middle East & North Africa	0.5	1.2	12.0	4.7
Bangladesh[a]	South Asia	15.2	38.9	NA	NA
Nepal[a]	South Asia	4.7	14.7	NA	NA
Pakistan[a]	South Asia	14.0	35.0	NA	NA
OECD average[b]		10.1	11.8	17.6	17.9

Source: UNESCO; EdStats (www.worldbank.org/education/edstats).
Note: The table shows most recent data available within two years of the year indicated.
a. Based on data from background paper prepared by the Aga Khan Foundation for the *Global Monitoring Report 2008*, UNESCO. Comparability across countries is limited because of different definitions of education expenditure. However, comparability within each country across years is assured.
b. Average estimate based on OECD countries for which data are available for both years.

figure 3.8 presents the same information, dividing the sample by country income level. It is noteworthy that a larger share of education is provided privately in low-income countries than in high-income countries.

Countries provide different examples of mixes between public and private sector roles in education financing and provision. Some countries make a sharp distinction between the role of the public sector as the education financier and the private sector as the education provider. For instance, in the Netherlands, all education is publicly

financed, including private schools, which enroll more than two-thirds of all students. In other countries, such as Chile, the private sector plays an important role in providing education, but the government subsidizes only some of the students who attend private schools. Several African countries have different types of nonpublic schools, including government-subsidized independent schools (for example, in the Gambia); partially subsidized mission or religious schools (for example, in Lesotho); and partially subsidized community-organized schools (for example, in Kenya). Elsewhere, public schools are supported financially by the private sector in the form of user fees or corporate sponsorship (for example, in Pakistan).

Examples of Innovation in Leveraging the Private Sector's Role in Education

Evidence on the impact of the private sector on the quality of education is limited and shows mixed results. Some of the evidence comes from cross-country studies that are mainly correlational studies. For instance, Woessmann (2009) shows that publicly operated schools deliver lower test scores than privately operated schools do, but publicly funded private schools are associated with higher academic achievement than publicly operated institutions. Therefore, one might conclude that partnerships in which the private sector is the operator and the public sector is the financier have the potential to increase the quality of education while keeping the education budget in check. Nonetheless, this evidence is correlational, and needs to be treated with caution.

Country studies provide a better source of evidence. The cases discussed below are examples of the delivery modalities shown in table 3.1, which help illustrate the issues regarding government role and capacities outlined in table 3.2. They are models either of government finance and private delivery or of private delivery and finance in which the government provides a framework for development.

FIGURE 3.7 Private enrollment share by region, 2006

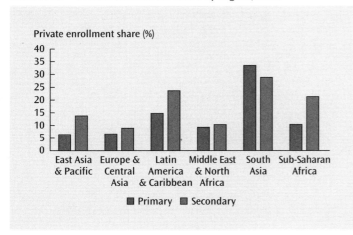

Source: UNESCO, EdStats (www.worldbank.org/education/edstats).

FIGURE 3.8 Private enrollment share by national income, 2006

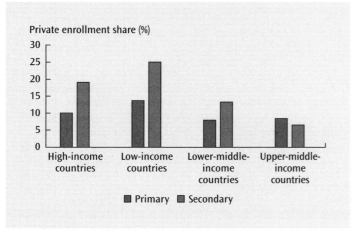

Source: UNESCO, EdStats (www.worldbank.org/education/edstats).

The cases presented are of two types. First are examples of *systemic* involvement of the private sector in the provision of education. Systemic involvement implies a clear strategy by the government to form alliances with the private sector. In these cases, the private sector typically provides a large share of education in the country, and the public sector serves as the financier. Universal voucher systems, such as the one in Chile, continue to be rare. They are also difficult to evaluate, thus leading to different conclusions in different studies (box 3.2). The bottom line seems to be that without targeting or special measures, the positive effects of vouchers on quality may be the result of sorting, because the best students leave their public schools to attend private institutions. Contracting programs, such as the ones for educational services in Côte d'Ivoire and Bangladesh, can increase the supply of schooling and enrollments (box 3.3). The case of Côte d'Ivoire is an example of a pragmatic approach to addressing a lack of public school capacity. The government retains the responsibility

for ensuring basic education but uses the private sector to make up for short-term gaps. In Bangladesh the government relies on private schools to deliver the great majority of secondary schooling; 97 percent of secondary school enrollment is in private schools. In addition, the government finances stipends to support girls' enrollment in secondary school. The stipend program has been credited with contributing to a significant increase in girls' enrollment and to reducing the male-female gap, but it has been less successful in terms of improving quality.

Overall, the evidence on the impacts of private partnerships from *systemic* interventions is mixed. On the one hand, the private sector is an efficient vehicle to increase access. On the other, the effects on the quality of education are unclear. The empirical evidence on the effects of vouchers on educational outcomes outside the United States is small, though growing. While there are few rigorous impact evaluations and even fewer random evaluations of voucher programs, the most rigorous studies available

---

BOX 3.2   Systemic involvement of the private sector in the public provision of education: vouchers in Chile

In the 1980s, Chile introduced a universal voucher system with the objective of making the education system more efficient. This reform enabled students to select the school of their choice, either public or private, and tied per-student public funding to school enrollment. The rationale behind this policy was that student choice would encourage school competition and increase accountability at the local level by making schools responsive to parental preferences. The provision of public funding to private schools led to the development of a school market in which more than 20,000 new private schools were created, and private enrollment rates increased from 32 percent of all enrollments in 1985 to 51 percent in 2005. Today 94 percent of all schools in Chile receive voucher funding, and 36 percent of those schools are private.

Evidence on the impact of the voucher system on the quality of education is mixed. Some studies found that the program had positive effects on beneficiaries' test scores, and others found no differences between private independent schools and public institutions. Moreover, there is evidence of sorting in private schools; that is, private schools choosing the best students and the rest remaining in public schools. There is evidence that the best students in public schools used the vouchers to attend private institutions.

More recently, Chilean students demonstrated significant improvements in their reading performance in the Program for International Student Assessment (PISA) tests between 2000 and 2006, making Chile the top Latin American country participating in PISA. The Chilean experience suggests that it may take some time for school choice policies to yield improvements in average academic achievement.

Source: Patrinos, Barrera-Osorio, and Guaqueta 2009.

BOX 3.3 Contracting out education programs: Bangladesh and Côte d'Ivoire

1. Bangladesh

The government subsidizes almost 90 percent of the base teacher salaries in community-managed, not-for-profit, nongovernment secondary schools. The government subsidizes enrollment increases by paying for additional teachers as long as the school meets the state criteria. Private schools are managed by local committees and are accountable to the government through the accreditation process required to be entitled to receive teacher salary subsidies.

A second type of public-private engagement is the provision of stipends to support girls' enrollment in secondary schools. Scholarships cover the cost of tuition of girls' secondary education. Additionally, girls receive a stipend expected to cover 50 percent of school fees. Stipend programs to support enrollment increases have been accompanied by curriculum reform, development of instructional materials, teacher training programs, improvement of school infrastructure, and institutional capacity-building initiatives. These are the main outcomes of the stipend program: (1) a significant increase in girls' secondary enrollment, from 442,000 in 1994 to more than 1 million in 2001; (2) a significant reduction in the enrollment gap between girls and boys; and (3) a significant reduction in the proportion of 13- to 15-year-old married girls, from 29 percent in 1992 to 14 percent in 1995.

Assessed weaknesses of the program include the low correlation between enrollment increases and improvement of completion and attainment rates at the secondary level, which suggests that access programs are not necessarily linked to the strengthening of core education components at the school level.

2. Côte d'Ivoire

The government established contracts with the private sector for education services with the objective of increasing the supply of education to meet student demand. In short, the government gives a payment to lower- and upper-secondary private schools for each public student that they enroll. Schools must be "chartered" to take on additional students, and placement depends in part on the educational performance of the school. The amount of the subsidy varies with school location and is loosely tied to the number of students enrolled. The number of students in the private school sponsorship program was 223,000 in 2001, up from 116,000 in 1993. Unfortunately, no systematic study has been done on the effects of this type of intervention, but research shows that the subsidy system is progressive, because it covers more of the expenditures for lower-income families. Thus the program promotes enrollment increases among the poor.

Sources: Sakellariou and Patrinos (2004) for Côte d'Ivoire; World Bank (2003) and Patrinos, Barrera-Osorio, and Guaqueta (2009) for Bangladesh.

show that voucher programs lead to significant improvements in access to secondary schooling for relatively poorer students. These programs can also lead to significant increases in test scores. Additionally, studies show that voucher recipients are more likely to complete secondary school, enter university, postpone marriage, and increase their earnings.

The second set of examples deal with public-private partnerships for *specific* programs. Usually, these are local programs without a systematic involvement of the private sector in the wider objectives of the government. For example, these programs may take advantage of the existing private sector to increase enrollment among underserved segments of the population, as is the case in the Punjab Education Foundation's program in Pakistan. A program partnership may also use the public sector in innovative ways, such as when the public sector constructs new buildings in underserved areas and contracts out the teaching to the private sector. This is the case of concession schools in Bogota, Colombia (box 3.4).

1. Concessions Schools in Bogota, Colombia

The concept of concession schools was introduced by the municipal authorities of Bogota in 1999 as a way to provide high-quality education to low-income and high-risk students. Concession schools are public but are managed by private school operators whose students have a record of scoring above average on the national secondary exit examination for five consecutive years. Private operators are granted autonomy over school management and receive a per-pupil payment. In Bogota, 25 public schools are run as concession schools under 15-year contracts. Empirical results from a rigorous impact study reveal significant increases in math scores; significant increases in reading scores; significant reductions in dropout rates; and some evidence of competition effects on nearby public schools.

2. The Punjab Education Foundation Assisted Schools Program, Pakistan

The Punjab Education Foundation was established in 1991 and restructured in 2004 into an autonomous institution to promote high-quality education for the poor through partnerships with the private sector. It is funded by the government of Pakistan's Punjab province, and it is headed by a 15-member, government-appointed board of directors, the majority of whom are from the private sector. The Foundation Assisted Schools Program aims to improve education quality by taking full advantage of the capacity of the mushrooming private schools in Punjab. Approximately 33 percent of children ages 6 to 10 who attend school are enrolled in private schools, and private enrollment shares are on the rise. The program attempts to improve quality through three fundamental components: vouchers, teacher training, and financial incentives to schools for improved academic performance. A preliminary evaluation of the initiative shows evidence of large positive impacts on the number of students, teachers, classrooms, and teaching materials.

Sources: www.pef.edu.pk; Barrera-Osorio and Raju 2008; Barrera-Osorio 2009.

Finally, the Kenya Private Schools Financing and Technical Assistance Program is an initiative of the International Finance Corporation (IFC) to provide local currency financing and technical assistance to private primary and secondary schools. In 2006 the IFC signed a risk-sharing agreement with K-Rep Bank of up to 120 million Kenyan shillings (US$1.7 million) on loans extended to eligible private schools in Kenya. Under this agreement, the IFC shares 50 percent of the risk on the pool of loans made to schools after an initial 5 percent first loss is taken by K-Rep Bank. Schools use these loans to finance construction projects, purchase educational materials, including computers, and cover other capital expenditures. To support the risk-sharing agreement, a technical assistance program was prepared.[16]

New Vehicles for Private Sector Contributions

The potential for leveraging the private sector role in human development outcomes extends well beyond service provision. Nongovernment actors are playing a variety of relatively new roles that include financing of both government and nongovernment actions and the introduction of new service delivery organizations and strategies. Private actors are increasingly visible and vocal in international, national, and local policy development and planning. New models of public-private partnership are also emerging internationally and nationally, although there is still limited evaluative evidence to help assess their benefits and costs. This section explores some of these new roles and their implications.

New Private Funders: Philanthropy, Health Insurance, Development Financing

The ascendance of the MDGs on the global stage has been accompanied by significant increases in development assistance in the last decade, redressing some of the previous declines. These increases have been particularly large for health, less so for education. Much of the increase has come from traditional sources of international funding—bilateral and multilateral agencies. But major new international philanthropies have also emerged as significant sources of new financing. Probably the best known of these is the Bill and Melinda Gates Foundation, but several others have also increased their funding for global health and education.[17] Beyond the obvious benefit of being a new source of funding, these new developments in private financing open up new avenues for innovation in delivering MDG-related health and education services.

The world's foundations contributed an estimated $4.5 billion to work in the development field in 2005. Of this amount, foundations from the United States contributed $3.8 billion, double the amount they gave in 1998. Prior to the current crisis, philanthropic contributions were increasing,

although this trend may not continue to the same extent. Greater contributions by U.S. foundations in the international arena could be driven by their availability of greater financial resources and experience in giving practices.[18]

Growing international philanthropy has taken several forms. In the recent scale-up of private giving for global health, significant funding has been provided to support existing and new international organizations as well as a variety of new global "alliances." For example, the Global Alliance for Vaccines and Immunization and the Global Fund to Fight AIDS, Tuberculosis, and Malaria have both received large contributions from government and nongovernment funders. Box 3.5 discusses the emerging role of the Bill and Melinda Gates Foundation in global health, and how it supports several new actors in this field.

The education sector receives a significantly smaller share of total philanthropic giving relative to the health sector. According to the Foundation Center, 43 percent of U.S. foundation support to international activities went to health programs, while 6 percent was earmarked for education. Nonetheless, recent major corporate and individual donations to education in developing countries

---

BOX 3.5   The growing role of the Bill and Melinda Gates Foundation in global health

One of the largest private foundations working in global health is the Bill and Melinda Gates Foundation, which has had a significant impact on the field since it was founded 14 years ago. Its other two focuses are reducing global poverty and increasing access to education for low-income Americans.

The foundation has committed over $11.6 billion since 1994 for global health programs. To date, the largest grants have been US$750 million for the Global Alliance for Vaccines and Immunization; followed by US$500 million for the Global Fund to Fight AIDS, Tuberculosis, and Malaria; and US$200 million each to the Aeras Global TB Vaccine Foundation and the Foundation for the National Institutes of Health. It was also a major founder of the Global Alliance for Improved Nutrition, a vehicle for collaborations with private organizations and industry, and it continues to give significant amounts in support of nutrition programs.

Source: www.gatesfoundation.org.

highlight the potential of philanthropic foundations to improve education outcomes and have attracted increasing interest from governments and multilateral agencies.

Private philanthropic contributions may have a significant impact on national education systems through several pathways. First, the flow of additional resources could ease resource constraints in education, and the resources can be targeted to underserved areas or populations. Second, private expertise in management can generate efficiencies in the implementation of education programs supported by philanthropy and provide useful lessons for greater efficiencies in public service delivery. Third, targeted support to research and analysis of policies and programs at the primary and secondary levels may be of added value to governments in developing countries that often lack the resources and expertise to invest in this area. Lastly, strategic involvement of the private sector may help redirect education policy toward the adoption and expansion of successful privately developed initiatives.

The role of new actors in the health and education sectors does not come without challenges. Uncoordinated and isolated actions of private donors may not generate systemic impacts and may benefit only selected groups of patients or students. There is a risk of overcrowding resources in certain countries or programs. The flow of private resources may substitute rather than supplement budgets, by creating incentives for governments to withdraw funding from public education or public health problems or to shift funding between levels within the sector. Withdrawal of resources from basic education, for example, may reduce the quality of the service provided and raise equity concerns. Finally, privately funded interventions raise the risk of lack of sustainability once the initial grants are exhausted.

Philanthropy is not the only form of private funding of public health and education activities. For example, in health, another (and somewhat different) form of private

financing is risk-pooling arrangements, such as health insurance and community financing/micro-insurance. To date, organized private financing has been of limited importance in low-income countries. Preker, Scheffler, and Bassett (2007) reviewed data from all developing regions and generally found that private health insurance accounted for a very small share of health expenditures. Private health insurance schemes in low-income countries primarily cover urban and more affluent populations and higher-cost services involving hospitalization, although some also have links with primary care services. The main relevance of these risk-pooling arrangements for the health-related MDGs is likely to be in relation to communicable diseases, especially HIV/AIDS and TB, which may be significantly prevalent in adults working in the formal sector. In higher-income Sub-Saharan countries such as South Africa, with high HIV/AIDS prevalence, private insurance arrangements can influence access to both prevention and treatment as well as make formal sector employers more aware of public health issues.

An emerging vehicle for private financing is community financing and micro-insurance. These are typically small-scale schemes initiated by NGOs with community linkages, although there are some examples of government promotion. These schemes typically involve community members in management and supervision and often cover the primary care services relevant to the various health-related MDGs. With a few exceptions, such as the "Mutuelles" found in Rwanda and West Africa, coverage of these schemes is still fairly low.[19] There are instances of these schemes purchasing insurance coverage through the formal private sector insurance providers. This provides a mechanism for formal private insurance to contribute to development of basic coverage. There is also growing interest in linking micro-insurance programs with financial services for rural communities, such as rural banking and micro-credit, exemplified by the programs of Basix in India, which provide financial services and technical assistance to the rural poor and women.[20]

Health insurance can also play an important role in reducing the financial risks of households experiencing serious illness. This financial risk protection is also related to the MDGs, especially MDG 1 on poverty reduction, because high out-of-pocket spending on health needs has been shown to be a significant cause of financial shocks to poor households (see, for example, Baeza and Packard 2006). This function can be carried out in different ways by both government and nongovernment entities funding different types of "demand-side" entitlements. For example, governments or NGOs could purchase insurance coverage from private insurers for targeted beneficiaries, such as informal sector workers and

families, or they could make direct payments for service charges at government or nongovernment hospitals. Investing the users of health care with such entitlements has added advantages of empowering them to demand greater quality and accountability from providers.

Private corporate financing for service delivery programs to achieve the MDGs in the wider population (in contrast to targeting corporate employees) is also emerging as a new area of innovation. Private corporate actors can be multinational or purely domestic. The health sector, in particular, has a large corporate element. Box 3.6 provides some examples of current corporate-supported programs, including one financed by a multinational pharmaceutical company, which target health outcomes in low-income countries.

BOX 3.6 Leveraging corporate finance for disease control

The following are two very different examples of corporate financing of health programs: one private corporate cofinancing of service delivery for HIV/AIDS; the other leveraging private research funding to develop new products for future purchase in public sector programs.

Debswana is a 50/50 partnership between the diamond mining company De Beers Group and the Botswana government to combat the HIV/AIDS epidemic. Debswana staffs and fully funds the Jwaneng Mine Hospital and HIV Clinic in Botswana that was opened in 2003. It originally was formed to treat employees of the mine, then it was extended to cover their families, and it now treats the public. In 2005, 30,000 free outpatient appointments were recorded, and by 2007, 3,100 patients were being treated with antiretroviral drugs, and the program had been expanded to support four satellite clinics offering HIV testing.[a]

Another innovative financing initiative tackles the failure of markets to develop and produce vaccines for the health needs of poor countries. Six donors (Canada, Italy, Norway, the Russian Federation, the United Kingdom, and the Bill and Melinda Gates Foundation) have committed $1.5 billion to an initiative to accelerate the development and production of a pneumococcal vaccine for use in developing countries by assuring vaccine manufacturers that funds will be available for poor countries to buy the vaccines at a predictable, long-term price. The initiative, titled the Advanced Market Commitment (AMC), is results-driven: payments will be made only for vaccines that work well in the poorest countries. It is also demand-led: developing countries have to want to purchase the vaccine.

AMC funds will be used to subsidize the purchase of pneumococcal vaccines that tackle the disease strains most prevalent in low-income countries in Africa and Asia and that meet a required public health efficacy level. When a vaccine meets these requirements and recipient countries want to buy it, the manufacturer is entitled to enter into a supply agreement for vaccines at a subsidized price in exchange for a commitment to provide an established volume level, at an established price, annually for 10 years. Once the private subsidy funds are depleted, the manufacturer must continue to provide the product at an established retail price to meet the continuing demand.[b]

a. Wilson 2007.
b. World Bank 2008b.

New Private Provision: International and National Nonprofits and For-profits

Much of the private health care provision described in this chapter is delivered by small, diverse, and often informal providers. But there are also private organizations that can be significant service providers for the health-related MDGs on a larger scale and scope. These include both international and domestic organizations and both the nonprofit and for-profit sectors.

Medecins san Frontieres, Save the Children, and the Program for Appropriate Technology in Health are just three of several well-known international nonprofits increasingly visible as service providers in developing countries.[21] These international groups may team up with traditional and new private funders as well as with domestic service providers, leveraging local capacities and international financing and often introducing innovative approaches to service delivery.

Nongovernment domestic service providers in developing countries, such as the widespread faith-based providers in Africa (for example, the Africa Religious Health Assets Program) and other regions, the Africa Medical and Research Foundation in Kenya, and the Bangladesh Rural Advancement Committee (BRAC) are also growing in scale and scope.[22] BRAC is a particularly interesting and important example. It provides a significant level of services addressing both the health- and education-related MDGs domestically in Bangladesh with a mix of financing sources, and it is increasingly active in other countries, such as Afghanistan (see box 3.7).

New Models of Public-Private Partnership

This brief review of the expanding landscape of private sector engagement in priority health and education issues in developing countries does not do full justice to the

---

BOX 3.7 | **The Bangladesh Rural Advancement Committee: An emerging global NGO**

The Bangladesh Rural Advancement Committee (BRAC) was launched in Bangladesh in 1972 and is the largest nonprofit organization in the developing world, employing 125,000 staff. It is funded through a combination of philanthropic support, income-generating enterprises, and borrowings. At present, it reaches more than 110 million people in Africa and Asia with its holistic approach to addressing poverty by providing micro-loans, self-employment opportunities, health services, and education.

BRAC is playing a major role in helping Bangladesh reach its MDGs; it offers preventive, curative, and reproductive health services to more than 92 million people. It helped immunize 82 percent of children under the age of two in Bangladesh, and trained women in 13 million households in how to treat diarrhea—the number one cause of death among children. The organization has been one of the pioneers implementing the "Directly Observed Therapy Short-Course" (DOTS) for treating TB, which has been described as a breakthrough by the World Health Organization. Concerning education, the BRAC Education Program targets out-of-school children and has graduated 3.9 million students from its primary schools (70 percent of whom are girls) and 2.3 million from its pre-primary schools, with nearly 1.6 million children currently enrolled in its 54,000 schools.

BRAC also operates in other countries such as Afghanistan, Liberia, Pakistan, Sierra Leone, Southern Sudan, Sri Lanka, Tanzania, and Uganda. In 2002, in solidarity with the refugees in Afghanistan, BRAC worked with Afghanis to launch microfinance and related programs, including health and education. BRAC is now the largest microfinance provider in Afghanistan, disbursing more than $96 million in small loans. In 2007, BRAC's annual program expenditure was $485 million. It used revenues from its microfinance program and pro-poor social enterprises, combined with debt, to self-finance 80 percent of the budget for its programs in Bangladesh.

Source: www.brac.net and BRAC-USA.

---

kaleidoscope of innovation and partnership that is emerging in many countries and around many different human development problems. Government and private sector roles are changing as both international and domestic economic and social conditions evolve. As the world strengthens its commitments to scaling up to achieve the MDGs, new models of public-private partnership are likely to come forward.

Several examples of this evolution have been emerging in relation to the World Economic Forum, which functions as a Swiss nonprofit foundation undertaking a range of initiatives in support of public and private action. This includes two major education partnerships: (1) the Global Education Initiative (GEI) brings together international and national private partners into education systems in Egypt, Jordan, Rajasthan (India), and the West Bank and Gaza, with the objectives of supporting national education reforms, developing information and communication technology in education, and demonstrating a model of education

reform that may be replicated in other countries; and (2) the Jordan Education Initiative (JEI) was launched in 2003 at the World Economic Forum, and it is now under the patronage of Jordan's Queen Rania. It is the most advanced of these partnerships, with over $25 million in contributions. The partnership model, supported by significant evaluation efforts, has led to the implementation of the Discovery Schools program, reaching over 50,000 students in 100 Discovery Schools with pedagogic methods centered on computers and digital and web-based technologies.

A related effort, the Global Education Alliance (GEA), is being implemented in Rwanda and has potentially significant implications for enhancing attainment of the education MDG (box 3.8).

Another new initiative is the United Nations' High Level Task Force on Innovative Financing for Health Systems.[23] This group, launched in September 2008, seeks to develop innovative mechanisms for raising additional funds to strengthen health

BOX 3.8 The experience of the Global Education Alliance in Rwanda

The Global Education Alliance (GEA) was created in 2007 by the World Economic Forum in collaboration with the Education for All Fast-Track Initiative, a partnership of bilateral and multilateral donors that supports poor countries in their efforts to achieve universal basic education by 2015. The GEA is intended to bring greater private sector support for education, along with the technical expertise needed to effectively integrate information and communications technology into education. The initiative is being implemented in Rwanda, which is far off track for meeting the MDG goal on universal primary education. The GEA recognizes the existence of a variety of initiatives to improve the use of information technology in education and seeks to add value in two ways—by coordinating the multiplicity of public and private stakeholders working on information technology in education in Rwanda, and by contributing business expertise to enhance service delivery and management.[a] Already, the Ministry of Education has released the first draft of a new policy that will govern the use of information technology in the country's education sector. The major aim of the policy is to guide the way information technology is used in the education sector, including the preparation of curricula and maintenance of student achievement records.[b]

Through the GEA, Rwanda has already partnered with companies such as AMD, Cisco, Edelman, Intel, and Microsoft. The country is also testing the One Laptop per Child technology developed by Massachusetts Institute of Technology Media Lab.

a. World Economic Forum 2009.
b. http://allafrica.com/stories/200901160133.html.

care delivery systems with the potential to reach millions of underserved women and children in developing countries. It will review the possibilities and make recommendations on opportunities for the private sector in both raising resources and channeling them to countries.

The Way Forward

The world is past the midpoint of the target date of 2015 for reaching the MDGs. As shown elsewhere in this report, progress toward many of the indicators is not on track to achieve the goals. Progress toward the health- and education-related MDGs especially needs to be accelerated.

Some believe that the financing and delivery of the health and education services needed to achieve the MDGs should be entirely the responsibility of governments. Shortcomings in government achievements in these areas then have a clear remedy—more public financing and expanding public provision, such as building more health facilities and schools; hiring more health workers for the civil service; and increasing public procurement of pharmaceuticals, school equipment, and other inputs.

The actual pattern of service financing and provision departs dramatically from this normative picture. Substantial funding and service delivery are already coming from outside government and making significant contributions to the health and education MDGs. Given the urgency of the human development challenges and costs (both human and economic) of shortfalls in their achievement, disregarding the potential of the nonstate sector to contribute to the health and education MDGs is shortsighted and wasteful. Leveraging the private sector role should be an essential element of pragmatic policies and programs for achieving the MDGs.

Engaging the private sector does not mean a lesser role for government, which will remain central in efforts to achieve the MDGs. To the contrary, it means additional responsibilities and somewhat different responsibilities for government as part of expanded efforts to increase access and improve the quality of MDG-related services. In a sense, expanding governments' efforts to leverage the private sector in health and education is analogous to moving from a more closed economy to a more open one. There are new risks but also potentially new rewards. Global partners need to support not only more innovation to leverage the private sector role but also investments to strengthen governments' abilities to design, manage, and evaluate new approaches, and to ensure adequate coordination and regulation across a wider range of actors.

For **education,** such a pragmatic approach has the potential to align and mainstream the activities of public and private stakeholders, with the private sector helping to fill gaps where the public sector may be weak, such as in managing programs cost-effectively. More attention could be given to strategies that go beyond the traditional form of public finance and private provision to define new ways of public-private collaboration to achieve the education MDGs. Although still small, nongovernment and philanthropic actors in the education sector increasingly support a significant flow of funds from nonofficial sources to champion such initiatives. New and ongoing international education initiatives, such as the GEI, show promise and some evidence of scale.

Many of these initiatives are dominated by technology companies, suggesting that the corporate sector can provide both financing and productive inputs. Technology in education is in short supply in many developing countries. Technology can help to improve quality, better train teachers, and make information flow more quickly. More engagement with the private sector in this area should be encouraged. Countries could make wider use of contracting out to utilize excess capacity in private schools and to educate more children, as well as to expand access to underserved areas and excluded populations.

International public-private partnerships in education, in combination with domestic contracting, can:

- Increase the flow of resources to the education sector and allow governments to reach goals more quickly
- Bring international expertise and best practice to the sector, and make better use of domestic capacity
- Promote research
- Bring all partners together with a common vision and set of goals

Better coordination of international and domestic public-private partnerships can help:

- Avoid isolated actions, giving the initiatives a greater chance of generating systemic impacts
- Reduce overcrowding of resources in certain areas
- Complement education budgets
- Address the sustainability issue before it becomes a problem

For **health**, the picture is more complex. Four separate MDGs emphasize health-related outcomes, and some of these, such as MDG 6, involve multiple diseases and health problems affecting different populations (and groups within populations) and requiring different technologies and service delivery strategies. The complexity of the health sector places large demands on state capacities to accelerate achievement across a broad scope of services, suggesting that leveraging contributions from the nonstate sector should be an essential part of national strategies where feasible.

Already the private sector role in *both* health care financing and delivery is larger than in education, even in the low-income countries. It is often significant systemwide, including in rural areas and among the poor. The scale and scope of new approaches is expanding, although given the large role of the private sector in health in many

countries, these efforts are still modest in terms of the overall health system. Governments in many low-income countries, where progress on the MDGs is most urgent, are increasing their engagement with the private sector, albeit cautiously.

Technical quality issues add a further complexity in the health sector. To be effective, services must be delivered according to technical standards. Not to do so is not only ineffective but can be very harmful both to individuals and to populations. Governments have to ensure quality in their own programs but face an added, and difficult, burden trying to ensure the quality provided by nongovernment partners. The capacities required of government in regulating the nonstate sector are quite different from those required for managing its own service providers.

Thus leveraging the private sector role to achieve the health MDGs requires government to chart a path combining the potential for increased access—especially for the poor—with the need for ensuring safety and quality. Some of the lessons of experience to date are the following:

- Health care financed and delivered solely by government has been expected to produce more equitable, efficient, and effective service delivery aimed at achieving the MDGs than that provided by private actors. There are many positive examples where this expectation has been met, but also many disappointing ones. Insufficient funding, poor governance, and other institutional failings have all been cited as major reasons that government programs fall short. In many circumstances, strong action to remedy weak government performance, including additional resources and innovations in governance and accountability, must be a key element of strategies to achieve the MDGs.
- Totally private financing and delivery arrangements, where feasible, make services physically available but often do not deliver good quality and may impose a

large financial burden on users. In some situations, such as remote rural areas, private formal alternatives are not available. Unitary private financing and provision favors locations and populations who can pay and will trade off quality when users cannot pay for it. There are many opportunities for private providers to take advantage of market imperfections, such as information asymmetry to the detriment of consumers' welfare and specific outcomes. Informal private sector providers raise additional concerns of poor quality, lack of accountability, and illegality. Governments and development partners may consider actions to support unitary private financing and delivery arrangements, but they should also pay adequate attention to regulation and safeguards to ensure quality and financial protection. Development of these arrangements should not work to the detriment of support for essential services for the poor.

■ Mixed models, involving government and private financial intermediaries working together, are producing a number of innovative approaches. One promising approach gaining wider acceptance is the use of public financing and private provision to expand access and ensure quality. Those making use of public financing and private provision (such as contracting out) have shown that good health outcomes and financial protection are possible under these arrangements and can be done efficiently compared with government delivery. Use of these approaches is spreading, although high-quality monitoring and evaluation is still limited. These types of public-private partnership place new demands on governments to manage these new relationships effectively. When government skills and capacities to do so are not sufficiently developed, there is a greater risk of poor quality, inefficiency, and inequity.

■ The range of experience is also growing for the reverse kind of partnership—private financing and public provision. Much international discussion has focused on one aspect of private financing—user fees for public services. But beyond user fees, there is a wide range of innovative new approaches to mobilize private financing in support of public provision for public health goals more broadly. These seem to be making positive contributions and are getting strong support from new private sector actors in global health. Governments and development partners should support these new initiatives while taking care to avoid duplication of efforts and competition among supplemental funds for scarce system resources like trained personnel.

Perhaps even more than education, in health there are many new vehicles for action in the nongovernment sector that promote innovative strategies. Large private funders have been more receptive to new approaches and to working with a broad range of partners. This is proving to be a promising engine of innovation to which governments are increasingly receptive. One emerging opportunity is the High Level Task Force on Innovative Financing for Health Systems, mentioned earlier, which will be considering a number of different strategies to increase both public and private sources of finance for increased investments in systems to accelerate MDG gains. Concurrently, there are new efforts under way to ensure better coordination and reduce transaction costs, like the International Health Partnership Plus (IHP+). The IHP+ has introduced new mechanisms at the country level to improve coordination among public and private sector partners, and to reduce the transaction costs accompanying increases in the number of partners, as new organizations become more active through joint acceptance of common national plans and reporting standards.

Common to both health and education, a key take-away message from this chapter is that improving service delivery via either the government or the private sector, or in public-private partnerships of various kinds, will require strengthening of government performance. Whether in terms of its own internal governance and accountability mechanisms, its ability to supervise contracts or diverse new funding sources, or its capacity to regulate nongovernment providers, government has a central role to play in accelerating progress toward the human development MDGs.

Leveraging the private sector role to achieve the human development MDGs is increasingly in the mainstream, and this trend is likely to continue. It does not mean a lesser government role in human development, but rather a somewhat different and even expanded role. It is not a panacea for the problems many countries face in accelerating MDG achievement, and it can be the cause of problems as well as a solution. But ample evidence demonstrates that the private sector can contribute substantially and in increasingly diverse ways to human development. The world needs to mobilize all its tools on the road to 2015.

Notes

1. A number of authors (for example, Bennett et al. 1997) define private sector providers as those not under the "direct control" of the government. While often used, this definition introduces some ambiguity in defining both "direct" and "control."

2. Barr 1993.

3. Bennett, McPake, and Mills 1997; Brugha and Zwi 1998.

4. Preker, Harding, and Travis 2000.

5. www.measuredhs.com.

6. Supon 2008. The distinction between formal and informal private providers captures whether service providers have formal (usually legally recognized) qualifications. In most cases these are qualified practitioners of allopathic medicine including both paramedics and physicians. In some countries where traditional medicine is formally recognized, traditional practitioners could also be classified as formal providers. Informal providers are typically legally unqualified or semiqualified and community based, such as traditional birth attendants or unlicensed village doctors and drug sellers. However, patients and communities may not understand these distinctions and may recognize many different types of providers without reference to this formal-informal distinction.

7. Mills and others 2002; Brugha and Zwi 1998.

8. Uplekar 2000.

9. Chabikuli and others 2002.

10. QAP 2002.

11. Das and Hammer 2004.

12. Boller, Wyss, and Tanner 2003.

13. Walker and others 2001.

14. Berman and Chawla 1999.

15. See Patrinos, Barrera-Osorio, and Guaqueta (2009) for a more detailed account of the private sector role in education.

16. Patrinos Barrera-Osorio, and Gauqueta 2009.

17. http://foundationcenter.org/newsletters/.

18. World Bank 2007.

19. Churchill 2006.

20. www.basixindia.com.

21. For more on these organizations, see their websites: www.msf.org; www.savethechildren.org; and www.path.org.

22. For more on these organizations, see their websites: www.arhap.uct.ac.za/; and www.amref.org.

23. www.internationalhealthpartnership.net/taskforce.html.

4

Scaling Up Aid to Poor Countries

The global financial crisis is impacting an increasing number of developing countries. Low-income countries, which had previously been relatively shielded from the immediate effects of the crisis, are now particularly vulnerable. They are facing shrinking export markets, sharply lower commodity prices, and declining growth rates. The global crisis has raised the risk of poverty and hardship for households in poor countries—about 40 percent of developing countries are highly exposed to the poverty effects of the crisis, and a majority of them are in Sub-Saharan Africa. At the same time, the weakening of economic activity is depressing fiscal revenues in these countries, even as social, infrastructure, and other public spending needs are rising. More than half of low-income countries could see a decline in revenue-to-GDP ratios in 2009. But most low-income country governments will not be able to make up the shortfall in their budgets by borrowing domestically or internationally. The increased fiscal pressures are placing the delivery of basic services at risk and constraining these countries' ability to undertake countercyclical spending.

Without additional external assistance, the impact on poor countries could be severe. Donors have a key role to play in helping low-income countries to protect hard-won gains on the Millennium Development Goals

(MDGs) through support of social safety nets and key development programs. However, concerns are growing that aid could be cut, precisely when an increase is sorely needed. Aid budgets are beginning to come under pressure as advanced economies implement large stimulus packages in response to the deepening global crisis. Donors must resist such pressures and deliver on aid commitments. But meeting existing commitments may not be enough. Indeed, there is a strong case for going beyond those commitments in view of the increased needs of countries hit hard by the crisis.

The Vulnerability Fund proposed by World Bank President Robert Zoellick is a mechanism that can be used to channel additional support. The fund, which would require developed countries to pledge 0.7 percent of their stimulus packages for developing countries, would assist vulnerable countries to protect critical spending.[1] By supporting growth in developing countries, the additional aid effort would be an investment in global economic recovery.

In light of the current global downturn, the need to make development assistance work better—predictable and timely aid that is aligned with country priorities and focused on results—has taken on added urgency. At the High-Level Forum on Aid Effectiveness held in Accra, donors and partner countries recognized the need to implement more reforms at a faster pace to meet the 2010 Paris Declaration targets. Within the context of a changing aid landscape, forum participants also sought to enhance aid effectiveness by acknowledging the need to embrace all development actors—bilateral, multilateral, private sector, global funds, and civil society organizations. Moving forward, the challenge will be to convert promises and intentions into actions.

Aid from private actors, particularly foundations and businesses, has grown rapidly in recent years, although there is some concern that the current crisis may interrupt this trend. Private participation brings new resources and innovative approaches to address pressing development problems. The size and impact of private donors' activities are influencing the aid agenda in profound ways. Public-private partnerships in aid programs are growing for key global priorities such as health, education, and climate change. As the role of private actors in the development arena expands, so does the need for improved aid coordination and alignment.

The Heavily Indebted Poor Countries (HIPC) Initiative and the Multilateral Debt Relief Initiative (MDRI) have substantially lowered the debt burdens of poor countries, but the current crisis could jeopardize gains in debt sustainability. Debt reduction combined with improved policies had created fiscal space to increase poverty-reducing spending in many HIPCs. Some countries may have scope for undertaking appropriate fiscal stimulus to cushion the impact of the global crisis, but many others are constrained by debt sustainability or resource availability. Creditors and borrowers need to ensure that new financing is on appropriate terms to maintain long-term debt and fiscal sustainability.

Rising Needs, Uncertain Aid Prospects

From the food and fuel crises to the financial crisis, global challenges are placing an extraordinary strain on poor countries. On the one hand, these crises are exposing households to the increased risk of poverty and hardship, especially where initial poverty levels are high. On the other, they are adversely impacting budgetary positions. Low-income countries, especially in Sub-Saharan Africa, are particularly vulnerable. Additional development assistance is essential to lessen the impact on these countries. But prospects for higher aid are uncertain amid heightened fiscal pressures in donor countries. Indeed, there is a risk that aid flows could decline.

Low-income Countries' Needs Are Increasing

Food crisis. The sharp rise in food prices between 2005 and 2008 pushed an estimated 160 million to 200 million more people into extreme poverty. Although food prices have since moderated, and some of the poverty effects have been reversed, the underlying problem of a sustainable global food supply persists.[2] The Comprehensive Framework for Action, which draws upon the World Bank's New Deal on Global Food Policy, represents a coordinated response to address the global food crisis.[3] It combines immediate actions to increase food availability to meet the needs of vulnerable populations with steps to strengthen food security in the longer run by addressing the underlying factors driving the food crisis. Preliminary estimates of the global incremental requirement for improving food security range from $25 billion to $40 billion a year. The High-Level Task Force on the Global Food Crisis has urged donors to double food assistance and to raise the share of agriculture in official development assistance (ODA) from 3 percent to 10 percent within five years.[4] It is important that the increase in resources for agriculture represent additional financing and not a diversion of funds from other sectors. Equally important, the resources should be provided in a predictable and flexible way.

Financial crisis. Following on the heels of the food crisis, the global financial crisis is straining countries even further. As the impact of the global slowdown on low-income countries intensifies in 2009, fiscal positions (already weakened by events in 2008) in these countries will come under increasing stress. The International Monetary Fund (IMF) estimates that about a quarter of low-income countries will face a fall in revenue of more than 2 percentage points of GDP in 2009.[5] Preliminary findings by the World Bank show that only 13 percent of low-income countries for which data are available will run a budget surplus in 2009 (compared with 28 percent in 2008 and 34 percent in 2007).[6] Countries in Sub-Saharan Africa and Europe and Central Asia are facing an especially large deterioration in their budget balances: budget deficits as a share of GDP are expected to rise on average by 4.7 percentage points in Africa and by 2 percentage points in Europe and Central Asia.

Under current crisis conditions, most low-income countries have little maneuvering room to secure more borrowing or raise revenues. Even countries that have the macroeconomic space and administrative capacity to support higher fiscal deficits will have difficulty securing financing.[7] This limited fiscal capacity will constrain poor countries'

ability to maintain basic services, let alone undertake countercyclical increases in spending. Without increased assistance, millions more could face malnourishment and slip into poverty. Investment in infrastructure and productive sectors will also be hit, threatening long-term growth prospects and progress on the MDGs.

The likely fiscal impact of the crisis on poor countries makes it all the more urgent to increase development assistance, including delivering on past aid commitments and responding to the additional needs arising from the crisis. For many poor countries, timely availability of increased assistance will be key in enabling them to protect essential social safety nets and support development programs critical for growth.

There Are Large Gaps between Aid Commitments and Delivery

Recent ODA trends show a wide implementation gap. Progress on aid volumes has been mixed in recent years. Preliminary estimates show that net ODA from Development Assistance Committee (DAC) members moved sharply higher in 2008 to $119.8 billion, an increase of 10.2 percent in real terms (figure 4.1). The uptick in ODA followed two years of declining aid, as official debt relief operations returned to more normal

FIGURE 4.1 DAC members' net ODA 1990–2008

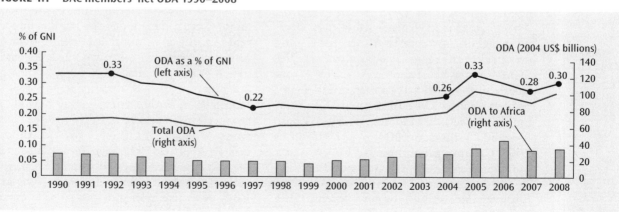

Source: OECD database.
Note: 2008 data are preliminary.

levels in 2006–07. The expansion in ODA boosted donors' ODA share in gross national income (GNI) from 0.28 percent in 2007 to 0.30 percent in 2008, but the share remains below the 0.33 percent level reached in 2005. At Gleneagles, and subsequent summits at Heiligendamm and Hokkaido, G-8 donors promised, with other donors, to double aid to Africa by 2010—an increase of $25 billion a year compared to 2004 amounts—and to increase overall aid by $50 billion a year by 2010. Measured against these pledges, net ODA would need to increase by $29 billion in 2004 terms by 2010. Some existing ODA commitments expressed as a share of GNI could be devalued by falls in expected GNI—consequently, the DAC estimates that the needed increase could be about $20 billion by 2010. ODA trends point to a continuing shortfall on aid commitments.[8]

With debt relief reverting to levels of the early 2000s, the pace of ODA growth will depend upon the expansion of other aid categories. Key among these will be country programmable aid (CPA), which includes program and project aid and technical assistance.[9] But this component of aid has shown only a modest increase in real terms, rising at an average rate of 4 percent per year since 2004. Substantial annual increases in CPA will be needed in 2009–10 to meet the 2010 aid targets. Two years before 2010, the prospects of reaching these targets are uncertain.

Mixed progress on ODA to Sub-Saharan Africa. Donors have made substantial commitments of assistance to Africa, but scaling up of aid to the region has been uneven. Net ODA flows to Sub-Saharan Africa rose from $26 billion to $40 billion during 2004–06, but fell back to $34 billion in 2007. Excluding debt relief, development assistance rose from $22 billion in 2004 to $31 billion in 2007. Country programmable aid grew at a more moderate pace, rising from $19 billion in 2004 to about $23 billion in 2008. Preliminary data show that net bilateral ODA from DAC donors to Sub-Saharan Africa was relatively unchanged in real terms in 2008 at $22.5 billion. But excluding debt relief, bilateral aid to the region was up by 10 percent. However, only one-third of DAC members have made substantial progress in scaling up aid to the region—that is, achieving a 50 percent or larger increase in their assistance to Sub-Saharan Africa. Most donors, including some large ones, are lagging in scaling up aid to the region. Significant growth in aid—25 percent per year—will be needed in 2009–10 to meet donor commitments to provide an additional $25 billion per year in aid to Africa by 2010.

Amid large infrastructure gaps in African countries, donors are beginning to step up support for infrastructure investment in the region.[10] The bulk (nearly 70 percent) of bilateral ODA to Sub-Saharan Africa is allocated to social sectors, and the share of infrastructure is modest at about 10 percent.[11] But a shift toward infrastructure spending appears to be under way, as key bilateral and multilateral donors increase infrastructure commitments under the aegis of the Infrastructure Consortium for Africa.[12] During 2005–07, consortium members increased concessional and nonconcessional infrastructure commitments to Africa by over 75 percent, to $12.4 billion—bilateral ODA increased from $2.2 billion to $3.5 billion and multilateral ODA rose from $2.9 billion to $5.9 billion (figure 4.2). Non-DAC donors such as China and India are playing an expanding role as well, particularly in the energy and infrastructure sectors. Donors' increased focus on infrastructure is welcome, but it is important that this shift not reduce the amount of resources available for much-needed spending on health and education.

Planned scaling-up falls short of targets. A perspective on future aid flows is available from the latest DAC Survey on Aid Allocation Policies and Indicative Forward Spending. The survey shows planned CPA flows, including which countries and regions are likely to receive more aid, and helps to assess whether aid targets are on track globally and for Africa.[13] The response rate to the

2009 survey was 85 percent; some donors have yet to provide indicative forward aid plans.[14] Preliminary survey findings suggest a nearly $30 billion shortfall in the CPA needed to meet the 2010 targeted increase in total net ODA (figure 4.3).[15] CPA will need to rise substantially more than planned if aid targets are to be met.

What do the forward spending plans imply for aid to Africa? Although planned scaling-up is largest for Sub-Saharan Africa, programmed increases fall far short of the required amounts for meeting aid targets for Africa. CPA to Africa increased by $6 billion from 2004 to 2008, and an additional $3 billion is planned during 2009–10. Assuming that debt relief and humanitarian assistance remain at their long-term levels, CPA to Africa would need to rise by about $17 billion for donors to meet the 2010 aid targets for the region.

Non-DAC official donors' aid—growing in importance. Aid from non-DAC donors continued on a strong upward trend in 2007, and preliminary data show that some donors posted large increases in 2008 as well. ODA for donors reporting to DAC was $5.6 billion in 2007, an increase of 7.5 percent over 2006 levels and 50 percent over 2004 volumes. Arab donors provided $2.6 billion in assistance, led by Saudi Arabia with $2 billion. ODA from non-DAC Organisation for Economic Co-operation and Development (OECD) countries was $2.1 billion, nearly double the 2004 level, with the Republic of Korea and Turkey providing well over $500 million each in aid. Among nonreporters, Brazil's assistance was estimated at $437 million, India's development cooperation expenditure was about $1 billion, and the Russian Federation's an estimated $210 million.[16] Official numbers are not available for China's aid, but estimates place this amount at about $1.4 billion in 2007.[17] South-South cooperation is beginning to provide larger amounts of resources for development, particularly in the productive sectors and infrastructure, areas that had received less attention from DAC donors

FIGURE 4.2 Increase in donor financing for infrastructure in Sub-Saharan Africa

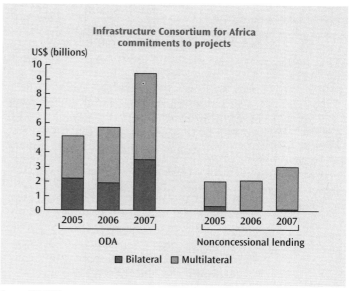

Source: ICA 2007.
Note: Consortium members include G-8 bilateral donors and multilateral agencies.

FIGURE 4.3 Gap between forward aid plans and required increases

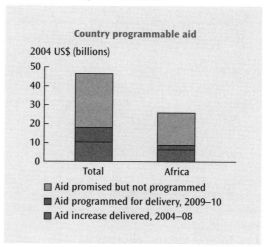

Sources: OECD 2009a and 2009b and staff estimates.
Note: The figure is based on survey results of donors' indicative aid plans.

in recent years. The rise in non-DAC ODA increases the importance of efforts to improve the availability of information about these flows and enhance coordination between all donors.

Sovereign wealth funds. The growth of sovereign funds holds the promise of an additional source of development finance. The IMF estimates that $2 trillion to $3 trillion is held in sovereign wealth funds (SWFs) and that this amount could reach $6 trillion to $10 trillion by 2013.[18] These valuations will now be lower as a result of the decline in asset values caused by the financial crisis. According to the Global Financial Stability Report, governments establish SWFs for several reasons: stabilization funds, savings funds for future generations, reserves investment corporations, development funds, and contingent pension reserve funds.[19] These objectives depend upon country circumstances and can change over time. Sovereign wealth funds have the potential to become a significant source of development finance.

Although the bulk of SWF resources are invested in industrial countries, these funds are beginning to invest in emerging markets as well, especially in Asia. Portfolio diversification could motivate these funds to invest in other developing countries, including those in Africa. Through its recently established Sovereign Funds Initiative, the International Finance Corporation (IFC) is attempting to connect long-term commercial capital from state-owned investors with the large and growing investment needs of private companies in developing countries. The initiative leverages IFC contributions of up to $200 million to raise $1 billion from sovereign saving pools—SWFs, superannuation funds, pension schemes—to invest in equity in "frontier emerging markets" in Africa and Latin America and the Caribbean.[20]

The Global Financial Crisis Is Jeopardizing ODA Prospects

Prospects for reaching the 2010 targets have become more uncertain. Even before the financial crisis, the gap between aid commitments and aid delivery was large. The crisis has heightened concerns that aid budgets will come under pressure, further jeopardizing attainment of the 2010 aid targets. In October 2008 the heads of OECD and DAC called on major donors to stand by their aid pledges. At the Monterrey Follow-up Conference on Financing for Development (in Doha), participants underscored the importance of meeting aid commitments. At the recently concluded London summit of the Group of Twenty (G-20), donors reiterated their commitment to meeting ODA pledges made at Gleneagles. But whether donor agencies will be able to hold the line in what are likely to be tough domestic budget negotiations and meet these pledges remains to be seen. Ireland has already announced a cut of nearly €100 million (a 10.6 percent decline) in its 2009 aid budget,[21] and there are indications that Italy's aid budget may also be cut.[22] An exception is Japan, which promised recently (at Davos) to augment its ODA by about 20 percent over the next three years.[23]

The impact of the current global crisis on development assistance will depend upon the severity and duration of the crisis. Evidence from recent slowdowns suggests that the association between aid disbursements and donor output is ambiguous, especially over shorter periods, and that aid is quite resilient to mild recessions—that is, it is not procyclical with respect to donor country output in a mild, short-duration crisis.[24] For example, ODA from the United States has actually increased in periods of declining national income; in 2001 and 2002, U.S. aid rose despite an eight-month recession in 2001 linked to the bursting of the dot-com bubble.[25]

But history also suggests that the longer and deeper the crisis, the larger the impact. Recent historical evidence shows that aid has contracted in periods of financial crisis. Finland, Norway, and Sweden all dropped their aid significantly following these countries' financial crises in 1991.[26] In the aftermath of the financial crisis, Finland's economy contracted by 11 percent and its aid by 60 percent. Moreover, aid recovery was slow following the financial crises in these countries: Norway and Sweden saw a recovery to precrisis aid levels in six to nine years, but

Finland's aid has yet to surpass precrisis levels (figure 4.4). Japan, which experienced a collapse of asset market prices in 1990, saw a sharp drop in aid flows as well. Based on these findings, the outlook for aid in the current global downturn is not encouraging.

The weight of empirical evidence suggests that deterioration in advanced countries' fiscal situation is likely to have adverse consequences for aid budgets. A study of the macroeconomic determinants of foreign aid notes that because aid is a discretionary item in government budgets, it is a function of a country's fiscal situation.[27] Using a sample of 15 donor countries for 1980–2004, the study finds that gross public debt is a significant determinant of aid: a 10 percent increase in the ratio of public sector debt to GDP is associated with a decline of 0.012 percent in the share of aid in GDP in the short run and of 0.023 percent in the long run (figure 4.5). Overall, the stance of fiscal policy has a statistically significant impact on aid. Thus a large deficit along with a high stock of public debt would be a drag on foreign aid. The study also finds that European Union countries' foreign aid is more sensitive to fiscal conditions than aid in other developed countries. With advanced-country governments poised to take on large amounts of debt stemming from stimulus packages and bank bailouts, the consequences for ODA in the medium term could be severe.

Aid volumes are affected by currency movements as well. Because aid budgets are set in donors' own currency, the recent appreciation of the U.S. dollar against most major currencies will deflate aid volumes measured in current dollar terms. Aid wiped out by currency movements in 2009 could be on the order of $3 billion to $5 billion (box 4.1). The analysis here is in U.S. dollars because international targets for ODA are in U.S. dollar terms. The outcome would be different if another currency was used as a benchmark.

Will public support for development aid remain high? Any discussion of the impact of the current global crisis on aid needs to

FIGURE 4.4   Financial crisis and aid response

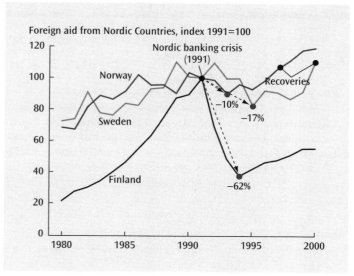

Source: Roodman 2008.

FIGURE 4.5   Ratios of public debt and ODA to gross national income for 22 DAC donors, 1980–2007

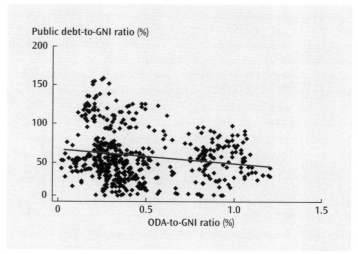

Sources: Faini 2006 and staff estimates.

address the importance of noneconomic factors, such as security and national concerns and public opinion, in motivating aid. Public opinion toward aid in donor countries is an important factor determining aid levels.[28] One examination of public attitudes toward foreign aid finds that individual

BOX 4.1   The indirect impact of the crisis on aid flows

Worries that the financial crisis may make some donors less willing to give aid are justifiable. But that direct effect of falling aid dollars may be compounded by the indirect effect that is happening through exchange rate movements. When donor governments allocate aid resources they do so in their local currency. Hence, the real value of aid to recipient countries hinges, in part, on currency exchange rates. Unfortunately, recent currency movements stand to lower the value of aid in 2009.

The global financial crisis has produced an appreciation of the dollar against many donor currencies. The euro, for example, was worth 18 cents less in February 2009 than its average for 2008. Even if European aid levels stay constant ($32.8 billion in 2007, in nominal terms, from Euro Area bilateral donors and the European Commission), this exchange rate adjustment translates to a $3.9 billion loss in the value of aid. Similarly, the pound sterling is worth 38 cents less, depressing U.K. aid contributions by $1.1 billion. And the SDR (special drawing right)—which is assumed to be a good proxy denomination for multilateral funds—has fallen by 8 cents against the dollar: a $1.4 billion loss. Smaller donors like Australia, Canada, and Norway have also seen their currencies drop. Among major donors, only the yen has appreciated, pushing up the value of Japan's contribution.

Aggregated across all donors, exchange rate movements could depress the value of aid by nearly $8 billion. Of course, not all aid resources are affected by currency movements in the same way. Technical cooperation, for example, is less sensitive to currency movements; more often than not, these resources are used to pay donor-country consultants in donor-country currency and so the real value may be unaffected. Debt relief and certain forms of humanitarian assistance operate in a similar way. Considering these types of aid, a rough estimate of aid wiped out by currency movements in 2009 is $3 billion to $5 billion.

Exchange rate changes and the value of aid

Donor	Currency	2007 ODA, nominal US$ (millions)	Exchange rate change (against dollar), 2008 average to 02/09/09	Change in value of aid, US$ (millions, held at 2007 levels)
DAC European Union members (less the United Kingdom)	euros	21,694	−0.177	−2,606
European Commission	euros	11,095	−0.177	−1,333
Multilateral funds	SDRs	27,457	−0.083	−1,437
United States	dollars	18,901		0
United Kingdom	pounds sterling	5,602	−0.376	−1,135
Japan	yen	5,778	0.001	709
Other donors		14,529		−1,913
All donors, total		105,056		−7,716

Source: Kharas 2009.

factors such as religiosity, attitudes toward poverty, attention to international news and events, and trust in others are important in influencing people's support of aid.[29] The good news is that public support for helping poor countries to develop has consistently been above 70 percent during 1983–2004

and was above 90 percent in 2004.[30] Recent evidence suggests that support for development assistance remains high in donor countries. For example, results from a French poll conducted in October 2008 reveal that over three-quarters of those polled favored maintaining or increasing aid to poor countries, despite the financial crisis, and only a fifth favored decreasing aid. These attitudes, however, may not be immune to the severity and duration of the crisis. Continued strong public support for development aid in donor countries will be an important element in the aid response to the current financial crisis.

Poor countries will be especially hard hit by any contraction in assistance. Aid constitutes a dominant share of external resources in these countries, despite the growing importance of other sources of development finance. Figure 4.6 shows that in nearly 50 percent of poor countries (IDA-eligible countries), the share of ODA is over 10 percent of recipient GNI. Over four-fifths of these highly aid-dependent countries are in Sub-Saharan Africa; several of them are also fragile countries. Aid also makes up a large share of fiscal revenues; for example, aid accounted for around 40 percent of budget revenues in Ghana and Mali in 2006. Many poor countries also rely heavily on remittances, so a slowdown in remittance

receipts is worrisome as well. Following a sharp deceleration in 2008, remittance growth is projected to turn negative in 2009. Sub-Saharan Africa could see a downturn of at least 4.4 percent. Varying country circumstances will translate into differential impacts on countries, but several countries could face both an aid and a remittance squeeze.

Aid Effectiveness Agenda: Improving Aid Delivery

The 2005 Paris Declaration on Aid Effectiveness has generated a common sense of purpose and a momentum for change, but concrete actions to advance aid effectiveness are lagging. Evidence from the OECD 2008 monitoring survey on aid effectiveness shows a lack of progress toward Paris targets.[31] The survey results point to considerable variation across both indicators and countries. One area of notable improvement is the quality of country systems for managing public funds. Substantial progress has also been made in untying aid and in coordinating technical cooperation.

FIGURE 4.6 Dependence on aid remains high in low-income countries

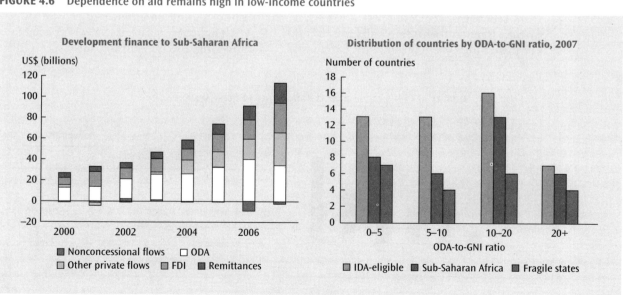

Sources: OECD database; World Development Indicators; Global Development Finance databases; staff estimates.
Note: Data on ODA/GNI are for 49 IDA-eligible countries. The Sub-Saharan Africa and fragile states groups are not mutually exclusive.

A recent study finds a strong relationship between the quality of country public financial management (PFM) systems and donors' use of those systems (figure 4.7).[32] The quality of PFM systems remains significant when controlling for donor characteristics, other recipient characteristics, and the donor share of aid in country. The study also finds that when donors have a larger presence in a country, they have a larger stake in overall country outcomes and in using country systems, which in turn strengthens country ownership and PFM capacity.

The monitoring survey presents a mixed picture for Africa. Progress on some indicators such as untying of aid is similar to the global average, but improvement is much slower in most other areas. Particularly sobering is the weaker performance, relative to the 2005 baseline, on the use of country systems and on donor coordination of missions and country studies.

At the Third High-Level Forum on Aid Effectiveness, held in Accra in 2008, donors and partner countries recognized the need to address three key challenges to accelerating progress on aid effectiveness: country ownership of development priorities, effective and inclusive partnerships, and achieving and accounting for development results. The Accra Agenda for Action calls for strengthening country ownership by broadening country-level policy dialogue to include parliaments, local governments, and civil society organizations; enhancing the capacity of developing countries to lead and manage development processes; and increasing the use of developing-country systems as a first option.

Building effective and inclusive partnerships for development will require partnerships that embrace all development actors—bilateral, multilateral, private sector, global funds, and civil society organizations. The action agenda recognized the changing aid landscape: the growing scale of South-South cooperation; the increasing role of non-DAC official donors, private philanthropy, and partnerships; and the associated need for improved coordination and better information on flows from different sources. It also recognized the need for reducing fragmentation of aid and further untying aid.

The need for better aid information could be helped by the International Aid Transparency Initiative, which was launched by the United Kingdom and other public and private donors at the High-Level Forum in Accra. The initiative is looking into ways to improve the reliability, detail, and timeliness of information on public and private aid.

A particular focus of the action agenda is delivering and accounting for development

FIGURE 4.7 Quality of PFM systems affects donors' use of those systems

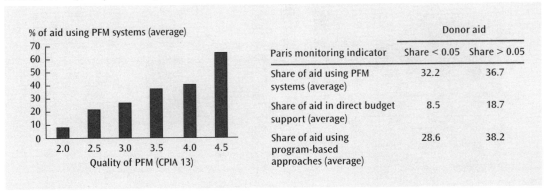

Paris monitoring indicator	Donor aid	
	Share < 0.05	Share > 0.05
Share of aid using PFM systems (average)	32.2	36.7
Share of aid in direct budget support (average)	8.5	18.7
Share of aid using program-based approaches (average)	28.6	38.2

Source: Knack 2009.
Note: Country Policy and Institutional Assessment (CPIA) data are for 2006. Higher rating denotes better performance.

results. The action agenda calls on donors to align their monitoring with country information systems and to support measures to strengthen developing countries' national statistical capacity and information systems. It also calls on donors and developing countries to jointly determine conditions for aid disbursements, with conditions to be based on developing countries' national development strategies. Other actions include increasing the medium-term predictability of aid—for example, donors providing three-to-five-year forward spending plans. The results of the latest OECD monitoring survey show that on average only 45 percent of aid is delivered on schedule.[33] Budget support survey data from the Strategic Partnership for Africa also show that forward projections of aid can be very unreliable. Using aid projections and outturns data derived from macroeconomic programming exercises by IMF staff, one study found that on average disbursements of budget aid differed from projected amounts by about 30 percent.[34] The follow-up conference at Doha also focused on improving the quality of aid. Participants reiterated a need to make aid more predictable by regularly providing developing-country partners with multiyear indicative information on forward spending plans.

Along with improving aid predictability, donors also need to turn their attention to the issue of aid volatility. Aid flows tend to be more volatile than other forms of revenue and output.[35] Uncertainty of aid flows diminishes the true value of these resources. One study uses the concept of "certainty equivalence" to estimate the cost of volatile flows at 15–20 percent of the total value of aid.[36]

Implementing the Accra Agenda for Action requires strong political support and coordinated action among all actors. The challenges to implementation are neither new nor simple. It remains to be seen whether donors will be able to step up the pace of reform. Improving the quality of aid has taken on an added urgency in the face of pressures on aid budgets. The current crisis should give an impetus to implementation of the Accra agenda.[37]

Mobilizing Private Aid for Development

Private actors, particularly foundations and businesses, are becoming increasingly important players in development finance. Along with new resources, private participation brings innovation. Private giving has shifted from the traditional charity approach to one of active participation by private donors in the aid community, including bringing a business approach to development assistance.

Trends in Private Giving

Comprehensive data on private giving are not available, but all indications point to a large and growing amount of private resources being devoted to development purposes. Private international giving as reported to the OECD shows a strong upward trend in grant making. Private giving for international purposes climbed to $18.6 billion in 2007, bucking the recent slide in official aid and representing more than a 25 percent increase over 2006 levels (figure 4.8). The 2007 increase was driven by a surge in private giving in the United States, which accounts for 65 percent of the total. Canada (7.5 percent) and Germany (7 percent) accounted for sizable shares in total private giving as well, closely followed by the United Kingdom (3.7 percent) and Australia (3.6).

Although large, these numbers do not capture the full extent of private giving. For example, corporations are not included, and some countries do not provide any reports. The Hudson Institute estimates that the extent of underreporting is large. For the United States alone the institute estimates that private international giving by foundations, corporations, educational institutions, religious organizations, and private and voluntary organizations was $36.9 billion in 2007—three times the $12.2 billion

FIGURE 4.8 Private grants data: undercounting philanthropy

Grants by private voluntary agencies as reported to the OECD
US$ (billions)

2002: 8.8
2006: 14.8
2007: 18.6

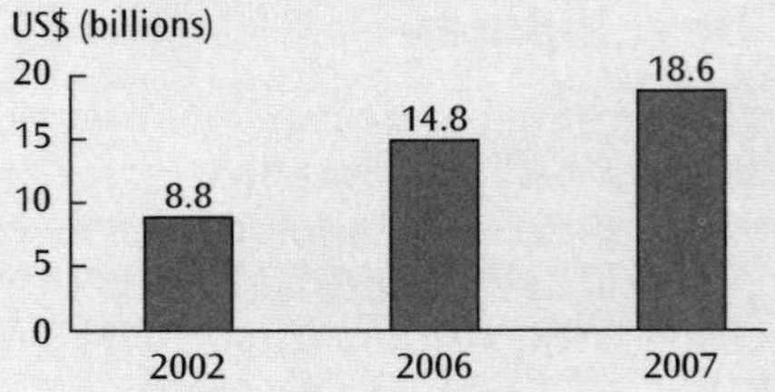

Gaps in grants data reported to the OECD in 2007
US$ (billions)

	Reported	Estimates
United States	12.2	36.9
United Kingdom	0.67	4.12
France	Not reported	1.03
Norway	Not reported	0.25
Spain	Not reported	0.36

Sources: OECD database; Hudson Institute 2009; GuideStar Data Services.

reported to the OECD.[38] Likewise, international giving by the United Kingdom was $4.1 billion, six times the reported amount. Private giving by France, Norway, and Spain is not captured in the DAC numbers but is estimated at a combined $1.6 billion.

Foundations and corporations are the most dynamic sectors of private philanthropy. U.S. giving is spurred by the activities of foundations.[39] According to the Foundation Center, there are over 72,000 grant-making private and community foundations in the United States, which contributed an estimated $5.4 billion in 2007.[40] The growth in international giving has far exceeded that of general foundation giving since 2002. The trend in giving is dominated by the Bill and Melinda Gates Foundation. At $2 billion in 2006 (and $2.4 billion in 2007), international grants awarded by this foundation are larger than the combined international grants of the next 14 largest foundations. Increased funding by the Gates Foundation accounted for most of the growth in the share of international giving in total giving by foundations: from 13.8 percent of total giving in 2002 to 22 percent in 2006. This share would have grown even without the Gates Foundation, albeit more modestly from 11 percent to 13 percent. A substantial part of funding to developing countries targets health, but support in other areas such as education and relief efforts has also increased.

Corporate giving is on the rise as well. Results from a survey of U.S.-based companies and corporate foundations indicate that these institutions contributed around $2.3 billion annually in 2006 and 2007 for international development assistance. About two-thirds of this amount was provided in the form of goods and services rather than as cash. The industry with the largest international donations was the pharmaceutical sector—10 pharmaceutical companies reported contributing $1.5 billion internationally in 2007.[41]

The European foundation sector has also been growing, and the number of public-benefit foundations increased by more than 54 percent between 2001 and 2005.[42] But data on European foundations are even more incomplete. Based on a 2007 survey by the European Foundation Centre, European foundations gave $607 million in 2005. Like the U.S. foundations, much of this was directed toward health, followed by education.

Injecting Entrepreneurship in Aid

Private involvement in aid is transforming philanthropy, with traditional giving being replaced by entrepreneurship in aid. The new philanthropists want to bring a business approach to aid and international development—"philanthrocapitalism."[43] The philanthrocapitalist model applies market-based principles to development: problem solving, taking risks, fostering innovation, managing organizational structures, mobilizing media attention to set the agenda, and measuring success.[44] Private engagement is particularly strong in health, education, humanitarian assistance, and climate change activities.

Global corporate citizenship is leading to an increased engagement of business in development. The concept of global corporate citizenship recognizes that businesses are stakeholders in development; in other words, development impacts business. Thus business needs to be committed to addressing global challenges such as public health care, climate change, and environmental sustainability. The involvement by business in development is manifested in several ways: engagement in the community, which is essentially philanthropic (businesses provide money to support good causes but also involve staff in fundraising activities or working on local community projects such as a school, health facility, or training center); commitment to corporate social responsibility, that is, adoption of minimum standards regarding labor practices, the environment, and transparency; enhancement of the development impact of business activity, particularly through research and development, supply chains and subcontractors, and distribution networks; and contribution to global public policy.[45] Because business involvement in development brings more than funding, these contributions are not adequately counted (box 4.2).

The Global Financial Crisis and Prospects for Private Aid

The current global crisis could interrupt the rising trend in private aid. As with official aid, the impact will depend upon the depth and duration of the crisis. Also, the short- and medium-term impacts of the crisis are likely to be different. Nonetheless, the crisis is likely to have a significant negative effect on the ability of foundations, corporations,

and individuals to make new and additional philanthropic commitments. Corporate profits are already adversely affected, and a broad-based decline in financial assets is likely to lower the value of foundations' endowments and their returns. Given difficult economic conditions in their home countries, many philanthropic organizations could pull back their international support and focus more of their resources on local or domestic causes.

Despite a difficult economic environment, some large foundations have issued statements indicating their intentions to maintain grant levels. For example, the Gates Foundation has announced an increase in its total giving for 2009—$3.8 billion compared with $3.3 billion in 2008, representing 7 percent of its assets as opposed to about 5 percent in previous years.[46] This increase comes in the face of a 20 percent decline in the foundation's assets in 2008. The MacArthur Foundation has announced that it plans to maintain grant-making levels in 2009 despite significant endowment losses.[47] But some other foundations have expressed difficulty in maintaining current levels and have even indicated a cutback. For example, the Hewlett Foundation has announced that grants will likely be 5–7 percent lower in 2009 than in 2008.[48]

Past patterns provide some insights on how grant making has been affected by economic crisis. A review of foundations' giving from 1975 to 2007 shows that during the previous recessionary periods of 1980, 1981–82, and 1990–91, grant making held up fairly well.[49] In the 2001 recession, grants declined slightly, but far less than the 10 percent decline in the value of foundations' assets during 2000–02 (figure 4.9). A large number of foundations base their grant budgets on a rolling average of their asset values over two to five years, a practice that helps smooth the effects of asset price fluctuations. Some foundations even increased their payout rate in the 2001 recession to provide resources for activities that they had been supporting over time. New gifts

---

BOX 4.2   Contributions of private actors to development in Sub-Saharan Africa

Early findings from an ongoing study sponsored by the W. F. Kellogg Foundation, the government of Norway, and the World Bank suggest that private actors in Sub-Saharan Africa are contributing to solving development problems in a variety of ways. Private corporations bring more than just funding. They provide opportunities, especially at the local level, to tackle problems that are meaningful for their company, the community, and the country. Trends indicate an increasing space for collaboration and attention to scale and sustainability.

The study finds that corporate contributions are often underrepresented in calculations that are based on corporate social responsibility (CSR) budgets or "giving" programs. Capturing the expenditures on other "core business" activities that have positive spillover effects is difficult, but the results are no less important.

■ In Ghana, the idea of harnessing mainstream business operations and not just CSR budgets for development impact is being adopted by some companies. A good example is Standard Chartered Bank (Gh). This bank has shifted from CSR to the concept of sustainability—a way of doing business that is fundamental to its strategy, is embedded across its businesses, and contributes to shareholder value. The bank realizes that it can have a positive impact on the environment and society, as well as on building a sustainable business, if it focuses on enhancing the economic development of the country in which it operates.

■ Another example of company activities that benefits both the affected communities and the company is the malaria program at AngloGold Ashanti's Obuasi mine (Ghana). This $1.3 million-a-year program has helped reduce malaria incidence at the local hospital from 79,000 cases in 2005 to 21,000 in 2007. The malaria incidence rate among the mine's employees dropped from 238 to 69 over the same period. In addition, the program created 116 jobs and developed ongoing community interaction to sustain the efforts.

■ In Uganda, early estimates show that the corporate sector provides basic services at the community level in which the companies work; however, specific investment figures are difficult to obtain.

Headquarter surveys of foundations, corporations, and nongovernmental organizations (NGOs) suggest that more attention is being given to increasing the impact of single interventions, replicating successful models, and ensuring the sustainability of benefits after the private programs are completed. Firms, foundations, and NGOs are looking for ways to leverage collaboration among themselves and with traditional donors and governments to strengthen the probability of achieving short- and long-term results.

Governments play an important role in facilitating private engagement in development and enhancing its effectiveness. In Sierra Leone, for example, the government is mapping how and where private actors are contributing to health care service delivery. The view is that by knowledge sharing and collaboration, scarce resources can be better allocated and opportunities for strengthening institutional systems or sharing lessons can be facilitated. In Liberia, strong leadership by the government is encouraging private actors to align their contributions in finance and capacity building to the country poverty reduction strategy.

Source: White, Bastoe, and Curry 2009.

---

and bequests and a growth in the number of foundations also helped to reduce the decline in grant volumes. A long and pronounced decline in foundation assets would have troubling consequences for grants, however.

The Foundation Center's analysis of trends in U.S. foundation grant making (excluding the Gates Foundation) also shows that the relative share of resources devoted to international giving remained fairly stable during the economic downturn in 2000–02.[50]

Public-Private Partnerships and Innovative Financing Mechanisms

The growing presence of private actors in aid and development is fostering partnerships between private entities and public institutions. Several factors are motivating this partnership. One is a recognition that official assistance is not enough for meeting the MDGs and related development goals and that private resources, both foreign and domestic, are also needed. A second is the

FIGURE 4.9 Trends in U.S. foundations' assets and giving

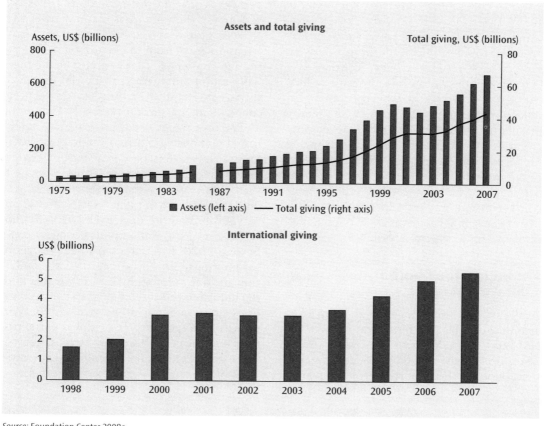

Source: Foundation Center 2008c.
Note: Data on foundations' assets and giving are not available for 1986. Data include the Gates Foundation.

recognition that private participation can bring an increased focus on efficiency and performance and spur innovation.

Through innovative instruments and mechanisms for development, progress is being made on a range of complex issues related to key global priorities, in particular in the areas of health, education, and climate change, as well as on specific country-level challenges. Innovative finance activities and mechanisms are tapping new sources of finance and new actors. Flows from innovative financing approaches are growing.[51] The International Finance Facility for Immunization has raised $1.6 billion, the Advance Market Commitments $1.5 billion, and (PRODUCT)RED™ over $100 million.

The Solidarity levy on airline tickets raised €160 million from France in 2008, and proceeds from auctioning or selling project-based carbon emissions permits under the European Union's Emission Trading System raised €120 million (for investment in climate protection measures in developing countries) from Germany in 2008.[52]

In addition to identifying and efficiently using new sources of public and private funding, innovative financing mechanisms help manage the risks and costs of vulnerability (for example, to weather and to currency and interest rate movements) facing developing countries and provide incentives for implementation. One way that these objectives are achieved is by leveraging private resources to support public purposes in developing countries. An example is the International Finance Facility for Immunization, which front-loads bilateral development aid by issuing bonds to finance high-return activity. Another way is by deploying public resources to reduce the costs and risks of private entry in developing-country markets, and thereby leveraging private investment in developing countries, through guarantees, risk-sharing facilities, and transactional support for public-private partnerships. Two examples are the use of carbon credits and Advance Market Commitments, which help mobilize private sector investment in vaccine development and production (box 4.3).

Financing for Combating Climate Change

Addressing climate change is central to attaining durable progress toward the MDGs and related development outcomes. *Global Monitoring Report 2008* provided a detailed discussion on the importance of integrating

environmental sustainability into core development work. As policy makers focus on addressing the immediate fallout from the current global crisis, they must not shift attention away from the longer-term climate change challenge. Tackling climate change will require mobilizing substantial financial flows—public and private—to developing countries, much beyond current levels.

The investment needs are large. To stabilize greenhouse gas atmospheric concentrations at levels that are considered reachable and manageable, the latest estimates suggest that additional investment required in developing countries will range from $150 billion to $200 billion per year over 2010–20 and will rise to $400 billion per year on average beyond 2020. Estimates vary depending on assumptions, especially regarding the ambition of long-term stabilization targets and the nature of policies adopted to curb greenhouse gas emissions, in particular, the type of instrument, the degree of global participation, and the contribution of various sectors. The estimates also vary depending on perceptions of the scope for cheap energy efficiency

---

BOX 4.3 Advanced market commitments: promoting private investments by leveraging public funds

An advance market commitment (AMC) tackles a long-standing development problem—persistent private sector failures to develop and produce goods needed in developing countries because of perceived insufficient demand or market uncertainty. The pilot focuses on the vaccine market, where research, development, and production of vaccines specific to the needs of the poorest developing countries are limited by the small number of manufacturers, high cost of product development and capacity scale-up, and demand uncertainty. With an AMC, public financing leverages private funds, spurring private sector investment in research, development, and distribution of vaccines.

Official and private donors—Canada, Italy, Norway, Russia, the United Kingdom, and the Bill and Melinda Gates Foundation—have pledged $1.5 billion for a pilot AMC for vaccines against pneumococcal diseases. (The Global Alliance for Vaccines and Immunization will support the AMC operationally and the World Bank will provide the financial platform.) The pilot AMC offers a subsidy to purchase eligible vaccines in exchange for a long-term commitment to supply the vaccine at a low price. For the pilot AMC, donors first commit funds appropriate for a predetermined market size and price with specifications targeting effectiveness and development impact in developing countries. Second, as and when the vaccine becomes available, a credible independent body will determine if the new vaccine meets the target specifications. Approval by that independent body entitles a manufacturer to enter into a supply agreement giving it access to AMC funds subsidizing the purchase of the vaccine. Finally, when AMC funding is depleted, the manufacturer will continue to provide the vaccine at an established price for a specified period to meet continuing demand.

measures and opportunity costs of mitigation measures in the forestry and agriculture sector as well as on the rate of technological change and deployment of climate-friendly technologies. Research, development, and demonstration of mechanisms for producing and using cleaner and safer energy would add anywhere from $10 billion to $100 billion a year to the needed investment.[53]

Financing the costs of adapting to the inevitable amount of warming that the world will experience will also be costly, albeit the estimates of adaptation costs are very incomplete and preliminary.[54] The World Bank puts investment needs in developing countries at $4 billion a year over the next several years, rising to $37 billion a year. Estimates from other international groups working on climate change range from as low as $8 billion a year to a high of $86 billion a year by 2015. Estimates so far are dominated by the cost of climate proofing future infrastructure investments; they thus tend to overlook other forms of adaptation, such as changes in behavior, adjustments in operational practices, or relocation of economic activity. They are also influenced by the estimated level of climate change and resulting effects as well as by the scope of adaptation strategies, which reflect competing understandings of the adaptation process, in particular its relationship to development dynamics.

These needs go far beyond current and upcoming resources. Current climate-related financial flows to developing countries, though growing, cover only a tiny fraction of the estimated amounts needed (table 4.1). The bulk of available and emerging resources dedicated to climate action relates to mitigation (at about $10 billion per year), mainly through carbon market transactions to reduce project-based emissions and to a lesser extent through the recently launched Climate Investment Funds. The Global Environment Facility has been the largest source of grant financing for energy efficiency and renewable energy, with an overall cumulative commitment of over $2.4 billion (since the early 1990s) in mitigation and capacity building. The amounts available for adaptation are about $1 billion per year.

Private sources through carbon markets are mobilizing the bulk of financial flows for mitigation. Recent years have seen strong growth in the carbon market and in private investment in clean energy. The carbon market, the largest share of which is accounted for by the European Union Emission Trading Scheme, was valued at about $120 billion in 2008 (over 12 times its 2005 value). About 2.1 billion metric tons of carbon dioxide equivalent emission reductions have been transacted over 2002–08 under the Clean Development Mechanism (CDM) for an approximate value of $24 billion.[55] It is estimated that some $52 billion in clean energy investment has benefited from this mechanism over 2002–07.[56]

TABLE 4.1 Current dedicated resources for climate change in developing countries
US$ (billions)

Mitigation		Adaptation	
Global Environment Facility, per year	0.25	Least Developed Country Fund, Special Climate Change Fund	0.3
Carbon market, per year	8+	Adaptation Fund	0.3–.0.5
Clean Investment Funds	5+	Clean Investment Funds	≈ 0.5
Other, per year	1+	Other, per year	0.4+
Total, per year	≈ 10	Total, per year	≈ 1

Source: World Bank 2008 and staff estimates.

Much of the financial support for adaptation comes from international donors. Donors have pledged resources through both bilateral and multilateral initiatives, but existing resources and financing instruments for adaptation are modest. An important development is the establishment of the Adaptation Fund, which should provide a boost to mobilizing resources for adaptation (box 4.4). Other sources are the United Nations Framework Convention on Climate Change Special Funds (administered by the Global Environment Facility), made up of a $180 million fund for least-developed countries and a $90 million Special Climate Change Fund, and the Global Facility for Disaster Reduction and Recovery ($40 million in fiscal 2008).

The international community had an estimated $9.5 billion invested in climate-friendly funds—public and private—in 2007, and the size of the funds grew in 2008. Several new bilateral funds have been created by donors to support climate change activities, primarily mitigation—pledges that total $2.7 billion a year over the next few years.[57] Official flows are important for correcting market imperfections, building capacity, and targeting certain areas. Because bilateral initiatives represent ODA, one issue that arises is whether these new flows dedicated to climate change are additional to other ODA commitments. Another issue involves the implications that the proliferation of specialized funds could have for effectiveness of resources. Among multilateral programs, the largest is the Climate Investment Funds Initiative (established by the World Bank jointly with the African Development Bank [AfDB], the Asian Development Bank [ADB], the European Bank for Reconstruction and Development [EBRD], and the Inter-American Bank [IDB]), which is designed to provide

BOX 4.4 The Adaptation Fund: country ownership in adaptation finance

Under the UN Framework Convention on Climate Change process, the Adaptation Fund is intended as a principal source of adaptation support for developing countries and a centerpiece of the international agenda on climate change. The fund is designed to finance concrete climate change adaptation projects and programs that are country driven and based on needs, views, and priorities of eligible developing-country parties to the Kyoto Protocol.

The fund's primary financing comes not from traditional development assistance, but from a 2 percent share of proceeds of certified emissions reductions (CERs) issued by the Clean Development Mechanism (CDM) under the Kyoto Protocol. The Adaptation Fund's financial base is thus precedent-setting: an international base arising from an international treaty. Using a share of the proceeds from CER sales to assist developing countries was envisioned when the Kyoto Protocol was agreed in 1997; the Adaptation Fund was allocated a 2 percent share in 2001.

As of January 12, 2009, the Adaptation Fund held about 4.9 million CERs. Current estimates by the UN Environment Programme's Riscoe Center suggest that the Adaptation Fund will receive about 30 million CERs by 2012. In November the center estimated that a total of 1.518 billion CERs would be issued by 2012, based on the current CDM pipeline and historic approval rates (http://www.cdmpipeline.org/).

The governance of the Adaptation Fund reflects its innovative source of financing. It assigns true ownership to developing countries. Accordingly, 75 percent of the Adaptation Fund Board is made up of representatives from developing countries, including the most affected countries (small island developing states and least-developed countries), and it provides that they can submit proposals directly to the Adaptation Fund Board. The World Bank serves as a trustee to the Adaptation Fund, performing two core functions, trust fund management and monetization of CERs for the Adaptation Fund. The Global Environment Facility serves as its secretariat. Monetization of CERs will start in 2009.

Source: Multilateral Trustee and Innovative Financing Group.

interim, scaled-up funding in the form of grants and concessional financing to help developing countries in their mitigation and adaptation efforts. In September 2009, donors pledged $6.3 billion for the Clean Investment Funds: $4.3 billion for the Clean Technology Fund and $2 billion for the Strategic Climate Fund.[58] Financial flows through CDM and these climate funds are still below required amounts.

The shortfall between needs and resources available for meeting the challenge of climate change in developing countries is enormous. Scaling up financing for climate change in the current global economic environment will be even more of a challenge. In this context it is important to explore synergies in proposed solutions and responses, for instance incentives for energy efficiency improvements, investments in renewable energy sources, and investments in greener infrastructures. Reforming existing market-based mechanisms to boost mobilization of funds and channel investments toward developing countries should also be a high priority, along with increased resource mobilization for adaptation.

Debt Relief: Progress and Challenges

The international community reached a consensus in Monterrey in March 2002 on a global response to address the challenges for financing development, including through debt relief. It was agreed at that time that external debt relief could play an important role in liberating resources that could help foster sustainable growth and development and accelerate progress toward the MDGs. More specifically, the consensus called for the speedy, effective, flexible, and full implementation of the HIPC Initiative, which should be fully financed through additional resources. In 2005, the HIPC Initiative was supplemented with the MDRI, whereby four multilateral financial institutions (IDA, the IMF, the AfDB, and the IDB) provide additional debt relief with the view to free more

resources for poverty reduction and achieving the MDGs.

Substantial progress has been made since 2002 in implementing debt relief. More than four-fifths of eligible countries (35 out of 41) have passed the decision point and qualified for HIPC Initiative assistance. Of those, 24 countries have reached the completion point and qualified for irrevocable debt relief under the HIPC Initiative and the MDRI. The debt relief committed to the 35 post-decision-point HIPCs amounts to $124 billion (in nominal terms, excluding Côte d'Ivoire), including $52 billion under the MDRI. On average this debt relief represents about 50 percent of these countries' 2007 GDP.

As a result, the debt burdens of many poor countries have been reduced markedly. On average, the debt burden of the 35 HIPCs is expected to be reduced by about 90 percent, compared to their pre-decision-point debt stock. HIPCs' debt service obligations have fallen on average by about two percentage points of GDP since the late 1990s, while poverty-reducing spending has increased on average by about the same amount during this period (figure 4.10).

To facilitate the HIPCs' advances toward debt relief, flexibility has been applied in implementing the initiative while preserving its core principles.[59] However, completing implementation of the HIPC Initiative will still require sustained efforts from the international community. Many of the 17 eligible, pre-completion-point HIPCs face substantial challenges, most in noneconomic areas. Almost half have been affected by war in recent years, and many remain at a high risk of conflict, political instability, or both. Most also have weak policies and institutions. Addressing these challenges will require continued efforts from these countries to strengthen their policies and institutions, together with sustained international support. Additional resources will also have to be marshaled to finance the cost of debt relief to all pre-decision-point HIPCs, including Somalia and Sudan, two countries

FIGURE 4.10   Average debt service and poverty-reducing expenditures

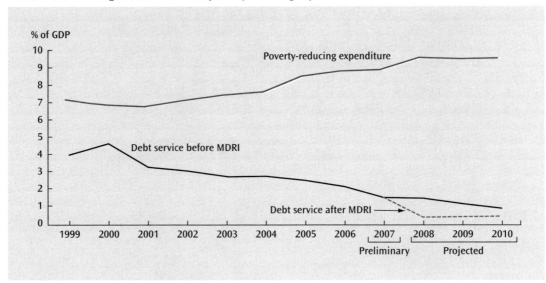

Source: IMF–World Bank 2008; HIPC documents; and IMF staff estimates.

with large and protracted arrears that were not included in the original framework for financing debt relief in the IMF.

Another challenge is to ensure that the HIPCs get full debt relief from all their creditors. Although the largest creditors (the World Bank, the AfDB, the IMF, the IDB, and all Paris Club creditors) provide debt relief in line with their commitments under the HIPC Initiative, and even beyond, others are lagging behind. Smaller multilateral institutions, non–Paris Club official bilateral creditors, and commercial creditors, which together account for about 25 percent of total HIPC Initiative costs, have delivered only a small share of their expected relief so far.[60] A number of commercial creditors have also initiated litigation against the HIPCs, raising significant legal challenges to burden sharing in the context of the initiative.

The World Bank's Debt Reduction Facility (DRF) for IDA-only countries has become one of the key instruments for promoting commercial creditor participation in the HIPC Initiative.[61] Since its establishment, the DRF has supported 24 operations in 21 countries, helping to extinguish about $9 billion of commercial external debt. Over the past 12 months, the DRF has financed a debt buyback for Nicaragua and has provided support for the preparation of debt buybacks for Liberia and Sierra Leone. The DRF-supported buyback for Nicaragua extinguished close to $1.4 billion of commercial external debt (97 percent of eligible claims) on terms consistent with the full delivery of HIPC Initiative debt relief. This operation is particularly important for the DRF in that it extinguished the claims of all litigating creditors.

Debt relief, while welcome, addresses only a relatively small part of the HIPCs' financing needs and cannot ensure debt sustainability permanently (box 4.5). Debt relief savings accrue through time and generally constitute only a moderate share of net aid inflows to the HIPCs. Addressing development needs of the HIPCs, and more generally low-income countries, therefore requires higher new aid flows in addition to debt relief. New flows also allow for a quick and targeted response to address any emerging issues, such as the impact of the current global crisis on poor countries.

BOX 4.5   Results from low-income country debt sustainability analyses

Debt sustainability analyses (DSAs) performed under the Debt Sustainability Framework provide a comprehensive view of the debt outlook for low-income countries. Between 2005, when the framework was introduced, and March 2009, 205 DSAs covering 68 low-income countries were completed; 173 DSAs were published. Recent joint World Bank–IMF DSAs for IDA-only countries and their ratings suggest that about 29 percent of these countries have a low risk of external debt distress (see the figure below). This share is higher for non-HIPCs (42 percent, or 8 countries) and post-MDRI countries (36 percent, or 8 countries). No pre-completion-point HIPC has a low risk rating. Post-MDRI countries perform nearly as well as non-HIPCs, thanks in large measure to the provision of debt relief, which has decreased their external debt ratio considerably. Another 32 percent of IDA-only countries have a moderate risk rating. This share is again higher for post-MDRI countries (45 percent, or 10 countries) and non-HIPCs (26 percent, or 5 countries). In these countries' DSAs, vulnerabilities appear in stress tests. Debt dynamics seem particularly sensitive to shocks to exports.

Debt sustainability is a major concern for the 39 percent (22 countries) of countries rated at high risk or in debt distress. Of these 22 countries, 12 are pre-completion-point HIPCs (80 percent of this country group), 6 are non-HIPCs (32 percent), and 4 are post-MDRI countries (18 percent). Again, debt dynamics seem particularly sensitive to shocks to exports.

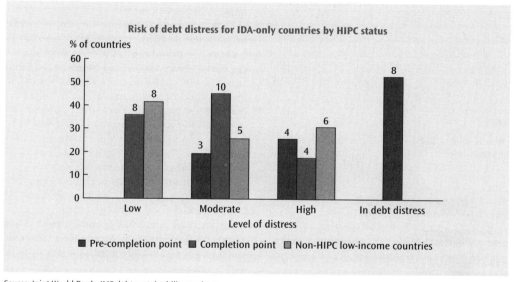

Risk of debt distress for IDA-only countries by HIPC status

Source: Joint World Bank–IMF debt sustainability analyses.
Note: Data are for 56 low-income countries. Numbers above bars indicate number of countries.

These new flows need to be on appropriate terms to ensure that debt sustainability, which has been restored through debt relief, is maintained in the future. The joint IMF–Bank Debt Sustainability Framework for low-income countries is an important tool that supports low-income countries in their efforts to achieve their development goals, while reducing the risks of future debt problems.

Maintaining debt sustainability after receiving debt relief highlights the need for strengthening debt management in these countries. The IMF and the World Bank have stepped up their efforts to assist low-income countries to enhance public debt management frameworks and have developed a comprehensive debt management tool kit for low-income countries.[62] One building block of this tool kit facilitates assessment of a country's debt management performance using 15 indicators that span the six core functions of public debt management. This assessment, known as DeMPA, has been applied in 20 low-income and 3 middle-income countries (as of December 2008). Early results from the assessment reports are helping to identify common priority areas for debt management reform across countries. Across the six core functions, operational risk management and cash flow forecasting and cash balance management appear as key weak spots (figure 4.11). Less than half of the sample complies with minimum requirements for sound governance and strategy development.[63] Countries appear to do better in the areas of coordination with macroeconomic policies and debt records and reporting, while roughly half scored a C or

higher with respect to borrowing and related financing activities.[64]

DeMPA can serve as an essential input for the second component of the tool kit—formulation of a debt management strategy that is consistent with long-term debt sustainability. The outputs from the assessment and the strategy formulation can also feed into the third building block—a reform plan. The recently established donor-funded Debt Management Facility will support a substantial scaling up of the World Bank–IMF's work in strengthening debt management capacity and institutions.

Notes

1. Robert B. Zoellick, "A Stimulus Package for the World," *New York Times*, January 23, 2009 (http://www.nytimes.com/2009/01/23/opinion/23zoellick.html).
2. Voluntary contributions to the World Food Programme jumped to over $5 billion in 2008 from $2.7 billion in 2007. Among the largest donors were the United States ($2.1 billion), Saudi Arabia ($503 million), the European Union ($355 million), and Canada ($275 million); see http://www.wfp.org/appeals/wfp_donors/2008.asp?section=3&sub_section=4). The World Bank established a $1.2 billion rapid financing facility—Global Food Response Program—in May 2008 to speed assistance to the neediest countries.
3. This framework has been developed by the U.N. Secretary General's High-Level Task Force on the Global Food Crisis.
4. The task force has proposed establishing a Financial Coordination Mechanism to facilitate quick mobilization and disbursement of additional donor resources.
5. IMF 2009.
6. PREM 2008, 2009a, 2009c.
7. Only a third of developing countries, and even fewer low-income countries, have reasonable fiscal capacity to expand fiscal deficits. See DEC-PREM 2009 and PREM 2009b.
8. See the UN's MDG Gap Task Force 2008 report.
9. CPA excludes debt relief, exceptional assistance such as humanitarian aid (which can rise and fall in response to unexpected events such as natural disasters) and food aid, some specific items including administrative costs, core funding

FIGURE 4.11 The DeMPA tool: assessing core functions of public debt management

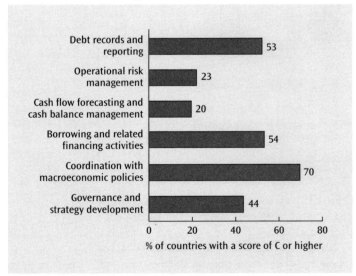

Source: IMF–World Bank 2009 forthcoming.
Note: A score of C indicates the minimum requirement for effective debt management.

of NGOs, imputed student costs and refugees in donor countries. In 2008, CPA constituted 68 percent of total DAC ODA.

10. Chapter 2 of the report estimates the regions' financing gap in infrastructure at about $40 billion, but it also notes that factors other than financing severely hamper infrastructure services.

11. The share of infrastructure was 25 percent in 1995.

12. The consortium was established in 2005 following the Gleneagles Summit.

13. OECD 2009a and 2009b.

14. The 2009 survey on planned CPA covered 41 bilateral and multilateral donors; 35 donors responded. The forward aid expenditures are conservative estimates of future aid flows. Donors' practices regarding forward aid planning vary with regard to periodicity of updating. Some donors have annual updates of multi-year schedules while others update multi-year schedules in the context of bilateral consultations with partner countries. The Accra Agenda for Action calls on donors to provide regular and timely information on their rolling 3-to-5-year forward planned expenditures and implementation plans to developing countries.

15. This estimate assumes debt relief and humanitarian assistance will be at long-term averages.

16. OECD 2009a.

17. Brautigam 2008.

18. IMF 2008.

19. IMF 2007.

20. Frontier economies are some of the poorest developing countries.

21. http://www.irishaid.gov.ie/latest_news .asp?article=1411.

22. "Less and worse aid? Financial crisis shows first impacts on European aid budgets" http://www .eurodad.org/whatsnew/articles.aspx?id=3285.

23. http://ipsnews.net/news.asp?idnews=45625.

24. Desai and Kharas 2008; Mold, Olcer, and Prizzon 2008.

25. Desai and Kharas 2008.

26. Roodman 2008.

27. Faini 2006.

28. McDonnell, Solignac-Lecomte, and Wegimont 2003.

29. Paxton and Knack 2008.

30. Zimmerman 2008; Eurobarometer 2005.

31. OECD 2008.

32. Knack and Eubank 2009. The study uses the unweighted average of all relevant donor-re-

cipient pairs, while the OECD results are based on aggregates for recipient countries.

33. OECD 2008.

34. Celasun and Walliser 2008. Several of the studies also suggest that while recipients' performance is an issue, many other factors, including technical, legal, and political, contribute to low predictability.

35. Bulir and Hamann 2003, 2006; Pallage and Robe 2001.

36. Kharas 2008.

37. Mold, Olcer, and Prizzon 2008.

38. Hudson Institute Center for Global Prosperity 2008.

39. There are three types of foundations—private, corporate, and community.

40. Foundation Center 2008b.

41. Conference Board annual surveys for 2007 and 2008. In 2007, 197 companies and corporate foundations participated in the survey, compared with 189 companies in 2006.

42. A public-benefit foundation is defined by the European Foundation Center as being an asset-based, purpose-driven institution that has no members or shareholders but has an established, reliable income source to carry out its work over a longer term than other institutions such as companies. In the 24 European Union member states, over 95,000 organizations are public-benefit foundations. Nearly three-fourths of the 54 percent increase in the number of these foundations from 2001 to 2005 can be attributed to European Union enlargement and the rest is a result of an increase in the number of foundations.

43. Bishop and Green (2008) describe philanthrocapitalism as a movement to harness the power of business and the market to the goals of social change. Also see Ben-Artzi (2008).

44. Marten and Witte 2008.

45. Schwab 2008; Maxwell 2008.

46. www.gatesfoundation.org/annual-letter/ Documents/2009-bill-gates-annual-letter.pdf.

47. www.macfound.org/site/c.lkLXJ8MQKrH/ b.4196225/apps/s/content.asp?ct=6334379.

48. A Note on the Economy at www.hewlett .org/AboutUs/News/A_Note_on_the_Economy .htm.

49. Foundation Center 2008c.

50. Foundation Center 2008a.

51. See Kiess (2008) and World Bank (2009c) for a detailed presentation of innovative financing mechanisms.

52. Not all new funds raised through these mechanisms represent additional financing with regard to conventional ODA.

53. International Energy Agency 2008.

54. United Nations (2008a); World Bank (2008). The forthcoming *World Development Report 2010* will present more complete evaluation of financing requirements and mechanisms.

55. The CDM is the main mechanism for encouraging private investment in mitigation in the context of developing countries.

56. World Bank Institute 2008.

57. Since December 2006 new bilateral funds have been established by Australia, the European Union, Germany, Japan, Spain, and the United Kingdom; see Bird and Peskett (2008).

58. The value of the pledges was $5.7 billion as of exchange rates on January 23, 2009. See World Bank 2009a.

59. Several rules have been adapted to take into account HIPCs' specific circumstances; for example, the policy track record required to qualify for debt relief has been shortened. Additional debt relief has been provided when debt indicators deteriorated because of factors beyond a country's control, such as negative terms-of-trade shocks or natural disasters.

60. Many creditors who have agreed to participate in the initiative are lagging in providing their share of debt relief. Given the voluntary nature of creditor participation in the HIPC Initiative, the IMF and the World Bank will continue to use moral suasion to encourage creditors to participate in the Initiative and to deliver fully their share of HIPC Initiative debt relief.

61. Established in 1989, the DRF aims to help reforming, heavily indebted, IDA-only countries reduce their commercial external debt, as part of a broader debt resolution program. Support from the DRF is provided through grants for the preparation and the implementation of commercial debt reduction operations. The DRF is financed by transfers from IBRD and grant contributions from other donors, as well as investment income earned on such contributions.

62. IMF–World Bank forthcoming.

63. Relates to 20 countries for which the assessment reports have been finalized.

64. The dimensions under the indicator for coordination with macroeconomic policies reveal a sample bias that is likely to unwind with future assessments. A number of the countries in the current sample are part of either the Economic and Monetary Community of Central Africa or the West African Economic and Monetary Union; as such the governments are bound by strict legislation that limits the availability of direct resources from the regional central banks.

Pressing Ahead with Trade Openness

External competitiveness and access to international markets are paramount for poor countries to realize the development promise of international trade. Pressing ahead with trade openness is a powerful means for countries to help mitigate the impact of the financial crisis and enhance prospects for economic recovery.

The recent food, fuel, and financial crises have put great strain on the global trading system, slowing—and at times reversing—progress in trade integration. In early 2008 sharp increases in world food and fuel prices triggered disorderly and sometimes harmful trade policy responses, including the imposition of export taxes, quotas, or outright bans by some large food-exporting countries. In late 2008 the financial crisis compounded the food crisis and led to a trade credit crunch and sharp increases in trade credit spreads. International trade slowed sharply in the last months of the year and is projected to contract in 2009—for the first time since 1982.

Risks of protectionism and other trade-distorting policies have heightened as economic activity collapses and unemployment soars in many countries. Although trade actions have remained relatively circumscribed so far, several countries have raised border barriers or subsidized automotive, steel, or other export-oriented industries.

A resurgence of "buy national" and other inward-looking policies risks retarding market corrections, distorting trade, and triggering retaliation. Maintaining and enhancing trade openness is key not only to preserving the mutual benefits of trade but to supporting the eventual economic recovery.

Even with bleak trade prospects, developing countries can improve their competitiveness and diversify their exports through trade facilitation measures and other behind-the-border reforms. The accelerating pace of globalization and erosion of preferences for poor countries associated with the expanding web of preferential trade agreements make improving domestic competitiveness through behind-the-border reforms imperative. In particular, efforts in the area of trade facilitation could do a lot—and perhaps even more than further reductions in tariff rates—to increase trade flows. The ease of moving goods internationally—including through improved border processing systems, logistics services, and trade infrastructure more generally—has become a key determinant of export competitiveness and diversification.

The crisis also increases the urgency of bolstering multilateral cooperation in the trade area. A Doha Round agreement would help keep markets open at a time of financial stress, ease protectionist pressures, and strengthen the rules-based multilateral trading system. It would also provide a much-needed boost in confidence to the global economy. Moreover, fulfillment of aid-for-trade commitments by high-income countries and international institutions is important to support both the multilateral trade liberalization agenda and domestic trade facilitation efforts. Given that many poor countries continue to face considerable infrastructure and other supply-side constraints to participating in global markets, donors should deliver on their aid-for-trade commitments in support of domestic reforms that address these constraints.

In its first part, this chapter reviews the recent sources of strain in the global trading system—the food, fuel, and financial crises—and discusses their impact on trade finance and policy, including the risk of trade protectionism. In the second part, it discusses possible avenues for transforming the current crisis into opportunities for reform, including completing the Doha Round of multilateral trade negotiations, pursuing domestic reforms aimed at enhancing trade openness and external competitiveness, and mobilizing more effective aid for trade in support of those reforms.

Strains in the Global Trading System

The multilateral trading system came under heightened strains in 2008 amid major international crises that eventually led to a global economic recession and a sharp drop in international trade.

FIGURE 5.1 Robust trade growth turned negative in most regions by late 2008

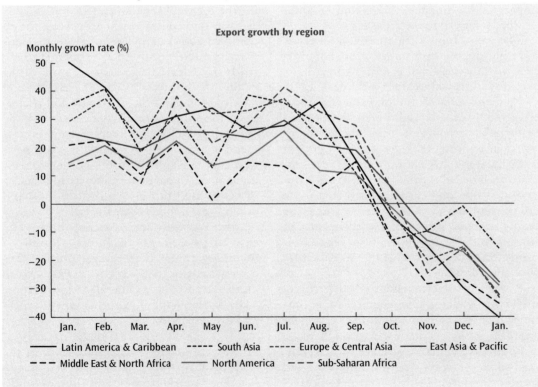

Source: Staff calculations, based on data collected from national sources.

Recent Developments in International Trade

The global recession has put great pressure on trade. In the fall of 2008 global demand suffered a sharp decline, most of the global economy went into recession leading to falling demand for both domestically produced goods and imports, and by early 2009 robust trade growth had turned negative in most countries.[1] International trade is forecast to decline in 2009, for the first time in 27 years (figures 5.1 and 5.2). Declining demand has been compounded by a contraction in the available finance for trade flows. Monitoring from the World Trade Organization (WTO) and the World Bank indicates that the contribution of protectionist and discriminatory policies to the decline in trade has remained limited to date. However, looking forward, there is a danger of a retreat from the relatively open border policies of the past decade.

The second half of 2008 saw a sharp slowdown in merchandise trade. For the year as a whole, growth in the volume of world trade moderated to 3.4 percent in 2008, from an average of 7.9 percent during 2003–07. According to the World Bank's *Global Economic Prospects* (April 2009), the world trade volume in goods and services is projected to decline by 6.1 percent in 2009, with a significantly sharper contraction in trade volumes of manufactured goods. While tourism is down in many regions, total trade in services appeared to be more resilient than in manufactures. These projections corroborate the WTO forecast of a 9 percent fall in world merchandise trade in 2009, with developed-economy exports falling by some 10 percent on average, and developing-country exports shrinking by 2–3 percent. With the global economy remaining weak throughout the year, a gradual pickup in trade volumes is not expected until 2010.

A number of leading indicators confirm this bleak trade outlook. In late 2008, a large oversupply of ships was reported in many ports, together with falling prices for shipping services. The Baltic Exchange Dry

FIGURE 5.2 World trade will contract in 2009

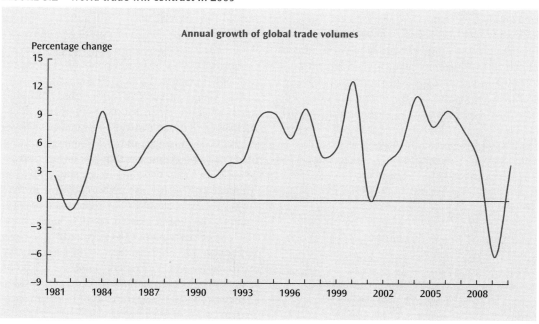

Source: World Bank 2009.

Index, a benchmark for global freight costs along key routes, fell by more than 90 percent between May and November 2008, and has yet to recover (figure 5.3).[2] Air cargo traffic, another possible early indicator of trade developments, has also registered its worst decline since the burst of the technology bubble in 2001. According to the International Air Transport Association, the volume of cargo traffic dropped by 13.5 percent in November 2008 (compared with November 2007). December was worse; cargo freight declined by 23 percent.

Falling commodity prices and exchange rate movements have compounded the sizable decline in world trade. In the second half of 2008 commodity prices decreased sharply, and the U.S. dollar appreciated against the currencies of major traders. The 27 percent decline in the International Monetary Fund (IMF) commodity price index between November 2007 and November 2008 is estimated to have contributed to an 11 percent drop in trade. The slowdown has been widespread, across regions and between developed and developing countries, as well as across exports and imports, implying that reduced demand is playing a major role. For instance, U.S. import data by sector indicate that, although the decline in commodity prices is evident, U.S. imports fell across nearly all industries. Declining demand and investment was especially evident among imports of transportation and machinery, electrical equipment, and stone and glass, all

of which fell by double digits. Small countries in Africa, Eastern Europe, and Central Asia have experienced the largest percentage declines in exports to the U.S. market.

Depending on the degree of trade and financial openness and the state of readiness to cope with shocks, the impact of the financial crisis has differed by country. Most at risk have been developing countries with large foreign banking and trade exposure combined with weak foreign exchange positions, rigid exchange rate systems, and fragile budgets. In the short run, emerging countries are particularly vulnerable. As a group, they have accounted for the bulk of global growth in 2007–08 and are therefore particularly exposed. Low-income countries appear less vulnerable in the short run because of their lower financial and trade integration. However, they are also often the least equipped to deal with crises. While net commodity importers will see some relief from the rapidly declining price of food and fuel, net exporters face the triple financial, fuel, and food crisis.[3]

Food and Fuel Crisis

International trade was significantly disturbed in 2007 and early 2008 by large terms-of-trade shocks as a result of surging prices of minerals and various food products. Oil prices doubled between January 2007 and August 2008. Grain prices also more than doubled between January 2006 and September 2008, including dramatic surges in staples such as wheat, rice, and soybean oil. A large number of developing countries that are net importers of food and fuel were severely affected by the increase in the prices of these commodities. Import bills increased and balance of payments deteriorated. In all countries, consumers, especially vulnerable consumers, were negatively affected by the rise in food prices. Both food and fuel prices have in recent months retreated from their mid-2008 peaks. However, food prices have remained and are projected to remain well above their 1990s levels for the next several years.[4]

FIGURE 5.3 Baltic Exchange Dry Index

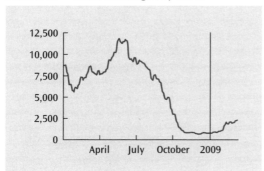

Source: Baltic Exchange Information Services Ltd. and Bloomberg L.P.

The 2008 global food price crisis had deep historical roots in the distortions of the world trading system (box 5.1). While several factors beyond trade combined to produce an upward global food price spiral (including high energy and fertilizer prices, depreciation of the U.S. dollar, biofuel production, changes in food buffer stocks, droughts, and increased world demand), the origins of the current spike in global food prices can be traced to decades of trade-distorting policies that have encouraged inefficient agricultural production in rich countries and discouraged efficient production in developing countries.[5] High-income countries have historically protected their domestic producers and subsidized inefficient production—most recently biofuels—dumping surpluses onto global markets. In turn, developing countries have often used trade and other domestic policies to simultaneously tax and protect their agricultural sector, with the net effect in many countries of taxing farmers. Overall, the world has suffered from overproduction in high-income countries and underproduction in poor countries.

BOX 5.1   Trade policies: A taproot of the global food price crisis

The global food price crisis had deep roots in the distortions of the world trading system. Historically, agricultural trade-distorting policies have taken the form of specific and ad valorem tariffs that are sometimes linked to quantities of imports (such as tariff rate quotas); quantitative restrictions or prohibitions on imports and exports; and domestic producer supports and export subsidies for farm products. Countries have also availed themselves of additional restrictions in the form of safeguard protection in case of import surges. The trading system in agriculture is further distorted and segmented by the existence of trade agreements whereby preferential tariff rates, market access conditions, or both, are offered on a reciprocal or nonreciprocal basis to a subset of partner countries. Overall, the trading system in agriculture is nontransparent, discriminatory, and highly distorted.

More recently, biofuel policies in high-income countries, which consist of import duties, subsidies, tax credits, and legislative mandates, have had the effect of further distorting global agricultural trade and contributing to the global food price crisis. Biofuel production in the United States from food crops such as maize and soybean oil and in the European Union from rapeseed and sunflower seed oils have fueled the rise in food prices by increasing the demand for these food crops and shifting land out of other crops. In the last three years, 5 million hectares of cropland that could have been used for wheat have gone to rapeseed and sunflowers for biofuels in major wheat producers, including Canada, the European Union, and the Russian Federation. Increased demand for biofuels is estimated to have accounted for 70 percent of the increase in corn prices and 40 percent of the increase in soybean prices. Although oil prices may have been somewhat higher in the absence of biofuels, these subsidies do not promote economic efficiency as an offset to their inflation impact.

The combined impact of these trade-distorting agricultural policies has been to displace and reduce the efficiency of agricultural production globally. While such policies are introduced for a wide range of domestic motives (economic, social, environmental, security), they are welfare-reducing—both in the country applying them and in the rest of the world—relative to direct, first-best policy instruments for achieving those domestic objectives. In distorting the incentives producers and consumers would otherwise face, they are also welfare-redistributing and inherently discriminatory. By promoting less efficient production in developed countries at the expense of investment in generally more efficient production in developing countries, world food prices have been kept artificially low, and domestic food prices in protected markets have been kept artificially high. Policies in developing countries have, until recently, generally taxed agriculture to channel resources into manufacturing, with the result that investment in increasing supply has not been adequate to provide for rapid responses to global price spikes. Furthermore, because agricultural production has taken place in relatively inefficient, thin, and insulated markets, global trade in food products is less resilient to exogenous shocks and less able to handle volatility in trade and output.

Source: Chauffour 2008.

While agricultural trade restrictions and direct subsidies in high-income countries have tended to decrease over time, they remain a major source of support for producers in these countries. In 2007 support to farmers in advanced countries from agricultural policies amounted to $258 billion, equivalent to 23 percent of the farmers' gross receipts, down from 26 percent in 2006 and 28 percent in 2005.[6] With prices for major agricultural commodities rising steeply on international markets, the gap between supported domestic prices and world prices has narrowed considerably, contributing to the lowest level of producer support since the estimates began in the mid-1980s. Yet, developed countries did not take advantage of this window of opportunity to structurally reform their agricultural policies. Some progress has been made in moving away from the most production- and trade-distorting policy measures, although they continue to dominate producer support in most developed countries.

The rapid rise in food and fuel prices led to diverse reactions in affected countries. Along with protests and riots, higher prices put macroeconomic stability in jeopardy. The impact of the food crisis across a significant share of the population in many developing countries generated social demands for broad-based action. Governments were pressured to reduce food prices through administrative measures, including lower import tariffs or taxes, subsidies, and price controls.[7] In some countries, the policy response reflected the lack of more targeted mechanisms such as conditional cash transfers or food-for-work programs, which require substantial preparation time and implementation capacity. Many poor countries have narrow tax bases and rely on tariffs and other trade taxes for a large part of government revenue. In such countries, it is important to ensure that the revenue losses from tariff or tax reductions can be accommodated without destabilizing the macroeconomic situation. Tariff reductions can also have adverse effects on poor farmers

who previously had a protected market, particularly if the tariff reductions are unanticipated. Such farmers may need targeted assistance as tariffs are reduced. In contrast, direct price controls or untargeted subsidies typically tend to be disincentives for producers, do not concentrate help on the poorest, and drain scarce fiscal resources.

In addition, some large food-exporting countries imposed export taxes, quotas, or outright bans.[8] While it can be difficult for countries with abundant supplies to allow international prices to filter through to consumers, especially when a large majority of the poor are urban, and there is temptation to keep food prices down by reducing exports, such measures reduce production incentives and can have unintended economic and social consequences. In particular, export restrictions tend to distort prices and the allocation of resources (impeding investment and the supply-side response) and prevent local farmers from receiving the higher world market price for their production (slowing the reduction of poverty in rural areas where most poor people live in most of the countries involved).[9] Export restrictions also displace local production to crops that are not subject to export restrictions (aggravating the very food security and price concern that justifies the measure in the first place); cut local production from global buyers and distribution chains (jeopardizing future reentry in once-secure markets); create space for illegal trade (fueling corruption and related forms of governance malpractices); exacerbate the rise and fluctuations of global food prices (creating a vicious incentive for trading partners to follow suit, curb exports, and hoard); and more generally hurt trading partners and the multilateral trading system (weakening the security of poor and vulnerable countries).[10]

Looking forward, trade policies that would help address the food crisis more fundamentally would involve correcting historical distortions in agricultural trade. Priority areas for action include disciplining export controls; reversing biofuel subsidies; lowering production subsidies; facilitating agriculture trade; investing in trade-related infrastructure; completing the Doha Round; and, in the longer run, further liberalizing agricultural trade on a multilateral basis. While all of these steps would lead to more efficient agricultural markets, the complex web of policy distortions in agriculture has many cross-cutting effects, and it is difficult, especially in the short term, to predict precisely the impact that unwinding these policies would have on food prices. In particular, net food-importing countries might be adversely affected because global agricultural trade liberalization could cause world prices of agricultural commodities—at least those that are highly protected—to rise (while domestic prices in the liberalizing countries fall). Yet, the current conditions of relatively high food prices provide an opportunity for implementing long-standing agricultural trade reform. Instruments such as the IMF's Trade Integration Mechanism exist to help mitigate the possible adverse effects of liberalization on net food importers.

Financial Crisis

In September 2008, with the impact of the food crisis still unfolding, the multilateral trading system had to cope with another major crisis—this time financial. The financial crisis, which originated in the developed world, fast spilled over to emerging markets and developing countries. The initial shock was a squeeze of liquidity, including for trade finance. The credit crunch in developed-country markets caused havoc in many low-income and emerging countries, as foreign banks abruptly reduced or stopped lending and stepped back from even the most basic banking services, including trade credits and guarantees. Net flows of private capital to emerging markets are projected to decline sharply in 2009. Although they are less financially integrated, low-income countries are also being hurt: trade finance, which is usually considered the lifeline of trade for

poor nations that lack other resources to finance their imports and exports, has been disrupted. While the crisis began and spread in the financial sphere, the real economy has not remained immune. With collapsing demand and economic activity, protectionist pressures have intensified.

Trade finance. As the financial crisis unfolded, the availability of trade finance tightened and its cost rose because of growing liquidity pressure in mature markets and a perception of heightened country and counterparty risks. The contraction in trade finance was also fueled by the loss of critical market participants, such as Lehman Brothers, a drying up of the secondary market for short-term exposure (as banks and other financial institutions deleveraged), and the volatility of commodity prices.[11] The implementation of the Basel II Accord on banking laws and regulations, with its increased risk sensitivity of capital requirements, in an environment of global recession is also generally considered to have put additional pressure on banks to hold back on trade finance. Regardless of the impact of Basel II, as companies continue to be downgraded, higher risk premiums increase capital requirements, further reducing access to trade credit, especially for small and medium enterprises and banks in emerging markets.[12]

With up to 20 percent of the $15.8 trillion world merchandise trade in 2008 involving secured documentary transactions, such as letters of credit (LCs), trade finance is critical to sustaining the multilateral trading system.[13] As the financial crisis spread, the demand for LCs, insurance, and guarantees increased, because exporters wanted to be certain importers would pay on schedule. This led to delays in international trade, with goods reportedly being docked for weeks before shipment, as terms of financing were finalized. Trade finance has tended to be highly vulnerable in times of crisis. For instance, trade finance to developing countries collapsed during the 1997–98 East Asian financial crisis. Bank-financed trade credits declined by about 50 percent and 80 percent in the Republic of

Korea and Indonesia, respectively, in 1997–98. During the 2001–02 crisis episodes in Argentina and Brazil, trade credits declined by as much as 30–50 percent.[14]

With no comprehensive and reliable data on trade finance available, an overall assessment of trade finance developments in 2008 remains difficult. Selected information indicates that—along with global demand—trade finance flows declined in the last quarter of 2008. According to Dealogic, "structured" medium- and long-term trade finance instruments (such as syndicated loans) contracted by about 40 percent in the last quarter of 2008 compared with 2007.[15] While structured trade finance represents only a fraction of medium- and long-term global trade finance, it appears to be indicative of a broader trend. On short-term trade finance, data from the Society for Worldwide Interbank Financial Telecommunication indicate that the number of trade finance messages declined by 4.8 percent in

December 2008, compared with the same period in 2007. This covers collection and cash letters as well as documentary credits and guarantees. According to a survey of 40 banks in developed and emerging markets undertaken by the IMF in collaboration with the Bankers' Association for Finance and Trade (BAFT) in December 2008, banks in developed countries reported roughly the same number of transactions of documentary credits, guarantees, and LCs in October and November 2008 compared with same period in 2007.[16] In contrast, emerging market banks reported a 6 percent fall in such transactions. These developments are consistent with the data released by the Berne Union of export credit and investment insurance agencies, which indicate that, in the last quarter of 2008, new insurance commitments increased strongly for high-income countries and decreased for developing countries (figure 5.4).[17]

At the same time, the price of trade finance and the need for securing transactions through guarantees and insurance has increased markedly. Tight credit conditions have allowed lenders to drive up interest rates for their loans in many countries, especially in emerging markets (figure 5.5). When banks are under pressure, the capital needed for trade finance may be allocated elsewhere on balance sheets. With no secondary market to offload loans, balance sheets have been constrained. In addition, global currency volatility and more rigorous counterparty risk assessment contributed to higher cost of trade finance for importers, exporters, and financial intermediaries. By the end of 2008, trade finance deals were offered at 300–400 basis points over interbank refinance rates—two to three times more than the rate a year earlier. The cost of LCs was reported to have doubled or tripled for buyers in emerging countries, including Argentina, Bangladesh, China, Pakistan, and Turkey. This assessment was confirmed in the IMF/BAFT survey, which found widespread increases in pricing of all trade finance instruments relative to

FIGURE 5.4 New insurance commitments (medium- and long-term) reported by Berne Union members on selected countries

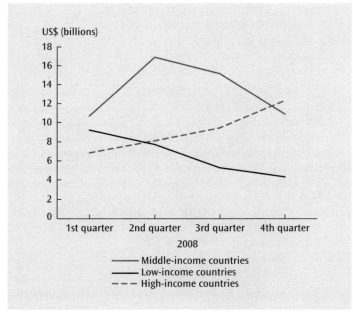

Source: Berne Union.

banks' costs of funds. More than 70 percent of respondents indicated that the price of various types of LCs increased because of an increase in their own institution's cost of funds (80 percent of respondents), an increase in capital requirements (60 percent of respondents), or both.

As part of the financial sector bailouts, given the rapidly deteriorating trade finance landscape, a number of national authorities started to intervene to provide blanket liquidity to banks and targeted trade credit lines and guarantees for exporters that have been cut from trade finance. For instance, in October 2008, Brazil's Central Bank was one of the first to issue loans in an attempt to provide relief to exporters. However, the financial interventions did not always lead to the desired results, because banks were concerned about increased counterparty risk and remained cautious, with many preferring to use the injected liquidity to purchase government paper. Moreover, as developed countries bailed out their banks, there has been political pressure to finance domestic transactions rather than provide trade finance that goes to developing countries.

Coordinating national interventions would send a powerful signal to market participants that would help restore confidence and eventually lower the overall cost of public intervention. When central banks lack the foreign exchange reserves to provide trade credit lines, other central bankers could offer currency swaps to help keep normal trade flows. The intervention of the U.S. Federal Reserve in support of Brazil and Mexico through currency swaps in late 2008 was a case in point. Export credit agencies from developed countries could be mobilized further to provide short-term insurance, and lending when possible, for bilateral trade credits. Promoting the use of local currencies in intraregional trade to reduce the dependence on the U.S. dollar and the euro as currencies of payment is another option to consider for reducing pressure on foreign exchange. When these

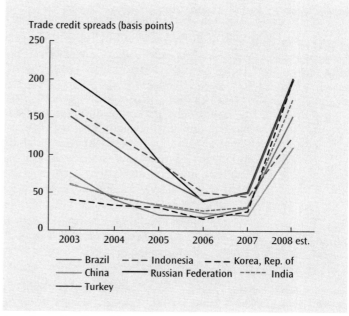

FIGURE 5.5 Cost of trade finance in selected emerging markets

Source: Data collected by staff from private bankers.

steps are not possible, hard-pressed countries could consider depositing a collateral fund offshore to encourage acceptance of LCs by local importers, as the Indonesian Central Bank did during the 1997–98 Asian crisis.

In parallel, there is scope for financial institutions and enterprises to promote other sources of short-term financing. Factoring is a type of supplier financing that could be particularly suited to a heightened risk environment. Because factoring involves the outright purchase of invoices at a discount rather than the collateralization of a loan, the creditworthiness of the seller becomes less important in the decision process than the value of the seller's underlying assets. Hence, factoring could become an instrument of choice when firms in developing countries have difficulty accessing trade financing. While still a relatively small source of credit in emerging markets, the crisis could be an opportunity to expand factoring in both low-income and emerging countries.

For sectors and products highly integrated in a global supply chain, supply-chain finance solutions should remain a relatively stable source of working capital and thus financing. Corporations already use credit across multiple transaction types as part of daily operations. Since these credits are not intermediated through banks and their underlying risks are borne among party constituents (absent factoring and insurance), they should be more resilient to the credit crunch, at least to its initial direct effect. They will, however, remain vulnerable to the global economic and financial prospects.

Development institutions have taken actions to help ease access to trade finance. For example, in response to the financial crisis, the International Finance Corporation (IFC) has, among other actions, doubled its Global Trade Finance Program to $3 billion to facilitate trade by providing guarantees that cover the payment risk in trade transactions with local banks in emerging markets. To deal with the liquidity constraint, the IFC has also introduced a Global Trade Liquidity Pool, which, in collaboration with official and private partners, is expected to provide up to $50 billion of trade liquidity support over the next three years. Regional development banks such as the African Development Bank (AfDB), the Asian Development Bank (ADB), the European Bank for Reconstruction and Development (EBRD), and the Inter-American Development Bank (IDB) have also launched or expanded their trade finance programs to extend guarantee facilities to international banks confirming local banks' LCs, with a focus on small transactions in low-income countries that have little access to international markets and no or low international ratings.[18]

The international community has recognized the importance of dealing with trade finance concerns in a coordinated fashion. At the Group of Twenty (G-20) meeting in London, in April 2009, leaders reached agreement to ensure $250 billion of support for trade finance.[19] They also asked their regulators to make use of available flexibility in capital requirements for trade finance under Basel II.

Protectionism temptation. If history is a guide, the economic stress and uncertainty that engulfed the international scene in 2008 could be a precursor to rising protectionist tendencies. Raising barriers at the frontier, starting with barriers to trade in goods or services, is often a tempting political option under such circumstances. Restricting capital movements, including for the more secure operations to finance imports and exports, is another inward-looking temptation. As governments consider their policy options, they should be mindful of the domestic and international consequences of such actions. In particular, developed countries can lead by example in avoiding protectionist responses. Less distorting policies to respond to the economic crisis would include the use of fiscal policy to stimulate domestic demand across the board. While trade and industrial policy may boost domestic consumption and production in certain sectors, on balance they tend to impose a net cost on the economy, have adverse domestic consequences on resource allocation and economic efficiency, and discriminate against foreign producers. They are likely to be met with retaliation from other countries, limiting their effectiveness and undermining the international trading system. Trade policy is not the appropriate instrument for pursuing equity objectives or for attaining goals such as employment protection; indeed, the distributional consequences of protectionism may be harmful to many poor households. Finally, once in place, tariffs and subsidies are difficult to remove, potentially creating a host of future difficulties.

Multilateral cooperation is therefore essential to ensure that disruptions to trade in goods and services and trade finance triggered by the global financial crisis remain circumscribed. Unlike in 1929, international trade is nowadays governed by rules and disciplines aimed at preventing the world economy from falling into another trade-induced Great Depression.[20] As noted by its director-general, Pascal Lamy, the WTO "provides the real economy, the everyday economy, with a collective insurance policy against the disorder caused by unilateral actions, whether open or disguised; a guarantee of security for transactions in times of crisis, henceforth an element of resilience that is vital to the running of a globalised world. In short, a global insurance policy for a global real economy."[21] Yet for the system to hold at times of crisis, all countries need to obey these multilateral rules and disciplines.

At the Summit on Financial Markets and the World Economy, Washington, DC, November 2008, the leaders of the G-20 underscored the critical importance of rejecting protectionism and not turning inward in times of financial uncertainty.[22] They committed to refrain, during the next 12 months, from raising new barriers to investment or to trade in goods and services, imposing new export restrictions, or implementing WTO-inconsistent measures to stimulate exports. However, many countries could increase their applied levels of tariffs and trade-distorting subsidies without breaching their bound rates or other relevant WTO disciplines.[23] According to the WTO monitoring of trade developments, there has been a marked increase in protectionist pressures globally since September 2008, including by a number of G-20 countries. Although there is no general trend, a pattern is beginning to emerge of increases in import licensing, import tariffs and surcharges, and trade remedies to support industries facing difficulties early on in the crisis. Examples of countries that have introduced trade restricting or distorting measures (see table 5.1) include Argentina (more stringent licensing requirements), Ecuador (higher rates on some 630 tariff lines), India (higher tariffs on some steel products), Indonesia (limitations on entry points for certain imports), Ukraine (possibility of an import surcharge), and the European Union (increased export subsidies for selected dairy products).[24]

While resisting outright protectionism, governments, mainly in developed countries,

TABLE 5.1 Trade distorting actions taken in selected countries

Country	Trade policies	Sector-specific support
Argentina	✔	
Australia		✔
Austria		✔
Azerbaijan	✔	
Brazil	✔	✔
Canada	✔	✔
China	✔	✔
Ecuador	✔	
Egypt, Arab Rep. of	✔	
European Union	✔	
France		✔
Germany		✔
India	✔	
Indonesia	✔	
Japan		✔
Kazakhstan	✔	
Libya	✔	
Malaysia	✔	✔
Mexico	✔	
Morocco		✔
Paraguay	✔	
Philippines	✔	
Portugal		✔
Romania		✔
Russian Federation	✔	✔
Spain		✔
Turkey	✔	
Ukraine	✔	
United States	✔	✔
Uzbekistan	✔	
Vietnam	✔	

Source: WTO. Report to the Trade Policy Review Body, March 26, 2009.
Note: Trade policy actions include WTO-consistent antidumping and countervailing duties, but do not include increases in overall domestic support to agriculture or financial sector measures.

have launched extensive domestic stimulus packages targeted at troubled export industries or competing import industries (such as airline, construction, steel, semiconductors, and automobile). While not barriers to trade in the traditional sense, these programs aimed at protecting businesses and jobs from the effects of the global slowdown could nevertheless restrict or distort trade, especially when they include "buy domestic" provisions.[25] In particular, industrial subsidies in one country (to the car industry, for example) provide an incentive for other countries to respond with their own subsidies or protection against imports from subsidized producers.[26] They are contagious and could result in a subsidy war that compounds the damage caused and leaves everyone worse off. In addition, they pull resources away from more productive uses. As noted by the WTO, when analyzing these support measures from a trade perspective, it must be recognized that at least some of the measures, which in most cases constitute some form of state aid or subsidy, may eventually have negative spillover effects on other markets or distort competition.

At the G-20 meeting in London, world leaders reaffirmed—and extended to the end of 2010—the commitment made in Washington, DC, to refrain from raising new barriers to investment or to trade, imposing new export restrictions, or implementing WTO-inconsistent measures to stimulate exports. In addition, they agreed to rectify promptly any such measures taken since their meeting in Washington, DC.

The number of antidumping actions rose significantly in 2008 (figure 5.6). Initiations of new antidumping investigations and application of new antidumping measures increased by 31 percent and 19 percent, respectively. With 73 percent of all new investigations, developing countries dominated the use of antidumping in 2008. Brazil, India, and Turkey were the top three initiators with some 100 cases combined. Exporters in developing countries were the most frequent target. Regarding the application of new antidumping measures, India, the United States, and the European Union applied the most measures, some 64 combined, most frequently targeted at China's products.

To strengthen confidence in global cooperation and institutions, it remains important that countries refrain from unilaterally restricting trade in areas where multilateral rules and disciplines do not exist or are not fully developed. For instance, the introduction of export restrictions on agricultural products by many large net food exporters contributed to the severity of the recent food price crisis. Countries should instead strive to keep their markets open and use the crisis as an opportunity to invest in trade-related infrastructure and to implement measures to facilitate trade. In particular, efforts in the area of trade facilitation could do a lot to increase global trade flows and partially counterbalance the effects of the global recession on trade.

In the same vein that multilateral cooperation leads to a global trade outcome superior to beggar-thy-neighbor policies, multilateral cooperation could help make trade finance more affordable and resilient in times of crisis. The Doha Round of negotiations under the General Agreement on Trade in Services could be used to increase the WTO's contribution to making the provision of trade financing more secure and more readily available, particularly in developing countries. Meanwhile, the WTO could continue

FIGURE 5.6 Growth of antidumping cases

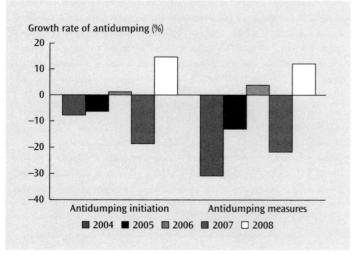

Source: WTO, Antidumping Database; Brown forthcoming.

to use its convening power to raise awareness and find ways to alleviate the situation if it were to deteriorate further.

Transforming Crises into Opportunities for Reform

As an old Chinese proverb says, a crisis is an opportunity riding the dangerous wind.[27] In the trade arena, the current crisis could provide an opportunity to complete the Doha Round of multilateral trade negotiations, accelerate national trade liberalization and trade facilitation reforms, and fulfill aid-for-trade commitments and improve their efficiency.

Doha Round

Central to the task of promoting inclusive globalization and making the multilateral trading system more resilient in times of crisis are bringing down barriers to the trade of goods and services that poor people produce and increasing the reliability and predictability of the system's rules and disciplines. A successful Doha Round would help to ensure open markets at a time of financial stress, ease protectionist pressures, and strengthen the rules-based multilateral trading system. It could also provide a much-needed boost in confidence to a global economy experiencing a sharp slowdown, financial uncertainty, and high food prices. The need for a successful outcome has become more urgent, because the circumstances and some of the challenges facing the world economy in 2009, such as disciplining export restrictions or support to industries, are different from those in 2001 when the round was launched.[28]

Seven years into the Doha Round, trade negotiators have remained unable to reach agreement on modalities to further open markets for goods and services and strengthen the rules of the multilateral trading system. Yet trade negotiators have never been so close to an agreement. In the thorny agriculture negotiations, gaps have been narrowed significantly on a number of critical issues, including key parameters for cutting tariffs and trade-distorting subsidies. The IMF and the World Bank have called on all parties to revive the significant package that was on the table in Geneva in July 2008 and work swiftly toward closure. After years of valuable technical work, there is a Doha deal to be seized. According to the World Bank, a deal based on the broad parameters discussed in Geneva would compare favorably with the Uruguay Round on market access and would surpass it in breadth of coverage and tangible benefits for developing countries.[29]

Despite progress leading up to it, the ministerial meeting held in Geneva in July 2008 failed to achieve a breakthrough. Though compromise appeared within reach, the tentative agreement on nonagricultural market access (NAMA) and agriculture reached an impasse in country positions on several issues, including the provisions governing the new agricultural special safeguard mechanism for developing countries.[30] Other areas of disagreement that were not addressed or resolved included domestic subsidies for cotton, tariff-cutting sectoral initiatives in NAMA, and protections for food products with geographical names.

While an opportunity has been missed, the very substantial progress achieved at and since the meeting should not be overlooked or wasted. The compromise package on the tariff and subsidy reduction parameters in agriculture and NAMA circulated during the meeting attracted broad support. Progress was made in the dispute over fisheries subsidies. The long-standing issue of the European Union's banana regime and the margin of preference for ACP (African, Caribbean, and Pacific) producers had also nearly been resolved. The "signaling conference" on services held in the context of the mini-ministerial to set out the possible scope and ambition of a services agreement was a success. Countries showed willingness to lock in actual market access and make new or improved commitments in a wide range of services sectors.

Given the amount of progress made during the July meeting and the G-20 pledge to conclude the round before year-end,[31] efforts to reconvene a ministerial meeting led to revised draft texts for both agriculture and NAMA in December 2008. However, consultation with key players revealed that substantial differences remained, particularly on whether to hold additional specific negotiations for particular sectors, the special safeguard mechanism, and cotton. Under the circumstances, Director-General Lamy decided against calling a ministerial meeting. At their London meeting, G-20 leaders reiterated their commitment to urgently reach an ambitious and balanced conclusion to the Doha Round.[32]

The extent of progress toward the final agreement differs across negotiating groups. In agriculture, developed countries under the agreement would, among other things, cut highest bound tariffs by 70 percent over five years, with an average cut of not less than 54 percent; lower subsidy limits by 70 percent (United States) to 80 percent (European Union); and eliminate all export subsidies by 2013. Developing countries' bound tariffs would be cut by somewhat less than two-thirds of the cuts required of developed countries, and these countries would be able to designate certain "special" products for differential treatment, exempting them fully or partially from tariff cuts. In NAMA, developed countries' average bound and applied tariffs would be cut by roughly a third over four or five years, with the highest cuts in peak tariffs, while developing countries would be subject to little or no cut in applied tariffs. "Rules" negotiations on revisions to the antidumping and subsidies and countervailing measures agreements have also produced a draft text, with the U.S. practice of "zeroing" remaining the primary source of disagreement.[33] Notwithstanding the signaling conference, the services negotiations remained at an early stage. Negotiations in the area of trade facilitation continued to proceed satisfactorily.

Much is at stake in the Doha negotiations. The December 2008 package would boost economic growth and expand opportunity by cutting subsidies drastically, lowering tariffs significantly, and opening up services markets. It would be a mistake for the world economy and harmful for developing countries not to revive it.[34] Existing gaps can be bridged. For instance, there are certainly ways to solve the special safeguard mechanism problem and to establish a user-friendly safety net against import surges of agricultural products to protect fragile farming systems while, at the same time, agreeing on disciplines so that it is not abused and does not hamper normal trade flows.[35] The major players have all indicated their resolve not to lose momentum. Agriculture and NAMA negotiations resumed in early 2009 and discussion is focused on areas of divergence while preserving agreed topics as tabled in the draft texts. Negotiations in other areas, such as services and rules, will continue in parallel.

Preferential Trade Agreements

With slow Doha Round negotiations toward a new multilateral agreement, the surge in preferential trade agreements (PTAs) is fast reshaping the architecture of the world trading system and the trading environment of developing countries.[36] Such proliferation of regional and bilateral trade agreements could pose serious challenges to the promotion of a more open, transparent, and rules-based multilateral trading system. While preferential agreements may in some instances promote development, they necessarily discriminate against nonmembers and can therefore lead to trade diversion in a way that hurts both member countries and excluded countries. The multitude of PTAs is also becoming cumbersome to manage for many developing countries. As agreements proliferate, countries become members of several different agreements. The average African country belongs to four different agreements; the average Latin American country to seven. This proliferation creates what has been referred to as a "spaghetti bowl" of overlapping arrangements, with often different tariff schedules, different exclusions of particular sectors or products, different periods of implementation, different rules of origin, and different customs procedures, among other differences. Notable PTAs that came into force in 2008 and early 2009 include bilateral agreements between the European Union and Bosnia and Herzegovina, the CARIFORUM states, Montenegro, and Côte d'Ivoire; between the United States and Peru and Oman; between Japan and Indonesia and the Philippines; and a number of agreements between developing countries, such as between Panama and Chile, Pakistan and Malaysia, and Turkey and Albania.

In 2008 the European Union negotiated a number of economic partnership agreements (EPAs) with ACP countries to replace the system of trade preferences under the Cotonou trade regime. Several interim agreements were initialed with individual countries rather than with full ACP regions. In Central Africa an interim agreement has been concluded with Cameroon (other countries in the region opted out). In Southern Africa, a regional agreement was agreed with Botswana, Lesotho, Mozambique, Namibia, and Swaziland. In West Africa, the European Union reached individual agreements with Côte d'Ivoire and Ghana. In East Africa, a regional agreement was agreed with the East African Community (Burundi, Kenya, Rwanda, Tanzania, and Uganda). In Eastern and Southern Africa, a regional agreement was agreed with Comoros, Madagascar, Mauritius, Seychelles, Zambia, and Zimbabwe (but with individual market access schedules). In the Pacific region, a regional agreement was reached with Papua New Guinea and Fiji (with individual market access schedules). The European Union's aim remains to conclude full regional EPAs. Negotiations over these full EPAs are ongoing with all African and Pacific regions and cover a wider range of topics, including any issues set out in the interim agreements that partners want to reexamine.

Developments in National Trade Policies

Governments use numerous instruments to regulate trade, including import tariffs, special duties, quotas, technical product regulations, antidumping duties, and discretionary licensing. The commonly used indicators of trade policy, such as average tariffs and frequency measures, capture only partially the impact of trade policies on trade flows. It is often preferable to use summary measures that take into account the effect of all policies affecting trade.

Measures of trade restrictiveness. As in previous reports, this section briefly presents two measures of the restrictiveness of trade policies affecting merchandise trade: the Overall Trade Restrictiveness Index (OTRI), and the Tariff Trade Restrictiveness Index (TTRI). Both provide a measure of the uniform tariff equivalent of observed policies on a country's imports: they represent the "tariff" that would be needed to generate the observed level of trade for a country. The level of restrictiveness confronting exporters is captured by two similarly constructed indicators: the Market Access OTRI (MA-OTRI), and the Market Access TTRI (MA-TTRI).

The OTRI captures ad valorem tariffs, specific duties, and nontariff measures (NTMs), such as price control measures, quantitative restrictions, monopolistic measures, and technical regulations.[37] The TTRI is narrower in scope; it takes into account only tariffs (both ad valorem and specific).[38] Because many NTMs are not protectionist in intent (or effect), the OTRI reflects net (overall) restrictiveness; it is not necessarily a measure of the level of protection that a government seeks for domestic industry. Some NTMs include border restrictions, such as quotas or bans, and are motivated by protectionist objectives. Others, such as standards for mercury content or fecal matter, are aimed at safeguarding human, animal, or plant health. Since distinguishing between objectives is not possible, protection is better measured by the TTRI; because of its limited coverage of trade policy instruments, however, it is best seen as providing a lower-bound estimate of the extent of protection prevailing in a market.

Measured by the OTRI and TTRI, trade policies are generally more restrictive in developing countries than in high-income economies (figure 5.7). This reflects both lower tariffs and the higher percentage of manufactures in the trade of high-income nations (manufactures generally face much lower trade restrictions than agricultural products, which are relatively more important in the export basket of developing countries). Trade restrictions on agriculture are, on average, highest in high-income countries.[39] With the exception of upper-middle-income countries, agricultural TTRIs and OTRIs substantially exceed those for manufactures. Nontariff measures are an important component of overall trade restrictiveness, especially for agricultural products, resulting in OTRI levels that exceed the TTRI by a significant margin. For high-income countries, the OTRI is about three times higher than the TTRI, while in lower-middle-income and low-income countries, the ratio is two or less.

The level of trade restrictiveness on average is higher for countries in South Asia and the Middle East and North Africa, and lower for countries in East Asia and Pacific and Europe and Central Asia. Sub-Saharan Africa and Latin America and the Caribbean have overall restrictiveness levels in between these two extremes (figure 5.8). The United States, European Union, Japan, and China account for about 60 percent of world trade. All have policies that are more restrictive of trade in agricultural products than manufactures, with Japan and the European Union imposing significantly higher restrictions (figure 5.9).

For all income groups and all regions, the overall OTRI has fallen since 2002 (figure 5.10). The greatest overall liberalization has been implemented by low-income countries, especially in manufacturing goods. Middle-income developing countries significantly reduced the restrictiveness of agricultural trade. In particular, there has been a significant reduction in China's OTRI, which fell by almost 8 percentage points between 2002 and 2007. This was in part explained by a dramatic reduction of 32 percentage points in China's agricultural OTRI, which led to a sharp reduction in the agricultural trade restrictiveness in East Asia and Pacific. In terms of the overall OTRI, South Asia improved the most followed by the Middle East and North Africa and Latin America and the Caribbean.

Changes in market access. The effect of trade policies on exporters' access to markets is different across trading partners and geographic

FIGURE 5.7   OTRI and TTRI by income group, 2007

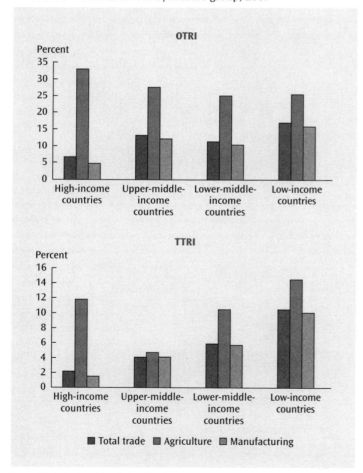

Source: World Bank and UNCTAD staff estimates.

FIGURE 5.8 OTRI and TTRI by region, 2007

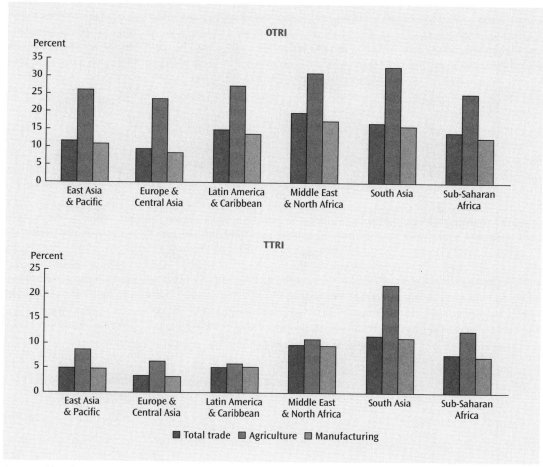

Source: World Bank and UNCTAD staff estimates.

regions, in part because of the discriminatory use of trade policies (trade preferences) and in part because of the composition of trade. Figures 5.11 and 5.12 report the MA-OTRI and change in MA-OTRI faced by exporters in each geographic region and country income group. The MA-OTRI measures the overall restrictiveness (including nontariff measures) faced by exports.

Sub-Saharan Africa countries benefit from relatively liberal market access as a result of preferential access to the major economies and a larger share of exports of commodities for which tariffs are low. Conversely, Sub-Saharan Africa's market access to other low-income countries is restricted

FIGURE 5.9 OTRI of the four largest traders, 2007

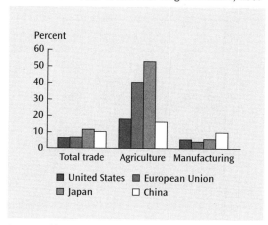

Source: World Bank and UNCTAD staff estimates.

FIGURE 5.10 Change of OTRI by income group and region, 2002–07

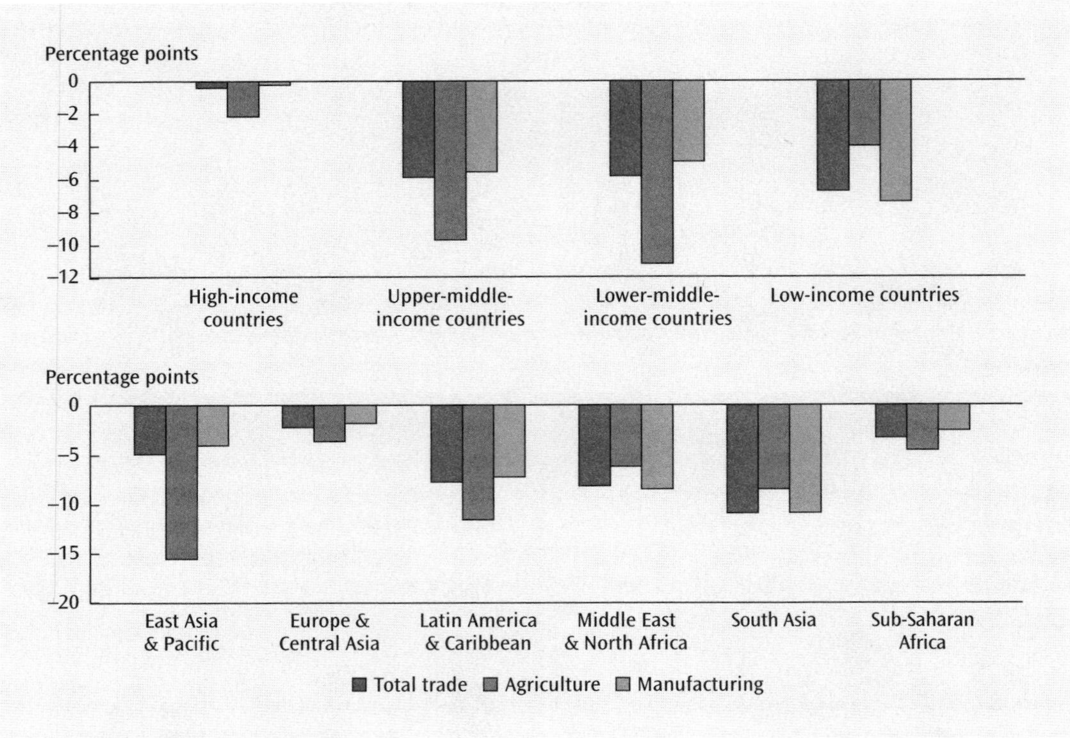

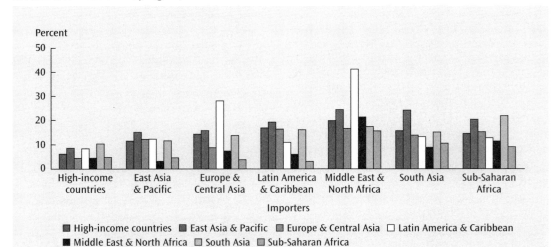

Source: World Bank and UNCTAD staff estimates.
Note: Most changes in OTRI in this figure reflect tariff changes.

FIGURE 5.11 MA-OTRI by region, 2007

Source: World Bank and UNCTAD staff estimates.
Note: The horizontal axis represents the importing area and the vertical bars show exporters into that area.

FIGURE 5.12   Change in MA-OTRI by region, 2002–07

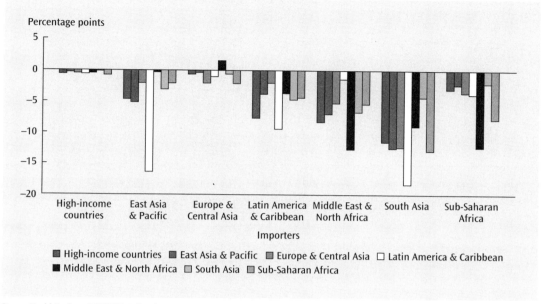

Source: World Bank and UNCTAD staff estimates.
Note: Most market access changes in the figure reflect tariff changes. The horizontal axis represents the importing area and the vertical bars show exporters into that area.

by relatively high tariffs. Among other regions, Europe and Central Asian market access to high-income countries is facilitated by preferences in the European Union, while the low MA-OTRI confronting Middle East and North African countries is largely attributable to the composition of exports—oil products are generally subject to low import tariffs. Latin America and the Caribbean faces relatively high market access barriers in Europe and Central Asia and the Middle East and North Africa. Interestingly, despite the multiplication of regional trade agreements, restrictions on intraregional market access remain high in many regions.

In terms of changes, market access has improved in recent years, with Latin America and the Caribbean benefiting the most in South Asia, East Asia, and within Latin America; and Sub-Saharan Africa gaining significantly in South Asia but also within Africa. High-income countries increased their market access in most regions. This is largely attributable to export composition,

because high-income countries' exports mainly consist of manufactures, for which restrictiveness has declined relatively more. Exports of lower-income countries are more oriented toward agriculture, which faces more restrictive barriers and for which liberalization has been more mute.

Policies in services markets. Permitting foreign firms to compete in services markets is another powerful potential channel for technology diffusion as well as a mechanism to reduce costs and raise the quality of services. As reported in *Global Monitoring Report 2008,* an ongoing research project by the World Bank is seeking to compile data on the extent to which policies discriminate against foreign services providers. To date, surveys have been conducted in 56 developing countries and comparable information obtained for 24 developed countries, covering five key sectors: financial services (banking and insurance), telecommunications, retail distribution, transportation, and professional services.[40] In

FIGURE 5.13 Restrictiveness of services trade policies by region, 2008

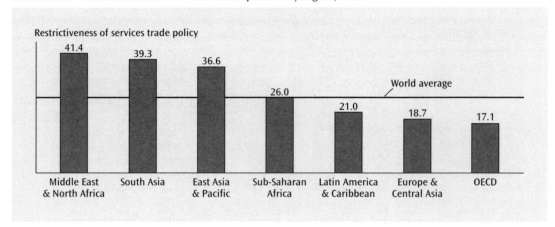

Source: Gootiiz and Mattoo 2009.
Note: The regional index is an average of individual countries' services trade restrictiveness index. This index incorporates indexes of financial services, retailing, maritime shipping, maritime auxiliary services, air passenger services, accounting, auditing, and legal services in domestic and foreign law.

each sector, the survey covered the most relevant modes of supplying that service: cross-border trade (mode 1 in WTO parlance) in financial, transportation, and professional services; commercial presence or foreign direct investment (mode 3) in each services sector; and the presence of service-supplying individuals (mode 4) in professional services.

The restrictiveness of services policies varies substantially across world regions (figure 5.13). Interestingly, some of the most restrictive policies today are visible in the fast-growing economies of Asia as well as in the Middle East. In contrast, policies are relatively liberal in Latin America, Sub-Saharan Africa, Eastern Europe, and the developed countries. Some of the poorest countries, like Cambodia, Ghana, Mongolia, Nigeria, and Senegal, are remarkably open, with World Bank–IMF reform programs and accession to the WTO probably playing a significant role. Despite significant liberalization in recent years, telecommunications, finance, and retail services are still relatively restricted in Asia; many Sub-Saharan African countries have opened up telecommunications, especially the mobile segment, to competition, but the sector is still relatively restricted in the region; and transport and

professional services are restricted all over the world, including in Latin America, Eastern Europe, and the developed countries (figure 5.14).

Behind-the-Border Agenda: Impact of Trade Policy vs. Other Trade Costs

The fast pace of globalization and the erosion of preferences for poor countries associated with expanding preferential trade agreements make improving domestic competitiveness through behind-the-border reforms imperative. In particular, efforts in the area of trade facilitation can do a lot to increase trade flows.[41] The ease of moving goods internationally has become a key determinant of export competitiveness and diversification.

There is much that developing countries can do in the area of trade facilitation to expand trade by reducing the transaction costs for their firms and farmers. High trade transaction costs and lack of capacity to rapidly move goods and services across borders prevent many developing countries from taking advantage of *existing* trade opportunities. In particular, outdated and inefficient border processing systems, problems

FIGURE 5.14 Restrictiveness of services trade policies by region and sector, 2008

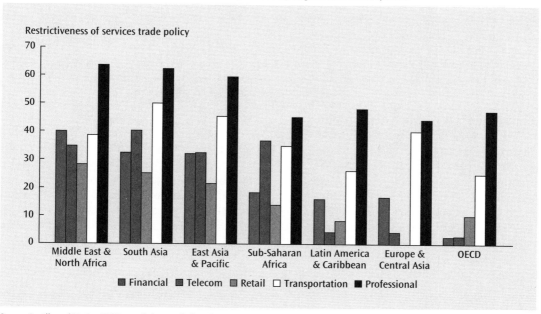

Source: Gootiiz and Mattoo 2009; restrictiveness index of cross-border air passenger policy came from the WTO QUASAR database (2007).
Note: Financial services = retail banking and life and automobile insurance; telecom services = fixed and mobile phones; retail services = retailing (commercial presence); transportation services = maritime shipping, maritime auxiliary services, and air passenger services; professional services = accounting, auditing, and legal services in domestic and foreign law.

associated with inefficient logistics services, and gaps in the trade infrastructure all result in higher transaction costs, delays, and unreliable supply chains. The high returns to action in this area are increasingly recognized, as reflected in increased levels of investment in trade-facilitation-related reforms by governments and the development community. The World Bank Group, in partnership with donors, is increasing its efforts to provide additional services and resources to help developing countries with trade facilitation activities, including provision of support for regional, multicountry projects.[42]

The available data on the level of trade restrictiveness implied by border policies indicate that nontariff measures are increasing in relative importance as a barrier to trade but that tariffs remain a significant factor, especially in developing countries. The tariffs and NTMs included in the indicators discussed above are only a subset of the policies that may affect trade. Internal

trade and transaction costs may be of equal if not greater importance as constraints to trade. Many of these trade costs reflect the domestic economic environment and the overall private investment climate: the legal and regulatory framework, the efficiency of infrastructure services and related regulation, customs clearance procedures, and administrative red tape, among other things.

A substantial amount of information on the extent of product market regulation is available for developed countries, but comparable data do not exist for developing country regulatory regimes. However, data are available for a large number of developing countries on the performance of logistics services and on the internal costs associated with shipping goods from the factory gate to the port, and from ports to retail outlets. The first is mainly captured by the Logistics Performance Index (LPI); the second is largely covered by the Doing Business database.[43] All of these indicators capture dimensions of prevailing domestic regulatory regimes that affect trade. While they overlap to some extent, they also inform about possible specific bottlenecks. The Doing Business "cost of trading" measures the fees associated with completing the procedures to export or import a 20-foot container, measured in U.S. dollars. These include costs for documents, administrative fees for customs clearance and technical control, terminal handling charges, and inland transport.[44] The LPI is based on a worldwide survey of global freight forwarders and express carriers and measures the logistics friendliness of countries on seven key dimensions (efficiency and effectiveness of the clearance process by customs and other border control agencies; quality of transport and information technology infrastructure for logistics; ease and affordability of arranging shipments; competence in the local logistics industry; ability to track and trace shipments; domestic logistics costs; and timeliness of shipments in reaching destination). Feedback from the survey is supplemented with data on the performance of key components of the logistics chain. Table 5.2 reports the average of these indexes by country income groups. Low-income countries generally have weaker trade facilitation performance than higher-income economies.

Hoekman and Nicita (2008) assess the effects of border barriers and trade costs indicators on merchandise trade flows using a gravity model framework where bilateral trade flows are a function of the economic size and distance between two countries. In addition to standard economic variables, they use both the TTRI and the NTM components of the OTRI (defined as the difference between the OTRI and the TTRI), as well as the Doing Business and LPI indicators as explanatory variables.[45] The results are typical of those of other gravity equation models.[46] Distance is an important determinant of bilateral trade, as are a common border and common language. Landlocked countries tend to trade less, especially in terms of exports, while larger and more populous countries tend to trade more.

Trade policies (tariffs and NTMs) are statistically significant determinants of trade volumes. On average, a reduction in the TTRI of 10 percent would increase trade volumes by a little more than 2 percent, while NTMs add another 1.8 percent.[47] Other trade costs are important. Coefficient estimates for the LPI suggest that a one point reduction in the LPI score would increase trade volumes by about 50 percent. Similar results are found for internal trade costs as captured by the Doing Business indicators. The elasticity of imports to the cost of importing is about 0.48, and that of exports to the cost of exporting is about 0.47. That is, a 10 percent reduction in the cost associated with importing (exporting) would increase imports (exports) by about 4.8 percent (4.7 percent). When including both the LPI and the Doing Business indicators in the estimation, all coefficients remain significant except for the LPI for the importers.

To assess the relative impacts of internal trade costs and the trade-impeding effect of border trade policies, table 5.3 reports the predicted effect on trade if low-income countries were to converge to a set of policies that would generate the observed average levels of the LPI and Doing Business indicators in middle-income countries. These results are compared with the average effect of a reduction in the TTRI and OTRI to 5

TABLE 5.2 Measures of domestic trade costs
averages by country group

Indicator	High-income countries	Middle-income countries	Low-income countries
LPI (score)[a]	3.9	3.0	2.8
Doing Business, import (US$)[b]	813.6	1,024.2	1,212.0
Doing Business, export (US$)[b]	774.4	867.2	949.3

Source: Hoekman and Nicita 2008.
a. On a 5-point scale (5 highest performance).
b. Fees associated with completing the procedures to export or import a 20-foot container (not including tariffs and trade taxes).

and 10 percent, respectively.[48] The predicted increases in trade volumes of low-income countries in this convergence experiment are substantial. The largest increases in trade are associated with actions to improve the logistics-trade facilitation scores (as measured by the LPI). Improving performance on the Doing Business measure of internal trade costs has an impact similar to what could be obtained by further traditional trade policy reform—reducing the TTRI or bringing down the restrictiveness of NTMs.

These results suggest that administrative and regulatory policies are at least as important as trade policies in impeding trade. This finding supports the recent focus of many developing countries on taking action to facilitate trade. The analysis also makes clear that large benefits are still to be gained from traditional trade liberalization, the focus of the ongoing Doha Round of WTO negotiations. As noted above, progress in the Doha Round has unfortunately been slow. Bringing the negotiations to a successful conclusion is important because it would imply improvements in market access to all export markets. Trade facilitation does not require multilateral (or bilateral) negotiations—the costs that are incurred by traders in developing countries can be reduced through unilateral actions. As Ikenson argues, there is great scope to enhance growth opportunities "while Doha sleeps."[49] The recent financial crisis makes this policy prescription even more important. Trade facilitation and supporting measures to enhance competitiveness are areas in which aid for trade can have an important impact.

The trade facilitation agenda facing developing countries is broad and can be defined as covering the infrastructure, institutions, regulations, policies, procedures, and services that allow firms to conduct international trade transactions—involving trade in either goods or services—on time and at low cost. Specifically, this agenda includes (1) modernizing and improving border management institutions, processes, and related supporting hardware (such as information

TABLE 5.3 Effects of convergence by low-income countries to middle-income average
percent

Indicator/policy area	Increase in imports	Increase in exports
LPI score	15.2	14.6
Doing Business, cost of trading	7.4	4.1
TTRI for low-income countries reduced to 5 percent	5.7	n.a.
OTRI for low-income countries reduced to 10 percent	8.4	n.a.

Source: Hoekman and Nicita 2008.
n.a. Not applicable.

technology), including customs, standards compliance, and transport security; (2) streamlining trade regulations and procedures, such as licensing, trade finance rules, documentary requirements, and work permits; (3) increasing the efficiency and capacity of trade gateways, such as ports and airports; (4) creating an enabling environment for the efficient provision of services such as logistics, transport security, trade finance, testing and certification, remittances, freight-forwarding, and customs brokering; (5) improving trade corridors, including multimodal freight transport and gateway infrastructure; and (6) establishing regional trade facilitation systems, such as transit regimes for landlocked countries, regional sanitary and phytosanitary management, and regional customs harmonization and standardization.

To help developing countries improve their competitiveness by reducing the costs of engaging in international trade, the World Bank, together with other development agencies, has scaled up its trade facilitation programs and launched a Trade Facilitation Facility. This facility, launched in April 2009, will enable the World Bank Group to respond to increased demands from developing countries to overcome trade bottlenecks imposed by weaknesses in trade logistics, customs, testing and certification, trade finance, and other aspects of trade facilitation regimes. An integral part of scaling up World Bank and IFC services in the trade facilitation area, the facility creates a one-stop shop by bringing together the different parts of the institution that provide trade facilitation-related assistance and establishing a dedicated facility that will allow the institution to deliver a coherent and expanded package of services, and respond more effectively to the increasing demand for support in this area.

Aid for Trade

In supporting the multilateral trade liberalization agenda as well as domestic trade facilitation efforts, aid for trade can produce positive cross-border externalities that benefit all trading partners. Although trade is an important engine of growth, many poor countries face considerable infrastructure and other supply-side constraints to participating in global markets. Trade reform is also a "global public good" in that all countries generally benefit from one country's policy and institutional reforms (such as lowering of tariffs and other trade barriers) and investments in trade infrastructure (such as customs reforms and ports). Those benefits are increased when reforms are undertaken by a number of countries concurrently. Because the benefits of reform are not fully captured by the reforming country itself, there is potentially "underinvestment" in reforms. Aid for trade can thus be an important complement to trade reform and global market opening.

To set in motion a process to help provide more and better aid for trade, trade ministers at the 2005 Hong Kong, China Ministerial called on bilateral and multilateral donors to increase the resources for aid for trade, endorsed the enhancement of the Integrated Framework for least developed countries, and established a Task Force on Aid for Trade. The Aid for Trade Task Force recommended, among other things, improvements in global monitoring efforts

to ensure that pledges on aid for trade were fulfilled.[50] As part of this effort, three regional reviews took place in 2007 to take stock of progress in the delivery of aid for trade, and a first WTO Global Aid for Trade review was held in Geneva in November 2007 to exchange ideas about best practices and to facilitate collective action to maximize the benefits of aid for trade. In 2008 the WTO announced an aid-for-trade roadmap aimed at monitoring overall aid-for-trade aggregates with a view to evaluating the initiative and mobilizing support for the trade agenda through national conferences.[51] A second global review will take place in early July 2009.

Common themes that emerged from the first global review included the importance of leadership in developing countries to integrate trade into national plans; priority setting in deciding on the projects that deliver the biggest return on investment; thinking regionally, because many capacity and connectivity problems, especially for small or landlocked countries, are regional in scope; ensuring increased and predicable financing, by following through on donor pledges made at the Monterrey, Gleneagles, and Hong Kong, China meetings; and mobilizing the private sector because it is businesses, not governments, that trade.

Leaving aside the methodological limitations in defining and tracking aid for trade discussed in last year's report, aid-for-trade flows increased by some $2 billion in real terms during 2007, or 21 percent relative to the baseline for 2002–05 established by the Aid for Trade Task Force (table 5.4). Total aid for trade in 2007 on the basis of the OECD Creditor Reporting System definition represented roughly 30 percent of total sector allocable official development assistance (ODA), below the 35 percent registered in 2002. A noticeable development in 2007 was the contrast between the performance of multilateral and regional donors, such as the World Bank and the regional development banks, and that of bilateral donors, including the European

TABLE 5.4 Aid-for-trade commitments: annual averages 2002–05 and totals for 2006 and 2007
US$ (millions), 2006 constant prices

	Average aid for trade 2002–05	Infrastructure		Capacity building		Trade policy and regulations		Total aid for trade		Change 2006 to 2007	As a share of total aid for trade in 2007	As a share of donor sector allocable ODA, 2007
		2006	2007	2006	2007	2006	2007	2006	2007	percent	percent	percent
Top 10 bilateral donors												
Denmark	387	95	167	142	145	0	1	237	314	32	1.2	25
France	681	517	507	310	738	1	4	828	1,249	51	4.9	21
Germany	1,160	797	501	1,062	968	18	38	1,877	1,508	−20	5.9	24
Japan	4,439	3,417	2,968	1,105	1,392	50	46	4,573	4,406	−4	17.3	65
Netherlands	529	134	86	664	508	63	44	861	638	−26	2.5	10
Norway	252	104	142	199	189	21	21	324	352	9	1.4	20
Spain	372	592	297	111	279	1	7	704	583	−17	2.3	32
Sweden	216	87	70	213	236	26	34	326	340	4	1.3	23
United Kingdom	757	108	110	445	374	81	26	634	510	−20	2.0	10
United States	3,594	2,307	2,482	1,897	1,967	316	183	4,520	4,632	2	18.2	35
Total bilateral	13,810	8,649	7,749	6,937	7,716	1,046	703	16,217	15,899	−2	62.0	27
Main multilateral donors												
AfDB	565	282	831	243	231	..	..	526	1,062	102	4.2	92
ADB[a]	717	166	340	216	257	..	5	382	603	58	2.4	45
European Commission	2,479	1,647	1,352	1,161	1,133	411	261	3,220	2,746	−15	10.8	29
World Bank (IDA)	3,166	1,724	3,233	1,120	1,431	..	..	2,844	4,663	64	18.3	44
Total multilateral	7,321	3,874	5,918	2,933	3,414	414	269	7,221	9,600	33	38.0	37
Total aid for trade	21,097	12,523	13,666	9,870	11,130	1,460	971	23,439	25,499	9	100	30

Source: OECD Creditor Reporting System (as of January 2009).
Note: .. = Negligible.
a. Data provided here are only indicative of ADB's expanding trend and position relative to other institutions. They do not necessarily reflect ADB's actual involvement in aid for trade, which is likely to be higher due to some limitation of current classification systems.

Union. While the main multilateral donors continued to scale up their aid-for-trade programs, several bilateral donors recorded a significant decline in their aid-for-trade commitments. Total commitments from bilateral donors decreased by 2 percent in 2007 while commitments from multilateral donors increased by more than 30 percent (figure 5.15).

The United States and Japan continued to dominate global aid-for-trade delivery, with $4.6 billion and $4.4 billion in 2007,

FIGURE 5.15   Aid-for-trade commitments: annual averages for 2002–05, and totals for 2006 and 2007

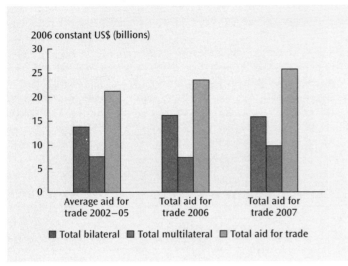

2006 constant US$ (billions)

■ Total bilateral   ■ Total multilateral   ■ Total aid for trade

Source: OECD Creditor Reporting System (as of January 2009).

respectively. Other important bilateral donors include France, Germany, the Netherlands, Spain, and the United Kingdom. The World Bank, through the International Development Association (IDA), was the largest provider of concessional aid for trade in 2007, closely followed by the United States; both provided about 18 percent of total aid for trade in 2007. IDA aid for trade has been driven by an increase in aid for infrastructure projects. The ADB and the AfDB are also important providers of aid for trade in their respective regions and among the top 10 donors globally. In 2007, the AfDB allocated more than 90 percent of its total sector allocable ODA to aid for trade. The 10 largest bilateral donors and multilateral agencies funded more than 90 percent of global aid-for-trade activities in 2007. In general, a greater portion of multilateral than of bilateral commitments goes to low-income countries.

In terms of composition, aid to support the development of economic infrastructure and productive capacity building dominated overall volumes of aid for trade, at 54 percent and 43 percent, respectively, in 2007. Aid for trade policy and regulations, usually delivered

through technical assistance, accounted for the smallest share. However, limitations in the data collection might underestimate this portion of aid for trade.

Iraq, India, Vietnam, Afghanistan, and Ethiopia were the top five recipients of aid for trade in 2007, accounting for almost 30 percent of the total. Asian countries received almost 50 percent of all aid for trade—$10 billion on average during 2002–07 (figure 5.16).[52] Africa followed with 32 percent ($7.14 billion). Ethiopia, with 3.17 percent of total aid for trade in 2007, was the only country from Sub-Saharan Africa among the top five recipients. The predominance of Asia largely reflects the volume of aid received for economic infrastructure—almost 60 percent of total aid for trade in the region. Even when excluding large recipient countries in Asia, Africa lags behind: the average Asian country received one-and-a-half times more than the average African country. Low-income countries received only about half of the total aid-for-trade commitments in 2002–07, slightly more than half of which went to least-developed countries.

Progress has been made in trade-related technical assistance for the least-developed countries with the establishment of the Enhanced Integrated Framework (EIF) in 2007, a new executive secretariat, and a trust fund to support its operations. The new EIF governance structure will emphasize country ownership by reinforcing and enlarging the involvement of the EIF national bodies at the country level, linking the WTO-based EIF secretariat to in-country processes, and encouraging recipient countries to lead projects.[53] In September 2007 a pledging conference was held for the EIF Trust Fund in Stockholm; 22 donors pledged $170 million over a five-year period. Since then, a further $3 million has been pledged. With the selections of the trust fund manager and head of the secretariat, the EIF is likely to be fully operational in early 2009.

To complement the EIF, the World Bank launched in November 2007 the Multi-Donor Trust Fund for Trade and

FIGURE 5.16 Commitments of aid for trade by region, income group, and category, average 2002–07

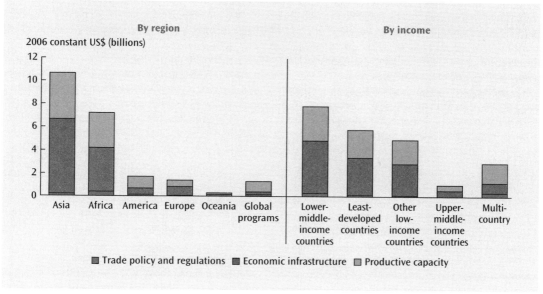

Source: OECD Creditor Reporting System and OECD/WTO Trade Capacity Building database.
Note: Asia includes East and South.

Development to provide additional resources in support of the Bank's trade strategy at the country, regional, and global levels.[54] In its first year of operation, the trust fund has supported work in many low-income countries and regional projects, and enhanced the World Bank's capacity to respond to client demand for trade-related technical assistance and capacity building; develop analytical tools to assist countries to define trade policy strategies; expand research and datasets on trade topics of importance to developing countries; and diffuse knowledge on international trade to developing countries. Some examples of work include a comprehensive program on trade in services in the Africa region; mainstreaming trade and competitiveness in Côte d'Ivoire, Madagascar, and Tanzania; technical assistance for trade policy reform and export promotion in North Africa; a regional study on services trade in South Asia; an assessment of trade facilitation and logistics in Mongolia; and new research on agriculture and poverty with a focus on gender.

Notes

1. Exports and imports of 45 countries that have reported trade data for January 2009 are uniformly weak, with an average drop of over 30 percent compared to January 2008. Based on a handful of countries that have reported February 2009 data, including China, trade continues to be very weak, and downside risks are large.

2. The Baltic Dry Index indirectly measures global supply and demand for the commodities shipped aboard dry bulk carriers, such as building materials, coal, metallic ores, and grains. The index is sometimes perceived as a leading economic indicator of global trade because dry bulk primarily consists of materials that function as raw material inputs to the production of intermediate or finished goods, such as concrete, electricity, steel, and food.

3. See chapter 1 for a more detailed account of the macroeconomic impact of the global economic crisis on developing countries.

4. World Bank 2009.

5. Chauffour 2008.

6. OECD 2008.

7. Additional information on food and fuel price impacts on individual countries is available in IMF 2008.

8. The world's major developing-country exporters of wheat (Argentina, Ukraine, Russian Federation, and Kazakhstan) and rice (Vietnam, India, and China) introduced various types of temporary export restrictions in an attempt to decouple domestic markets from global markets and rein in domestic food prices.

9. In the case of large exporters, this impact may be less significant as agriculture export is often carried out by large commercial farms that have few links to the rural poor.

10. Export restrictions had a particularly strong impact on the rice market, for which global trade is less than 10 percent of total production. After China, the Arab Republic of Egypt, India, Pakistan, and Vietnam (among others) restricted exports, small countries that relied on imports were unable to ensure adequate supplies. Subsequent bilateral agreements between important trading partners, such as Bangladesh and India, were insufficient to alleviate this problem.

11. The secondary market plays a key role in helping banks undertake transactions that are larger than their current credit and cross-border limits.

12. Whether the contraction of trade finance in late 2008 contributed to the decline in world trade or was a consequence of this decline remains an open question. However, the latter force appears to have been dominant: overall demand for trade finance has decreased with lower trade volumes and higher prices.

13. According to Global Business Intelligence, a consulting firm specializing in international supply chain matters, accounts receivable and payable (that is, open accounts) represent 78 percent of international trade, LCs 15 percent, and finance for export collection (another paper-based transaction similar to LCs but without credit) 7 percent.

14. IMF 2003.

15. In total only 116 trade finance loans (excluding aircraft and shipping) were signed in the last quarter, the lowest quarterly count since 2004.

16. IMF 2009.

17. Evidence of liquidity pressure on trade finance has also been reported by the banks participating in the IFC's Global Trade Finance Program. Major international banks participating in the program have been unwilling to assume a portion of the risk in a particular transaction, leaving the underlying risk to the IFC alone.

18. See chapter 6 for more details on actions taken by the international financial institutions.

19. Leaders agreed to "ensure availability of at least $250 billion" over the next two years to support trade finance through our export credit and investment agencies and through the MDBs.

20. The 1930 U.S. Smoot-Hawley Act that raised tariffs is widely blamed for intensifying the Great Depression.

21. Pascal Lamy, "WTO Is Global Insurance Policy for a Global Economy," speech before the Finance Commission of the French National Assembly, Paris, October 1, 2008.

22. Statement from the G-20 Summit on Financial Markets and the World Economy, Washington. DC., November 15, 2008.

23. It is estimated that if WTO members were to increase their applied tariffs up to their bound rates, the average global rate of duty would double and the value of global trade would be cut by about 7.7 percent; see Bouet and Laborde 2008.

24. Newfarmer and Gamberoni 2009; WTO 2009.

25. For instance, a "Buy American" provision made it into the final $787-billion fiscal stimulus bill passed by the United States in February 2009. It requires the purchase of U.S.-made iron, steel, and manufactured goods for projects of construction, alteration, maintenance, or repair of a public building or public work financed by the bill. However, it also requires that the measure be applied in a manner consistent with U.S. obligations under international trade agreements.

26. Major U.S. and European carmakers received various forms of financial support in late 2008 and early 2009.

27. In the same vein, when meeting with the Swiss president on January 27, 2009, Chinese Premier Wen Jiabao underscored that the word "crisis" in Chinese is made of two characters meaning danger and opportunity.

28. Mattoo and Subramanian 2008.

29. Martin and Mattoo 2008.

30. The special safeguard mechanism allows developing countries to raise tariffs temporarily to deal with import surges and price falls. The blockage in the July 2008 negotiations was about import surges in the particular instance where the mechanism raises tariff above commitments made in the Uruguay Round. A number of countries opposed breaching the pre-Doha Round commitments, while others insisted on being able to do this.

31. Statement from the G-20 Summit on Financial Markets and the World Economy, Washington DC, November 15, 2008.

32. Statement from tthe G-20 Summit, London, April 2, 2009.

33. In calculating the dumping margin of a product (that is, the average of the differences between the export prices and the home market prices), the practice of zeroing puts a value of zero on instances when the export price is higher than the home market price.

34. According to Bouet and Laborde (2008), there would be a potential loss of $1.064 trillion in world trade if world leaders were to fail to conclude the Doha Round and if countries were to subsequently revert to the trade policies in place at the end of the Uruguay Round.

35. Statement of World Bank Group President Robert B. Zoellick on Doha WTO Negotiations, August 18, 2008 at http://web.worldbank.org/ WBSITE/EXTERNAL/NEWS/0,,contentMDK:21 874660~pagePK:34370~piPK:34424~theSitePK: 4607,00.html.

36. As of December 31, 2008, some 421 regional trade agreements had been notified to the World Trade Organization.

37. For more detail, see World Bank–IMF 2008.

38. The OTRI and TTRI are calculated as a weighted sum of ad valorem tariffs and ad valorem equivalent of specific duties, and nontariff measures (for the OTRI), where the weights are import volumes and import demand elasticities (Kee, Nicita and Olarreaga 2008). The OTRIs by country and the data used to calculate the OTRI are posted on the DECRG Trade Research Website under "data and statistics"; see http://go.worldbank.org/ C5VQJIV3H0.

39. One characteristic of the OTRI to keep in mind is that it is calculated using weights that reflect actual imports. This may distort the picture about the geographic pattern of protection. An appropriate measure of the OTRI and TTRI is the one that breaks it down by product category, not by source.

40. Gootiz and Mattoo 2009.

41. Djankov, Freund, and Pham, 2006; Ikenson 2008.

42. World Bank 2008b.

43. World Bank 2007; World Bank 2008a.

44. The cost measure does not include tariffs or trade taxes or "unofficial" costs such as briberies. The indicator is part of the Doing Business trading-across-borders index, which compiles the number of documents, the cost, and the time necessary for procedural requirements for exporting and importing a standardized cargo of goods by ocean transport. Local freight forwarders, shipping lines, customs brokers and port officials pro-

vide information on required documents and cost as well as the time to complete each procedure. Inland transport costs are based on distance to the shipping port. The methodology, surveys, and data are available at http://www.doingbusiness.org.

45. Hoekman and Nicita 2008. Standard variables include GDP and population of the country pairs, distance between them, controls for adjacency, common language, and access to the sea. Because the OTRI is calculated at the bilateral level, it captures the effect of preferential trade agreements. In the analysis only two components of the LPI are used: indicators of the efficiency of customs and a measure of access to (choice of) and affordability of international shippers. The dataset used spans 104 importers and 115 exporters.

46. For example, Limão and Venables 2001; Wilson, Mann, and Otsuki 2003; Anderson and Marcouiller 2002; Anderson and van Wincoop 2003; Francois and Manchin 2007.

47. The effect of NTMs is captured at the margin, that is, given the effect of the existing tariff structure.

48. The 5 and 10 percent thresholds correspond to the levels that would bring the TTRI and OTRI of low-income countries to that of middle-income countries.

49. Ikenson 2008.

50. Monitoring takes place at three levels: (1) global monitoring, carried out by the OECD; (2) donor monitoring, in the form of self-evaluations; and (3) in-country monitoring, also in the form of self-assessments.

51. For an update of the ongoing work, see WTO, 2008 Aid-for-Trade Roadmap, Annotated Update, July 23, 2008 at http://www.wto.org/ english/tratop_e/devel_e/a4t_e/a4t_roadmap_ feb08_e.doc

52. In the OECD Credit Reporting System database, Asia includes Middle East Asia, South and Central Asia, and Far East Asia.

53. The Enhanced Integrated Framework (EIF) is a multi-agency (IMF, ITC, UNCTAD, UNDP, the World Bank, and the WTO), multidonor program to assist least-developed countries in addressing national competitiveness priorities through trade diagnostic. The enhancement of the EIF was recommended by the WTO Task Force to improve governance as well as communication and coordination between the various partners.

54. The current donors to the MDTF are Norway, Sweden, and the United Kingdom for a total contribution of approximately $30 million over three years (2007–10).

International Financial Institutions: Crisis Response and Support for the Private Sector

The international financial institutions (IFIs) have a crucial role to play in supporting an effective response to the global crisis and the development emergency that now confronts many developing countries.[1] As a result, the focus of the IFIs has shifted to counteracting and mitigating the global private credit crunch and recession. This contrasts with 2007, when the impact of the IFIs stemmed largely from their ability to leverage private capital, which reached record levels of about $1 trillion in net terms in that year.

In 2008 credit conditions for developing countries deteriorated sharply as private flows dried up. Cross-border syndicated bank loans fell from $410 billion to $167 billion. Bond issuances fell from $170 billion to $72 billion. Equity investments fell from $269 billion to $174 billion. In 2009 net private capital flows to developing countries could fall still further, to less than one-fifth of the 2007 peak level, as private credits continue to contract.[2] Indeed, net private flows could even turn negative in 2009 if difficulties in rolling over maturing debt intensify.

The immediate priority for the IFIs is to respond to the crisis and deal with an unprecedented rise in demand for financing. The World Bank estimates that developing countries face a financing gap of $270 billion–$700 billion in 2009 depending on the severity of the economic and financial crisis and the strength and timing of policy responses.[3] Should a more pessimistic outcome occur, the financing gap could increase to as much as $1 trillion. Some middle-income countries had relied heavily on private finance to fund large current account deficits in 2008. They have been the first to feel the impact of the global crisis. They need funding to smooth a reduction in deficits, as well as to roll over existing debts and manage reduced liquidity in their banking systems.

In 2009 another round of impacts is expected to hit all developing countries. Reflecting the global recession, this round will come through reductions in export volumes and prices, remittances, tourism, foreign investment, and reduced public revenues and hence expenditures.

The immediate priority for the IFIs is to limit the fall in economic growth in developing countries, to maintain public infrastructure assets, and to assist poor households. The negative effect on human capital of growth collapses seems to be greater than the positive effect from growth accelerations.[4] Thus the ability of the IFIs to offset recent shocks is critical to sustaining recent gains toward achieving the Millennium Development Goals (MDGs).

Before the crisis hit, one-third of all developing countries had current account deficits surpassing 10 percent of gross domestic product (GDP). These countries will face growing problems in financing such deficits and will need to restrict demand. Private capital for trade, infrastructure, microfinance, and health care has been sharply cut. All told, the reduction in net private capital could amount to about 5 percentage points of developing-country GDP in 2009.

The private sector in developing countries finds itself in a particular squeeze. The flight to quality means that financing is more expensive or simply unattainable for many firms. The International Finance Corporation (IFC) estimates that its clients have postponed or cancelled about $100 billion worth of projects because of lack of finance.

The boom, and now bust, of private financial flows to developing countries highlight the complexity of tapping the development potential of the private sector. On the one hand, in a normal year, private capital far exceeds official aid and is viewed as indispensable to achieve the MDGs, especially for big-ticket items like infrastructure and social services. On the other hand, private capital has been volatile and is allocated on commercial terms rather than according to where the development impact is greatest.

The resources of the multilateral development banks (MDBs) flow largely to the public sector, so these institutions must be careful that any crisis response not undermine the long-term strategy of support for the private sector and that the response builds long-term productivity improvements into the projects they finance. The MDBs need to find what the African Development Bank (AfDB) refers to as the growing "sweet spot" between traditional public and private domains.

Although differentiated according to country circumstance, the core IFI strategy must have four components:

■ Stabilize the macroeconomy and, where appropriate, encourage stimulus

■ Protect development assets, by avoiding stop-go expenditures on new projects and maintaining existing infrastructure assets spending
■ Protect poor households and help maintain social and political stability
■ Maintain the long-term focus on market development and strengthening of the private sector.

The IFIs have responded with agility to country needs to stabilize the balance of payments so far. The International Monetary Fund (IMF) has provided $49 billion since mid-2008 and the MDBs (the World Bank Group and the four major regional development banks) had record gross disbursements of $55 billion in 2008. Much of this increase took the form of budget support to maintain public expenditure, including improvements in social safety nets to mitigate the effects of the crisis on the poorest. But IFI capacity to continue to expand operations in response to the crisis is declining. Some MDBs may require significant capital increases because crisis lending has reduced available headroom. In this context, the Group of Twenty (G-20) leaders at the recent summit in London took timely action in agreeing to support sizable increases in resources available to the IMF and the MDBs.

Low-income countries, while less affected by the crisis so far, have not had access to additional resources to the same extent. Disbursements of concessional funds from MDBs were relatively flat in fiscal 2008 at about $12.5 billion. The IMF provided about $260 million in additional Poverty Reduction and Growth Facility funds in 2008. While disbursements may pick up thanks to generous replenishments of the International Development Association (IDA), the African Development Fund, and the Asian Development Fund, existing resources may not be sufficient to meet low-income country needs. Accordingly, agreements reached at the G-20 summit in London also sought to boost resources available to support low-income countries.

Along with greater resources, the MDBs have made progress in the effectiveness of their interventions, including in terms of the indicators relevant for the Paris Declaration on aid effectiveness. In some areas, however, such as the use of country systems, use of project implementation units, and predictability of aid, the MDBs still fall short. The Development Assistance Committee suggests that efforts will have to be geared up considerably to meet the Paris Declaration targets set for 2010.

The role of the IFIs of course extends beyond financing. Knowledge is a core IFI comparative advantage. A crucial role for the IFIs in the context of the current global crisis is to inform policy making by analyzing the international spillovers of national policy actions and bringing out the interconnected nature of the challenges, and to highlight the need to ensure that national responses are consistent with the global good. Amid rising pressures for policies to turn inward, the IFIs' role in warning against the risks of trade protectionism and financial mercantilism is indispensable. Drawing policy lessons from the current crisis, especially but not only in financial regulation, will be another key area. The IMF has a particularly important role in enhanced surveillance of risk in the globalized financial markets.

The crisis has highlighted the need for a reform of the Bretton Woods institutions and indeed all the IFIs to fill the gaps in development finance—especially in risk management instruments and facilities for low-income countries—that have been revealed and to better integrate private sector development with public sector lending and reform. The central issues are the mandates, instrumentalities, and governance of the institutions to allow them to play a more effective role. A vigorous crisis response in 2009 can set the stage for a new multilateralism, one that embraces finance, trade, development, and climate change.

Strategic Overview: Crisis Response and Medium-Term Strategies to Support the Private Sector

The crisis has only reinforced the IFI focus on private sector activity as the critical driver of development. When the private sector is strong and vigorous, development progress is made, but when the private sector falters, the key strategy is how to protect development against reversals. Fiscal stimulus packages in response to the crisis will catalyze sustainable economic growth only if they result in a reawakening of private and business sector activities. The private sector, in turn, will rebound only if it is supported by an adequate financial sector and by an appropriate enabling environment. Hence, structural reform of the business environment is an important complement to macroeconomic and fiscal policies in dealing with the crisis. The most effective strategies will be those that link the crisis response with long-term productivity enhancements and with a vision of how to nurture the private sector over the long term.

At the heart of the IFI approach toward private sector development is the realization that growth is central to poverty reduction and that private sector development in a properly regulated environment is the main engine of growth. As the Asian Development Bank (ADB) has put it: "Thriving businesses create jobs. Jobs provide incomes. Steady incomes reduce poverty and provide opportunities for new generations."

The approach to private sector development has evolved as countries move beyond first-round macroeconomic and trade integration reforms to second-round microeconomic and institutional reforms such as administrative, legal, and regulatory functions. The latter require private sector input to determine priorities and impact, and presuppose in-depth knowledge of the sector. Thus, public policy increasingly relies on a healthy dialogue with and understanding of the private sector. The IFIs have understood this and adapted their strategies accordingly, raising the share of financial and human resources dedicated to private sector development and changing approaches to build partnerships and broaden engagement.

Nevertheless, the IFIs have not always found it easy to develop effective operational approaches. In a 2005 evaluation of development effectiveness, the Independent Evaluation Group of the World Bank noted that private sector development projects had one of the lowest success rates of any sector.[5]

Partly, these findings reflect the tensions involved in providing public support to private companies. First and foremost, as some MDB funding is on terms that are generally more favorable to companies than purely commercial finance, questions have been raised about the distortionary effects of implicit public subsidies. The benefits from lending to the private sector are clear. New theories of the importance of "self-discovery"[6] and the potential for market failure in introducing new products and processes into an economy provide the underpinnings for public funds to support demonstration projects. But there can also be costs. Direct credit lines may distort broader credit markets and create unsustainable financial intermediaries.[7]

The MDBs have also been concerned about whether their funding to the private sector is additional to private funding, or simply a cheaper option that could undermine market discipline. Additionality of funding has been fostered by aggressively expanding into underserved market segments such as micro, small, and medium enterprise funding; big-ticket infrastructure; social sectors; and, increasingly, underserved areas. For example, the European Bank for Reconstruction and Development (EBRD) was initially the only market-oriented lender in transition economies, so its activities were additional almost by definition. The IFC has put an increased focus on poor countries and Africa in its strategy, explicitly aiming at having 50 percent of its new projects in these countries by 2011. Such strategies

promote additionality but also call for flexibility. As markets mature and demonstration effects take hold, the rationale for public intervention diminishes.[8]

More fundamentally, the MDBs have moved to sharpen the identification of the public policy rationale for supporting private firms. In this, they have shifted from support for specific firms to support for market development, with a focus on creating the right enabling environment for business, setting standards for environmental and social assessments for firms, reducing capital flight and corruption, and widening the scope of markets.

Accordingly, a broader, more comprehensive approach toward private sector development has been adopted. Broadly speaking, IFI efforts to catalyze the private sector can be classified under two headings:

- Extending the reach of markets, through risk mitigation, improvement in the enabling environment, and direct support for demonstration projects; and
- Improving basic infrastructure and social service delivery through introducing private sector management and incentives, including innovative finance, to induce faster speed of implementation and expansion of access of the poorest segments of society.

The strategic challenge today is to respond to the financial crisis while remaining committed to the long-term goals of private sector development. Table 6.1 shows some of the main elements of IFI support for the private sector. It should be noted that many IFI operations bundle finance, knowledge, and partnerships. Moreover, some elements might be more significant as instruments for mobilizing other elements (for example, partnerships for finance and advisory services) than as a means of support in themselves. Many new mechanisms have been introduced in 2008, particularly to stabilize markets, in risk management and finance, but knowledge and partnership activities

TABLE 6.1 Selected elements of IFI support to the private sector

Area of engagement	Extending the reach of markets			Improving basic service delivery	
	Risk management	Enabling environment	Direct project support	Infrastructure	Social services
Finance	Countercyclical lending/ balance of payments support	Financial market development	Equity	Public-private partnerships	Innovative financing
	Flexible Credit Line[a]	Public sector reform	Loans	Sustainable Infrastructure Action Plan	Health for Africa
	DPOs/deferred drawdown		Guarantees		Vulnerability Financing Facility[a]
	Disaster insurance		Micro-, small, and medium enterprise funds	Energy for the Poor Initiative	Advance Market Commitment for Vaccines[a]
	Microfinance Liquidity Facility[a]				
	Trade Finance Facilitation Program				
	Global Trade Finance Program				
	Global Food Response Program[a]				
	IDA Fast-Track Initiative[a]				
Knowledge	Macroeconomic policy	Doing Business	Technical assistance	Risk management frameworks	Social performance indicators[a]
	Debt Sustainability Framework	Financial Sector Assessment Program	Small and medium enterprise toolkit		
	International Tax Dialogue	Standards and codes			
	Saving mobilization	Regulatory reform			
	Extractive Industries Transparency Initiative++	Foreign investment promotion			
Partnerships	Climate change	Corporate social responsibility	Carbon markets	Public-Private Infrastructure Advisory Facility	Global Partnership for Output-Based Aid
	Stolen Asset Recovery[a]	Equator principles	Aid for trade		Global Fund to Fight AIDS, Tuberculosis, and Malaria
	Ethics in business	Corporate governance	Consultative Group to Assist the Poor	Global Gas Flaring Reduction	Global Alliance for Vaccines and Immunizations
	Global Emerging Markets Local Currency Bond Program		Sovereign Fund Facility[a]		

a. Mechanism introduced in 2008 or 2009.

have also evolved. At the same time, the institutions have intensified activities under existing mechanisms.

As the crisis unfolds, the IFIs have responded in flexible ways, but some weaknesses in each area of engagement—finance, knowledge, and partnerships—have also been revealed.

Finance

On financing, several key strategic issues emerged during 2008:

■ Are IFI resources adequate to meet the needs caused by a major global slowdown?
■ Does the crisis alter long-term projections of demand for MDB activities?

- Are modalities of support sufficiently flexible?
- Is MDB capital leveraged and deployed to minimize risk?
- Are low-income countries adequately protected?
- Do MDB activities adequately protect vulnerable groups within countries?

The IFIs have had the financial capability to respond to the crisis but are now approaching resource limits. While the IMF's liquidity position remained satisfactory at the end of 2008, G-20 leaders at the recent summit in London agreed to support a large expansion in the IMF's precrisis lending capacity to enable the institution to face the expected unprecedented rise in demand for financing. As an immediate measure, bilateral financing from members will be increased to $250 billion. In the near term, the immediate financing from members will be incorporated into an expanded and more flexible New Arrangements to Borrow and will be increased by up to $500 billion. The G-20 leaders also supported consideration of market borrowing by the IMF to be used if necessary in conjunction with other sources of financing to raise resources to the level needed to meet demands. The IMF's concessional lending capacity for low-income countries and access limits will be doubled. The leaders committed to using additional resources from agreed-on IMF gold sales, together with surplus income, to provide $6 billion additional concessional and flexible finance for the poorest countries over the next two to three years. In addition to these steps, G-20 leaders agreed to support a general allocation of special drawing rights (SDRs) equivalent to $250 billion to increase global liquidity, $100 billion of which will go directly to emerging market and developing countries.

Among the MDBs, the ADB is already short of resources, and without a general capital increase it cannot conduct regular multiyear programming discussions with major clients. The EBRD is also reviewing its capital resources. The AfDB is already finding that it may need to bring forward its plans for a capital increase in 2012. The International Bank for Reconstruction and Development (IBRD) estimates it could use its $100 billion in available resources over the next three years. At the London summit in April 2009, the G-20 leaders agreed to support a 200 percent general capital increase at the ADB and to review the need for capital increases of the AfDB, EBRD, and the IDB. The G-20 statement supported additional lending by the MDBs, including to low-income countries, of $100 billion over the next three years.

From a strategic perspective, MDB capital increases should be based on longer-term business needs rather than a crisis response. To illustrate, IBRD lending after the East Asia crisis fell to one-half of its crisis-lending levels, so crisis-lending levels should not be the basis for capital need. At the same time, the crisis may be changing the nature of demand from middle-income clients, who may now see the MDBs as more reliable development finance partners than private capital markets and look to them for a larger part of their financing needs. Demand for risk-based instruments, such as deferred drawdown options and guarantees, has been especially strong and may well continue after the current crisis is over.

The issue of capital increases is therefore tied to the issue of adequately flexible and speedy modalities of MDB engagement. A striking feature of 2008 was that even in the face of dramatic shocks, some IFI facilities were underused. A number of precautionary instruments, such as the World Bank's deferred drawdown option, and various trade financing arrangements, which have had slow uptake in times of ample private liquidity, are now seen as useful additions for MDBs. Clients are increasingly requesting such credit lines. The crisis has highlighted the need for speed and transparency in access to resources. But the standard MDB lending model is built around negotiated agreements and safeguard procedures that take considerable time, although in emergencies the response can be rapid.

The strategic issue is how to ensure that MDB facilities complement the leading role of the IMF in countercyclical lending and are provided only in the context of viable macroeconomic programs. The broader trend toward ex ante certification of policies rather than ex post conditionalities may make this task easier. In countries with good policies, MDB finance could be directly targeted at fiscal expenditures that need to be supported during a crisis to avoid long-lasting development setbacks.

The MDB role in crises is to protect public assets and the most vulnerable households so that welfare and economic losses are minimized. For example, one estimate suggests that $45 billion in road asset value in developing countries was lost between 1970 and 1989 for lack of $10 billion in maintenance spending.[9] The MDBs do not have the resources, however, to offset private capital swings in most countries. From this perspective the MDB role is to provide resources to fund budget priorities, not to provide countercyclical balance of payments financing per se.

One of the benefits of the shift of MDB financing toward nonconcessional, nonsovereign lending, documented in the 2008 *Global Monitoring Report*, was the increase in leverage that could be brought about by partnering with the private sector. With the crisis, leverage options have narrowed. For that reason, the IFC has shifted its focus by launching a broad and targeted set of initiatives to help shore up the private sector through support for trade financing, recapitalization of banks, and financing for small and medium enterprises. There are better prospects for guarantees and other innovative financing instruments to generate leverage by mitigating risk. While there has been an expansion of such instruments, the crisis has highlighted the ample scope for scaling up in a more systematic way if balance sheets permit.

Low-income countries have far fewer options than middle-income countries to access new funds during crisis periods. They are constrained by fixed limits on grants and concessional credits. There is therefore an asymmetry in treatment between low- and middle-income countries and a much greater risk that low-income countries will be forced to adjust through domestic demand contraction, risking recent development gains. Poor households in low-income countries will then be left with no relief. For that reason, the World Bank established a Global Food Crisis Response Program based on additional trust funds in May 2008 and is now proposing a flexible Vulnerability Fund as a way of responding to the current crisis.[10]

Several technical solutions have been advanced to deal with the limited availability of incremental resources for poor countries: front-loading of new commitments, contingent debt service clauses in concessional credits, emergency procedures to accelerate disbursements on existing projects, relaxation of budget support ceilings, and access to nonconcessional financing (with or without buy-down arrangements to lower future debt service costs) subject to limits under the Debt Sustainability Framework.

The crisis has revealed areas where a cutback of private capital can be particularly damaging to development: trade, infrastructure, banks (including those dealing with micro-, small, and medium enterprise finance), energy, and household safety nets. Options to ensure that these areas can be managed through future cycles should be a strategic priority for MDBs. In this way, the crisis may drive considerations of selectivity and comparative advantage of MDBs.

Knowledge

In recent years, all IFIs have emphasized their knowledge and learning contributions to development and their desire to shift toward more knowledge-based institutions. Knowledge services, such as country analytical work, technical assistance, and global data and research, provide countries with analytic, diagnostic, and capacity-building support. Shared knowledge on the development vision, policies, and expenditure frameworks to link programs with budget resources has become indispensable in the current volatile environment.

In fact, provision of knowledge is one of the core comparative advantages of multilateral agencies.[11] The IFI reorientation toward knowledge services focuses on building country absorptive capacities, strengthening country strategies, underpinning aid effectiveness, and disseminating and sharing global practices and experiences in implementing development. Four areas stand out:

- Understanding of the global economic system and development of risk mitigation
- Country-level implementation of global standards and codes
- Country-level development of robust markets
- Social and environmental assessments

Many countries are struggling to understand the nature of the current financial crisis and the channels through which they could be affected. For example, middle-income countries in the Middle East and North Africa region have asked for help in understanding the factors behind the large swings in oil prices and the implications of the financial crisis.

Growing economic nationalism and financial mercantilism in the face of the crisis are pressuring the open, global economy. The IFIs have a valuable role to play in documenting cooperative, collective solutions and the pitfalls of beggar-thy-neighbor policies. The implementation of new forms of state aid to industry, regulatory forbearance for banks, temporary trade and capital account restrictions (even those permitted under the World Trade Organization), incentives for foreign investments, and exchange rate policies are all areas where the IFIs can monitor developments on a global basis and provide advice and information to countries and regional peer review groups.

The IMF, in particular, has a critical role to play in enhanced surveillance of macroeconomic and financial risks. The IMF will closely collaborate with a new Financial Stability Board (including G-20 countries, members of the Financial Stability Forum, Spain, and the European Commission) to monitor progress in implementing the G-20 Action Plan for strengthening financial supervision and regulation. Both institutions will also prepare joint semiannual Early Warning Exercises (EWEs), which integrate macrofinancial and regulatory perspectives and identify macrofinancial risks; the first of these joint exercises was completed in March 2009 in collaboration with the Financial Stability Forum. At the same time, financial sector advice given under the joint IMF–World Bank Financial Sector Assessment Program (FSAP) will be better integrated into country surveillance activities and policy dialogue. To further bolster its macroeconomic analysis, the IMF has also expanded its semiannual vulnerability analyses to advanced economies. Many emerging economies have been surprised at the dimensions of their exposure to a global recession. For low-income countries, the joint IMF–World Bank Debt Sustainability Framework provides a key tool for assessing fiscal risk.

The crisis has underlined the benefits of financing development in ways that do not create debt. Self-reliance echoes calls from many developing-country policy makers but is undermined by tax evasion and illicit capital flows.[12] These were a major topic of discussion at the Doha Conference on Financing for Development, and the international tax dialogue and anticorruption efforts are examples of how IFI knowledge activities can have impact on broad development policies.

Increasingly IFIs are viewed as useful vehicles for monitoring the application of global standards and codes and other forms of international benchmarking. Financial Sector Assessment Programs (FSAP), associated Reports on Observance of Standards and Codes, and business and foreign investment promotion rules and regulations have been valuable tools for this dialogue. With new regulatory approaches to the financial sector certain to emerge out of the global crisis discussions, the IFIs will be well placed to monitor individual country compliance and to assist developing countries with implementation.

Strengthening country systems, especially on financial management and public expenditure, are important pillars of the IFI agenda of leveraging knowledge with financial resources to maximize development impact.

Sound markets with well-developed regulatory systems are the best form of insurance against risk. IFI knowledge can help countries implement institutional reforms to build more robust markets.[13] All the MDBs have technical assistance programs that help entrepreneurs understand the responsibilities and risks they bear as business people. This work has helped advance an understanding of how social and environmental standards can help businesses contribute to sustainable development in a cooperative fashion without losing competitiveness.

Partnerships

Before the crisis, the scale of private capital was already driving MDBs to seek new partnerships to advance development. As the crisis unfolds, the strategic need to engage coherently with partners in shaping strategies and carrying out specific programs becomes more critical. Strategic partnerships are evolving around:

- Resources for development to fill financing gaps
- Division of labor according to comparative advantage among agencies
- Innovative and scaled-up approaches
- Global public goods

The MDBs engage in partnerships to achieve common development objectives, under agreed-upon shared and joint responsibilities. Partnerships are meant to augment the MDBs' own development initiatives, but they also facilitate harmonization of efforts between donors, recipient countries, and various other stakeholders at global, regional, and country levels. The MDBs are slowly moving toward expanding partnerships in this broad sense. There are now many instances of partnerships among and between multilaterals, bilaterals, and private agencies: as of fiscal 2008, the World Bank alone had more than 1,000 trust funds with donor commitments totaling $26.3 billion. But private resource mobilization remains limited. World Bank Group trust fund contributions from foundations and corporations totaled only $1 billion between 2002 and 2008, and the development gains from trying to expand these resources significantly appear small. Hence, resource mobilization is no longer seen as the main driver of private partnerships.[14]

More scope exists to build partnerships in response to specific challenges. Earlier successes with public-private partnerships include the Consultative Group on International Agricultural Research and the Onchocerciasis (River Blindness) Control program. Along the same lines, the Global Alliance for Vaccines and Immunizations, the Global Fund to Fight AIDS, Tuberculosis, and Malaria, and new commitments to agricultural research in Africa offer much promise and exemplify the MDB approach of reaching out to world-class corporations. Another example is the IFC's Global Emerging Markets Local Currency Bond program. But these approaches work only when there is a full understanding of the comparative advantage of various partners, in terms of either sectoral expertise or the nature and terms of the financing they provide.

Partnerships are especially important in the delivery of global public goods. In those cases, the voice of developing countries in shaping international goals is important. A recent example is the UN Office on Drugs and Crime/World Bank Stolen Asset Recovery (StAR) program, where bank secrecy rules in developed countries were adapted to enable developing countries to reclaim stolen assets which, by some counts, could exceed $1 trillion.[15] StAR (along with the Extractive Industries Transparency Initiative) helps promote transparency and better governance across the developing world (box 6.1).

IFI Operational Results and New Initiatives

The IFI crisis response has prioritized stabilizing markets. The medium-term support for private sector strategies falls under two categories—extending the reach of markets, and improving basic service delivery. This section summarizes IFI activities in 2008 and recent new initiatives along these dimensions.

Extending the Reach of Markets

Stabilizing markets, countercyclical financing, and risk management

In 2008 the IFIs played an important role in countercyclical financing (table 6.2) and in financing emerging development needs. The IMF has taken the lead with its strong encouragement of additional fiscal stimulus in countries with healthy balance of payments and public debt profiles. Since mid-2008, it also has provided financial support, amounting to about $49 billion, to nine emerging countries to permit orderly adjustment to payments crises.[16] Requests for such support are expected to rise sharply in 2009. The IMF moved quickly to establish a new Flexible Credit Line (FCL) to provide large and up-front financing to emerging economies with very strong fundamentals and policies. The facility can be used on a precautionary basis or for actual balance-of-payment needs. Because access to the FCL is restricted to those countries that meet strict qualification criteria, drawings under it are not tied to policy goals agreed with the country. Countries not qualifying for the FCL can count on new High Access Precautionary Stand-By Arrangements (SBAs) as a regular lending window. Like the FCL, precautionary SBAs can be frontloaded and take account of the strength of a country's policies and the external environment. Decisions have been taken on a doubling of access levels for emerging markets and low-income countries, and conditionality has been reformed to make it more focused and tailored to country circumstances. Furthermore, the IMF has made substantial progress with a comprehensive review of the

---

BOX 6.1   Stolen Asset Recovery Initiative

Corruption and asset theft are development problems of the first magnitude. The direct economic impact is huge. An even greater impact probably results from the insidious effects of degrading public institutions, tainting and destabilizing financial systems, and undermining the rule of law.

The StAR Initiative, launched by the World Bank and the United Nations Office on Drugs and Crime in October 2007, works with financial centers and developing countries to reduce the barriers to asset recovery and facilitate developing countries' efforts to secure the return of stolen assets. Programs have been started in six countries, and discussions with many more are under way. The StAR initiative is about justice and the prospect of taking legal action after years of impunity for corrupt officials, even when the prospects for the return of stolen assets are low. StAR is exploring how financial centers can strengthen regulations and improve compliance and enforcement of authorities to trace the beneficiary ownership of bank accounts and to enhance supervision of accounts of politically exposed persons. At the same time, StAR provides legal assistance and training to developing countries to strengthen their capacity to manage asset recovery programs as part of broader anti-corruption efforts.

In a first success, Haiti appears to be on its way to recovering $6 million after the Swiss Federal Office of Justice ruled that account holders had failed to prove that the funds were legally acquired. The order may be appealed.

---

lending framework and external debt policies for low-income countries.

The Fund also modified its Exogenous Shocks Facility to speed up access, given the limited uptake of demand for resources from this facility in early 2008 when commodity prices started to soar. As a result, $261 million has been committed under this facility as of the end of 2008. There were twelve cases of augmentation under Poverty Reduction and Growth Facility arrangements in 2008, increasing financial commitments under these arrangements by about $214 million.

The MDBs also expanded their activities, in the first instance to help countries manage food and fuel price increases. The World Bank and the ADB both announced major initiatives to help countries manage higher food prices. The World Bank's Global Food

TABLE 6.2 Examples of IFI crisis response programs in 2008

Agency	Program	Amount	Key features
IMF	Flexible Credit Line	No formal access limits	Eligibility based on strong macroeconomic fundamentals
IMF	Modified Exogenous Shocks Facility	Up to 75 percent of quota	Rapid access component with streamlined conditionality
IMF	High-Access Precautionary Stand-By Arrangements (SBAs)	Access above normal limits for SBAs	Emergency financing procedures Only core macroeconomic conditions
IMF	Poverty Reduction and Growth Facility Augmentation	Flexible within annual and cumulative ceilings	Balance of payments support
IBRD	Development Policy Operations	$100 billion over 3 years	Budget and payments support
IBRD	Global Food Crisis Response Program	$200 million + $1 billion (other donors)	Trust funds from net income for social protection and food production
IBRD	Energy for the Poor	Trust fund	Increase energy access
IDA	Fast-track Facility	$2 billion	Support critical public spending. Front-loading of IDA 15
IFC	Global Trade Finance Program	$3 billion	Guarantees of trade credits
IFC/Japan	Bank recapitalization fund	$3 billion	Equity and subordinated debt for banks
IFC	Infrastructure Financing Facility	$500 million	Equity and loans for private and PPP infrastructure
ADB	Trade Finance Facilitation Program	$150 million	Support for trade transactions
ADB	Budget support	$717 million	Budgetary support for food security/safety nets
IDB	Liquidity Program for Growth Sustainability	$6 billion	Balance of payments support to member governments
EBRD	Crisis response	€7.0 billion	Expected 2009 financing of €7 billion (€1.6 billion over 2008), mainly for crisis response, including expanded Trade Facilitation Program
AfDB	Trade Finance Initiative	$1 billion	Lines of credit to financial institutions
AfDB	Emergency Liquidity Facility	$1.5 billion	Short-term emergency finance support

Source: IMF and MDBs.
Note: The indicated amounts do not include mobilization from partners.

Crisis Response Program has already committed $856 million for 29 countries, including $325 million for African countries. IDA has also provided $4.1 billion in new commitments of concessional financing in the second half of 2008. While helpful, that still leaves low-income countries vulnerable to global shocks. Nonconcessional lending by the IBRD has risen sharply and could reach $35 billion in fiscal 2009, triple the level of the previous year.

The World Bank has rapidly implemented a Vulnerability Financing Facility to provide an umbrella structure under which specific initiatives can be formed to pool grant resources from donors with World Bank funds in a rapid-response program to expand and strengthen social safety nets and protect

---

BOX 6.2   World Bank Group's Vulnerability Framework

The World Bank Group's Vulnerability Framework is an umbrella mechanism that includes a comprehensive range of ongoing and new programs to support growth and poverty reduction in countries impacted by the global economic crisis. A key component is a Vulnerability Financing Facility (VFF) with a focus on mitigating the impact on the poor and vulnerable through strengthening safety nets and basic social services. It comprises the Global Food Crisis Response Program (GFRP) and the Rapid Social Response Fund. A second key component is the Infrastructure Recovery and Assets Platform (INFRA) that aims to support infrastructure spending critical for growth, including energy for the poor programs. A third key component aims to strengthen support to the private sector through IFC programs. The Vulnerability Framework draws on the full range of the World Bank Group's financial, technical, advisory, and coordinating resources. The framework has an open, flexible architecture that would facilitate ready adaptation to evolving needs. Support for programs in the Vulnerability Framework would be one option for donors wishing to contribute additional resources to help developing countries respond to the global economic crisis. At the London summit in April 2009, G-20 leaders committed to supporting the Vulnerability Framework through voluntary bilateral contributions.

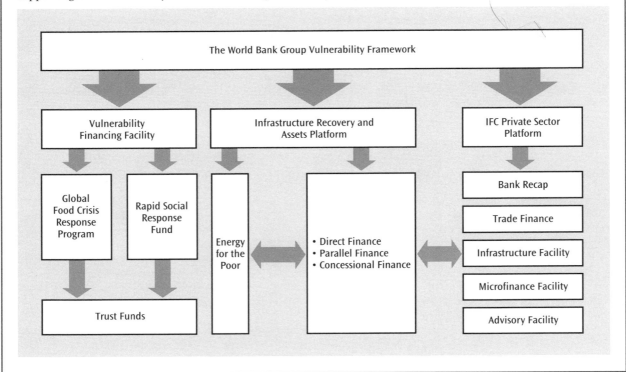

ATJELERO, S

0825

2 3 APR 2019

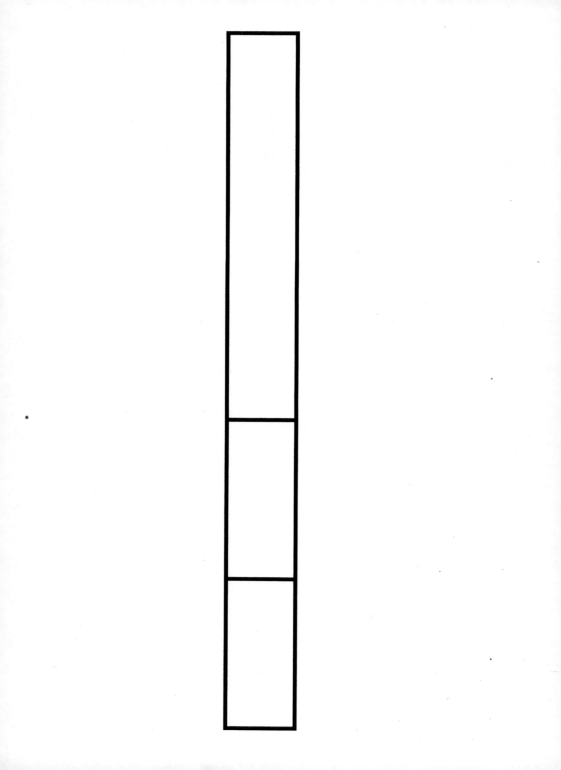

other critical public programs (box 6.2).[17] The facility is part of a broader Vulnerability Framework to assist vulnerable countries to deal with the impact of the global economic crisis. A supporting initiative is the IDA Financial Crisis Response Fast-Track Facility, set up in late 2008, which aims to fast-track up to $2 billion of financial assistance, with the potential to increase this amount in the future, depending on the need.

The MDBs have also responded to cutbacks in private trade credits. Private trade finance was hurt as counterparty risk rose and spreads on trade finance soared even for creditworthy borrowers. The ADB, EBRD, and IFC have moved to strengthen trade financing facilities and the Inter-American Development Bank (IDB) and the AfDB have new trade finance facilities under preparation (box 6.3).

Other areas that have been sharply affected are infrastructure, banks, and micro-, small, and medium enterprises. The MDBs have focused programs to respond to the needs in these sectors. The IFC established a new infrastructure crisis facility to ensure that viable privately funded infrastructure projects in emerging markets will have access to finance to weather the global crisis, and it partnered with the Japan Bank for International Cooperation to help recapitalize banks in smaller emerging markets through equity and subordinated debt (box 6.4).

Volume and Allocation of MDB Lending

Overall, MDB gross disbursements in 2008 reached a record volume of $55.1 billion, up from 48.7 billion in 2007 (figure 6.1). Of this, $42.5 billion was in nonconcessional resources, up from $36.7 billion in 2007. Gross concessional flows rose by only 3.5 percent to $12.5 billion, compared with the 17.2 percent increase in nonconcessional lending to sovereign borrowers. Total MDB lending is expected to rise sharply in the next three years, in response to the global economic crisis, to an annual average of as much as $100 billion.

Nonconcessional lending to sovereigns. Nonconcessional lending to sovereigns totaled about $27.8 billion in 2008, up from $23.7 billion in 2007, with increases spread across all regions. But nonconcessional

---

BOX 6.3 MDBs and trade finance

The World Bank Group has ramped up its support to the private sector by doubling the IFC's Global Trade Finance Program from $1.5 billion to $3.0 billion. Trade guarantees issued under the program will have an average duration of six months, thereby supporting up to $18 billion of trade finance over the next three years. The program offers banks guarantees covering the payment risk in trade transactions. Since the program's inception in September 2005, $3.2 billion in trade guarantees have been issued to support 2,600 transactions. Of the total transactions, 48 percent were for banks in Africa, 70 percent involved small and medium enterprises, 50 percent supported trade with the world's poorest countries, and 35 percent facilitated trade between emerging markets.

The EBRD's trade facilitation program guarantees political and commercial risk of 100 issuing banks and factoring companies. As of the end of 2008, the program had facilitated more than 7,600 trade deals worth more than €4.5 billion.

The ADB trade finance facilitation program started operations in 2004 and consists of three products: a Credit Guarantee; a Revolving Credit Facility; and a Risk Participation Agreement under which ADB shares risk with international banks to support trade in challenging and frontier markets. The program has supported over 1,000 international trade transactions for a total value of about $500 million and has grown exponentially over the past 12 months.

The IDB has recently approved a two-year mandate for the Structured and Corporate Finance department to support trade finance largely through credit guarantees. The AfDB is in the process of preparing a $1 billion trade finance initiative.

BOX 6.4   IFC response to the crisis

The IFC has ramped up four facilities with about $30 billion in new financing over the next three years, combining its own funds with those from partners. The facilities include:

- **Bank Recapitalization Fund ($3 billion).** This is a global equity and subordinated debt fund managed by the IFC that aims to recapitalize distressed banks. It will also provide advisory services. Japan will be a key founding partner and provide $2 billion to the fund.
- **Infrastructure Crisis Facility ($10 billion).** This facility will help ensure that viable privately funded infrastructure projects in emerging markets can weather the financial crisis. The facility will comprise a loan financing trust, an equity facility, and an advisory facility. The loan and equity components are expected to provide rollover financing and to substitute temporarily for commercial financing for new projects. Funding for existing projects would have a three- to six-year maturity. The IFC expects to invest a minimum of $300 million and mobilize between $1.5 billion and $10 billion from other sources.
- **Microfinance Liquidity Facility ($500 million).** The IFC expects to invest $150 million of its own money with contributions from Germany's KfW development bank and other donors for a total investment of $500 million, to provide refinancing to more than 100 strong microfinance institutions in 40 countries, which reach 60 million poor borrowers. The facility will be managed by three of the industry's leading fund managers.
- **Expanded Global Trade Finance Program ($18 billion over 3 years).** (See box 6.3 on trade finance.)
- **Global Trade Liquidity Pool (up to $50 billion over 3 years).** The IFC is working with a number of partners—global and regional banks—to create a global trade liquidity pool that will fund trade transactions for up to 270 days and will be self-liquidating once conditions for trade finance improve. The initiative involves $1 billion of IFC's own resources. G-20 countries have agreed to provide $3 billion to $4 billion in voluntary, bilateral contributions.

FIGURE 6.1   MDB gross disbursements, 2000–08

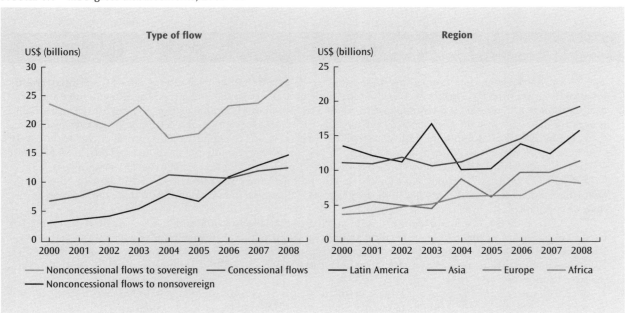

Source: Staff of the big five multilateral development banks.

lending has sharply accelerated recently. The IBRD lending pipeline has doubled since the start of fiscal 2009. Commitments in the first half of fiscal 2009 reached $12.4 billion, compared with $3.3 billion in the first half of fiscal 2008. Lending of $100 billion is envisaged for fiscal years 2009–11, almost triple the annual rate before the crisis. An acceleration in lending is also taking place at other MDBs. For example, the ADB has proposed $4 billion–$5 billion in additional commitments in 2009.

Concessional lending. Despite the crisis and record levels of donor pledges for recent replenishment of MDB concessional windows, gross concessional flows from MDBs were relatively flat in 2008 at about $12.5 billion. A sharp upward trend is expected as disbursements from new commitments start to rise. Credits and grants from the Asian Development Fund grew by 33 percent, and by 10 percent from the African Development Fund. Flows from IDA, however, declined.

IDA is in a strong position to increase support—thanks to the nearly $42 billion in commitment authority agreed for IDA 15 replenishment for the next three years—with scope for front-loading. It has up to $20.3 billion of resources available in fiscal 2009; while it committed only $4.1 billion in the first half of the fiscal year, commitments are expected to accelerate in the second half. IDA has a significant undisbursed portfolio against past commitments, amounting to $33 billion at the end of fiscal 2008.

Direct support to firms. MDB nonconcessional loans and guarantees to nonsovereign entities, mainly to the private sector, increased by about $2 billion in 2008 to $15 billion (figure 6.2). MDB nonsovereign flows (lending and equity investments) have grown by almost fourfold since 2000. The EBRD plans a 33 percent increase in commitments for 2009, to €7 billion. With the slump in private capital flows, demand for support from the private sector arms of the MDBs in likely to be strong in the period ahead.

The top two sectors for MDB private sector operations are infrastructure and financial institutions. Between them, these two

FIGURE 6.2 MDB gross disbursements to nonsovereign borrowers, by region, 2000–08

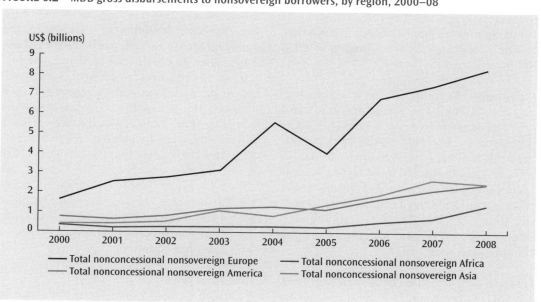

Source: Staff of the big five multilateral development banks.

sectors account for over 60 percent of total commitments.

Sixty percent of MDB nonconcessional, nonsovereign flows were directed to Europe, but there is an encouraging increase even in Africa. Geographically, the IFC has recently placed the poorest countries at the top of its agenda, and this led to commitments of $3.5 billion in IDA countries in fiscal 2008, of which $1.4 billion was in Africa across 25 countries. This is matched by AfDB's private sector operations, which grew to $1.5 billion in 2008.

In the current context, there are also good opportunities to provide nonsovereign public entities at the subnational level with long-term finance. The World Bank Group has integrated its approach to subnational financing by offering financial and guarantee products using the IFC balance sheet,[18] but this mechanism has not yet seen significant growth, and volumes are still modest, with a total exposure of $350 million. A number of countries have asked for support for nonsovereign lending to subnationals, extending beyond finance to include enhanced capital market access, especially in cases where administrative responsibilities for basic infrastructure services have been devolved to local governments. The EBRD has a longstanding and successful municipal finance business, with total commitments of €2.8 billion to date.

Guarantees. Beyond countercyclical financing, the MDBs have moved forward with other programs to reduce risk in emerging markets. The role of the Multilateral Investment Guarantee Agency (MIGA), for instance, has expanded in countries such as Ukraine and the Russian Federation, where private insurance has become more expensive (box 6.5). The IFC is also stepping up its guarantee operations, including increased collaboration with MIGA.

Coordination of MDB crisis support. The MDBs have stepped up coordination of their support to countries impacted by the global crisis. An important example of such coordination is a €24.5 billion program of support to the banking sector and bank lending to businesses hurt by the crisis in Central, Eastern, and Southern Europe jointly announced by the World Bank Group, the EBRD, and the European Investment Bank (EIB) in February 2009. The coordinated program of support will include contributions of €6 billion from the EBRD, €11 billion from the EIB, and €7.5 billion from the World Bank Group (IBRD €3.5 billion, IFC €2 billion, and MIGA €2 billion).

The Enabling Environment for Private Sector Development

MDB support for private sector development has shifted from a focus on privatization and restructuring of state-owned enterprises to one of improving the enabling environment for the private sector. The new focus is on supporting regulatory reforms, encouraging competitive and business-friendly environments, and redefining the public sector role as a catalyst and facilitator for the private sector rather than a competitor.

The IFIs use a full range of instruments to pursue a better enabling environment for private sector development. Lending for the financial sector and for public sector reform helps provide conditions in which the private sector can operate effectively. Analytical work, such as country diagnostics, metrics and global benchmarking, and specific advisory services, such as the World Bank Group's Foreign Investment Advisory Service and the Public-Private Infrastructure Advisory Facility, help countries pursue reforms to create a more efficient private sector. Partnerships, such as the introduction of global standards and codes, help ensure that the playing field is level across countries, as well as within countries.

Financial sector

Although banks in developing countries in general have not suffered severe direct losses

BOX 6.5 MIGA's contributions to supporting investment in developing countries

The Multilateral Investment Guarantee Agency (MIGA) is a specialized agency within the World Bank Group that offers political risk insurance to foreign long-term investors in developing countries. Guarantees issued by MIGA cover against the risks of inconvertibility of local currency into foreign exchange and its transfer out of developing countries, expropriation (including so-called "creeping expropriation" related to a series of governmental actions that eventually lead to the abandonment of an investment), breach of contract by the sovereign or its agents, and destruction of assets or interruption of business activities arising from politically motivated violence or civil unrest. By assuming these risks, MIGA aims at encouraging productive foreign investments into developing countries.

MIGA can manage these political risks better than private insurance providers can, but its administrative costs are higher. For this reason, MIGA is best positioned in the riskiest developing countries, where private insurers charge very high premiums.

The figures below show that MIGA is "overweight" with respect to foreign direct investment (FDI) stocks in high-risk countries—in the sense that its exposure in risky countries is far higher than these countries' share of total FDI to developing countries or their share of total developing country gross national income (GNI). By contrast, MIGA is "underweight" in low-risk, middle-income countries, which receive 72 percent of all FDI of developing countries but account for only 30 percent of MIGA's exposure.

Share of FDI stocks, GNI, and MIGA exposure in developing countries by income and risk, 2007

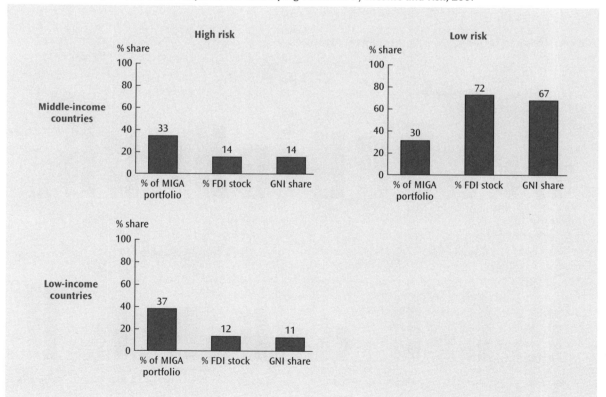

Source: MIGA.
Note: Low risk is defined as an Institutional Investor score greater than 50. Income per capita cutoff is $1,785.

from the current global financial crisis, they are increasingly suffering from the indirect fallout from reduced credit availability, higher counterparty risks, and slower real growth domestically. In addition to the shocks from the crisis, the difficulties faced by developing-country banks reflect shortcomings and vulnerabilities in developing countries' financial systems identified in assessments under the joint IMF–World Bank Financial Sector Assessment Program (FSAP).

Financial sector assessments have now been made for over 40 percent of developing countries—over 87 percent if weighted by GDP (figure 6.3). These assessments will now become a truly global program thanks to the recent G-20 agreement to apply the FSAP to all countries, including the major industrial countries. Since August 2007, the assessments have paid particular attention to crisis management, cross-border supervisory cooperation, exposure to subprime mortgages, and tighter funding conditions, in addition to the traditional focus of macrofinancial stability, regulatory and supervisory issues, and financial market infrastructure. Recently concluded assessments have found weak risk management, insufficient tools to assess borrower creditworthiness or collateral, inadequate contingency planning, and weak payment infrastructure, all underscoring the need to accelerate financial sector reforms.

All the regional development banks have a strong focus on the financial sector. For example, over 40 percent of the operations of the EBRD have supported the financial sector, especially micro- and small enterprises (box 6.6). Similarly, the IFC has supported micro-, small, and medium enterprises throughout the years—in fiscal 2008, the IFC's clients provided 8 million loans

FIGURE 6.3 Financial Sector Assessment Program country coverage

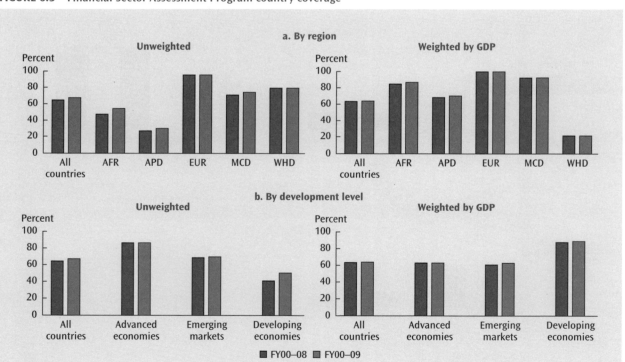

Source: IMF–World Bank database.
Note: AFR = Africa; APD = Asia and Pacific; EUR = Europe; MCD = Middle East and Central Asia; WHD = Western Hemisphere.

BOX 6.6   EBRD's micro- and small enterprise lending program

EBRD support to private business development through its micro- and small enterprise (MSE) lending program provides individual entrepreneurs and firms with access to otherwise scarce finance. The EBRD implements MSE lending through local commercial banks and nonbank microfinance institutions. The programs are currently being expanded to help rural areas and small farming enterprises. Loans are accompanied by technical assistance to strengthen partner institutions and to establish efficient credit procedures for lending to small businesses. A new focus on risk management and corporate governance is being introduced in response to the global crisis.

Currently, there are MSE lending programs with commercial banks in 13 countries. Nonbank microfinance institutions have proven to be efficient intermediaries. The EBRD has to date partnered with 29 microfinance institutions providing loans, equity, and technical assistance for institutional strengthening, risk management, asset and liability management, and upgrades of management information systems and operational procedures.

for almost $100 billion to such enterprises. The AfDB is preparing a facility to provide short-term emergency finance to financial institutions.

Business Climate

The MDBs have collaborated on a number of Investment Climate Assessments and Enterprise Surveys. In the past six years, over 70,000 enterprises across 104 countries have been surveyed, providing valuable information on how regulations affect firms' economic performance. Middle-income countries, faced with an increasingly competitive environment, have been among the most active partners in these diagnostics.

All the regional development banks have active programs to support the broad enabling environment. Examples are the ADB's Making Markets Work Better for the Poor program, designed to understand the links between growth, poverty, and market dynamics; the EBRD's Turn-Around Management and Business Advisory Services programs that are focused on medium and smaller enterprises; and the AfDB's engagement on continent-wide programs such as the Infrastructure Consortium for Africa, the Africa Water Facility, and the African Fertilizer Financing Mechanism.

Doing Business is the World Bank Group's flagship to benchmark business environment reforms. Low-income countries have become the major source of demand for business advisory services. Africa was identified as the second most reforming region in *Doing Business 2009*, with 28 countries implementing 58 reforms. Botswana, Burkina Faso, Ghana, Kenya, and Senegal have been cited as top reformers. Another example of the growing impact of analytical work is seen in the marked improvement in the implementation rate of recommendations made by the World Bank Group's Foreign Investment Advisory Service: from 47 percent in 2001 to 70 percent in 2006.[19]

Social, Environmental, and Ethical Standards

The IFC has an active role in setting social and environmental standards and promoting good corporate governance. Its Equator principles are a benchmark for the financial industry to manage social and environmental issues in project financing and have been adopted by 66 of the largest global banks. The agency supports the management of social, environmental. and labor dimensions of its companies' business practices. Along with other development finance institutions, the IFC signed on to a Corporate Governance Approach Statement in 2007 to promote good corporate governance practices.[20] This approach supports the rights and equitable treatment of shareholders, disclosure and transparency, and the role of boards of directors. The Extractive Industries Transparency Initiative gives additional prominence to transparency for natural resource development.

Despite progress, the approach that MDBs should adopt to support private sector development activities still generates controversy. For example, the ADB has been holding consultations with multi-stakeholders since 2005 on updating its safeguards. The bank has proposed articulating policy principles and then separating these from procedural requirements; balancing a front-loaded procedural approach with one that is also focused on results during implementation; and introducing flexibility that is tailored to different clients with varying capacities as well as to different financing products and modalities. The bank's intent is to enhance effectiveness and strengthen the relevance of safeguards to changing client needs. These proposals have met with resistance from some NGOs, demonstrating the complex nature of MDB efforts to support private sector development. The challenge to MDBs is to keep processes simple but at the same time ensure that the highest safeguard standards are met.

Improving Basic Service Delivery

Infrastructure

Between 2003 and 2007, investment commitments to infrastructure projects with private participation in developing countries grew by almost 1.5 times—amounting to $158 billion in 2007,10 percent higher in real terms than the previous peak in 1997. Recent private activity also showed more diverse investors and projects. Companies from developing countries mobilized half of funding for infrastructure projects with private participation in 2005–06, in contrast to the 1990s, when large international companies from the developed world played a dominant role.

In the current economic crisis, additional infrastructure spending can provide a short-term stimulus and address long-term development needs. So far infrastructure spending accounts for about two-thirds of the stimulus programs in emerging economies. Stimulus spending should prioritize maintenance and can benefit poor households by providing short-term employment and income generation through labor-intensive public works programs. Successful examples in Argentina (Trabajar), Indonesia (Urban Poverty Project), and the Republic of Korea show the potential.

The funding gap for new infrastructure projects has risen by about $20 billion per year as prospects for private sector financing recede as a result of the financial crisis. In response, the World Bank is launching a new infrastructure initiative—Infrastructure Recovery and Assets (INFRA) Platform—which could provide an incremental $2 billion to $4 billion per year over the next three years. Embedded in the bank's Sustainable Infrastructure Action Plan (SIAP), the new platform would be an umbrella for mobilizing additional finance for energy, transport, water, and information and communications technology infrastructure in developing countries over and above the targets envisaged in SIAP (box 6.7).

The current crisis occurs just as infrastructure had been afforded a higher priority by MDBs. One area of focus is the reengagement of IDA with hydropower in Bujugali (Uganda), Resumo Falls (Rwanda), and Inga (Democratic Republic of Congo). Clean coal is being supported in Botswana. Other MDBs share this focus. The ADB is financing the first Ultra Mega Power Project in India, at Mundra, with participation by the Korean Ex-Im Bank and the IFC. The EBRD has launched a sustainable energy initiative with a focus on industrial energy efficiency, firm-level energy audits, and technical cooperation. This program has been extended to a multidonor, multi-IFI initiative coordinated in the World Bank. The IFC supported a 50 megawatt wind park in Mongolia.

The AfDB, along with others, is responding to the shrinking share of infrastructure

BOX 6.7   World Bank's Sustainable Infrastructure Action Plan
and the Infrastructure Recovery and Assets Platform

The Sustainable Infrastructure Action Plan (SIAP) was approved in July 2008 to leverage private and public funding of $109 billion to $149 billion over fiscal 2008–11 based on World Bank Group financing of $59 billion–$72 billion. This would represent a major increase compared with lending of $28 billion in fiscal 2000–03 (leveraged to $45 billion). However, estimates in December 2008 were already showing that investment commitments in private infrastructure projects were 40 percent below levels just a year earlier, putting the SIAP at risk.

To mitigate this risk, the World Bank Group is establishing a framework initiative for infrastructure recovery and assets during the crisis. This framework will serve as an umbrella for the World Bank's crisis response in infrastructure. The objectives of the three-year program are to stabilize existing infrastructure assets by restructuring current portfolios; ensure delivery of priority projects by accelerating disbursements and identifying additional financing, and by seizing opportunities for "green infrastructure" through access to carbon finance leveraging facilities; support public private partnerships in infrastructure through advisory and restructuring support, use of guarantees, and innovative instruments (in coordination with the IFCs' Infrastructure Crisis facility); and support new infrastructure project development and implementation by providing financing and advice to governments launching growth and job enhancement programs.

World Bank Group average annual infrastructure financing and leverage: crisis impact

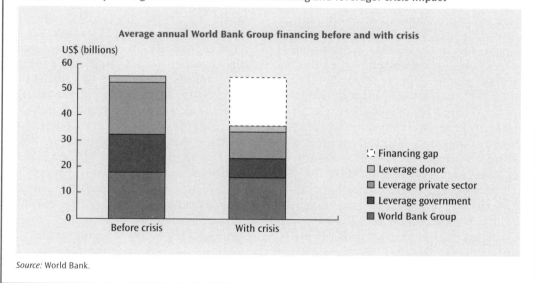

Average annual World Bank Group financing before and with crisis

Source: World Bank.

in total development assistance to Africa, which dropped from 23 percent in the mid-1980s to 13 percent by 2006. The AfDB hosts the Infrastructure Consortium for Africa, the Africa Water facility, and the NEPAD Infrastructure Project Preparation Facility.

Water and sanitation are two other focus areas for infrastructure. The number of countries that are off track to meet the MDG in sanitation is second only to the number off track in reducing mortality indicators. To meet the needs in these areas, the MDBs have experimented with new forms of innovative financing, including public-private partnerships, working more closely with subnational finance, output-based aid or performance-based grant initiatives, and political risk guarantees. Output-based aid is oriented toward a results focus by providing subsidies for externalities or redistribution only after prespecified results have been achieved. But these new instruments have yet to be adequately scaled up.

The World Bank's target under the Africa Action Plan is to connect 2.5 million more people to clean water by 2015. With more than 300 million Africans lacking access to clean water (and 500 million lacking sanitation), progress at this rate will leave large unmet needs except in the very long run.

Social Sectors

Education and health are two other sectors where much needs to be done to achieve the MDGs (see chapter 3). In both cases, scaling-up approaches envisage leveraging the private sector for service delivery. Private providers in these areas are not a new phenomenon, but organized, scaled-up, or franchised private delivery of social service is still at an early stage in most developing countries. That provides an opportunity that the IFC and the AfDB have incorporated into their strategies. Social sector operations involving the private sector are still modest, with 2 percent of lending in 2008 for the EBRD and the IFC and with less than 1 percent for the other MDBs. In general, empirical evidence and best practices from around the world support more active private provision of services under appropriate regulatory systems, and there is scope for greater MDB engagement in this area.

The AfDB has proposed an increased focus on higher education and technology and vocational training. The IFC is focused more on health and has recently partnered with IDA and the Bill and Melinda Gates Foundation to develop a significant Africa health initiative. The IFC is supporting the first private hospital in Bosnia and the first student loan program in Jordan.

Evaluation and Assessments

Evaluation of MDB responses to previous crisis episodes suggests seven points to consider:

- Quality is as important as scale of crisis-response support
- The implications for poverty and social safety nets should be given priority
- Opportunities for greener development activities should be developed
- Collaboration within and across groups is necessary but not always easy
- Safeguards continue to be vital to ensure that funds reach intended beneficiaries
- A focus on results is even more important when resources are scarce
- Preparedness and early warning make interventions more effective.[21]

The current financial crisis may affect support for the private sector as the main driver of development. Although all the MDBs are making strong efforts to reorient their strategies toward support for the private sector, they may face some difficulties among recipient countries about whether this is the best way of advancing development. To illustrate, in a recent Gallup World Poll, the private sector arms of the World Bank Group, the IFC, and MIGA, suffered from much lower perceptions of development effectiveness (figure 6.4) than the rest of the World Bank Group. This could be because the single greatest priority cited by respondents is poverty reduction rather than growth or strengthening the economy. The MDBs need to do a better job of linking these priorities.

Perceptions may improve as more efforts are devoted to a focus on development effectiveness in private sector projects. The IFC introduced a development outcome tracking system in 2005 to measure its development results. This shows that in fiscal 2008 the percentage of projects with high development outcomes increased from 63 to 71 percent (81 to 87 percent when weighted

FIGURE 6.4 Effectiveness and future importance of donor institutions

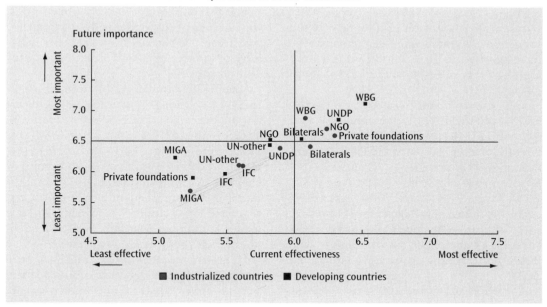

Source: Gallup World Poll 2008.

by dollar value of projects). In general, evaluations show there is no trade-off between investment profitability and development results. Significantly, both improve when the overall investment climate is improving.[22]

All the MDBs have independent evaluations of their private sector support operations. The EBRD's Evaluation Department recommended a range of actions in 2008, covering financial sector operations policy, business advisory services, private equity funds, and technical cooperation programs. The AfDB established a new function in the chief economist's office in 2008 to review development outcomes for new private sector operations. Additionality and complementarity are also reviewed. A recent review of the ADB's private equity funds found "unsatisfactory" returns and weak monitoring of environmental and other safeguards. The Independent Evaluation Group of the World Bank found that the private sector portfolio was among the weakest in terms of development results.[23]

These examples illustrate the practical difficulties in implementing a strategy focused on private sector development. One common finding in evaluation is the presence of overlaps and limited coordination between different parts of an institution in providing an integrated and consistent program of support for the private sector.

As a direct consequence, the World Bank Group has consolidated its investment climate reform work and investment promotion work under a single entity—the Investment Climate Department. A new IDA-IFC secretariat was established in fiscal 2008 to improve coordination of private sector operations in low-income countries and to promote more joint IDA-IFC operations. In the decade ending in 2008, the World Bank Group approved just 17 projects in IDA countries that leveraged both public (IDA and other donors) and private (IFC and other private partners) resources. In the past couple of years, the pipeline of such projects has grown to 35, most of them in Africa. Global practice groups in oil, gas, chemicals and mining, information and communications technology, and global capital markets bring together different parts of the World

Bank Group in these areas. The IDB and
ADB also face issues in ensuring consistency
within each institution in how private sector support is conducted; recent assessments
have pointed to fragmentation and overlapping areas of responsibility across bank
groups.[24]

Coordination and harmonization across
and within agencies are key issues for multilateral aid effectiveness, and all the multilaterals have signed on to the Paris Declaration on Aid Effectiveness.[25] That declaration
set out specific indicators to be achieved by
2010. Seven of the twelve indicators are relevant for multilateral agencies. Progress on
these indicators has been monitored in two
surveys: a benchmark survey conducted in
2006, and a follow-up survey conducted in
2008.

Table 6.3 shows the 2008 survey results
based on responses from 54 aid recipient

countries. Because each multilateral agency
operates in a different number of countries,
the number of respondents for each agency
is different. Nevertheless, the data are indicative of the strengths and weaknesses of the
multilaterals.

The MDBs do reasonably well on aligning aid to national priorities and including
aid in government budgets but still fall well
short of the 2010 target. They have also
made good progress on coordinating their
technical cooperation to strengthen country
capacity. As with all donors, use of country
financial management and procurement systems still lags behind. The World Bank is a
leader among multilaterals, and indeed all
donors, on this score; others have followed
with more caution. Multilaterals have been
trying to reduce the number of independent
project implementation units and now score
better than bilaterals on this indicator, but

TABLE 6.3 Paris Declaration survey results, 2008

	Align aid flows[a]	Coordinate technical cooperation[b]	Use country PFM system[c]	Use country procurement system[d]	Avoid parallel PIUs[e]	Predictable aid[f]	Program-based approaches[g]	Joint field missions[h]	Joint analytical work[i]
ADB	80	61	61	36	40	79	59	18	25
AfDB	57	28	44	42	121	45	38	17	44
IDB	55	60	52	26	108	54	52	35	44
WB	66	85	62	52	101	65	54	31	59
All multilaterals	48	63	48	40	1,193	45	48	35	60
All bilaterals	43	57	47	50	1,267	41	40	24	49
All donors	46	59	48	44	2,460	43	44	31	55
2010 targets	85	50	80	80	611	71	66	40	66

Source: DAC 2008.
Note: The category "All multilaterals" includes vertical funds, UN agencies, and other multilaterals.
a. Percent of aid on budget.
b. Percent of coordinated technical assistance.
c. Percent of aid using country's public financial management system.
d. Percent of aid using country's procurement system.
e. Number of project implementation units (PIUs).
f. Percent of aid delivered on schedule.
g. Percent of aid using program-based approaches.
h. Percent of joint missions.
i. Percent of joint country analytic work.

all donors continue to rely heavily on such mechanisms, with likely costs in terms of weakening other areas of recipient country government. The MDBs have high scores on aid predictability, but progress since 2006 has been mixed on this indicator. The MDBs lead all donors in terms of program-based approaches to their flows. They tend to lag behind other donors in coordinating field missions and undertaking joint analytical work. Their stronger in-house capabilities permit them to do independent work. But this may perpetuate the problems of overlap and waste and of excessive claims on government officials' time.

Overall, multilateral agencies, and the MDBs in particular, are closer than bilateral donors to reaching the Paris Declaration performance targets, but considerable progress is still required if they are to meet the 2010 commitments. The target for coordinated technical cooperation has already been met by three of the MDBs, and the ADB has met the target for aid predictability. In all other cases, the MDBs still have work to do. The DAC suggests that the multilaterals will have to gear up their efforts considerably to achieve the 2010 targets.

To sharpen the MDBs' focus on results, a common performance assessment system (or COMPAS) was designed in 2005 as a self-assessment framework to track MDB capacities to manage for development results. COMPAS reviews show progress: the MDBs have been improving the quality of project design and supervision, strengthening results frameworks, better managing risk in project portfolios, and increasing staff training in managing for results. The 2008 COMPAS reports that for most MDBs more than 80 percent of projects have baseline data, monitoring indicators, and clearly defined outcomes. Moreover, between 57 and 84 percent of MDB-funded projects receive satisfactory or better ratings in reaching their intended development objectives. In addition, MDBs have made improvements in assessing and strengthening partner countries' capacities in managing for results.[26]

Notes

1. The IFIs covered in this chapter include the International Monetary Fund (IMF), the World Bank Group, and the four big regional development banks (AfDB ADB, EBRD, and IDB).
2. IIF 2009.
3. World Bank 2009b. See also Birdsall 2009.
4. Arbache and Page 2007.
5. IEG 2005. The evaluation covered IBRD and IDA operations.
6. Hausmann and Rodrik 2003.
7. IEG 2006. IEG found that in over 90 percent of projects, there was at least one form of additionality in IFC projects. Providing funding on commercial terms is an important discipline for MDBs and goes a long way toward ensuring that they are indeed additional.
8. The Independent Evaluation Group found that IFC additionality was less than satisfactory in one-fifth of cases; see IEG 2008.
9. World Bank 2009c.
10. Robert Zoellick, "Time to Herald the Age of Responsibility," *Financial Times,* January 25, 2009.
11. DAC 2008.
12. Tandon 2008.
13. The IFC has rapidly expanded its advisory services programs (including the Foreign Investment Advisory Service and the Global Partnership on Output-Based Aid) since 2002 to become a second leg of its core business alongside investments.
14. World Bank 2009a.
15. Kar and Cartwright-Smith 2008.
16. Belarus ($2.5 billion), El Salvador ($800 million), Georgia ($700 million), Hungary ($15.7 billion), Iceland ($2.1 billion), Latvia ($2.4 billion), Pakistan ($7.6 billion), Serbia ($500 million), and Ukraine ($16.4 billion).
17. World Bank 2008a.
18. A three-year pilot World Bank–IFC subnational development facility provides loans to municipal and regional governments, public utilities, and financial institutions without sovereign guarantees.
19. Recommendations adopted within one year of completion of advisory project.
20. The statement endorses the OECD Principles of Corporate Governance.
21. IEG 2008b.
22. IEG 2008a
23. Like other parts of the development agenda, promoting private sector development can be a

high-risk activity, and significant failure rates are to be expected. While success rates may be somewhat lower than for other sectors, evaluation evidence also shows that, when successful, improvement in the enabling environment for private sector development can be very large, with high benefit-to-cost ratios.

24. See the Office of Evaluation and Oversight, IDB, "Synthesis of OVE Evaluations of Bank Action for Support of Private Sector Development"; and ADB, "Private Sector Development: A Revised Strategic Framework," February 2006.

25. The Paris Declaration is relevant for official aid. Hence the EBRD, which lends largely to the private sector, is not separately identified here.

26. To be published in April, the 2008 COMPAS report, as well as previous years' reports, can be found at ww.mfdr.org/COMPAS/.

References

Chapter 1

Arbache, Jorge, and John Page. 2007. "More Growth or Fewer Collapses? A New Look at Long-Run Growth in Sub-Saharan Africa." Policy Research Working Paper 4384, World Bank, Washington, DC.

Bartsch, Ulrich. 2006. "How Much Is Enough? Monte Carlo Simulations of an Oil Stabilization Fund for Nigeria." Working Paper WP/06/142, International Monetary Fund, Washington, DC.

Davis, Jeffrey M., Rolando Ossowski, and Annalisa Fedelino, eds. 2003. *Fiscal Policy Formulation and Implementation in Oil-Producing Countries*. Washington, DC: International Monetary Fund.

Drummond, Paulo, and Anubha Dhasmana. 2008. "Foreign Reserve Adequacy in Sub-Saharan Africa." Working Paper WP/08/150, International Monetary Fund, Washington, DC.

Hoggarth, Glenn, and Jack Reidhill. 2003. "Resolution of Banking Crises: A Review." *Financial Stability Review* (December).

ILO (International Labour Organization). 2009. "Global Employment Trends: January 2009." Geneva.

IMF (International Monetary Fund). 2007. *Global Financial Stability Report: Market Developments and Issues*. Washington, DC: International Monetary Fund.

———. 2009a. "Global Policy Response to Financial Crisis: Range of Interventions." Washington, DC.

———. 2009b. "Market Liquidity and Related Measures in Emerging Market Economies," Washington, DC.

Ravallion, Martin. 2008. "Bailing Out the World's Poorest." Policy Research Working Paper 4763, World Bank, Wahington DC.

World Bank. 2008a. *Global Economic Prospects*. Washington, DC: World Bank.

———. 2008. Migration and Development Brief 8. Washington, DC.

———. 2009. "The Expected Impact of the Global Financial Crisis on the World's Poorest," a note prepared by the Development Economics Vice Presidency, World Bank, Washington, DC (February).

Chapter 2

AICD (Africa Infrastructure Country Diagnostic). 2009. "Africa's Infrastructure: A Time for Transformation." Public-Private Infrastructure Facility, World Bank, Washington, DC.

Andrés, Luis A., J. Luis Guasch, Thomas Haven, and Vivien Foster. 2008. *Private Sector Participation in Infrastructure: Light, Shadows and the Road Ahead*. Washington, DC: World Bank.

Armendariz de Aghion, Beatriz, and Jonathan Morduch. 2005. *The Economics of Microfinance*. Cambridge, MA: MIT Press.

Arvis, Jean-Francois, Gael Raballand, and Jean-Francois Marteau. 2007. "The Cost of Being Landlocked: Logistics Cost and Supply Chain

Reliability." Policy Research Working Paper 4258, World Bank, Washington, DC.

Aterido, Reyes, Mary Hallward-Driemeier, and Carmen Pages. 2008. "Big Constraints to Small Firm Growth?" Working paper, World Bank, Washington, DC.

Ayyagari, Meghana, Asli Demirgüç-Kunt, and Vojislav Maksimovic. 2006. "Firm Innovation in Emerging Markets: Role of Governance and Finance." Policy Research Working Paper 4157, World Bank, Washington, DC.

———. 2007. "How Important Are Financing Constraints? The Role of Finance in the Business Environment." Policy Research Working Paper 3820, World Bank, Washington, DC.

Barseghyan, Levon. 2008. "Entry Costs and Cross-country Differences in Productivity and Output." *Journal of Economic Growth* 13 (2): 145–67.

Barth, James R., Gerard Caprio, Jr., and Ross Levine. 2006. *Rethinking Bank Regulation: Till Angels Govern.* New York: Cambridge University Press.

Beck, Thorsten, Asli Demirgüç-Kunt, Luc Laeven, and Vojislav Maksimovic. 2006. "The Determinants of Financing Obstacles." *Journal of International Money and Finance* 25 (6): 932–52.

Beck, Thorsten, Asli Demirgüç-Kunt, and Ross Levine. 2007. "Finance, Inequality, and the Poor." *Journal of Economic Growth* 12 (1): 27–49.

Beck, Thorsten, Asli Demirgüç-Kunt, and Vojislav Maksimovic. 2004. "Financing Patterns around the World: Are Small Firms Different?" World Bank, Washington, DC.

———. 2005. "Financial and Legal Constraints to Firm Growth: Does Firm Size Matter?" *Journal of Finance* 60: 137–77.

Beck, Thorsten, Asli Demirgüç-Kunt, and Maria Soledad Martinez Peria. 2007. "Banking Services for Everyone? Barriers to Bank Access and Use around the World." Policy Research Working Paper 4079, World Bank, Washington, DC.

Besley, Timothy, and Robin Burgess. 2004. "Can Labor Regulation Hinder Economic Performance? Evidence from India." *Quarterly Journal of Economics* 119 (1): 91–134.

Bruhn, Miriam. 2008. "License to Sell: The Effect of Business Registration Reform on Entrepreneurial Activity in Mexico." Policy Research Working Paper 4538, World Bank, Washington, DC.

Buvinic, Mayra, and Elizabeth King. 2007. "Smart Economics." *Finance and Development* 44 (2).

Buys, Piet, Uwe Deichman, and David Wheeler. 2006. "Road Network Upgrading and Overland Trade Expansion in Sub-Saharan Africa." Policy Research Working Paper 4097, World Bank, Washington, DC.

Calderón César, and Luis Servén. 2003. "The Output Cost of Latin America's Infrastructure Gap." In *The Limits of Stabilization,* ed. W. Easterly and L. Servén. Washington, DC: World Bank.

———. 2008. "Infrastructure and Economic Development in Sub-Saharan Africa." Policy Research Working Paper 4712, World Bank, Washington, DC.

Caprio, Gerard, and Asli Demirgüç-Kunt. 1997. "The Role of Long-Term Finance: Theory and Evidence." *World Bank Economic Review* 10 (2): 291–321.

Caprio, Gerard, Jonathan Fiechter, Robert Litan, and Michael Pomerleano, eds. 2004. *The Future of State-Owned Financial Institutions.* Washington, DC: Brookings Institution.

Chari, A. 2008. "License Reform in India: Theory and Evidence." Department of Economics, Cornell University, Ithaca, New York.

Claessens, Stijn, and Eric Feijen. 2006. "Finance and the MDGs." NFX and World Bank, Washington, DC.

———. 2007. "Finance and Hunger: Empirical Evidence of the Agricultural Productivity Channel." Policy Research Working Paper 4080, World Bank, Washington, DC.

Claessens, Stijn, and Enrico Perotti. 2007. "Finance and Inequality: Channels and Evidence." *Journal of Comparative Economics* 35 (4) 748–73.

Clarke, George R. G., Robert Cull, and Maria Soledad Martinez Peria. 2001. "Does Foreign Bank Penetration Reduce Access to Credit in Developing Countries: Evidence From Asking Borrowers," Policy Research Working Paper Series 2716, The World Bank, Washington, DC.

Cull, Robert, Asli Demirgüç-Kunt, and Jonathan Morduch. 2007. "Financial Performance and Outreach: A Global Analysis of Leading Microbanks." *Economic Journal* 117: F107–33.

Dal Bó, Ernesto, and Martin A. Rossi 2007. "Corruption and Inefficiency: Theory and Evidence from Electric Utilities." *Journal of Public Economics* 91 (5–6): 939–62.

Datta, Saugato. 2008. "The Impact of Improved Highways on Indian Firms." World Bank, Washington, DC.

de la Torre, Augusto, Juan Carlos Gozzi, and Sergio Schmukler. 2007. "Innovative Experiences in Access to Finance: Market Friendly Roles for the Visible Hand?" Policy Research Working Paper 4326, World Bank, Washington, DC.

de la Torre, Augusto, Maria Soledad Martinez Peria, and Sergio Schmukler. 2007. "Bank Lending to SMEs." World Bank, Washington, DC.

Dell'Ariccia, Giovanni, Deniz Igan, and Luc Laevan. 2008. "Credit Booms and Lending Standards: Evidence from the Sub-Prime Mortgage Market." IMF Working Paper 2008/106, Washington, DC.

Dercon, Stephan, Daniel Gilligan, John Hoddinott, and Tassew Woldehanna. 2007. "The Impact of Roads and Agricultural Extension on Consumption Growth and Poverty in 15 Ethiopian Villages." WPS 2007-01, Centre for the Study of African Economies, Oxford University, U.K.

Djankov, Simeon, Caralee McLiesh, and Andrei Shleifer. 2007. "Private Credit in 129 Countries." *Journal of Financial Economics* (May).

Dollar, David, Mary Hallward-Driemeier, and Taye Mengistae. 2005. "Investment Climate and Firm Performance in Developing Economies." *Economic Development and Cultural Change* 54 (1): 1–31.

Eberhard, A., V. Foster, C. Briceño-Garmendia, F. Ouedraogo, D. Camos, and M. Shkaratan. 2008. "Underpowered: The State of the Power Sector in Sub-Saharan Africa." Background paper, Africa Infrastructure Country Diagnostics (AICD), World Bank, Washington, DC.

Eberhard, Anton, and Katherine Gratwick. 2006. "The Experience of IPPs across Africa." Working paper, Management Programme in Infrastructure Reform and Regulation, Graduate School of Business, University of Cape Town.

Ebinger, Jane O. 2006. "Measuring Financial Performance in Infrastructure: An Application to Europe and Central Asia." Policy Research Working Paper 3992, World Bank, Washington, DC.

Eifert, Benjamin. 2009. "Do Regulatory Reforms Stimulate Investment and Growth? Evidence from the Doing Business Data, 2003–07." Working Paper 159, Center for Global Development, Washington, DC.

Escribano, A., J. L. Guasch, and J. Pena, J. 2008. "Impact of Infrastructure Constraints on Firm Productivity in Africa." Working paper, AICD, World Bank, Washington, D.C.

Estache, Antonio, Vivien Foster, and Quentin Wodon. 2002. *Accounting for Poverty in Infrastructure Reform: Learning from Latin America's Experience.* Washington, DC: World Bank.

Foster, Vivien, and Tito Yepes. 2006. "Is Cost Recovery a Feasible Objective for Water and Electricity? The Latin American Experience." Policy Research Working Paper 3943, World Bank, Washington, DC.

Galdo, Virgilio, and Maximo Torero. 2006. "The Impact of Public Telephones in Rural Areas: The Case of Peru." In *Information and Communication Technologies for Development and Poverty Reduction: The Potential of Telecommunications,* ed. Maximo Torero and Joachim von Braun. Baltimore: Johns Hopkins University Press for International Food Policy Research Institute.

Gassner Katharina, Alexander Popov, and Nataliya Pushak. 2008. "Does Private Sector Participation Improve Performance in Electricity and Water Distribution?" PPIAF Trends and Policy Options 6. Public-Private Infrastructure Advisory Facility, Washington, DC.

Giannetti, Mariassunta, and Steven Ongena. 2005. "Financial Integration and Entrepreneurial Activity: Evidence from Foreign Bank Entry in Emerging Markets." Tilburg University, Tilburg, the Netherlands.

Gulati, Mohinder, and Mark Rao 2006. "Checking Corruption in the Electricity Sector." World Bank, Washington, DC.

Hallward-Driemeier, Mary and Yue Li. 2009. "Regulations, Access to Finance, and Investment across Countries." World Bank, Washington, DC.

Honohan, Patrick. 2004. "Financial Sector Policy and the Poor." Working Paper 43, World Bank, Washington, DC.

IEG (Independent Evaluation Group). 2008. *Doing Business: An Independent Evaluation.* Washington, DC: World Bank.

Igan, Deniz, and Eisuke Okada. Forthcoming. "Housing Choice and Securitization." IMF working paper, Washington, DC.

IMF (International Monetary Fund). 2009. "Lessons of the Financial Crisis for Future Regulation of Financial Institutions and Markets and for Liquidity Management." Washington, DC.

Kaufmann, Daniel, Aart Kraay, and Massimo Mastruzzi. 2008. "Governance Matters VII: Aggregate and Individual Governance Indicators, 1996–2007." Policy Research Working Paper 4654, World Bank, Washington, DC.

Kenny, Charles. 2006. "Measuring and Reducing the Impact of Corruption in Infrastructure." Policy Research Working Paper 4099, World Bank, Washington DC.

———. 2007. "Construction, Corruption, and Developing Countries." World Bank, Washington, DC.

Kenny, Charles, and Tina Søreide. 2008. "Grand Corruption in Utilities." Policy Research Working Paper, World Bank, Washington, DC.

Klapper, Leora, Luc Laeven, and Raghuram Rajan. 2006. "Entry Regulation as a Barrier to Entrepreneurship." Journal of Financial Economics 82 (3): 591–629.

Komives, Kristin, Vivien Foster, Jonathan Halpern, and Quentin Wodon, with support from R. Abdullah. 2005. Water, Electricity and the Poor: Who Benefits from Utility Subsidies? Washington, DC: World Bank.

Levine, Ross, Norman Loayza, and Thorsten Beck. 2000. "Financial Intermediation and Growth: Causality and Causes." Journal of Monetary Economics 46 (1): 31–77.

Levine, Ross, and Sara Zervos. 1998. "Stock Markets, Banks, and Economic Growth." American Economic Review.

Mason, Andrew, and Elizabeth King. 2001. "Engendering Development through Gender Equality in Rights, Resources, and Voice." Policy Research Report 21776, World Bank, Washington, DC.

Narayan, Deepa. 2000. Voices of the Poor: Can Anyone Hear Us? Washington, DC: World Bank.

Olken, Benjamin, and Patrick Barron. 2007. "The Simple Economics of Extortion: Evidence from Trucking in Aceh." Working Paper 13145, National Bureau of Economic Research, Cambridge, MA.

Perry, Guillermo E., Omar Arias, Pablo Fajnzylber, William F. Maloney, Andrew Mason, and Jaime Saavedra-Chanduvi. 2007. Informality: Exit and Exclusion. Washington, DC: World Bank.

PPIAF (Public-Private Infrastructure Advisory Facility). 2008. "PPI Data Update." Note 13, World Bank, Washington, DC (November).

Ramachandran Vijaya, Alan Gelb, and Manju Kedia Shah. 2009. "Africa's Private Sector: What's Wrong with the Business Environment and What to Do about It," Center for Global Development, Washington, DC.

Ravallion, Martin. 2001. "Growth, Inequality, and Poverty: Looking beyond Averages." World Development 29 (11): 1803–15.

Stiglitz, Joseph, and Nicholas Stern. 2009. "Obama's Chance to Lead the Green Recovery." Financial Times. March 2.

Straub, Stephane. 2008. "Infrastructure and Growth in Developing Countries: Recent Advances and Research Challenges" Policy Research Working Paper 4460, World Bank, Washington, DC.

Vagliasindi, Maria. 2008. "Governance Arrangements for State-Owned Enterprises." Policy Research Working Paper 4542, World Bank, Washington, DC.

Von Klaudy, Stephan, Apurva Sanghi, and Georgina Dellacha. 2008. "Emerging Market Investors and Operators: A New Breed of Infrastructure Investors." PPIAF Working Paper 7, Public-Private Infrastructure Advisory Facility, World Bank, Washington, DC.

Wagstaff, A., and M. Cleason, M. 2004. "The MDGs for Health: Rising to the Challenges." World Bank, Washington, DC.

West Africa Trade Hub. 2007. "Report on the First Results of the Improved Road-Transport Governance (Irtg) Initiative on Interstate Highways." http://www.watradehub.com/images/stories/downloads/studies/Report%20on%20first%20IRTG%20results,%20English,%20jw.pdf.

WHO (World Health Organization). 2004. "Facts and Figures: Water, Sanitation and Hygiene Links to Health," http://www.who.int/water_sanitation_health/publications/factsfigures04/en/.

World Bank. 2001. Finance for Growth: Policy Choices in a Volatile World. Washington, DC: World Bank.

———. 2004. World Development Report 2005: A Better Investment Climate for Everyone. Washington, DC: World Bank.

———. 2007a. Finance for All: Policies and Pitfalls in Expanding Access. Washington, DC: World Bank.

———. 2007b. "Indonesia Public Expenditure Review." Washington, DC.

———. 2008a. "Banking the Poor: Measuring Banking Access in 54 Economies." Washington, DC.

———. 2008b. Doing Business in 2009. Washington, DC: World Bank.

———. 2008c. *Doing Business in the Arab World 2009: Comparing Regulation in 20 Economies.* Washington, DC., World Bank.

World Bank Group. 2008. *Sustainable Infrastructure Action Plan.* Washington, DC: World Bank.

Chapter 3

Baeza, C., and T. Packard. 2006. *Beyond Survival: Protecting Households from Health Shocks in Latin America.* Washington, DC: World Bank.

Barr, N. 1993. *The Economics of the Welfare State.* Stanford, CA: Stanford Press.

Barrera-Osorio, F. 2009. "The Concession Schools of Bogota, Colombia." In *School Choice International*, ed. R. Chakrabarti and P. E. Peterson, 193–218. Cambridge, MA: MIT Press.

Barrera-Osorio, F., and D. Raju. 2008. "Evaluating a Test-based Public Subsidy Program for Low-cost Private Schools: Regression-discontinuity Evidence from Pakistan." Word Bank, Human Development Network, Washington, DC.

Basix: http://www.basixindia.com

Bennett, S., B. McPake, and A. Mills. 1997. *Private Health Care Providers in Developing Countries: Serving the Public Interest?* London: Zed.

Berman, P., and M. Chawla. 1999. "A Model for Analyzing Strategic Use of Government Financing to Improve Health Care Provision." Partnerships for Health Reform, Harvard School of Public Health, Boston (April).

Bhat, R., A. Singh, S. Maheshwari, and S. Saha. 2006. *Maternal Health Financing—Issues and Options: A Study of Chiranjeevi Yojana in Gujarat.* Indian Institute of Management, Ahmedabad India.

Boller C., K. Wyss, and M. Tanner. 2003. "Quality and Comparison of Antenatal Care in Public and Private Providers in the United Republic of Tanzania." *Bulletin of the World Health Organization* 81: 116–22.

Brugha R., and A. Zwi. 1998. "Improving the Quality of Privately Provided Public Health Care in Low and Middle Income Countries: Challenges and Strategies." *Health Policy and Planning* 13: 107–20.

Chabikuli N., H. Schneider, D. Blaauw, A. Zwi, and R. Brugha. 2002. "Quality and Equity of Private Sector Care for Sexually Transmitted Disease in South Africa." *Health Policy and Planning* 17: 40–46.

Churchill, C., ed. 2006. *Protecting the Poor: A Microinsurance Compendium,* Geneva: International Labour Organization and Munich Re Foundation.

Danel, I., and G. La Forgia. 2005. "Contracting for Basic Health Care in Rural Guatemala: Comparison of the Performance of Three Delivery Models." In *Health System Innovations in Central America: Lessons and Impact of New Approaches*, ed. G. La Forgia. Washington, DC: World Bank.

Das J., and J. Hammer. 2004. "Strained Mercy: The Quality of Medical Care in Delhi." Policy Research Working Paper 3228. World Bank, Washington, DC.

IFC (International Finance Corporation). 2007. *The Business of Health in Africa: Partnering with the Private Sector to Improve People's Lives.* Washington, DC: World Bank.

Lonnroth K., M. Uplekar, and L. Blanc. 2006. "Hard Gains through Soft Contracts: Productive Engagement of Private Providers in Tuberculosis Control." *Bulletin of the World Health Organization* 84: 879–83.

Mills A., R. Brugha, K. Hanson, and B. McPake. 2002. "What Can Be Done about the Private Health Sector in Low-income Countries?" *Bulletin of World Health Organization* 80: 325–30.

QAP (Quality Assurance Project). 2002. "Vendor-to-Vendor Education to Improve Malaria Treatment by Drug Outlets in Kenya." Bethesda, MD.

Patrinos, H., F. Barrera-Osorio, and J. Guaqueta. 2009. *The Role and Impact of Public-Private Partnerships in Education.* Washington, DC: Word Bank.

Preker, A., R. Scheffler, and M. Bassett. 2007. *Private Voluntary Health Insurance in Development: Friend or Foe?* Washington, DC: World Bank.

Sakellariou, C., and H. A. Patrinos. 2004. "Incidence Analysis of Public Support to the Private Education Sector in Côte d'Ivoire." Policy Research Working Paper 3231. World Bank, Washington, DC.

Schwartz, B., and I. Bhushan. 2004. "Reducing Inequality in the Provision of Primary Health Care Services: Contracting in Cambodia." Paper presented at a World Bank conference on Reaching the Poor with Effective Health, Nutrition, and Population Services, Feb. 18–20, Washington, DC.

Supon, L. 2008. "Private-Public Mix in Woman and Child Health in Low-income Countries: An Analysis of Demographic and Health Surveys." Results for Development Institute, Washington, DC.

UNESCO (United Nation Educational, Scientific, and Cultural Organization). 2007. "Non-State Providers and Public-Private-Community Partnerships in Education." Background paper for the *Education for All Global Monitoring Report 2008: Education for All by 2015: Will We Make It?* A. K. F. Team. Paris.

Uplekar, M. 2000. "Private Health Care." *Social Science and Medicine* 51: 897–904.

Walker, D., H. Muyinda, S. Foster, J. Kengeya-Karondo, and J. Whitworth. 2001. "The Quality of Care by Private Practitioners for Sexually Transmitted Diseases in Uganda." *Health Policy and Planning* 16: 35–40.

Wilson, B. 2007. "The Private Sector Responds to AIDS in Botswana." *Lancet* 7: 766.

Woessmann, L. 2009. "Public-Private Partnerships and Student Achievement: A Cross-Country Analysis." In *School Choice International,* ed. R. Chakrabarti and P. E. Peterson, pp. 13–46. Cambridge, MA: MIT Press.

WHO (World Health Organization). 2009. "Global Tuberculosis Control." Geneva.

World Bank. 2003. "Project Performance Assessment Report." Bangladesh, Female Secondary School Assistance Project. Sector and Thematic Evaluation Group, Operations Evaluation Department. Report 26226. World Bank, Washington, DC.

———. 2007. *Global Development Finance 2007. The Globalization of Corporate Finance in Developing Countries.* Washington, DC: World Bank.

———. 2008a. "Pilot Advanced Market Commitment for Vaccines against Pneumococcal Disease." World Bank, Washington, DC (December).

———. 2008b. *World Development Indicators.* Washington, DC: World Bank.

Chapter 4

Ben-Artzi, Ruth. 2008. "The Aid Challenge: The Role of Non-Governmental and Philanthropic Actors." Paper presented at ISA's 49th Annual Convention, "Bridging Multiple Divides," San Francisco, CA.

Bird, Neil, and Leo Peskett. 2008. "Recent Bilateral Initiatives for Climate Financing: Are They Moving in the Right Direction?" ODI Paper 112, Overseas Development Institute, London.

Bishop, Matthew, and Michael Green. 2008. *Philanthrocapitalism: How the Rich Can Save the World.* http://www.philanthrocapitalism.net.

Brautigam, Deborah. 2008. "China's Foreign Aid in Africa: What Do We Know?" In *China into Africa: Trade, Aid, and Influence,* ed. Robert I. Rotberg. Washington, DC: Brookings Institute Press.

Bulir, Ales, and A. Javier Hamann. 2003. "Aid Volatility: An Empirical Assessment." Working Paper 01/50, International Monetary Fund (IMF), Washington, DC.

———. 2006. "Volatility of Development Aid: From the Frying Pan onto the Fire." Working Paper 06/65, IMF, Washington, DC.

Celasun, Oya, and Jan Walliser. 2008. "Predictability of Aid: Do Fickle Donors Undermine Aid Effectiveness?" *Economic Policy* 23 (55): 545–94.

Conference Board. Various years. "Annual Survey." New York.

DEC-PREM (Development Economics and Poverty Reduction and Economic Management vice presidencies). 2009. "Developing Countries Face Increasing Macro and Fiscal Policy Challenges: Proposed Responses." World Bank, Washington, DC.

Desai, Raj, and Homi Kharas. 2008. "More Excuses from Donors at Doha." Brookings Institution, Washington, DC.

Eurobarometer. 2005. "Attitudes towards Development Aid." http://ec.europa.eu/public_opinion/archives/ebs/ebs_222_en.pdf.

Faini, Riccardo. 2006. "Foreign Aid and Fiscal Policy." Development Studies Working Paper 212, Centro Studi Luca D'Agliano, Turin.

Foundation Center. 2008a. "Do Foundation Giving Priorities Change in Times of Economic Distress." New York.

———. 2008b. "International Grantmaking IV: An Update on U.S. Foundation Trends." New York.

———. 2008c. "Past Economic Downturns and the Outlook for Foundation Giving." New York.

Hudson Institute. 2009. The Index of Global Philanthropy and Remittances, 2009. Center for Global Prosperity, Washington, DC.

ICA (Infrastructure Consortium for Africa). 2007. *Annual Report 2007.* Tunis.

IEA (International Energy Agency). 2008. "Energy Technology Perspectives." Paris.

IMF (International Monetary Fund). 2007. "Global Financial Stability Report." Washington, DC. http://www.imf.org/external/pubs/ft/gfsr/2007/02/pdf/annex12.pdf.

———. 2008. "IMF Intensifies Work on Sovereign Wealth Funds." IMF Survey. http://www.imf.org/external/pubs/ft/survey/so/2008/POL03408A.htm.

———. 2009. "The Implications of the Global Financial Crisis for Low-Income Countries." Washington, DC.

IMF–World Bank. 2008. "Heavily Indebted Poor Countries Initiative and Multilateral Debt Relief Initiative: Status of Implementation." Washington, DC.

———. Forthcoming. "Managing Public Debt: Formulating Strategies and Strengthening Institutional Capacity." Washington, DC.

Kharas, Homi. 2009. "The Financial Crisis, a Development Emergency, and the Need for Aid." Brookings, Washington, DC.

Kiess, Johannes Sebastian. 2008. "Innovative Financing Development: The Landscape." Background paper prepared for the Multilateral Trusteeship and Innovative Financing Group, World Bank, Washington, DC.

Knack, Stephen, and Nicholas Eubank. 2009. "Aid and Trust in Country Systems." Unpublished paper, World Bank Research Department. Washington, DC.

Lin, Justin. 2008. "The Impact of the Financial Crisis on Developing Countries." Paper presented at the Korea Development Institute, Seoul October 31, 2008.

Marten, Robert, and Jan Martin Witte. 2008. "Transforming Development? The Role of Philanthropic Foundations in International Development Cooperation." Research Paper Series 10, Global Public Policy Institute, Berlin.

Maxwell, Simon. 2008. "Stepping Up the Ladder: How Business Can Help Achieve the MDGs." Overseas Development Institute, London.

McDonnell, Ida, Henri-Bernard Solignac Leomonte, and Liam Wegimont. 2003. "Public Opinion and the Fight against Poverty." OECD Development Centre, Paris.

MDG Gap Task Force 2008. "Delivering on the Global Partnership for Achieving the Millennium Development Goals." United Nations, New York.

Mold, Andrew, Dilan Olcer, and Annalisa Prizzon. 2008. "The Fallout from the Financial Crisis (3): Will Aid Budgets Fall Victim to the Credit Crisis?" Policy Insights 85, OECD Development Centre, Paris.

OECD (Organisation for Economic Co-operation and Development). 2008. "2008 Survey on Monitoring the Paris Declaration." Paris.

———. 2009a. "Development Co-operation Report 2009." Paris.

———. 2009b. "Results of the 2009 DAC Survey on Donor's Forward Spending Plans." Paris.

Pallage, Stéphane, and Michel Robe. 2001. "Foreign Aid and the Business Cycle." *Review of International Economics* 9 (4): 641–72.

Paxton, Pamela, and Steve Knack. 2008. "Individual and Country-Level Factors Affecting Support for Foreign Aid." Policy Research Working Paper 4714, World Bank, Washington, DC.

PREM (Povery Reduction and Economic Management network). 2009a. "Emerging Impacts of the Financial Crisis on Low-Income Countries Preliminary Findings." World Bank, Washington, DC.

———. 2009b. "The Global Economic Crisis: Assessing Vulnerability with a Poverty Lens." World Bank, Washington, DC.

———. 2009c. "Low-Income Countries and the Financial Crisis: Vulnerabilities and Policy Options." World Bank, Washington, DC.

Roodman. David. 2008. "History Says Financial Crisis Will Suppress Aid." Center for Global Development, Washington, DC. http://blogs.cgdev.org/globaldevelopment/2008/10/history-says-financial-crisis.php.

Schwab, Klaus. 2008. "Global Corporate Citizenship Working with Governments and Civil Society." *Foreign Affairs* (Jan/Feb).

United Nations. 2008. "Investment and Financial Flows to Address Climate Change: An Update." http://unfccc.int/resoource/docs/2008/tp/07.pdf.

White, Elizabeth, Per Bastoe, and Herbert Curry. Forthcoming. "The Role of Private Actors in Sub-Saharan Africa."

World Bank. 2008. "Development and Climate Change: A Strategic Framework for the World Bank Group." Development Committee Paper. Washington, DC.

———. 2009a. "Climate Investment Funds Financial Status as of January 26, 2009." Washington, DC.

———. 2009b. Draft Following Up On Accra: A World Bank Action Plan On Aid Effectiveness." Operations Policy and Country Services, World Bank, Washington, DC.

———. 2009c. "Innovative Development Finance: From Financing Sources to Financial Solutions." Report prepared by the Working Group on Innovative Finance, Washington, DC.

World Bank Institute. 2008. "State and Trends of the Carbon Market 2008.

Zimmerman, Robert. 2008. "The Fallout from the Financial Crisis (5): The End of Public Support for Development Aid?" Policy Insights 87, OECD Development Centre, Paris.

Chapter 5

Anderson, James, and Douglas Marcouiller. 2002. "Insecurity and the Pattern of Trade: An Empirical Investigation." *Review of Economics and Statistics* 84 (2): 342–52.

Anderson, James, and Eric van Wincoop. 2003. "Gravity with Gravitas: A Solution to the Border Puzzle." *American Economic Review* 93: 170–92.

Bouet, Antoine, and David Laborde. 2008. "The Potential Cost of a Failed Doha Round." Issue Brief 56, International Food Policy Research Institute, Washington, DC.

Brown, Chad. Forthcoming. Global Antidumping Database. World Bank, Washington, DC.

Chauffour, Jean-Pierre. 2008. "Global Food Price Crisis—Trade Policy Origins and Options." Trade Note 134, World Bank, Washington, DC.

Djankov, Simeon, Caroline Freund, and Cong Pham. 2006. "Trading on Time." Policy Research Working Paper 3909 (update), World Bank, Washington, DC.

Francois, Joseph, and Miriam Manchin. 2007. "Institutions, Infrastructure, and Trade." Policy Research Working Paper 4152, World Bank, Washington, DC.

Gootiiz, Batshur, and Aaditya Mattoo. 2009. "Services in Doha: What's on the Table?" World Bank Working paper series, Washington, DC.

Hoekman, B., and A. Nicita. 2008. "Trade Policy, Trade Costs, and Developing Country Trade." Policy Research Working Paper 4797, World Bank, Washington, DC.

Ikenson, Daniel. 2008. "While Doha Sleeps: Securing Economic Growth through Trade Facilitation." Trade Policy Analysis 37, Cato Institute, Washington, DC.

IMF (International Monetary Fund). 2003. *Trade Finance in Financial Crisis: Assessment of Key Issues.* Washington, DC: IMF.

———. 2008. *Food and Fuel Prices—Recent Developments, Macroeconomic Impact, and Policy Responses.* Washington, DC: IMF.

———. 2009. "Survey of Private Sector Trade Credit Developments." Washington, DC.

Kee, Hiau Looi, Alessandro Nicita, and Marcelo Olarreaga. 2008. "Import Demand Elasticities and Trade Distortions." *Review of Economics and Statistics* 90 (4): 666–82.

Limão, Nuno, and Anthony J. Venables. 2001. "Infrastructure, Geographical Disadvantage, Transport Costs, and Trade." *World Bank Economic Review* 15 (3): 451–79.

Martin, Will, and Aaditya Mattoo. 2008. "The Doha Development Agenda: What's on the Table?" Policy Research Working Paper 4672, World Bank, Washington, DC.

Mattoo, Aaditya, and Arvind Subramanian. 2008. "Multilateralism beyond Doha." Working Paper WP 08-8, Peterson Institute, Washington. DC.

Newfarmer, Richard, and Elisa Gamberoni. 2009. "Trade Protection: Incipient but Worrisome Trends." Trade Note 37, World Bank, Washington, DC.

OECD (Organisation for Economic Co-operation ande Development). 2008. *Agricultural Policies in OECD Countries: At a Glance 2008.* Paris: OECD.

Wilson, John S., Catherine Mann, and Tsunehiro Otsuki. 2003. "Trade Facilitation and Economic Development: A New Approach to Measuring the Impact." *World Bank Economic Review* 17 (3): 367–89.

World Bank. 2007. *Connecting to Compete: Trade Logistics in the Local Economy.* Washington, DC: World Bank.

———. 2008a. *Doing Business Report 2009.* Washington, DC: World Bank.

———. 2008b. "Trade Facilitation at the World Bank: Moving the Agenda Forward." Washington, DC (August).

———. 2009. *Global Economic Prospects 2009: Commodities at the Crossroads.* Washington, DC: World Bank.

World Bank–IMF (International Monetary Fund). 2008. *Global Monitoring Report, 2008.* Washington, DC: World Bank.

Chapter 6

Arbache, Jorge, and John Page. 2007. "More Growth or Fewer Collapses: A New Look at Long-run Growth in Sub-Saharan Africa." Policy Research Working Paper 4384, World Bank, Washington, DC.

Birdsall, Nancy 2009. "How to Unlock the $1 Trillion that Developing Countries Urgently Need to Cope with the Crisis." Center for Global Development, Washington, DC (February).

DAC (Development Assistance Committee). 2008. "DAC Report on Multilateral Aid, 2008." Organisation for Economic Co-operation and Development, Paris.

Gallup World Poll. 2008. www.gallup.com/consulting/worldpoll/24046/About.aspx.

Hausmann, R., and D. Rodrik. 2003. "Economic Development as Self-Discovery." Kennedy School of Government, Harvard University, Cambridge, MA (April).

IIF (Institute for International Finance). 2009. "Capital Flows to Emerging Market Economies." Washington, DC.

Independent Evaluation Group. 2005. "Improving the World Bank's Development Effectiveness: What Does Evaluation Show?" World Bank, Washington, DC.

———. 2006. "World Bank Lending for Lines of Credit." World Bank, Washington, DC.

———. 2008a. "Independent Evaluation of IFC's Development Results 2008: IFC's Additionality in Supporting Private Sector Development." World Bank, Washington, DC.

———. 2008b. Lessons from World Bank Group Responses to Past Financial Crises. Washington, DC: World Bank.

Kar, Dev, and Devon Cartwright-Smith. 2008. Illicit Financial Flows from Developing Countries: 2002–2006. Washington, DC: Global Financial Integrity Project, Center for International Policy. http://www.gfip.com.

Tandon, Yash. 2008. Ending Aid Dependence. Oxford, U.K.: Fahamu Books.

World Bank. 2008. "Global Financial Crisis: Responding Today, Securing tomorrow." Background Paper for the G20 Summit on Financial Markets and the World Economy, Washington DC, November 15, 2008.

———. 2009a. "Strengthening World Bank Group Partnerships with the Private Sector." SecM2009-0116, World Bank, Washington, DC (March 10).

———. 2009b. "Swimming against the Tide: How Developing Countries Are Coping with the Global Crisis." World Bank, Washington, DC.

———. 2009c. "World Bank Group Infrastructure Response to the Crisis." World Bank, Washington, DC.

Annex

Arbache, Jorge, and John Page. 2007. "More Growth or Fewer Collapses? A New Look at Long-run Growth in Sub-Saharan African Countries." Policy Research Working Paper 4384, World Bank, Washington, DC.

Baird, Sarah, Jed Friedman, and Norbert Schady. 2007. "Infant Mortality over the Business Cycle in the Developing World." Policy Research Working Paper 4346, World Bank, Washington, DC.

Bourguignon, François, Agnès Bénassy-Quéré, Stefan Dercon, Antonio Estache, Jan Willem Gunning, Ravi Kanbur, Stephan Klasen, Simon Maxwell, Jean-Philippe Platteau, and Amedeo Spadar. 2008. "Millennium Development Goals at Midpoint: Where Do We Stand and Where Do We Need to Go?" European Union, Brussels.

Chen, Shaohua, and Martin Ravallion, 2008. "The Developing World Is Poorer than We Thought, but No Less Successful in the Fight against Poverty." Policy Research Paper 4703, World Bank, Washington, DC.

Fallon, Peter, and Robert Lucas. 2002. "The Impact of Financial Crises on Labor Markets, Household Incomes, and Poverty: A Review of Evidence." World Bank Research Observer 17 (1): 21–45.

Ferreira, Francisco, and Norbert Schady. 2008. "Aggregate Economic Shocks, Child Schooling and Child Health." Policy Research Working paper 4701, World Bank, Washington, DC.

UNAIDS. 2008. Report on the Global AIDS Epidemic. Geneva: UNAIDS.

United Nations. 2008a. "Committing to Action: Achieving the Millennium Development Goals." 2008. Background paper by the Secretary-General for the High-level event on the Millennium Development Goals, September 25, in New York, New York.

———. 2008b. Delivering on the Global Partnership for Achieving the Millennium Development Goals, MDG Gap Task Force Report 2008. New York: United Nations.

———. 2008c. The Millennium Development Goals Report 2008. New York: United Nations.

United Nations, MDG Africa Steering Group. 2008. Achieving the Millennium Development Goals in Africa: Recommendations of the MDG Africa Steering Group. New York: United Nations.

World Bank. 2008. *World Development Indicators, Poverty Data: A Supplement to World Development Indicators 2008.* Washington, DC: World Bank.

World Bank Development Economics Vice Presidency. 2009. "The Expected Impact of the Global Financial Crisis on the World's Poorest." Note, World Bank, Washington, DC (February).

World Bank Development Economics Vice Presidency and the Human Development Network. 2009. "The Impact of the Financial Crisis on Progress towards the Millennium Development Goals in Human Development." Note, World Bank, Washington, DC (February).

World Bank Poverty Reduction and Economic Management Network. 2009. "The Global Economic Crisis: Assessing Vulnerability with a Poverty Lens." Note, World Bank, Washington, DC (February).

Monitoring the MDGs: Selected Indicators

This annex contains **DataLinks**, a feature that provides access to the Excel files corresponding to each figure. To make use of this feature, simply locate the link below each figure (beginning with http://dx.doi.org), and type it into your Internet browser.

Eradicate Extreme Poverty and Hunger

Projections based on the new 2005 purchasing power parity (PPP) poverty data reveal that the share of people living on less than $1.25 a day will fall from 41.7 percent in 1990 to 15.1 percent in 2015. The greatest poverty reduction has occurred in East Asia and the Pacific and is largely attributable to China.

If China were excluded from the global calculation, the drop in poverty would be less drastic, from 35.2 percent in 1990 to 18.2 percent in 2015. East Asia and the Pacific exceeded its target; Latin America and the Caribbean and South Asia are projected to be on target.

MDG 1 FIGURE 1   Poverty rates by region, based on new PPPs

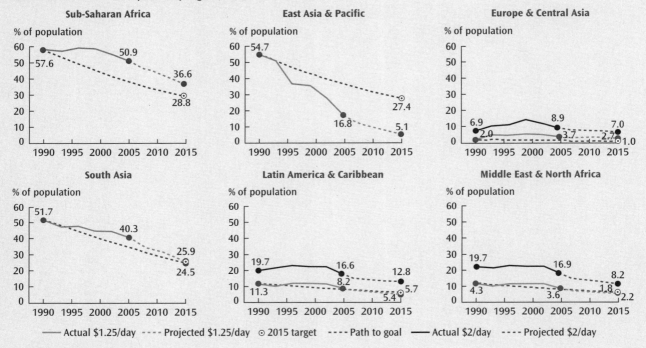

— Actual $1.25/day ---- Projected $1.25/day ⊙ 2015 target ---- Path to goal — Actual $2/day ---- Projected $2/day

http://dx.doi.org/10.1596/978-0-8213-7859-5_F1
Source: World Development Indicators.

▲ **Extreme poverty is defined as the proportion of individuals in developing countries who live on less than $1.25 a day (based on purchasing power parity 2005 constant prices). Poverty estimates are computed based on data covering 96 percent of developing countries' population. MDG 1 Figure 1 shows that Sub-Saharan Africa lags behind, and based on current projections, this region will reduce poverty by only 20 percent between 1990 and 2015.**

▶ **Of the 84 countries with available data (out of 144), 45 have already achieved or are on track to meet the poverty reduction target, but 40 are either off track or seriously off track. Four of 8 countries in East Asia and the Pacific, and 4 of 5 countries in South Asia with available data are not on track. Fifteen of 21 countries in Europe and Central Asia have achieved or are on track to achieve the target. Ten of the 12 fragile states with available data are not on track, so the prospect is bleak for fragile states to meet MDG 1. Fragile states are low-income countries or territories with no Country Policy and Institutional Assessment (CPIA) score or a CPIA score of 3.2 or less.**

MDG 1 FIGURE 2   Proportion of countries on track to achieve the poverty reduction target

Fragile states
Sub-Saharan Africa
South Asia
Middle East & North Africa
Latin America & Caribbean
Europe & Central Asia
East Asia & Pacific

0   25   50   75   100
% of countries

■ No data ■ Seriously off track ■ Off track ■ On track ■ Achieved

http://dx.doi.org/10.1596/978-0-8213-7859-5_F2
Source: World Development Indicators.

TARGET 1.A Halve, between 1990 and 2015, the proportion of people whose income is less than $1.25 a day

TARGET 1.B Achieve full and productive employment and decent work for all, including women and young people

TARGET 1.C Halve, between 1990 and 2015, the proportion of people who suffer from hunger

MDG 1 FIGURE 3 Share of poorest and richest quintiles in national consumption

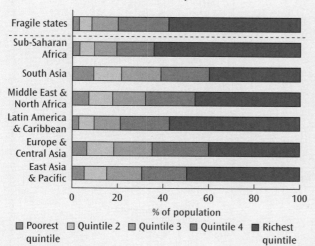

■ Poorest quintile □ Quintile 2 □ Quintile 3 □ Quintile 4 ■ Richest quintile

http://dx.doi.org/10.1596/978-0-8213-7859-5_F3
Source: World Bank staff estimates.

▲ Poverty data based on the new PPP estimates reveal that for all regions, the richest population quintile has a 40 percent or larger share in national consumption, which is far greater than the 2 to 9 percent consumed by the poorest quintile. Sub-Saharan Africa and the fragile states have the greatest disparity between the richest and poorest quintiles.

MDG 1 FIGURE 4 Proportion of countries on track to halve under-five malnutrition

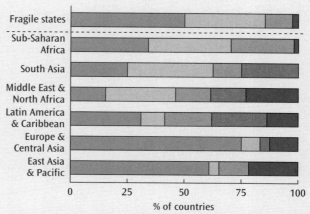

■ No data □ Seriously off track ■ Off track ■ On track ■ Achieved

http://dx.doi.org/10.1596/978-0-8213-7859-5_F4
Source: World Bank staff estimates based on data from UNICEF.

▲ The prevalence of child malnutrition is measured by the percentage of children under the age of five whose weight-to-age ratio is more than two standard deviations below the international median. Standards of child growth were revised in 2006, and estimates of child malnutrition that conform to the new standard are being computed. The current assessment of progress toward MDGs achievement is based on child malnutrition estimates conforming to old child growth standards. According to this assessment, more than half of the countries with available data are not on track to achieve the target by 2015.

MDG 1 FIGURE 5 Ratio of employment to population, by gender

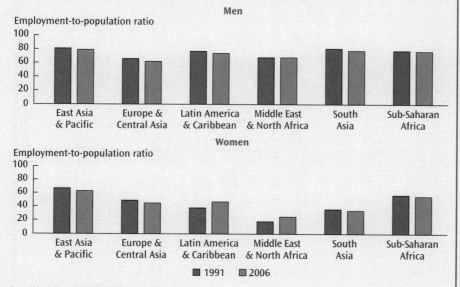

◄ The employment-to-population ratio is the proportion of a country's working-age population (ages 15 years and older) that is employed. Between 1991 and 2006, this ratio fell in most regions, with the exception of the Middle East and North Africa for both genders and Latin America and Caribbean for females. For all regions, the ratio has consistently been lower for females than males.

■ 1991 ■ 2006

http://dx.doi.org/10.1596/978-0-8213-7859-5_F5
Source: World Development Indicators.

Achieve Universal Primary Education

Progress toward the primary education goal has varied across regions. East Asia and the Pacific and Latin America and the Caribbean have both progressed well in achieving the primary completion rate target, although some countries in these regions are not on track. Europe and Central Asia and the Middle East and North Africa have had slow progress. Neither Sub-Saharan Africa nor South Asia is on track to achieve the target, but a few countries in these regions have shown significant progress.

MDG 2 FIGURE 1   Primary school completion rates, by gender

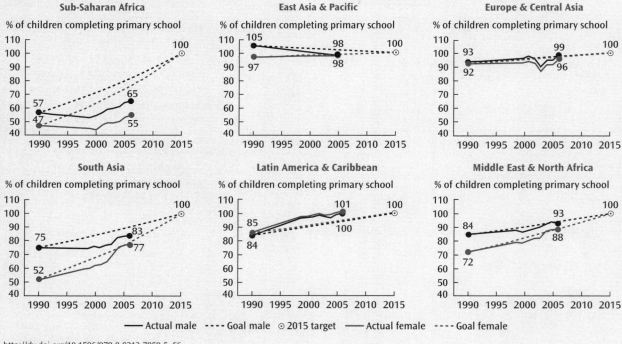

http://dx.doi.org/10.1596/978-0-8213-7859-5_F6
Source: World Development Indicators.

▲   The primary school completion rate is the percentage of children completing the last year of primary schooling. It is computed by dividing the total number of students in the last grade of primary school minus repeaters in that grade by the total number of children of official completing age. Under certain circumstances, the computation can overestimate the actual proportion of a given cohort completing primary school and sometimes exceeds 100 percent.

TARGET 2.A Ensure that by 2015, children everywhere, boys and girls alike, will be able to complete a full course of primary schooling

MDG 2 FIGURE 2 Proportion of countries on track to meet the primary education target

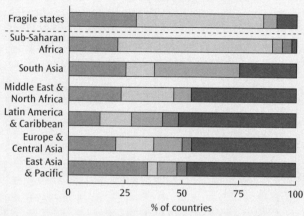

% of countries

☐ No data ☐ Seriously off track ☐ Off track ■ On track ■ Achieved

http://dx.doi.org/10.1596/978-0-8213-7859-5_F7
Source: World Development Indicators.

▲ Seventeen of 24 countries in Latin America and the Caribbean, 13 of 18 countries in Europe and Central Asia, and 12 of 14 countries in East Asia and the Pacific (for which data exist) have already met or are on track to meet the target. Other regions have shown little progress; 3 of 5 countries in South Asia and 33 of 36 countries in Sub-Saharan Africa are not on track. Fragile states also lag behind—only 3 of 22 countries with available data have achieved the target.

▶ The youth literacy rate is the percentage of people ages 15–24 that can, with comprehension, both read and write a short, simple statement about their everyday life. For countries with data available for the 2005–07 period, literacy rates in most Sub-Saharan African countries were lower than 80 percent for both males and females. All countries in that region besides Liberia have lower literacy rates for females than males.

MDG 2 FIGURE 3 Literacy rates, ages 15–24, by gender

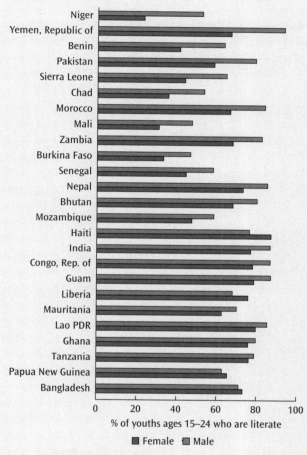

% of youths ages 15–24 who are literate

■ Female ■ Male

http://dx.doi.org/10.1596/978-0-8213-7859-5_F8
Source: World Development Indicators.

MDG 2 FIGURE 4 Adjusted net enrollment ratio in primary education

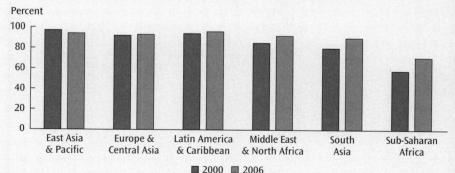

■ 2000 ■ 2006

http://dx.doi.org/10.1596/978-0-8213-7859-5_F9
Source: World Development Indicators.

◀ Adjusted net enrollment rates in primary education measure the proportion of children of official primary school age who are enrolled in any level of education. Although higher values indicate that more children of primary school age attend school, these rates do not capture issues such as repetition and late enrollment, as long as children enter school before the official age of completion. For all regions except Sub-Saharan Africa, net enrollment ratios met or exceeded 90 percent in 2006. In Sub-Saharan Africa, the rate only rose from 58 to 71 percent from 1990 to 2006.

Promote Gender Equality and Empower Women

Most of the progress in achieving gender parity in education has been made at the primary school level, but regions such as East Asia and the Pacific, Europe and Central Asia, and Latin America and the Caribbean have had fairly good progress at all education levels. Female participation in the labor force has increased, but labor force participation rates, occupational levels, and wages reveal continuing significant gender gaps.

MDG 3 FIGURE 1   Gender disparity at primary and secondary education, by regions

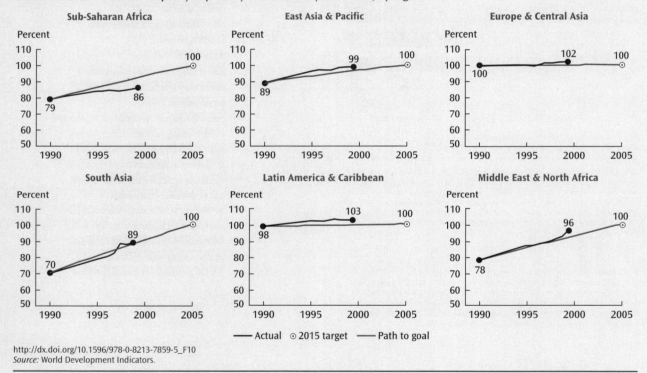

— Actual   ⊙ 2015 target   — Path to goal

http://dx.doi.org/10.1596/978-0-8213-7859-5_F10
Source: World Development Indicators.

▲   Gender disparity is measured by the ratio of girls to boys enrolled in primary and secondary schools. Most regions are on track to achieve this target by 2015.

MDG 3 FIGURE 2   Gender parity disaggregated by education levels

Ratio of female to male enrollment, 2006

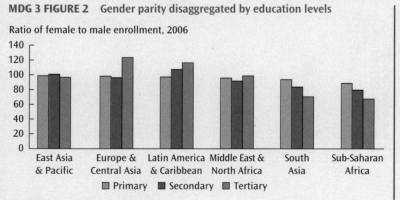

◄   East Asia and the Pacific and Europe and Central Asia are close to reaching the gender parity target for all education levels. The Latin America and Caribbean region is well on track to achieve the target at the primary level, but gender bias against boys is apparent at the secondary and tertiary levels. Regions with higher primary and secondary gender parity ratios have exhibited better performance at the tertiary level. South Asia and Sub-Saharan Africa lag behind at all levels for this target, particularly at the tertiary level.

http://dx.doi.org/10.1596/978-0-8213-7859-5_F11
Source: World Development Indicators.

TARGET 3.A Eliminate gender disparity in primary and secondary education, preferably by 2005, and in all levels of education no later than 2015

MDG 3 FIGURE 3 Proportion of countries on track to achieve gender parity in education

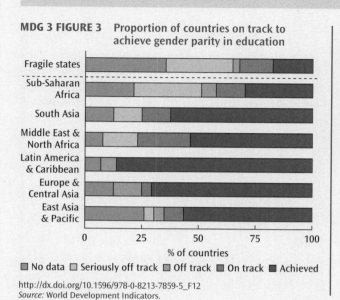

% of countries

■ No data ▢ Seriously off track ▢ Off track ■ On track ■ Achieved

http://dx.doi.org/10.1596/978-0-8213-7859-5_F12
Source: World Development Indicators.

◀ Twenty-five of 27 countries for which data exist in Latin America and the Caribbean have achieved gender parity in primary and secondary education. Eighteen of 21 countries in Europe and Central Asia and 15 of 17 countries in East Asia and the Pacific with available data are on track or have achieved this target. In Sub-Saharan Africa, 20 of 37 countries for which data exist are not on track, and another 10 countries lack data. Ten of the 22 fragile states (for which data exist) are seriously off track, and only 6 have achieved the target. Combining primary and secondary education for some countries masks gender bias at either the primary or secondary level of education. This progress assessment also does not take into account the gender bias for boys, but male underenrollment is a concern in many countries, especially at the secondary level. The methodology for assessing this target is currently being revised.

MDG 3 FIGURE 4 Women in the labor force

Share of female in total employment (%)

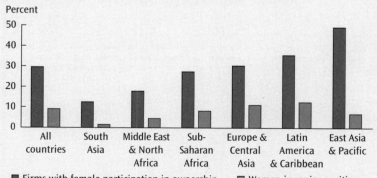

■ 1991 ■ 2006

http://dx.doi.org/10.1596/978-0-8213-7859-5_F13
Source: World Development Indicators.

◀ The total labor force participation rate measures the proportion of the population between ages 15 and 64 that is economically active, employed, or actively seeking a job, while the share of females in total employment shows the extent to which women are active in the labor force. The percentage of females in the labor force is below 50 percent for all regions and is lowest in the Middle East and North Africa and in South Asia. South Asia showed no improvement in the ratio from 1990 to 2006, while several regions had slightly lower ratios in 2006 than in 1990. The only regions to show improvements were the Middle East and North Africa and Latin America and the Caribbean.

MDG 3 FIGURE 5 Disparity in occupational level by gender

Percent

■ Firms with female participation in ownership   ■ Women in senior positions

http://dx.doi.org/10.1596/978-0-8213-7859-5_F14
Source: World Bank Enterprise Surveys.

◀ The Enterprise Surveys indicate that about half of the firms in East Asia and the Pacific have female participation in ownership, compared to only 13 percent in South Asia and 18 percent in the Middle East and North Africa. The percentage of women in senior positions is far smaller, ranging from only 2 percent in South Asia to 13 percent in Latin America and the Caribbean.

Reduce Child Mortality

The under-five mortality rate has fallen in all regions since 1990, and some regions have come close to being on track to meet MDG Target 4.A. However, in most countries, the rate has not declined fast enough to meet the target by 2015, and over three-quarters of countries with available data are not on track. Nearly half of all deaths of children under five occur in Sub-Saharan Africa. Malnutrition, as well as lack of access to water and sanitation infrastructure, contributes to the poor health and death of young children. The leading cause of childhood deaths, including pneumonia, diarrhea, malaria, and measles, can easily be prevented through basic health service improvements and interventions, such as insecticide-treated mosquito nets and vaccinations.

MDG 4 FIGURE 1   Under-five mortality rate, by region

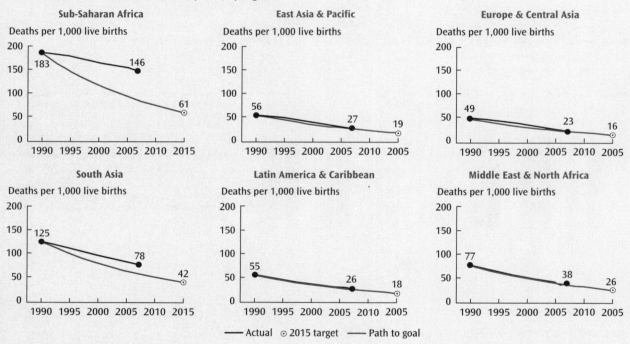

http://dx.doi.org/10.1596/978-0-8213-7859-5_F15
Source: World Development Indicators.

▲   The under-five mortality rate is the probability that a newborn will die before reaching age five (expressed as a rate per 1,000). At an aggregate level, none of the regions is on track to achieve the under-five mortality target, though all regions except South Asia and Sub-Saharan Africa have come close. However, as MDG 4 Figure 2 shows, most countries are off track. Regional estimates of child mortality are based on data covering 99.9 percent of developing countries' total population.

TARGET 4.A Reduce by two-thirds, between 1990 and 2015, the under-five mortality rate

MDG 4 FIGURE 2 Proportion of countries on track to achieve the child mortality target

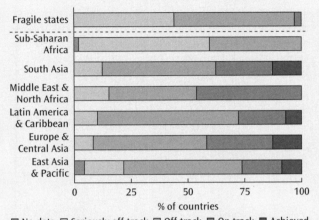

% of countries

■ No data ☐ Seriously off track ☐ Off track ■ On track ■ Achieved

http://dx.doi.org/10.1596/978-0-8213-7859-5_F16
Source: World Development Indicators.

▲ Data are available for all but 2 countries on the under-five child mortality rate, but only 33 of the 142 countries with available data have achieved or are on track to achieve the target by 2015. None of the 46 Sub-Saharan African countries with available data is on track to reach the target. None of the fragile states has attained the target and only 1 of 34 is on track to reduce by two-thirds the 1990 under-five mortality rate.

MDG 4 FIGURE 3 Proportion of countries on track for measles vaccination

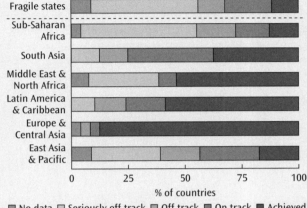

% of countries

■ No data ☐ Seriously off track ☐ Off track ■ On track ■ Achieved

http://dx.doi.org/10.1596/978-0-8213-7859-5_F17
Source: World Development Indicators.

▲ Assessment of measles immunization rates shows a more positive picture for some regions. Though an official target has not been set, assessment is based on a target of achieving a 95 percent measles immunization rate by 2015. Twenty-one of 23 Europe and Central Asian countries with available data have already achieved this target, while 6 of 8 South Asian countries are either on track or have already achieved the target. About half of the countries in East Asia and the Pacific are not on track. Sub-Saharan Africa and fragile states also lag behind.

MDG 4 FIGURE 4 Measles vaccination coverage

Measles immunization rate (% of children ages 12–23 months)

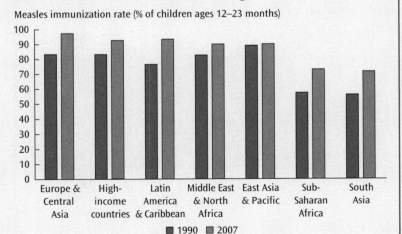

■ 1990 ☐ 2007

http://dx.doi.org/10.1596/978-0-8213-7859-5_F18
Source: World Development Indicators.

◄ Measles vaccination coverage is defined as the percentage of children ages 12–23 months who received measles vaccinations before 12 months or at any time before the survey was administered. Since 1990, the coverage of measles vaccinations has increased in all six regions, with the greatest improvements occurring in Sub-Saharan Africa and South Asia. Measles vaccination coverage in South Asia increased from 56 percent in 1990 to 71 percent in 2007. The vaccination rate for Europe and Central Asia (83 percent) surpassed the average rate for high-income countries (97 percent) in 2007.

Improve Maternal Health

Among all the MDGs, the least progress has been made in improving maternal health, and a full achievement of the MDG 5 targets remains a challenging task. Every year, more than 500,000 women die from complications during pregnancy, childbirth, or in the six weeks after delivery. Most of these women live in low-income countries. Progress in Sub-

Saharan Africa—a region with the highest maternal mortality rate—has been negligible. Improving the access to and quality of births attended by skilled personnel, providing prenatal care, and reducing the number of pregnancies (particularly among adolescents) can all contribute to reducing the number of maternal deaths.

MDG 5 FIGURE 1   Maternal mortality rates

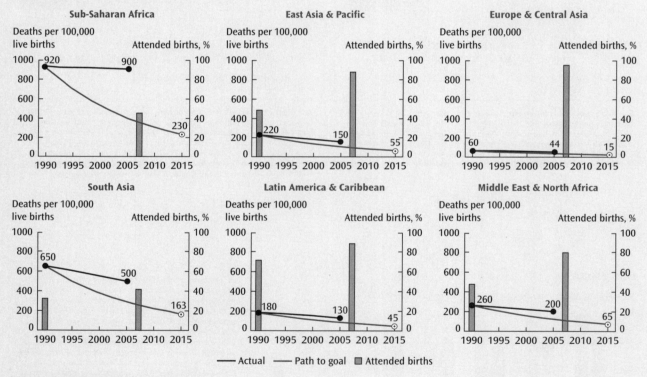

— Actual   — Path to goal   ▉ Attended births

http://dx.doi.org/10.1596/978-0-8213-7859-5_F19
Source: World Development Indicators.
Note: Only data for 2007 are available for attended births in Europe and Central Asia and Sub-Saharan Africa.

▲   The maternal mortality rate is the number of women who die from pregnancy-related complications during pregnancy or delivery, per 100,000 live births. Such statistics are very difficult to collect through surveys, and data reported here rely on modeling techniques developed by the World Health Organization, United Nations Children's Fund, and United Nations Population Fund. The increased share of attended births contributes to declines in maternal mortality rates. See MDG 5 Figure 3 for information on attended births.

TARGET 5.A Reduce by three-quarters, between 1990 and 2015, the maternal mortality ratio
TARGET 5.B Achieve by 2015 universal access to reproductive health

MDG 5 FIGURE 2   Contraceptive prevalence by income groups

% of married women ages 15–49 using contraception

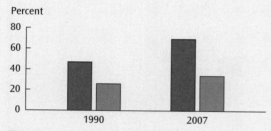

■ 1990 ■ 2007

http://dx.doi.org/10.1596/978-0-8213-7859-5_F20
Source: World Development Indicators.

▲   The contraceptive prevalence rate is the percentage of married women ages 15–49 who use, or whose sexual partners use, any form of contraception. This rate has increased for all income groups between 1990 and 2007, but is still quite low at only 33 percent for low-income countries in 2007.

MDG 5 FIGURE 4   Prenatal care coverage in South Asia

Percent

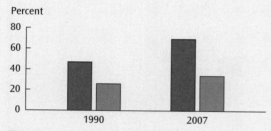

■ Pregnant women receiving prenatal care at least once
■ Pregnant women receiving prenatal care at least four times

http://dx.doi.org/10.1596/978-0-8213-7859-5_F22
Source: World Development Indicators.

▲   Maternal death is correlated with poor health care during pregnancy and childbirth. Prenatal care coverage is the percentage of women attended during pregnancy by skilled health personnel for pregnancy-related issues. One of the regions with the highest maternal mortality rates, South Asia, has shown improvements in the percentage of pregnant women who have received prenatal care at least once, increasing from 47 to 69 percent from 1990 to 2007. Although this shows progress, a healthy pregnancy requires much more than one or two prenatal visits. The number of women who received prenatal care at least four times increased only marginally, from 26 to 34 percent between the two years.

MDG 5 FIGURE 3   Proportion of countries on track to achieve attended births target

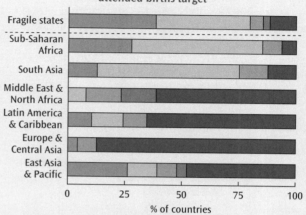

■ No data □ Seriously off track □ Off track ■ On track ■ Achieved

http://dx.doi.org/10.1596/978-0-8213-7859-5_F21
Source: World Development Indicators.

▲   Births attended by skilled health staff are the percentage of deliveries attended by personnel trained to give the necessary supervision, care, and advice to women during pregnancy, labor, and the postpartum period. Increasing attended births helps decrease the maternal mortality rate. Twenty-one of 23 countries in Europe and Central Asia and 19 of 26 countries in Latin America and the Caribbean have achieved the target to lower the nonattendance rate to 10 percent by 2015, but most South Asian and Sub-Saharan African countries are not on track.

MDG 5 FIGURE 5   Adolescent fertility rate, by region

Births per 1,000 women, ages 15–19

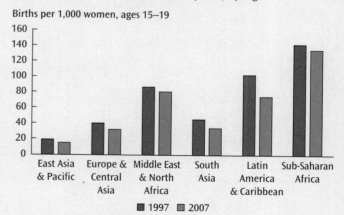

■ 1997 ■ 2007

http://dx.doi.org/10.1596/978-0-8213-7859-5_F23
Source: World Development Indicators.

▲   Giving birth at an early age puts young women at an increased risk of pregnancy complications and, in some cases, death. The adolescent fertility rate is defined as the number of births per 1,000 women ages 15–19. From 1997 to 2007, the rate has marginally declined in all regions. The largest decrease between the two years is in Latin America and the Caribbean, where the rate dropped from 102 to 74. Progress was less dramatic in the most fertile region, Sub-Saharan Africa, where the rate only decreased from 141 to 134.

Combat HIV/AIDS, Malaria, and Other Diseases

In 2007, around 33 million people globally were living with HIV, and about 2 million people, the majority in Sub-Saharan Africa, died from the disease. Most countries face difficulty in reaching the MDG targets related to HIV/AIDS. Less than half of the individuals in these countries have correct knowledge about

HIV transmission and prevention. Women from the poorest income quintile are the least knowledgeable. Achieving the target to halt and reverse the incidence of major diseases such as malaria and tuberculosis has also been challenging.

MDG 6 FIGURE 1 HIV prevalence rates and estimated deaths

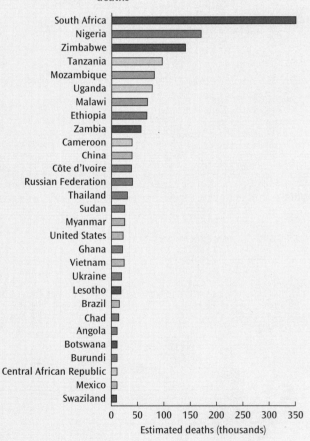

Estimated deaths (thousands)

% of population ages 15–49 living with HIV

☐ < 1 ■ 1–4.9 ☐ 5–9.9 ■ 10–14.9 ■ ≥ 15

http://dx.doi.org/10.1596/978-0-8213-7859-5_F24
Source: World Development Indicators.

▲ HIV prevalence is the percentage of individuals ages 15–49 who are infected with the HIV virus. South Africa had the highest number of estimated deaths from AIDS (350,000) and a prevalence rate of 18.1 percent in 2007. Other Sub-Saharan African countries also exhibited high death rates and prevalence rates greater than 1 percent.

MDG 6 FIGURE 2 Proportion of population aged 15–24 years in Sub-Saharan Africa with comprehensive HIV/AIDS knowledge, by gender and income quintile

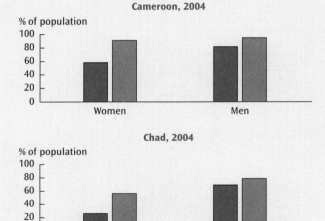

■ Poorest quintile ■ Richest quintile

http://dx.doi.org/10.1596/978-0-8213-7859-5_F25
Sources: HNPStats database, World Bank, based on household surveys.

▲ HIV/AIDS knowledge is defined as the percentage of individuals who have comprehensive, correct knowledge about HIV (ability to describe two ways to prevent infection and to reject three misconceptions concerning HIV). Estimates from household surveys in Sub-Saharan African countries such as Cameroon, Chad, and Mozambique reveal the disparity in knowledge about the sexual transmission of HIV/AIDS by household income levels and gender of the respondents. Women from the poorest income quintile have the least amount of knowledge, while men from the richest income quintiles have the most knowledge. Men and women from the richest quintiles have more knowledge than their counterparts in the poorest quintile. A higher percentage of men and women in Cameroon have HIV/AIDS knowledge compared to Mozambique, and subsequently the prevalence and estimated death rates in Cameroon were both lower in 2007.

TARGET 6.A Have halted by 2015 and begun to reverse the spread of HIV/AIDS

TARGET 6.B Achieve by 2010 universal access to treatment for HIV/AIDS for all those who need it

TARGET 6.C Have halted by 2015 and begun to reverse the incidence of malaria and other major diseases

MDG 6 FIGURE 3 Tuberculosis detection and treatment

Tuberculosis cases detected under DOTS (%)

Tuberculosis treatment success rate
(% of registered cases)

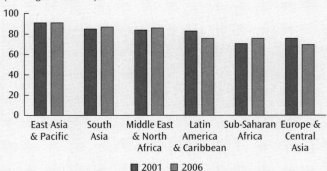

http://dx.doi.org/10.1596/978-0-8213-7859-5_F26
Source: World Development Indicators.

▲ To effectively halt and lower the tuberculosis (TB) incidence rate, early detection and successful treatment of the disease are vital. The TB cases detected under the Directly Observed Treatment Short-course (DOTS) increased dramatically in East Asia and the Pacific (40 to 77 percent) and South Asia (29 to 67 percent) from 2002 to 2007. The detection rate in Sub-Saharan Africa only rose marginally from 42 to 47 percent. The TB treatment success rate has fallen in Latin America and the Caribbean and Europe and Central Asia, but has slightly improved in the other regions.

MDG 6 FIGURE 4 Bednet use by children

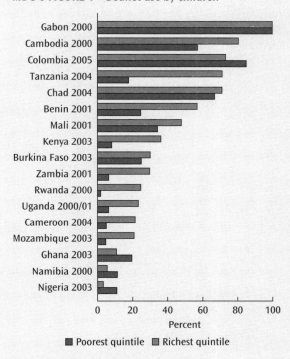

http://dx.doi.org/10.1596/978-0-8213-7859-5_F27
Source: Country household surveys.

▲ The majority of malaria cases that plague the developing world occur in tropical or subtropical regions. Malaria causes over 1 million deaths each year, predominantly in Sub-Saharan Africa, to children under age five. Because bednets protect humans from contact with mosquitoes, which are the vector for malaria transmission, they are one of the best malarial prevention strategies. In most countries, children in the richest quintile have a greater usage of bednets, but the reverse is true in Colombia, Ghana, Namibia, and Nigeria.

Ensure Environmental Sustainability

Based on current trends, the world and a few regions will meet the water access target by 2015. However, achieving the improved sanitation access target remains a challenge. There are disparities among regions, and South Asia and Sub-Saharan Africa have made the least progress on both targets. Reducing deforestation and carbon dioxide emissions are

important to mitigate the effects of climate change. However, global carbon dioxide emissions levels have gradually increased since 1990 and reached 28 billion metric tons in 2005. The rate of deforestation has been highest in Latin America and the Caribbean and Sub-Saharan Africa—two regions that contain over 40 percent of the world's forest area.

MDG 7 FIGURE 1   Population without access to an improved water source or sanitation facilities

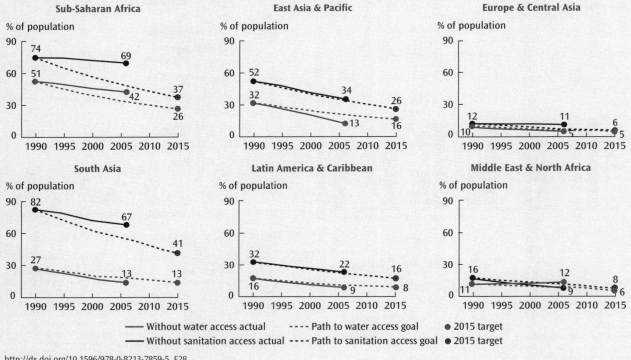

http://dx.doi.org/10.1596/978-0-8213-7859-5_F28
Source: World Development Indicators.

▲ Access to sanitation refers to the percentage of population with at least adequate access to excreta facilities (private or shared, but not public) that can effectively prevent human, animal, and insect contact with excreta. Access to improved sources of water refers to the percentage of population with reasonable access to a permanent source of safe water in their dwelling or within a reasonable distance from it. Regional estimates for both indicators are computed using country data covering 97 percent of developing countries' total population. All regions but Sub-Saharan Africa and the Middle East and North Africa are on track to achieve the water access target, based on current trends. Prospects are bleaker for the sanitation access target, with only the Middle East and North Africa on track and Sub-Saharan Africa and South Asia lagging far behind.

TARGET 7.A Integrate the principles of sustainable development into country policies and programs and reverse the loss of environmental resources

TARGET 7.B Reduce biodiversity loss, achieving by 2010 a significant reduction in the rate of loss

TARGET 7.C Halve by 2015 the proportion of people without sustainable access to safe drinking water and basic sanitation

TARGET 7.D Have achieved a significant improvement by 2020 in the lives of at least 100 million slum dwellers

MDG 7 FIGURE 2 Proportion of countries on track to achieve the targets for access to improved water and sanitation

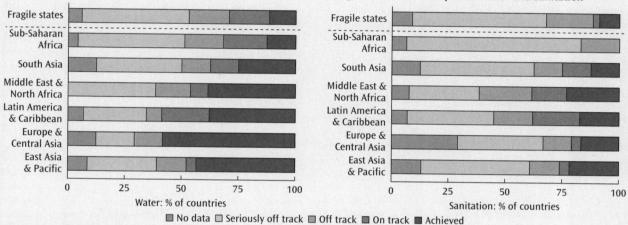

http://dx.doi.org/10.1596/978-0-8213-7859-5_F29
Source: World Development Indicators.

▲ Forty-nine percent of the developing countries with available data have achieved or are on track to achieve the improved water target, while 23 percent have achieved or are on track to achieve the improved sanitation target. Fourteen of 21 countries with available data in Europe and Central Asia have achieved the target to improve water access. In the Middle East and North Africa, 7 of 13 countries with available data are not on track. Progress has been much slower for the improved sanitation target, and no Sub-Saharan African country and almost two-thirds of countries in the other regions are not on track, based on available data.

MDG 7 FIGURE 3 CO₂ emissions disaggregated by largest emitters and the rest of the world

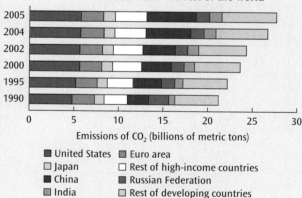

http://dx.doi.org/10.1596/978-0-8213-7859-5_F30
Source: World Development Indicators.

▲ Carbon dioxide (CO₂) emissions are derived from burning fossil energy and manufacturing cement. The United States, Euro Area, and Japan produce almost 75 percent of the CO₂ emissions from all high-income countries. However, about half of the total global CO₂ emissions comes from the developing world, particularly from China, the Russian Federation, and India. China's share of global emissions has risen from 11 to 20 percent between 1990 and 2005.

MDG 7 FIGURE 4 Forest lost and gained

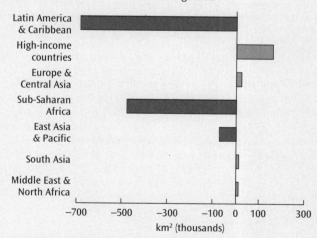

http://dx.doi.org/10.1596/978-0-8213-7859-5_F31
Source: World Development Indicators.

▲ Deforestation, resulting largely from land use change, has been about 13 million hectares a year, and net forest lost has been 7.3 million hectares. Because forests are important to mitigating climate change, deforestation creates challenges to fostering sustainable development. The fastest rates of forest lost from 1990 to 2005 were in Sub-Saharan Africa (7.1 percent), Latin America and the Caribbean (7.0 percent), and East Asia and the Pacific (1.6 percent). The other regions had increases in their forest areas.

Develop a Global Partnership for Development

According to preliminary estimates, the share of official development assistance (ODA) in GNI rose from 0.28 in 2007 to 0.30 in 2008, but falls below the 0.33 level reached in 2005. ODA in 2005 was boosted by the exceptional debt-relief initiatives for heavily indebted poor countries (HIPC). Donors will need to increase programmable aid (which excludes debt relief) in order to meet the 2010 aid target to increase total aid by $50 billion overall and aid to Sub-Saharan Africa by $25 billion a year (in 2004 dollars). The HIPC Initiative and Multilateral Debt Relief Initiative

(MDRI) have drastically decreased the debt burdens of many low-income countries, but maintaining long-term debt sustainability will be difficult. Mobile phone subscriptions have more than doubled in low- and middle-income countries, but large gaps remain for improving access to technologies such as broadband Internet. Substantial infrastructure investments by the private sector will facilitate the growth of information and communications infrastructure and access to mobile phone technology.

MDG 8 FIGURE 1   Evolution of global aid, as a percentage of GNI in DAC countries

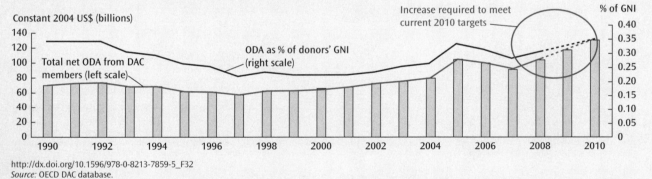

http://dx.doi.org/10.1596/978-0-8213-7859-5_F32
Source: OECD DAC database.

▲   In 2005, G-8 leaders at the Gleneagles Summit agreed to increase the annual aid allocations to developing countries by an additional $50 billion by 2010, compared with 2004. From 2005 to 2007, the ratio of ODA to gross national income for DAC donors fell from 0.33 to 0.28, but the ratio must be 0.35 in 2010 to meet the target. The total net ODA from DAC donors increased from 1990 to 2005, but has declined since then; aid in 2005 was high because of the one-time debt relief to Nigeria and Iraq.

MDG 8 FIGURE 2   Aid to small island states and landlocked developing countries

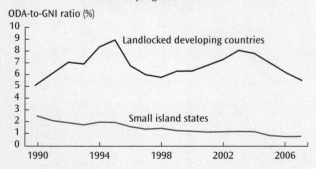

http://dx.doi.org/10.1596/978-0-8213-7859-5_F33
Source: OECD DAC database.

▲   The ODA-to-GNI ratio for landlocked developing countries has fluctuated between 5 and 9 from 1990 to 2007 but has not changed much over the period. The ratio has decreased for small island states from 1990 to 2007.

MDG 8 FIGURE 3   Debt service as a percentage of exports of goods and services

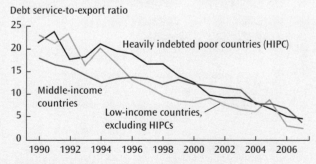

http://dx.doi.org/10.1596/978-0-8213-7859-5_F34
Source: OECD DAC database.

▲   Debt relief under the HIPC Initiative reduced burdens of external debt service for 34 post-decision-point highly indebted poor countries. Assistance under the MDRI Initiative further reduced the external debt of 23 post-completion-point counties. High commodity prices and strong growth in the world economy before the onset of the global financial crisis have improved export revenues of many developing countries. The debt-service-to-export ratios for all developing country groups shown in the figure have declined since 1990, with low-income countries and HIPCs enjoying the largest declines.

TARGET 8.A Develop further an open, rule-based, predictable, nondiscriminatory trading and financial system

TARGET 8.B Address the special needs of the least developed countries

TARGET 8.C Address the special needs of landlocked developing countries and small island developing states

TARGET 8.D Deal comprehensively with the debt problems of developing countries through national and international measures in order to make debt sustainable in the long term

TARGET 8.E In cooperation with pharmaceutical companies, provide access to affordable essential drugs in developing countries

TARGET 8.F In cooperation with the private sector, make available the benefits of new technologies, especially information and communications

MDG 8 FIGURE 4 Average tariff imposed by developed countries on least developed countries

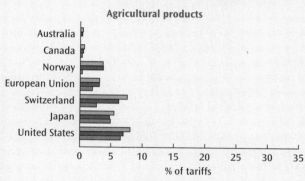

Agricultural products

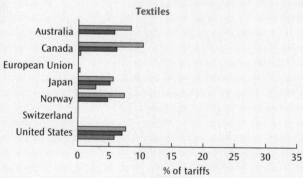

Textiles

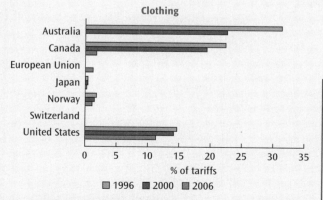

Clothing

http://dx.doi.org/10.1596/978-0-8213-7859-5_F35
Sources: United Nations Conference on Trade and Development, World Trade Organization, and International Trade Center.

MDG 8 FIGURE 5 Cellular subscribers per 100 people

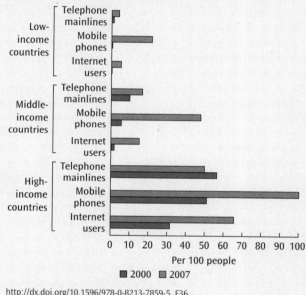

http://dx.doi.org/10.1596/978-0-8213-7859-5_F36
Source: World Development Indicators.

▲ Compared with telephone mainlines, the number of mobile phone subscribers and Internet users has rapidly increased in low- and middle-income countries, although the levels remain much lower than those of high-income countries. Between 2004 and 2007, mobile phone subscribers increased from 3.7 to 23.1 per 100 people in low-income countries and 22.2 to 46.9 per 100 people in middle-income countries.

◀ The average tariffs imposed by industrial countries on least developed countries' (LDC) agricultural, textile, and clothing products have fallen from 1996 to 2006. Tariffs on agricultural products have decreased only slightly. Tariffs on clothing products have been the highest, and the rates of reduction the largest. Although these reductions eroded the preferential access to high-income markets that some LDCs had previously exclusively enjoyed, the overall reduction of tariffs benefit production and exporting sectors of all LDCs.